SECOND EDITION

MANAGING BUSINESS PROCESS FLOWS

Principles of Operations Management

Ravi Anupindi

Stephen M. Ross School of Business
The University of Michigan, Ann Arbor

Sunil Chopra

Kellogg School of Management
Northwestern University

Sudhakar D. Deshmukh

Kellogg School of Management
Northwestern University

Jan A. Van Mieghem

Kellogg School of Management
Northwestern University

Eitan Zemel

Stern School of Business
New York University

D0082383

PEARSON

Prentice
Hall

Upper Saddle River, NJ 07458

Library of Congress Cataloging-in-Publication Data
Managing business process flows: principles of operations management/
  Ravi Anupindi . . . [et al.].—2nd ed.
    p. cm.
  Includes bibliographical references and index.
  ISBN 0-13-067546-6 (paperback)
    1. Production management. 2. Process control. I. Anupindi, Ravi.

TS155.M33217 2004
658.5—dc22   2004060088

VP/Editorial Director: Jeff Shelstad
Executive Editor: Mark Pfaltzgraff
Senior Sponsoring Editor: Alana Bradley
Senior Editorial Assistant: Jane Avery
Senior Media Project Manager: Nancy Welcher
AVP/Executive Marketing Manager: Debbie Clare
Managing Editor: John Roberts
Production Editor: Suzanne Grappi
Manufacturing Buyer: Michelle Klein
Production Manager, Manufacturing: Arnold Vila
Cover Design Manager: Jayne Conte
Cover Design: Bruce Kenselaar
Composition/Full-Service Project Management: GGS Book Services, Atlantic Highlands
Printer/Binder: Hamilton

Credits and acknowledgments borrowed from other sources and reproduced, with permission, in this textbook appear on appropriate page within text.

Screen shots and icons reprinted with permission from the Corel Corporation. © 2004 Corel Corporation. All rights reserved. Corel, iGrafx, iGrafx Process, and the iGrafx logo are trademarks or registered trademarks of Corel Corporation and/or its subsidiaries in Canada, the United States, and/or other countries. All other product, font and company names, and logos are trademarks or registered trademarks of their respective companies. This book is not sponsored or endorsed by or affiliated with the Corel Corporation.

Pearson Education LTD.   Pearson Education Australia PTY, Limited
Pearson Education Singapore, Pte. Ltd   Pearson Education North Asia Ltd
Pearson Education, Canada, Ltd   Pearson Educación de Mexico, S.A. de C.V.
Pearson Education–Japan   Pearson Education Malaysia, Pte. Ltd

10 9 8 7 6 5 4 3 2 1
ISBN 0-13-067546-6

Contents

Preface

In this book, we present a novel approach to studying the core concepts in operations, which is one of the three major functional fields in business management, along with finance and marketing. We view operations management in terms of design, control, and improvement of business *processes* and use the process view as the unifying paradigm to study operations. We address manufacturing as well as service operations in make-to-stock as well as make-to-order environments.

We employ a logical, rigorous approach to discuss the core operations management concepts in three steps:

1. Model and understand a business process and its flows.
2. Study causal relationships between the process structure and operational and financial performance metrics.
3. Formulate implications for managerial actions by filtering out managerial "levers" (process drivers) and their impact on operational and financial measures of process performance.

Our objective is to show how managers can design and control process structure and process drivers to improve the performance of any business process. The book consists of four parts.

In Part I, "Process Management and Strategy," we introduce the basic concepts of business processes and management strategy. Processes are core technologies of all organizations for producing and delivering products that satisfy customer needs. Processes involve transforming inputs into outputs by means of capital and labor resources that carry out a set of interrelated activities. Process management strategy then involves establishing competitive priorities and matching the process capabilities with the desired product attributes.

In Part II, "Process Flow Measurement," we examine key process measures, their interrelationships, and managerial levers for controlling them. In particular, process flow time, flow rate, and inventory are three operational measures that affect the financial measures of process performance. Flow time can be decreased by shortening critical activity times, flow rates can be increased by increasing the process capacity, and inventory can be decreased by reducing the batch sizes. Throughout this part, the focus is on the average values, ignoring for now the impact of variability in process performance.

In Part III, "Process Flow Variability," we study the effect of variability in flows and processing on the process performance and the managerial levers to plan for and control it. Safety inventory is used to maintain the availability of materials and products in spite of variability in inflows and demands in the make-to-stock environment. Safety capacity is used to minimize waiting times due to variability in inflows and processing times in the make-to-order environment. Safety time is used to provide a reliable estimate of the response time to serve a customer. Finally, feedback control is used to monitor and respond to variability in process performance dynamically over time.

In Part IV, "Process Integration," we conclude with principles of synchronization of flows of materials and information through a network of processes most economically. The ideal is to eliminate waste in the form of excess costs, defects, delays, and inventories. Instead of responding to the economies of scale and variability in flows, the long-term approach is to eliminate the need for such responses by making processes lean, flexible, and predictable. It requires continual exposure and elimination of sources of inefficiency, rigidity, and variability and use of information technology to integrate various subprocesses. The goal is to design and control the process for continuous flows without waits, inventories, and defects. We close with the different philosophies of process improvement toward achieving this goal.

In Appendix I, we give a summary of the "levers" to manage business processes. We hope that this checklist will be useful to the practitioner. We assume that our readers have knowledge of some basic concepts in probability and statistics; for completeness, we summarize these as background material in Appendix II.

▪▪▪ Changes in the Second Edition

The first edition of this book was published in 1999 and reflected our experiences from teaching the core Operations Management course at the Kellogg School of Management of Northwestern University. For this second edition, while the core content remains as before, we have made extensive changes to sharpen the development of the ideas in each chapter and improve exposition:

- To enliven the exposition, we start each chapter with an opening vignette and include several current examples of how the theory can be applied in practice.
- We have improved the exposition of the quantitative material with technical derivations relegated to the chapter appendices.
- In Chapter 5, we now give an explicit treatment of the impact of setup times on flow rate.
- We have added several end-of-chapter features. These include a summary, a list of key symbols and equations, a list of key terms, a new set of discussion questions, and an expanded set of exercises.
- We have added a new glossary of terms at the end of the book.

▪▪▪ Modeling Software

We have included a CD-ROM containing a student evaluation version of iGrafx® Process™ with this edition. iGrafx Process will help the reader document, model, simulate, and analyze business processes in order to make more effective use of people and resources, reduce cycle times, and reduce costs. Logical and intuitive, iGrafx Process software should enable the reader to document and analyze most business processes, manufacturing or transactional. To validate possible changes in a safe, risk-free environment, the software provides powerful "what-if" modeling capabilities and rich graphical reporting. The software helps a user do the following:

- Build intelligent and robust process models with ease.
- Understand process dynamics with trace mode.
- Create lifelike business models using flexible transaction generators.
- Gain better insight into process interactions using the transaction window.
- Make more effective management decisions.

The software comes with an electronic version of the User Guide as well as two Quick Reference Guides in Appendices III and IV.

▪▪▪ Acknowledgments

We gratefully acknowledge the feedback from our full-time, part-time, and executive management students at our respective institutions. Our colleagues Krishnan Anand (now at Wharton School), Martin (Marty) Lariviere, Andy King (now at Dartmouth College), and Matt Tuite (now retired) have, over time, given us many suggestions for improvement. In particular, Anand suggested the original Loan Application Flow example in Chapter 3, while Marty offered us several new exercises. (Instructors know that good problem sets are golden.) Andy pointed out the need to explicitly account for setup times in determining flow rate more accurately. In addition, we also benefited from the suggestions by several colleagues at other universities. We are particularly indebted to Larry Robinson at Cornell University, George Monahan at the University of Illinois at Urbana–Champaign, Kevin Gue and Ken Doerr of the Naval Postgraduate School at Monterey, and Marty Puterman at the University of British Columbia.

The manuscript has benefited significantly from extensive and meticulous reviews from Amy Whitaker, developmental editor at Pearson Prentice Hall. We are thankful to her for suggesting, among other things, the idea of a glossary of terms and helping us prepare this list. Several people from the staff at Pearson Prentice Hall have really worked hard in patiently coordinating the entire project. In particular we are thankful to Jane Avery, Senior Editorial Assistant; Suzanne Grappi, Production Editor; and Tom Tucker and Alana Bradley, Senior Editors. We also thank Trish Finley of GGS Book Services for her assistance with the production of the manuscript. We acknowledge Kim Scott, Mark Stanford, and Cindy Valladares at iGrafx for developing some of the exercises in the problem sets using the iGrafx Process software.

Finally, all of us have been influenced in various ways by the way we were taught operations at our respective alma maters. Parts of the book reflect what each of us imbibed from the various classes we took. So we thank our mentors and other faculty at Carnegie Mellon University, Stanford University, the State University of New York at Stony Brook, and the University of California at Berkeley. Last, but not least, we would like to thank our families for their support during this effort.

Ravi Anupindi
Stephen M. Ross School of Business
The University of Michigan, Ann Arbor

Sunil Chopra, Sudhakar D. Deshmukh, and Jan A. Van Mieghem
Kellogg School of Management
Northwestern University

Eitan Zemel
Stern School of Business
New York University

About iGrafx® Process™

iGrafx® is a comprehensive suite of business management tools that help organizations understand, analyze, and optimize their processes. It combines the ease-of-use of a graphical driven tool with advanced modeling techniques and robust simulation capabilities. It enables you to identify, explore, and validate how to gain and maintain sustainable business advantage through better business processes.

iGrafx® Process™ enables the creation of business process models that reflect process behavior and the effects of change. In a way not possible with other modeling techniques such as even the most complex spreadsheet, process models respond to changing schedules of resource availability, customer demand patterns, or random events such as machine downtime. Some of the capabilities that you will be able to use include the following:

- Create, test, and simulate any process using its infinite "what-if" analysis.
- Track and model cycle times, costs, queue, and other user-definable statistics.
- Analyze process performance for value added, non–value added, and more.
- Understand process dynamics through easy-to-use tracing of simulations in action.
- Create hierarchical mapping and modeling.
- Create data-driven cause–effect charts linked to Pareto diagrams.
- Publish your content to Web or print in presentations or word-processing applications.

iGrafx creates a team-based collaborative process visualization and analysis environment. iGrafx transforms business owners into process owners by providing the necessary tools to engage in successful decision making and communicating powerful recommendations.

iGrafx, a division of Corel Inc.
7585 SW Mohawk Street
Tualatin, OR 97062
Phone: (503) 404-6050
E-mail: info@igrafx.com
www.iGrafx.com

PART

Process Management and Strategy

CHAPTER 1

Products, Processes, and Performance

Introduction

Toyota and Wal-Mart are two companies that have been successful at generating best-in-class profits over an extended period of time. Toyota's estimated profits in 2003 were $7.2 billion, the highest in the automotive industry. Wal-Mart's profits in 2003 were the best in the retailing sector at around $8 billion. Both firms have achieved financial success by providing products that meet customer expectations at a production and delivery cost that is significantly lower than the value perceived by customers. To be successful, all organizations—software manufacturers, park districts, automakers, postal services, tax-collection agencies, and even churches—must provide products and services that meet customer expectations, whether physical (comfort, safety, convenience), psychological (relaxation, peace of mind), social, or spiritual, and they must do so within a budget.

The performance of both Toyota and Wal-Mart illustrates that the success of organizations is closely linked to their business processes that produce and deliver goods to their customers. The Toyota Production System has been credited with producing high-quality cars, in a short time, and at a relatively low cost. Wal-Mart's purchasing and distribution processes allow it to provide a high availability of products at its stores at low cost. In this book, we focus on how organizations can improve business processes to produce and deliver products that better meet customer expectations.

How do organizations categorize customer expectations they seek to fulfill? What types of metrics do they use to monitor and manage process performance? How do organizations structure their processes to deliver superior financial performance?

2

This chapter provides a framework for answering these questions. In Section 1.1, we discuss how every organization can be viewed as a process. In Section 1.2, we describe performance measures that help managers to evaluate processes. In particular, we discuss financial measures, external or customer-focused measures, and internal or operational measures of performance. In Section 1.3, we look at four product attributes that customers value: product cost, delivery-response time, variety, and quality. In Section 1.4, we study the corresponding process competencies that managers can control: processing cost, flow time, resource flexibility, and process quality. We also outline the differences between two types of processes: job shop and flow shop. Section 1.5 concludes the chapter by defining process design, planning, control, and improvement decisions that are discussed in detail in the rest of the book.

▮▮▮ 1.1   The Process View of Organizations

The process view considers *any organization, or any* part *of an organization*, to be a **process** that transforms inputs into outputs (see Figure 1.1). To evaluate and improve the performance of a process—the two key objectives of this book—we must examine the transformation of inputs into outputs. The following five elements of a process characterize the transformation:

1. Inputs and outputs
2. Flow units
3. Network of activities and buffers
4. Resources
5. Information structure

Inputs and Outputs   To view an organization as a process, we must first identify its inputs and outputs. **Inputs** refer *to any tangible or intangible items that "flow" into the process from the environment;* they include raw materials, component parts, energy, data, and customers in need of service. Steel, tires, and other parts are examples of inputs from the environment into an auto assembly plant. **Outputs** are *any tangible or intangible items that flow from the process back into the environment,* such as finished products, processed information, material, energy, cash, or satisfied customers. For example, cars leave as output from an assembly plant to the environment. So an organization's inputs and outputs shape its interaction with its environment.

As inputs flow through the process they are transformed and exit as outputs. For example, raw materials flow through a manufacturing process and exit as finished goods. Similarly, data flows through an accounting process and exits as financial statements, and invoiced dollars (accounts receivable) flow through a billing and collection process and exit as collected dollars (cash).

Flow Units   The second step in establishing a process view is obtaining a clear understanding of the **flow units**—*the item*—being analyzed. Depending on the process, the flow unit may be a unit of input, such as a customer order, or a unit of output, such as a

▮▮▮▮▮▮▮▮▮▮▮ **FIGURE 1.1 The Process View of an Organization (Black Box)**

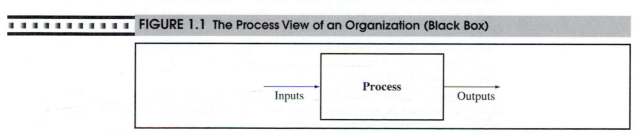

Inputs → **Process** → Outputs

TABLE 1.1 Examples of Generic Business Processes

Process	*Flow Unit*	*Input–Output Transformation*
Order fulfillment	Orders	From the receipt of an order to the delivery of the product
Production	Products	From the receipt of materials to the completion of the finished product
Outbound logistics	Products	From the end of production to the delivery of the product to the customer
Shipping	Products	From the shipment of the product to the delivery to the customer
Supply cycle	Supplies	From issuing of a purchase order to the receipt of the supplies
Customer service	Customers	From the arrival of a customer to their departure
New product development	Projects	From the recognition of a need to the launching of a product
Cash cycle	Cash	From the expenditure of funds (costs) to the collection of revenues

finished product. The flow unit can also be the financial value of the input or output. For example, the flow at an Amazon warehouse can be analyzed in terms of books, customer orders, or dollars. Determining what the flow units are is important in process analysis and performance evaluation. Table 1.1 lists some generic business processes and identifies the flow units that move through the input–output transformation.

Network of Activities and Buffers   The third step in adopting the process view is describing the process as a network of activities and buffers.

An **activity** is *the simplest form of transformation; it is the building block of a process.* An activity is actually a miniprocess in itself, but for our purposes of process evaluation and improvement, we are not concerned with the details of any specific activity, so a black box view of the activities will suffice. For example, when studying a supply chain, an interorganizational process that includes suppliers, manufacturers, distributors, and retailers, it is enough to view each organization as one activity or black box rather than looking at all the activities that take place within each organization. When studying each organization more fully, however, we must study its particular transformation process by looking closely at its specific activities. At this level, we would look at activities such as spot welding sheet metal to an auto chassis, checking in passengers at airport terminals, entering cost data in accounting information systems, and receiving electronic funds transfers at collection agencies.

A **buffer** *stores flow units that have finished with one activity but are waiting for the next activity to start.* For example, a patient who has registered waits in a buffer to see the doctor at an emergency room. Similarly, cars that have been painted wait in a buffer before entering the assembly line. For physical goods, a buffer often corresponds to a physical location where the goods are stored. A process, however, may also have a buffer, such as a set of customer orders waiting to be processed that do not correspond to any physical location. You can think of storage in a buffer as a special activity that transforms the time dimension of a flow unit by delaying it. *In business processes, storage is called* **inventory**—*the total number of flow units present within process boundaries.* The amount of inventory in the system is an important performance measure that we discuss in detail in Chapter 3.

Process activities are linked so that the output of one becomes an input into another, often through an intermediate buffer—hence the term a **network of activities and buffers**. This network describes the specific **precedence relationships** among activities—*the sequential relationships that determine which activity must be finished before another can begin.* As we will see later, the precedence relationships in a network structure strongly influence the time performance of the process. In multiproduct organizations, producing each product requires activities with a specific *set* of precedence relationships. Each network of activities, then, can have multiple "routes," each of which indicates precedence relationships for a specific product.

Figure 1.2 shows a process as a network of activities and buffers and the routes or precedence relationships among them.

Resources   The fourth element of the process view consists of organizational resources. From an operations perspective, **resources** are *tangible assets that are usually divided into two categories:*

- **Capital**, *fixed assets such as land, buildings, facilities, equipment, machines, and information systems*
- **Labor**, *people such as engineers, operators, customer-service representatives, and sales staff*

Resources facilitate the *transformation* of inputs to outputs during the process. Some activities require multiple resources (a welding activity, for instance, requires a worker and a welding gun), and some resources can perform multiple activities (some workers can not only weld but also drill). The allocation of resources to activities is an important decision in managing any process.

Information Structure   The fifth and final element of the process view of an organization is its **information structure**, which shows what information is needed and is available in order to perform activities or make managerial decisions.

▪ ▪ ▪ ▪ ▪ ▪ ▪ ▪ ▪ ▪ ▪ **FIGURE 1.2 A Process as a Network of Activities and Buffers**

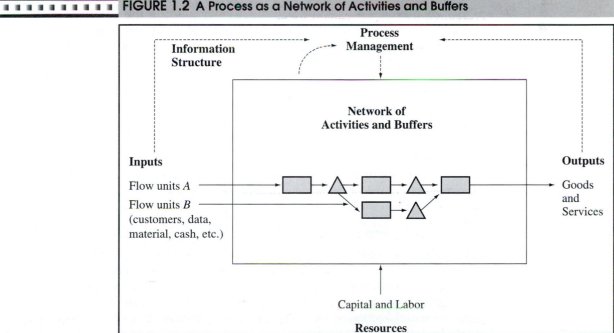

Now, we can define a **business process** as *a network of activities performed by resources that transform inputs into outputs.* **Process flow management**, therefore, is *a set of managerial policies that specify how a process should be operated over time and which resources should be allocated over time to the activities.* This is the process view of organizations that will be our basis for evaluating and improving organizational performance. We will see how process structure and process flow management significantly affect the performance of every organization.

The process view is applicable to a variety of organizations. This view can represent a manufacturing process that transforms raw materials into final products as well as services performed by accounts receivable departments, product design teams, computer rental companies, and hairdressing salons. The process view is also a convenient tool for representing *cross-functional processes* within an organization, including production, financing, and marketing-related functions and supplier relationships. By incorporating buffers, we also account for handoffs or interfaces between different people or activities—typically the areas where most improvements can be made. In addition, the process view can be adopted at a very broad level, such as the supply chain, or at a very micro level, such as a workstation in a plant. The process view is "customer-aware"—it always includes the customer—the person who receives the outputs. The process view of organizations is our main tool for the following:

1. Evaluating processes
2. Studying the ways in which processes can be designed, restructured, and managed to improve performance

▪▪▪ 1.2 Performance Measures

What determines the effectiveness of a process? Any reasonable answer to this question must be based on two factors:

1. Evaluation and measurement of the firm's current and past performance
2. Future goals as expressed by the firm's strategy

In order to assess and improve the performance of a business process, we must measure it in quantifiable terms. In this section, we identify several quantifiable measures of process performance—financial, external, and internal.

1.2.1 The Importance of Measurement: Management by Fact

Longtime General Motors chairman Alfred Sloan defined a "professional manager" as someone who manages by fact rather than by intuition or emotion. By capturing facts in an objective, concrete, and quantifiable way, we get a clear picture of the relationship between controllable process competencies and desired product attributes and thus are able to set appropriate performance standards (see Table 1.2). Performance measurement is essential in designing and implementing incentives for improving products and processes and for assessing the result of our improvements.

1.2.2 Types of Measures: Financial, External, and Internal

The financial performance of a process is based on the difference between the value that outputs of the process (products) provide to customers and their cost of production and delivery. Solid financial performance depends on satisfied customers and an effective process. Thus, process management requires *external* measures that track customer satisfaction and *internal* measures that gauge the effectiveness of the process. External measures indicate the effectiveness of products at meeting customer expectations,

TABLE 1.2 The Importance of Measurement

"When you can measure what you are speaking about, and express it in numbers, you know something about it."

—Lord Kelvin (1824–1907)

"Count what is countable, measure what is measurable, and what is not measurable, make measurable."

—Galileo Galilei (1564–1642)

"Data! Data! Data! I can't make bricks without clay."
—Sherlock Holmes in *The Adventure of Copper Beeches*
by Sir Arthur Conan Doyle

"In God we trust, everyone else must bring data."

—W. Edwards Deming

whereas internal measures identify areas where the process is performing well and areas where improvement is necessary.

Financial Measures

Financial measures track the difference between the value provided to customers and the cost of producing and delivering the product. The goal of every organization is to maximize this difference. For a profit-making enterprise, the key financial measure is profit. For a not-for-profit organization, the key financial measure is the value provided to its clients given the budget constraint. Each quarter, most organizations report three types of financial measures to shareholders and other stakeholders:

1. *Absolute performance* (revenues, costs, net income, profit)
2. *Performance relative to asset utilization* (accounting ratios such as return on assets, return on investment, and inventory turns)
3. *"Survival" strength* (cash flow)

Though the ultimate judge of process performance, financial measures are inherently lagging, aggregate, and more results than action oriented. They represent the goal of the organization but cannot be used as the sole measures to manage and control processes. Managing and controlling a process using only financial measures would be like driving a car while looking in the rear-view mirror. Thus, it is important to link financial measures to external measures that track customer satisfaction with process output and internal measures that track operational effectiveness.

External Measures

To improve its financial performance, a firm must attract and retain customers by providing goods and services that meet or exceed their expectations. Customer expectations can be defined in terms of four critical attributes of the process output (products)—product cost, response time, variety, and quality. For example, FedEx customers expect speed and reliability and are willing to pay more for it than, say, customers of the U.S. Postal Service, who expect a lower cost and are willing to tolerate a longer delivery time. A person buying a Lexus expects high quality, a range of options, and very responsive service. A person buying a Toyota Corolla, in contrast, expects to pay a much lower price and is willing to compromise on features, options, and responsiveness of service. Customer satisfaction is then linked to whether the performance of the product along the four attributes meets or exceeds customer expectations.

External measures track customer expectations in terms of product cost, response time, variety, and quality as well as customer satisfaction with product performance along these dimensions. External measures can be used to estimate the value of goods or services to customers. For example, the American Society for Quality and the University of Michigan have developed the American Customer Satisfaction Index, which tracks overall customer satisfaction in several manufacturing and service industries and public sectors. Each score is a weighted average of customer responses to questions relating to perceptions of service, quality, value, and the extent to which products meet expectations.

Measures that track customer dissatisfaction with a product are also good external measures that can help guide future improvement. Number of warranty repairs, product recalls, and field failures are some measurable signs of potential customer dissatisfaction. Although number of customer complaints received is a direct measure of customer dissatisfaction, research shows that only about 4% of dissatisfied customers bother to complain. Those who do complain, therefore, represent just the tip of the iceberg. Customer dissatisfaction decreases customer retention, leading to lower revenues and increased costs. It is estimated that organizations typically lose 20% of their unsatisfied customers forever and that the cost of attracting a new customer is about five times that of serving a current customer.

Customer-satisfaction measures represent an external market perspective that is objective and bottom-line oriented because it identifies competitive benchmarks at which the **process manager**—*the person who plans and controls the process*—can aim. However, they measure customer satisfaction at an *aggregate*, not at an *individual customer*, level. They are also more results oriented than action oriented: in other words, they cannot indicate *how* the manager might improve processes. Finally, they are *lagging* rather than *leading* indicators of success, as they are "after-the-fact" assessments of performance. To be operationally useful, they must be linked to internal measures that the process manager can control.

Internal Measures

A process manager does not directly control either customer satisfaction or financial performance. In order to meet customer expectations and improve financial performance, a manager requires internal operational measures that are detailed, that can be controlled, and that ultimately correlate with product and financial performance. Customer expectations in terms of product cost, response time, variety, and quality can be translated into internal measures that track the performance of the process in terms of cost, flow time, flexibility, and quality. Internal performance measures can thus be a predictor of customer (dis)satisfaction (and thus financial performance) if customer expectations have been identified accurately.

For example, an airline's on-time performance may be translated into the following internal goal: "Average arrival and departure delays should not exceed 15 minutes." The responsiveness of its reservation system could be measured by "the time taken to answer the telephone," with a specified goal of "30 seconds or less 95 percent of the time." Similarly, waiting time for service at a bank teller's window or for registration and admission at a hospital can all be measured, monitored, and standardized. Likewise, product availability at a retailer can be measured by such standards as "fraction of demand filled from the stock on hand" or "average number of stockouts per year." At a call center, service (un)availability can be measured by the proportion of customer calls that must wait because "all operators are busy." The goal might be to reduce that proportion to "no more than 20 percent." At an electric utility company, service availability might be measured by "frequency or duration of power outages per year" with a target of "no more than 30 minutes per year." In each case, the internal measure is an indicator of how satisfied the customer is likely to be with process performance.

Process flexibility can be measured either by the time or cost needed to switch production from one good or service to another or by the number of different products that can be produced.

When measuring product quality, managers must be specific as to which of the many quality dimensions they are concerned with: product features, performance, reliability, serviceability, aesthetics, and conformance to customer expectations. Reliability, for example, is measured in terms of durability and frequency of repair and can be assessed by technical measures like the following:

- *Failure rate*, which measures the probability of product failure
- *Mean time between failures* (MTBF), which indicates how long a product is likely to perform satisfactorily before needing repair

Serviceability can be measured using *mean time to repair* (MTTR), which indicates how long a product is likely to be out of service while under repair.

Although customers can readily identify product features, performance can be assessed only through actual experience; evaluating reliability usually requires long-term experience. In a restaurant, the main service transformation (the "product") is "feeding" hungry customers, and ambiance, menu, and a cocktail lounge are among the features. Tasty food prepared by experienced chefs and served by knowledgeable, friendly, attentive waiters provides a quality dining experience; consistency of quality from one visit to the next proves reliability. McDonald's, for example, is a highly reliable fast-food restaurant featuring a limited menu and a dining experience of a very specific kind.

Knowing the external product measures expected by customers, the process manager must translate them into appropriate internal process measures that affect external measures. In order to be effective, internal measures must meet two conditions:

1. They must be linked to external measures that customers deem important.
2. They must be directly controllable by the process manager.

Obviously, measuring and improving a feature that the customer does not value is a waste of time and resources. Moreover, if we do not know how an internal process variable affects a product measure, we cannot control it. Ignoring one or both of these conditions has sabotaged many process improvement programs (see Kordupleski et al., 1993).

▪▪▪ 1.3   Products and Product Attributes

Products are *the desired set of process outputs.* (The process may also produce by-products, such as heat, pollution, or scrap, which are not desired by or delivered to customers.) Given that products may be physical goods, services performed, or a combination of both, there are some differences (and many similarities) between goods and services that managers must consider when designing or managing the processes that deliver them. One difference is that unlike tangible goods, services include tangible and intangible aspects experienced by the customer, such as being treated by a doctor or receiving investment advice. Another difference is that some services, such as a haircut, are often produced and consumed simultaneously and cannot be produced in advance, whereas goods can be produced and stored for later consumption.

Different customers may have different expectations for a specific product. If the process is to produce and deliver products that satisfy all customers, the process manager must know what these expectations are. External measures help a process manager identify key **product attributes**—*those properties that customers consider important*—that define customer expectations. For example, external measures help FedEx define customer expectations in terms of delivery time, reliability, and price for its next-day-delivery product. We categorize product attributes along the following four dimensions:

1. **Product cost** is *the total cost that a customer incurs in order to own and experience the product*. It includes the purchase price plus any costs incurred during the lifetime of the product, such as costs for service, maintenance, insurance, and even final disposal. Cost is important because customers usually make purchase decisions within budget constraints.

2. **Product delivery-response time** is *the total time that a customer must wait before receiving a product for which he or she has expressed a need to the provider*. Response time is closely related to product availability and accessibility. If a manufactured good is on store shelves, the response time is effectively zero. If it is stocked in a warehouse or a distribution center, response time consists of the transportation time needed to get it to the customer. If a firm does not stock the product and produces only to order, response time will also include the time required to produce the product.

   With services, response time is determined by the availability of resources required to serve the customer. If resources are not immediately available, the customer must wait. For example, in the absence of an idle checkout clerk, a customer has to wait in a checkout line for service. Generally, customers prefer short response times, as immediate gratification of needs is typically preferred over delayed gratification.

3. **Product variety** is *the range of choices offered to the customer to meet his or her needs*. Variety can be interpreted and measured at different levels. At the lowest level, we can measure variety in terms of the level of customization offered for a product. This includes options offered for a particular car model or the number of colors and sizes for a style of jeans. At a higher level, variety can be measured in terms of the number of product lines or families offered by a firm. For example, a car manufacturer like General Motors offering a full range like compacts, sports cars, luxury sedans, and sport-utility vehicles (SUVs) provides more variety of product lines than a manufacturer like Ferrari offering only sports cars. Similarly, a retail store offering the full range from casual to business to formal wear offers more variety than a store focused on providing only tuxedoes. Whereas standard, commodity products have little variety, custom products may be one-of-a-kind items tailored specifically to customers' unique needs or wishes. For example, when purchasing consumer items such as clothing in a department store, customers must choose from a limited selection. In contrast, when ordering a suit at a custom tailor, each customer can provide different specifications that meet personal needs and desires that constitute, in effect, an almost endless range of product variety.

4. **Product quality** is *the degree of excellence; how well the product performs*. Product quality is a function of effective design as well as production that conforms to the design. It may refer to tangible, intangible, and even transcendental

TABLE 1.3 What Is Quality?

"Quality is recognized by a non-thinking process, and therefore cannot be defined!"
—R. M. Pirsig in *Zen and the Art of Motorcycle Maintenance*

"That which makes anything such as it is."
—*Funk and Wagnall's Dictionary*

"Fitness for use."
—J. Juran and American Society of Quality Control

"Conformance to requirements."
—P. Crosby

"Closeness to target—deviations mean loss to the society."
—G. Taguchi

"Total Quality Control provides full customer satisfaction at the most economical levels."
—A. Feigenbaum

"Eight dimensions of quality are: Performance, Features, Conformance, Reliability, Serviceability, Durability, Aesthetics, and Perception."
—D. Garvin

characteristics. Product quality is often the most difficult product attribute to define and measure because subjective judgment and perception play important roles in the estimation of quality. Table 1.3 lists some definitions of quality. Each definition tries to capture something that is elusive and all-inclusive, largely because quality is a dimension that must be seen from both the customer's and the producer's perspective.

From the customer's perspective, quality depends on a product's features (what it can do), performance (how well it functions), reliability (how consistently it functions over time), serviceability (how quickly it can be repaired), aesthetics, and conformance to expectations. Whereas product features and performance are influenced by quality of design, reliability is more heavily influenced by how well the production process conforms to the design. The styling, size, options, and engine rating of an automobile are its features. Acceleration, emergency handling, ride comfort, safety, and fuel efficiency are aspects of performance, while durability and failure-free performance over time represent its reliability.

A product may be defined as a bundle of the four attributes—cost, time, variety, and quality. When these four attributes are measured and quantified, we can represent a product by a point in the associated four-dimensional matrix, or *product space*, of cost, time, variety, and quality. (The "product space" image will be a useful metaphor to define strategy in Chapter 2.) Sound external measures track product performance along these four attributes at an absolute level relative to the competition and relative to customer expectations.

The value of a product to the customer is measured by the utility (in economic terms) that he or she derives from buying some combination of these attributes. In general, high-quality products available in wide varieties that are delivered quickly and at low cost provide high customer value. Product value or utility is a complex function of the four product attributes. It may be easy to define qualitatively, but it is difficult to measure in practice. *A reasonable estimate of* **product value** *is the price that a specific* *customer is willing to pay for a product*. Of course, this willingness to pay varies from customer to customer, giving rise to the familiar price–quantity market-demand relationship described by economists.

Customers prefer products with all the attributes—they want products that are good, fast, and cheap. But all products have trade-offs. (Some products are good but not delivered as fast; some are cheap but not as good.) When customer expectations depend on the availability of competing products, an important strategic business decision is selecting the right combination of product attributes that will result in a product that appeals to a particular segment of the market (see Chapter 2). Moreover, because of competition, there must be continuous improvement in product variety and quality and a decrease in cost and delivery-response time.

▪▪▪ 1.4 Processes and Process Competencies

Processes produce and deliver products by transforming inputs into outputs by means of capital and labor resources. *The process of producing goods is typically called* **manufacturing** *or* **production operations**. *Processes that deliver services are called* **service operations**. We refer to *business processes that design, produce, and deliver goods and services* simply as **operations**. Given the many similarities, we highlight some of the unique aspects of service operations. Many service operations, such as a hospital, require the physical presence of the customer who undergoes or participates in at least part of the process. This introduces variability from one customer to the next and increases the importance of factors such as the attractiveness of the process environment and friendliness of the labor resources. (The term "backroom operations" refers to those aspects of service operations that are hidden from customers.) Setting effective internal measures of performance for service operations is particularly difficult because services involve significant interaction with the customer and are often produced and consumed simultaneously. This makes it harder to identify internal measures that could be leading indicators of customer satisfaction.

A process manager aims to improve financial performance by effectively producing products that satisfy customer expectations in terms of the four product attributes—product cost, response time, variety, and quality. In this section, we describe process competencies according to the corresponding four product attributes. Internal measures track the competency of a process in terms of cost, flow time, flexibility, and quality. Internal measures are thus an indicator of how well the process output is likely to meet customer expectations.

1.4.1 Process Competencies

As with products, we use four dimensions for measuring the competence of processes to produce and deliver the corresponding product attributes:

1. **Process cost** is *the total cost incurred in producing and delivering outputs*. It includes the cost of raw materials and both the fixed and the variable costs of operating the process. (For our purposes, this is as specific as we need to be about the ways accounting practices allocate costs to time periods and products.)
2. **Process flow time** is *the total time needed to transform a flow unit from input into output*. It includes the actual process time as well as any waiting time a flow unit spends in buffers. Process flow time depends on the number of resource units as well as the speed of processing.
3. **Process flexibility** measures *the ability of the process to produce and deliver desired product variety*. Process flexibility depends on the flexibility of its

resources: flexible resources (such as flexible technology and cross-trained workers or "generalists") can perform multiple different activities and, often, produce a variety of products. Dedicated or specialized resources, in contrast, can perform only a very restricted set of activities, typically those designed for one product. Another dimension of process flexibility is its ability to deal with fluctuating demand. A steel mill cannot readily alter the amount of steel it produces at a time. An auto repair shop, in contrast, finds it easier to change the number of cars repaired each day.

4. **Process quality** refers to *the ability of the process to produce and deliver quality products*. It includes process accuracy (precision), conformance to design specifications, process reliability, and maintainability.

The competencies of a process identify products that the process will be particularly good at supplying. For example, McMaster-Carr, a materials, repair, and operations (MRO) products distributor, has a process that has high flexibility, short flow time, and high-quality competencies. It does not, however, have a low-cost competency. The process competencies at McMaster-Carr allow it to supply a large variety of MRO products quickly and reliably. The company charges its customers a premium price. Customers looking for a large quantity of a single item at low price do not go to McMaster-Carr.

Shouldice Hospital in Canada focuses on hernia operations for otherwise healthy patients. The founder developed and standardized a repeatable surgical procedure that requires only local anesthesia and encourages patient movement, participation, and socialization through excellent ambulatory care provided in a non-hospital-like environment. The Shouldice process provides very high quality service at relatively low cost. It is, however, very inflexible and will not accept patients who have any risk factor and certainly does not treat patients for anything other than hernia. The competencies required in an emergency room process are very different from those of Shouldice. Given the wide variety of patients that an emergency room has to treat, its process competencies must include flexibility and high quality.

1.4.2 Process Architectures: Job Shop versus Flow Shop

Process architecture is defined by *the types of resources used to perform the activities and their physical layout in the processing network*. Automobile assembly plants have process architecture with specialized resources laid out in a rigid sequence that is common for all cars produced. A tool and die shop, in contrast, has process architecture that uses flexible resources to work on a large variety of products, each with a different flow sequence. Process competencies are strongly influenced by the process architecture. The link between customer expectations, desired process competencies, and required process architecture is discussed in Chapter 2. Most process architectures fall somewhere on the spectrum between two extremes: the *job shop process* and the *flow shop process*.

Job Shops

At one extreme, a **job shop** uses *flexible resources to produce low volumes of customized, high-variety products*. Job shops include artisan bakeries, tool and die shops, management consulting firms, law firms, and architectural and design companies. Job shops use general-purpose resources that can perform many different activities and locate similar resources in close proximity. This design is called a **functional layout** or **process layout** because it *groups organizational resources by processing activity or "function" in "departments."* For example, a job shop manufacturing process (say, a tool and die or machine shop) will group all its presses together in a stamping department and all its mills in a milling department.

A job shop usually has many products simultaneously flowing through the process, each with its own route. Therefore, it is often more practical to represent a job shop as a network of resources instead of a network of activities. In a network of resources, the rectangular boxes represent resources grouped into departments (such as an X-ray, accounts payable, or stamping department) instead of activities. The flowchart on the left in Figure 1.3 shows an example of the functional layout of a process with four resource groups (labeled A, B, C, and D) that produces two products. Resources A, D, and B perform product 1's activities, while product 2 calls for resources C, B, and A. The set of activities for each product is now assigned to the resources with the routes representing the precedence relationships as before.

Because the sequence of activities required to process each product (i.e., the routes) varies from one job to the next, job shops typically display jumbled work flows with large amounts of storage and substantial waiting between activities. To direct work flow, job shops typically use highly structured information systems.

Because of the high variety of products flowing through the job shop, resources often need setups before they can be changed over from the activities required for one product to those required for another. This changeover results in loss of production and a fluctuating workload. In terms of process competencies, a job shop typically has high process flexibility that permits product customization but has high processing costs and long flow times.

Flow Shops

At the other extreme, a **flow shop** uses *specialized resources that perform limited tasks but do so with high precision and speed*. The result is a standardized product produced in large volumes. Because of the specialized resources and expertise developed by workers through repetition, quality tends to be more consistent. Although the high-processing capacity needed to produce large volumes entails high fixed costs for plant and equipment, these costs are spread over larger volumes, often resulting in the low variable processing cost that characterizes economies of scale. Resources are arranged according to the sequence of activities needed to produce a particular product, and limited storage space is used between activities. *Because the location of resources is dictated by the processing requirements of the product, the resulting network layout is called a* **product layout**. The flowchart on the right in Figure 1.3 shows the two-product

FIGURE 1.3 Functional Layout (left) versus Product Layout (right)

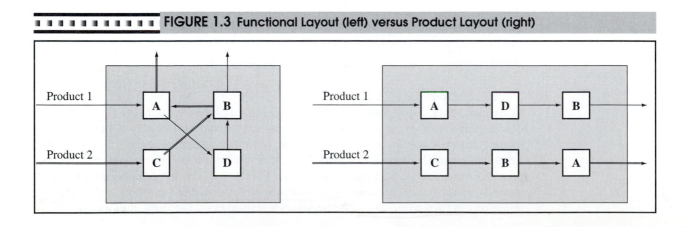

process now in product layout. Each product is now produced on its own "production line" with product-dedicated resources. Notice that dedicating resources to a product may necessitate duplication (and investment) of a resource pool, such as for resources A and B in Figure 1.3. On the positive side, limiting the product variety allows specialization of dedicated resources. Therefore, flow shops typically have shorter process flow time than job shops.

The most famous example of a flow shop is the automobile assembly line pioneered by Henry Ford in 1913. An *assembly line* is actually an example of a *discrete flow shop:* products are produced part by part. In contrast, beverage companies, steel plants, oil refineries, and chemical plants are *continuous flow shops:* sometimes called "processing plants," they produce outputs, such as beer and oil, in a continuous fashion. Although the rigid layout of resources and their highly specialized nature prevent the process from providing significant product variety, the flow shop remains the crown jewel of the industrial revolution—its hallmark is low unit-processing cost, short flow time, and consistent quality at high volumes.

Not surprisingly, real-world processes generally fall somewhere along the spectrum between these two extremes. In the early stages of a product's life cycle, for example, because volumes are low and uncertain, high capital investment in specialized resources cannot be justified. Consequently, a job shop is often the appropriate process. As the product matures, however, volume increases and product consistency, cost, and response time become critical. The flow shop then becomes the more appropriate process architecture. At the end of the product life cycle, volumes have declined, and perhaps only replacements are needed. Again, the job shop becomes more attractive.

▮▮▮ 1.5   Process Design, Planning, Control, and Improvement

A process manager has four important questions to consider:

1. What should the process architecture be?
2. What policies should govern process operations?
3. How should process performance be controlled over time?
4. How should process performance be improved?

During **process design**, *managers select the process architecture that best develops the competencies that will meet customer expectations.* Process design decisions include plant location and capacity, product and process design, resource choice and investment (capital/technology and labor), and scale of operation. For example, Toyota has plants in most major markets that produce large volumes of the Corolla using a line flow process. This allows Toyota to provide a large volume of Corollas quickly at a low cost but with a limited amount of variety. In contrast, Ferrari manufactures all its cars in Italy using more of a job shop. Even though it takes longer to produce a car (that is very expensive!), Ferrari is able to accommodate a high degree of customization. Given the small volume of sales, a single plant allows Ferrari to achieve some economies of scale relative to having plants in every major market.

Process planning is *identifying internal measures that track process competence and specifying the managerial policies that ensure process competence along desired dimensions.* Managerial policies specify the operation of the process and use of resources over time to best meet customer demand. At a retail store, managerial policies specify how many units of each product should be carried in stock and when replenishment orders should be placed. At a call center, managerial policies specify the number of customer service representatives that should be available by day of week and time of day.

Process control *is the aspect of process management that is focused on continually ensuring that in the short run, the actual process performance conforms to the planned performance.* The objective is to ensure that the actual process performance continually conforms to the planned performance. Ensuring conformance means monitoring the actual performance over time, comparing it to the planned performance, and taking corrective action when deviations occur. Control decisions include monitoring and correcting product cost, delivery performance, customer waiting time, inventory levels, and quality defects.

For **process improvement**, managers identify internal measures that need to be improved in the long run and work on changes in process design or planning that are required to achieve this improvement. For example, Toyota has identified that it is important for its suppliers to be more flexible, operate with lower inventories, and be able to respond to a Toyota order quickly. Toyota works with its suppliers to reduce changeover times in all production lines and detect defects as soon as they are introduced. These process changes improve performance in terms of flexibility, inventories, and time.

▪▪▪ 1.6 The Plan of the Book

The remainder of this book focuses on the management of operations in general and process flows in particular. Chapter 2 focuses on strategic decisions about product attributes and matching process competencies to product decisions. In Part II, we analyze key process measures in detail. Part III is devoted to process planning and control and stresses the means by which managers achieve desired performance in the presence of uncertainty. In conclusion, Part IV focuses on the principles of process synchronization, integration, and improvement.

SUMMARY ▪▪▪▪▪▪▪

A process is a network of activities and buffers that uses resources to transform inputs into outputs. Any organization or any part of an organization can be viewed as a process. The effectiveness of a process is ultimately determined by its financial performance—the difference between the value provided to customers and the cost of producing and delivering the product. Any financial measure, however, is a lagging measure of performance and thus cannot be used to manage and control the process.

To improve financial performance, a firm must attract and retain customers by providing goods and services that meet or exceed customer expectations. Customer expectations are defined in terms of key product attributes—cost, delivery response time, variety, and quality. From a customer's perspective, a product is thus a bundle of the four attributes. The value of a product is measured by the utility that the customer derives from buying some combination of these attributes. To improve financial performance, a firm must identify and deliver attributes that are valued by customers.

Product attributes are the output of a process and can be measured only after the process is complete. As leading indicators of performance, the manager must thus internally track competency of the process in terms of cost, flow time, flexibility, and quality. The competencies of a process identify the products that the process will be particularly good at supplying. Different process architectures result in different process competencies. At one extreme, a job shop has high process flexibility that permits product customization but with high processing costs and long flow times. At the other extreme, a flow shop provides low cost, short flow times, and consistent quality but cannot produce significant variety.

KEY TERMS ▪▪▪▪▪▪▪

- Activity
- Buffer
- Business process
- Capital
- Flow shop
- Flow units
- Functional layout
- Information structure
- Inputs
- Inventory
- Job shop
- Labor
- Manufacturing
- Network of activities and buffers

- Operations
- Outputs
- Precedence relationships
- Process
- Process architecture
- Process control
- Process cost
- Process design
- Process flexibility
- Process flow management
- Process flow time
- Process layout
- Process manager
- Process planning

- Process quality
- Product attributes
- Product cost
- Product delivery-response time
- Product layout
- Product quality
- Product value
- Product variety
- Production operations
- Products
- Resources
- Service operations

DISCUSSION QUESTIONS ▪▪▪▪▪▪▪

1.1 Several examples of organizations are listed here. For each, identify underlying business processes in terms of inputs, outputs, and resources employed. Who are the major competitors of each? What financial, external, and internal performance measures should each organization use? Who are their customers, and what product attributes do they consider important? What process competencies should each organization aim for?
- Personal computer manufacturer
- Telephone company
- Major business school
- Federal penitentiary
- Red Cross
- Law firm
- Fast-food restaurant
- Inner-city school
- Local bank
- Art museum
- Public park
- Toothpaste manufacturer

1.2 Compare Wal-Mart and a convenience store chain like 7-Eleven in terms of the product attributes that customers expect. What process competencies does each organization aim to develop?

1.3 Compare McDonald's and a high-end restaurant in terms of the product attributes that customers expect. What process competencies should each organization aim to develop? Would you expect each process to be more like a job shop or a flow shop? Why?

1.4 As a product moves through its life cycle from introduction to maturity to decline, how do the attributes that customers consider important change? What are the implications in terms of the process competencies that need to be developed? What process type is appropriate in the introductory phase? In the maturity phase? Why?

SELECTED BIBLIOGRAPHY ▪▪▪▪▪▪▪

Kordupleski, R. E., R. T. Rust, and A. J. Zahorik. 1993. "Why Improving Quality Doesn't Improve Quality (or Whatever Happened to Marketing?)." *California Management Review*, Spring, 82–95.

Leavitt, T. 1976. "The Industrialization of Service." *Harvard Business Review* 54, no. 5: 63–74.

Schmenner, R. W. 1994. *Plant and Service Tours in Operations Management.* Upper Saddle River, N.J.: Prentice Hall.

Schmenner, R. W. 1995. *Service Operations Management.* Upper Saddle River, N.J.: Prentice Hall.

Wheelwright, S. C. 1978. "Reflecting Corporate Strategy in Manufacturing Decisions." *Business Horizons*, February, 57–66.

2

Operations Strategy and Management

Introduction

In early 1984, Michael Dell started a company that only 20 years later has become the worldwide leader in the computer industry with a global market share nearing 18% in 2004. In the 1980s, the computer sales process was tremendously inefficient, and it was not uncommon for new technology to take more than a year before it would reach end customers. In terms of the product attributes discussed in Chapter 1, Dell's initial focus was to improve product delivery-response time while keeping product cost low and product variety and quality acceptable. To best deliver that specific value proposition, Dell designed a new operational process that involved direct sales coupled with a lean and responsive assemble-to-order system. According to Carpenter (2003), Dell explains that "his key to success was putting the focus on the customer and building a custom computer that was exactly what the user needed." The perfect fit between intended strategic positioning and the process used to deliver the products has yielded impressive returns: "Dell said his business grew by 80 percent for the first eight years, 60 percent for the next six and about 20 percent each year since then." While the Dell system seems deceptively simple and has been analyzed by many managers and researchers, no other computer company has been able to copy it successfully.

How does a company's strategic market positioning affect the choice of its business processes? How can a company verify that its processes have the appropriate competencies to support its competitive strategy? How can a company use the inherent trade-offs in process competencies to its advantage when designing its business processes?

In this chapter, we examine the relationship between strategy and operations management and trace their historical development. Section 2.1 starts with a discussion of the concepts of strategic positioning and operational effectiveness. Section 2.2 then defines *business strategy* in terms of markets, customers, and products and *operations strategy* as planning the process structure necessary to produce and deliver those products. In Section 2.3, we emphasize the importance of *strategic fit* among three pivotal aspects of a firm's operations:

1. Business strategy
2. Operations strategy
3. Process architecture and operating policies

In Section 2.4, we show how focusing on narrow market segments and structuring business processes accordingly facilitate this strategic fit. Section 2.5 presents an important example of matching products and processes according to variety and volume. In Section 2.6, we discuss the concept of *operations frontier* in the competitive product space of product cost, response time, variety, and quality. Section 2.7 concludes the chapter by tracing the historical evolution of operations strategy and process improvements.

▪▪▪ 2.1 Strategic Positioning and Operational Effectiveness

The word *strategy* derives from the Greek military term *stratégia*—"the general's art." It is the art or science of planning a war, and much of the original management thinking on strategy treated business as something of a war and the goal was to win. However, times have changed. Chief executive officers are no longer generals, and workers are not soldiers. Today, strategy is a plan to achieve an objective (Hindle, 1994).

The *plan* specifies precisely what managers must do in order to reach corporate objectives. Often, the implicit objective of a business strategy is to deliver sustained *superior*, not just average, performance relative to the competition. To outperform one's rivals, one must be—and remain—different from and better than them. Because similar firms, especially those in the same industry, perform in much the same way, a sustainable competitive advantage requires some form of differentiation.

Competitive Product Space   **Competitive product space** is *a representation of the firm's product portfolio as measured along four dimensions or product attributes— product cost, response time, variety, and quality*—that were introduced in Chapter 1. Figure 2.1 represents a firm's product portfolio in the competitive product space, but for graphical simplicity, we show only variety and cost while holding response time and quality constant. (In fact, instead of representing product cost directly, the figure shows the reciprocal of cost [1/cost] as a proxy of cost efficiency.) An organization may, for example, differentiate itself by offering customers value through a product with a unique combination of the four product attributes. Measuring and quantifying the portfolio of current product offerings along these four dimensions yields a set of *points*, one per product, in the competitive product space.

Strategic Positioning   **Strategic positioning** *defines those positions that the firm wants to occupy in its competitive product space;* it identifies the product attributes that the firm wants to provide to its customers. Figure 2.1 depicts strategic positioning of two firms—A and B. Firm A provides a low-cost standardized product, whereas Firm B provides an expensive but customized product. The arrow shows the intended direction of movement for the firm's strategy.

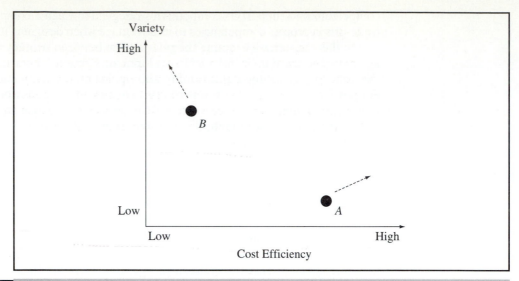

▪▪▪▪▪▪▪▪▪▪▪▪ **FIGURE 2.1** Current Position and Strategic Directions of Movement in the Competitive Product Space

Competitors also occupy positions in the competitive product space. One could conceivably measure the product performance of each competitor, deduce its strategic positioning from the attributes of its products, and represent its current position in the competitive space. Occupying a differentiated position, then, entails producing and delivering different product attributes. This approach requires the firm's business processes to be structured and operated in ways that differ from those of competitors. In the automotive industry, for example, Hyundai aims to occupy a low-cost position, and Rolls-Royce strives for the highest-quality cars. As we will see, each company's business processes will also differ. To *sustain* competitive advantage, a firm must ensure that its competition finds it hard to imitate its chosen position.

Operational Effectiveness   To deliver superior performance, a firm must strive to select product attributes that are distinct from those of its competition and create business processes that are more effective than its competition. **Operational effectiveness** means *developing processes and operating policies that support the strategic position better than the processes and policies of competitors do.* "Operational effectiveness includes but is not limited to efficiency. It refers to any number of practices that allow a company to better utilize its inputs by, for example, reducing defects in products or developing products faster" (Porter, 1996). It is important to understand that operational effectiveness does not necessarily mean the lowest-cost process. A firm such as FedEx, with a strategic position focused on speed and reliability, develops operational effectiveness with processes having competencies in speed and reliability, not low cost. In practice, gaining and sustaining a competitive advantage requires that a firm have a good strategic position *and* operational effectiveness to support that position.

▪▪▪2.2   The Strategy Hierarchy

Strategic planning spans different levels in an organization. At the highest level of a diversified company, **corporate strategy** *defines the businesses in which the corporation will participate and specifies how key corporate resources will be acquired and allocated* *to each business*. Corporate strategy formation is thus like portfolio selection—choosing a mix of divisions or product lines so as to ensure synergy and competitive advantage.

At the next level, **business strategy** *defines the scope of each division or business unit in terms of the attributes of the products that it will offer and the market segments that it will serve.* Here, strategy includes what we describe as *strategic positioning:* selecting the key product attributes on which the business unit will compete. Since the goal is to differentiate the firm from its competition by establishing competitive priorities in terms of the four product attributes, business strategy entails a two-pronged analysis:

1. Competitive analysis of the industry in which the business unit will compete
2. Critical analysis of the unit's competitive skills and resources

At the next level, we have **functional strategies** that *define the purpose for marketing, operations, and finance—the three main functions in most organizations:*

- *Marketing* identifies and targets customers that the business unit wants to serve, the products that it must supply in order to meet customer needs, and the competition that it will face in the marketplace.
- *Operations* designs, plans, and manages processes through which the business unit supplies customers with desired products.
- *Finance* acquires and allocates the resources needed to operate all a unit's business processes.

Each of these functions must translate midlevel business strategy into its own functional requirements by specifying what it must do well in order to support the higher-level strategy.

In particular, **operations strategy** *configures and develops business processes that best enable a firm to produce and deliver the products specified by the business strategy.* This task includes selecting activities and resources and combining them into a *network architecture* that, as we saw in Chapter 1, defines the key elements of a process, such as inputs and outputs, flow units, and information structure. Operations is also responsible for developing or acquiring the necessary process competencies—process cost, flow time, flexibility, and quality—to support the firm's business strategy. Whereas business strategy involves choosing product attributes on which to compete, operations strategy focuses on the process competencies required to produce and deliver those product attributes.

Thus, business strategy is concerned with selecting *external* output markets and the products with which to supply them, whereas operations strategy involves designing *internal* processes and *interfaces* between input and output markets. An operations strategy must establish operational objectives that are consistent with overall business goals and develop the processes that will accomplish them. For example, a business strategy based on product cost as a top competitive priority calls for an operations strategy that focuses on efficient and lean business processes. Similarly, if a firm seeks competitive advantage through product variety, its business processes must be flexible enough to produce and deliver customized products. If the goal is to provide short response times, processes must include greater investment in inventories (for manufactured goods) or greater process availability through excess capacity (for both manufacturing and service operations) as we will show in the remainder of this book. Finally, a strategy that calls for producing and delivering high-quality products requires high-quality processes with precision equipment and highly trained workers. In every case, process competencies must be *aligned* with desired product attributes—operations strategy must be *consistent* with business strategy. Example 2.1 describes how Wal-Mart achieved such consistency.

▪▪▪▪▪▪▪▪▪▪ **FIGURE 2.2** The Wal-Mart Strategy and Operations Structure

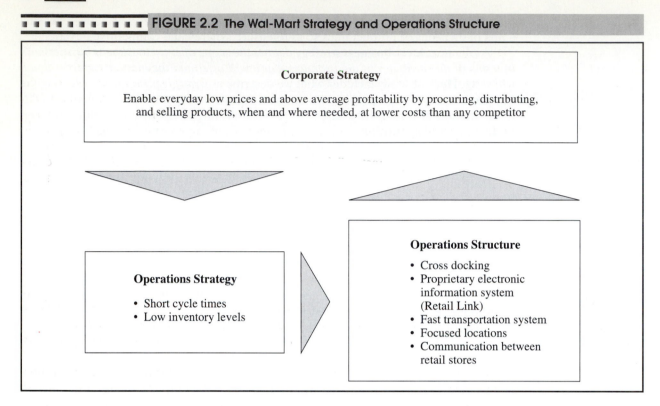

Example 2.1

As an example of consistency in hierarchical strategy, consider the case of Wal-Mart, the well-known retailing and distribution company. Figure 2.2 shows how Wal-Mart has positioned itself as a low-cost retailer of medium-quality goods supplied with high accessibility and availability in terms of both store locations and continuous product availability on store shelves. To support this business strategy, Wal-Mart operations strategy calls for an efficient distribution process featuring short response times and low inventory levels.

To accomplish both of these seemingly contradictory objectives, Wal-Mart's logistic process calls for its own transportation fleet and information network, complete with satellite communications system to connect stores in well-chosen locations. To ensure close communication among retail outlets and suppliers—and thus fast replenishment of depleted stocks—*point-of-sales* (*POS*) *data* are transmitted via a proprietary information system called Retail Link. Low pipeline-inventory levels are achieved by a system called *cross-docking* distribution centers: incoming trucks dock opposite outgoing trucks so that goods are distributed directly from incoming to outgoing trucks without intermediate storage.

The overall result is impressive: a high inventory turnover rate (four times the industry average), improved targeting of products to markets (resulting in fewer stockouts and markdowns), significantly higher sales per square foot of store space ($455 in 2002—twice the discount store average of $224), dominant market share, and growth (from 20% in 1987 to 47% in 1995 to 63% in 2002, while its rival, the second-largest discounter Kmart, had a share of only 10.6% in 2002). Wal-Mart is thus an outstanding example of a strategically well-positioned firm that has carefully orchestrated operations strategy and process structure in support of business strategy.

▪▪▪ 2.3 Strategic Fit

The hierarchical framework described in the previous section reflects a *top-down* approach to strategy formulation: once the firm's business strategy has defined its position in the competitive space (as defined by price, time, variety, and quality), its business processes are then designed and managed to attain and maintain that position. It is worth pursuing this point because it helps us answer a fundamental question: *What distinguishes an effective business process?* In manufacturing, the common tendency is to equate an effective process with an *efficient* process. Although **cost efficiency**— *achieving a desired level of outputs with a minimal level of inputs and resources*—is obviously an important competitive advantage, firms may also compete on a number of other strategic positions, such as those based on response time, product variety, or quality. Thus, a business process that is effective for one company may be a poor choice for another company pursuing a different strategy in the same industry.

How, then, does "effective" differ from "efficient"? A process is efficient if it operates at low cost. A process is effective if it supports the execution of the company's strategy. Thus, the key condition for process effectiveness is the existence of a *strategic fit* among three main components of a firm's strategy:

- Its strategic position
- Its process architecture
- Its managerial policies

Strategic fit means *consistency between the competitive advantage that a firm seeks and the process architecture and managerial policies that it uses to achieve that advantage*. Consistency may be absent if top-level managers lack knowledge about basic business processes or if they delegate important process decisions to managers who are unfamiliar with the firm's overall strategy. In either case, the company's strategic position and network of business processes may be incompatible. For instance, Jaikumar (1986) gives examples of firms that had invested in flexible manufacturing systems but were still producing only a handful of products in fairly large volumes. Flexible manufacturing systems should be used to support a strategy of increased product variety at lower volumes. Otherwise, they would simply result in an increased product cost.

The potential conflict between the top-down strategy and the principle of strategic fit was first described in 1969 by Skinner, who argued that "too often top management overlooks manufacturing's potential to strengthen or weaken a company's competitive ability." As a result, concluded Skinner, "manufacturing becomes the missing link in corporate strategy" (Skinner, 1969). Among other things, Skinner was criticizing the perception of operations as a technical discipline concerned only with cost reduction and low-level day-to-day decisions.

Even though that misperception is still fairly widespread, consultants, educators, and practicing operations managers have made substantial progress in understanding the strategic importance of operations. Indeed, the *business process reengineering* movement of the early 1990s stressed the fundamental rethinking and redesign of business processes as a means of improving performance in such areas as time, cost, quality, and service. This theory advocates radical changes in processes (and, in fact, in organization as a whole) as an effective means of formulating strategy and designing processes that will result in significant improvements in performance. By equating organizations with processes, this view has put business process management on the strategic agenda of top management at numerous firms (Harrison & Loch, 1995).

Market- and Process-Driven Strategies   Although the top-down view is convenient for explaining the concept of strategic fit, some experts urge that the relationship be reversed. Management, contends one team of researchers, should emphasize that "the building blocks of corporate strategy are not products and markets but business processes. Competitive success then depends on transforming a company's key processes into strategic competencies that consistently provide superior value to the customer" (Stalk et al., 1992).

Strategic fit may be achieved using either of two approaches:

1. **Market-driven strategy**: *A firm starts with key competitive priorities and then develops processes to support them.*
2. **Process-driven strategy**: *A firm starts with a given set of process competencies and then identifies a market position that is best supported by those processes.*

Whereas producers of commodity products tend to be market driven, technologically innovative companies tend to drive markets. Sony, for example, has a core set of process technologies that allow miniaturization of electronic products. It has leveraged this competency to develop new products and even new consumer markets. Had Sony relied solely on market analysis of current customer needs, the Walkman would never have been introduced.

In general, however, strategic fit requires both market- and process-driven strategies. It entails identifying and developing external market opportunities along with internal process competencies until the two are mutually consistent, and it means doing so repeatedly. The resulting view of strategy and fit, argues one review of the field, "inextricably links a company's internal competencies (what it does well) and its external industry environment (what the market demands and what competitors offer)" (Collis & Montgomery, 1995).

▪▪▪ 2.4   Focused Operations

The concepts of strategic fit and strategic positioning are rooted in the very existence of trade-offs and the need to make choices. As discussed, strategic fit requires business processes that are consistent with a given business strategy. However, because no single process can perform well on every dimension, *there cannot be a process that fits all strategies.* Choosing a strategy, therefore, involves *focus:* "The essence of strategy," observes Michael Porter, "is what to do and what *not* to do" (Porter, 1996).

Focused Strategy and Focused Processes   Not surprisingly, it is easier to design a process that achieves a limited set of objectives than one that must satisfy many diverse objectives. This fact underlies the concept of **focused strategy**: *committing to a limited, congruent set of objectives in terms of demand (products and markets) and supply (inputs, necessary process technologies and volumes).* In other words, this approach concentrates on serving limited market segments with business processes specifically designed and operated to meet their needs.

In turn, a focused strategy is supported by a **focused process**—*one whose products all fall within a small region of the competitive product space.* All products emphasize the same competitive priorities. If the *area* occupied in the product space by the process's product portfolio is small, then the process is focused. Conversely, if the product portfolio is more dispersed in the competitive space, then the process is less focused. The Aravind Eye Hospital in Madurai, India, offers a good example of a service operation that is focused on providing high quality and low price at the expense of variety. Aravind provides 180,000 cataract operations each year. According to Rubin (2001), its founder, Dr. Govindappa Venkataswamy (also known as "Dr. V.") specialized his surgical instruments and his "process of cataract surgery" allowing him to do as many as 100 surgeries a day! Aravind's operational excellence yields gross margins of 40% despite the fact that 70% of its patients pay nothing or almost nothing and that the hospital does not depend on donations.

An example of a ferocious cost competitor is Aldi, an international retailer specializing in a limited assortment of private label, high-quality products at the lowest possible prices. The first Aldi store opened in 1948 in the German town of Essen. Today, Aldi is a leader in the international grocery retailing industry with more than 5,000 stores and has operations in Europe, the United States, and Australia. Its secret to success is found in a lean operating structure with emphasis on frugality and simplicity that yields a very low cost structure. Brandes (1998) describes Aldi founder Theo Albrecht as "a man who uses paper on both sides and likes to turn off the lights when leaving a room." Low prices, however, come at the expense of much smaller variety and assortment and lower availability (in terms of stockouts) than competitors.

While offering a narrow product line is the most intuitive example of focus, a focused process need not produce a limited number of products. A job shop can be a focused operation, yet its mission is to provide variety as long as all its products have similar quality, cost, and timeliness attributes so that they all fall in a small area in the product space. Similarly, emergency rooms in hospitals focus on variety and responsiveness in the service sector. In July 2000, the emergency department at Oakwood Hospital in Dearborn, Michigan (www.oakwood.org), began guaranteeing that an emergency room patient will see a physician and have treatment started within 30 minutes. Oakwood completely revamped emergency room processes. The result was that the average wait to see a physician in the emergency room shrank from several hours to 22 minutes, and a year later, all but 32 out of 60,000 emergency room patients saw a physician within the guaranteed 30 minutes. Another example of a firm focused on providing speed and variety but not low cost is materials, repair, and operations products distributor McMaster-Carr, which we discussed in Chapter 1.

Even if a strategy calls for serving broader market segments, each of which requires a different strategic emphasis (or positions in the competitive product space), it can be separated into *substrategies*, each focusing on a limited, consistent, and clear set of objectives. Each substrategy can then be supported by its own consistent—or *focused*—business process. Depending on the scale of the business, this approach leads either to a *focused plant* that performs one specific process or to a **plant-within-a-plant (PWP)**, *in which the entire facility is divided into several "miniplants," each devoted to its own specific mission by performing a process that focuses strictly on that mission.*

Most general hospitals, for example, have realized the benefits of focus by separating the emergency room and trauma units from the rest of the facility. Some hospitals (such as Massachusetts General) have gone even further by developing separate units to focus on such routine operations as hip or knee replacement and rehabilitation. Specialty hospitals, such as Shouldice Hospital that we mentioned in Chapter 1, which provides only hernia repairs, have only one such focused unit. Large manufacturers usually operate multiple plants that support the entire *product life cycle:* research and development, prototype labs, production plants, sales and marketing units, financing-service offices, and repair facilities—all housed in physically separate facilities.

This divide-and-conquer strategy can also be implemented on a smaller scale by separating product lines within a plant. Harley-Davidson maintains two separate flow processes: one for its small 833cc engine and transmission systems and one for its large 1,340cc power trains. This strategy is logical because each product line requires a different process and has sufficiently high volume to warrant the investment. Similarly, engine maker Briggs & Stratton separates its various production plants and, within each plant, separates product assembly lines in PWPs.

Finally, the practice of achieving strategic fit through focused operations provides firms with a powerful deterrent against competitors' efforts to imitate them. Their competitive advantage, therefore, is more sustainable. Although any single activity may be vulnerable to imitation, the greater the number of activities involved, the harder wholesale imitation becomes. Supporting a firm's strategic position with multiple, mutually reinforcing activities creates sustainable competitive advantage because it is, according to Porter, "harder for a rival to match an array of interlocked activities than it is merely to imitate a particular [activity]" (Porter, 1996). Indeed, copying a focused business process—a complete *network* of activities, resources, and managerial infrastructure—amounts to cloning the entire organization. If a firm's process and strategy are both focused, its position is already the result of carefully considered trade-offs made when managers chose their position and its supporting process. (We will say more about trade-offs in Section 2.6.) A competitor, therefore, can copy that position only by making similar trade-offs. In so doing, it will inevitably be giving up its own position. Example 2.2 describes Continental Airlines' unsuccessful attempt to imitate low-cost focused competitor Southwest Airlines.

Example 2.2

Porter cites the case of Continental Airlines' efforts to imitate Southwest Airlines by creating a low-budget carrier called Continental Light: meals and first-class service were eliminated, departure frequency was increased, fares were reduced, and turnaround time at the gate was shortened. Porter indicates that "because Continental remained a full-service airline on other routes [its own position], it continued to use travel agents and its mixed fleet of planes and to provide baggage checking and seat assignments. . . . An airline," Porter concludes, "can copy activities (say, deciding to drop meal service), but it cannot do both (say, having meal service on some flights and not on others) without bearing major inefficiencies" (Porter, 1996).

In short, Continental failed to treat Light as an independent, focused plant-within-a-plant. Granted, financial considerations may have forced Continental to keep its low-budget operations aligned with its full-service operations. But by trying to do both—by refusing to make a choice—Continental engineered a "hybrid" process that could not compete with Southwest's focused operations. Continental aborted Continental Light shortly after takeoff.

Today, many airlines have set up a subsidiary that is designed to compete on low cost: Ted started by United Airlines, Song by Delta, Basiq Air by KLM, Tiger Airways by Singapore Airlines, and so on. It remains to be seen whether these ventures will be successful in competing with such "pure" low-cost airlines as Southwest and RyanAir.

▮▮▮ 2.5   Matching Products and Processes

Focused operations make it easier to match the products that a firm produces with the processes it uses to produce them. *A useful tool for matching processes to products* is the **product–process matrix** proposed by Hayes and Wheelwright (1979). A model of this matrix is shown in Figure 2.3.

The horizontal axis charts product variety from "low variety" (representing standardized products produced at high volume) to "high variety" (representing one-of-a-kind products produced at low volumes). At the right end, we would find such unique products as skyscrapers, tailor-made suits, consulting reports, and plastic-surgery procedures. Such highly customized products are demanded and produced to order in very low volumes. At the left end is the other extreme: highly standardized commodity products demanded and produced in large volumes. Beer breweries and commercial paper mills produce products at this end of the spectrum. Between these extremes fall products with intermediate degrees of customization and volume. Thus, houses built by a real estate developer may be largely similar to a limited variety of model homes while permitting some degree of customization and upgrades.

The vertical axis measures process flexibility, the process competency on the supply side that corresponds to product variety. At the bottom, low process flexibility results from a process architecture with rigid, fixed routes and specialized resources that can perform only a narrow set of tasks repeatedly, as in a flow shop. At the top,

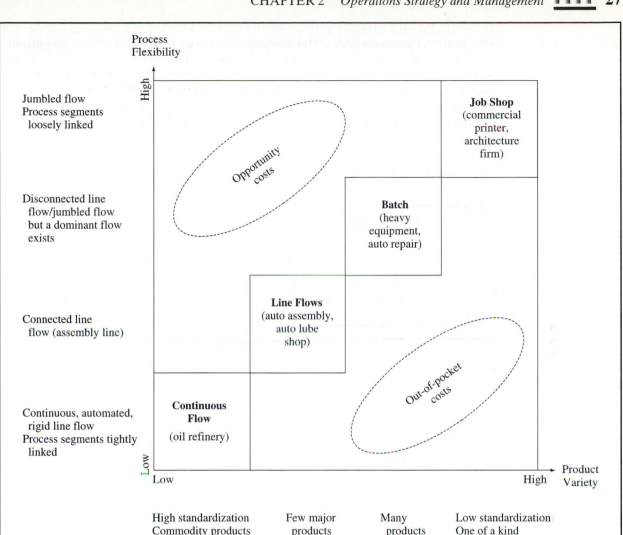

FIGURE 2.3 The Product–Process Matrix

high flexibility results from processes that employ general-purpose resources that are loosely linked so that products can flow along many different routes, yielding "a jumbled work flow," as in a job shop (see Chapter 1). Intermediate processes differ in the degree of specialization, volume capability, and interlinkage of resources.

Ideally, each process type fits a specific product demand: job shops, for instance, are ideally suited to produce custom products in low volumes, while flow shops work best for more standardized products demanded in high volumes. Effective product–process matches occur on the diagonal of the product–process matrix. An off-diagonal position represents a mismatch that can result in unnecessarily high costs—a job shop that produces only one product (resulting in opportunity costs of not producing wider variety) or a flow shop that undergoes numerous equipment changeovers in order to produce several products demanded only in very low volumes (resulting in out-of-pocket costs due to excessive changeovers). A diagonal position, though, corresponds to a proper match between the desired product variety and the necessary process flexibility.

Note that the product–process matrix connects only one product attribute with one process competency. A correlation exists between process flexibility and product cost: standardization typically results in economies of scale and thus lower variable product cost. Likewise, there is a correlation between process flexibility and product response time: flow shops typically have shorter flow times than job shops. Product quality, however, bears no direct correlation to layout of resources and connecting routes. Both job shops and flow shops can produce high quality.

■■■ 2.6 The Operations Frontier and Trade-Offs

Once the firm has chosen its operations strategy and process architecture, it must manage the process to execute the strategy. As discussed, a strategic position supported by consistent business processes that are managed effectively is essential for superior performance. Sustained competitive advantage requires *both* strategic positioning and operational effectiveness. Strategic positioning is about choosing a different set of activities or choosing to perform activities in a different way—which entails choosing a different business process architecture. Firms change strategic positions quite infrequently. When managers are considering such a change, they ask, "*What* should we do and not do?" Operational effectiveness, on the other hand, is about structuring processes to best support the strategic position and then executing these processes better than rivals. When managers are considering changes to the operating policies of a process structure already in place, they ask, "*How* could we better design and manage it?"

The Operations Frontier Earlier, we represented strategic position by the location of the firm's products in the competitive product space. An empirical study of a particular industry might measure and position each firm's product offerings in that space. As in Figure 2.4, the measurement could apply to two competitive dimensions (with product quality and product variety or customization regarded as constant). One could then define the **operations frontier** as *the smallest curve that contains all current industry positions*. Clearly, the operations frontier then represents the current best practices of world-class firms. Firms located on the same ray share strategic priorities. But firms on the operations frontier boast superior performance: they have the highest operational effectiveness—*the measure of how well a firm manages its processes*. Their processes provide superior performance along the desired product attributes. Operational effectiveness is thus related to the distance of the current position from the (current) operations frontier. The closer a firm is to the frontier, measured along its direction of improvement (whose slope represents the relative strategic priorities assigned by the firm to the four dimensions), the higher its operational effectiveness. In Figure 2.4, the companies delivering products A, B, and C share strategic priorities, yet the company delivering product A has the highest level of operational effectiveness. It defines the current set of best practices to manage its business processes (it is on the frontier), while the product C company has the lowest level (farthest from the frontier, as measured along its direction of movement).

Trade-Offs A **trade-off** is *a decreasing of one aspect to increase another*. Because the operations frontier is typically concave, any point *on* the frontier represents a trade-off: to increase performance along one product dimension, one must give up some performance along the others. It thus follows that firms that are not on the frontier do not face strict trade-offs: they can improve along multiple dimensions simultaneously.

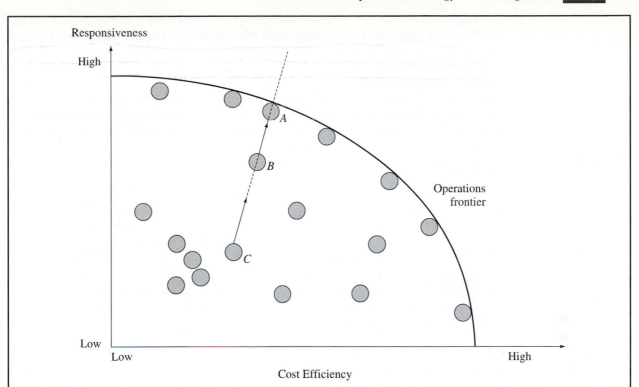

FIGURE 2.4 **The Operations Frontier as the Minimal Curve Containing All Current Positions in an Industry**

Trade-offs, therefore, are typically reflected most clearly in the strategies of world-class companies, such as Toyota as described in Example 2.3.

Example 2.3

In the late 1960s and early 1970s, Toyota, a small Japanese automobile maker, was facing a depressed economy in a country where space was at a premium. Because no firm can survive producing only a single product for small, depressed markets, product variety was a necessity. So Taiichi Ohno and his coworkers developed the *Toyota Production System* (*TPS*). The key idea behind TPS was to produce exactly what you need (regardless of variety) exactly when you need it. The potential problem was equally simple: there was no room for error. Suppliers and equipment had to be reliable, production had to be flexible, quality had to be high, and consistency was necessary in every respect. Critical to the success of the system were precisely coordinated relations with suppliers, who had to meet both precise schedules and precise performance specifications while remaining as flexible as the automaker itself.

TPS was in fact the reinvention of Henry Ford's assembly line or process-flow concept (see Section 2.7), though with an important modification: instead of focusing on low cost and no variety, TPS *allowed product variety through process flexibility*. TPS simultaneously permitted wide variety, high quality, low cost, and short response time. In effect, it so completely redefined the operations frontier that competitors all over the world had to scramble to catch up. Having established TPS as the world-class flow process for discrete manufacturing, Toyota remains the best example of a company that used manufacturing as a competitive weapon in rising from obscurity to the top ranks of its industry.

Initially, when competitors began copying elements of TPS, they saw dramatic improvements in *both* cost and quality. They thought that if such operational effectiveness was possible, perhaps the traditional trade-offs between cost and quality or cost and variety were no longer valid. Since most of these rivals were far from the best in their class, they originally did not have to make genuine trade-offs in their quest for operational effectiveness. Their operations were so ineffective that they could simultaneously improve on several dimensions of their processes.

Improved operational effectiveness is not the same as improved strategic positioning. Whereas strategic positioning defines the *direction* of improvement from the current position, operational effectiveness measures the *distance* of the current position to the current operations frontier along the direction of improvement. When a firm's position on the operations frontier is developed according to the "state of best practices," it represents the best attainable *compromise* between the two dimensions at a given point in time. Any change in such a position necessarily entails trade-offs between the two dimensions. Example 2.4 describes the trade-offs that differentiate an emergency room from other hospital processes.

Example 2.4

If a general hospital tries to handle emergency and nonemergency cases with a *single* process, the products of that process will have very different strategic emphases. Consequently, such a process will undoubtedly cover too large an area in the competitive product space and make it difficult for the hospital to be competitive on both dimensions. Suppose, however, that the hospital divides its operations into two distinct plants-within-a-plant (PWPs)—emergency-room and nonemergency facilities. Suppose, too, that each PWP has both its own competitive priority (time or cost) and a consistent process to support the priority. Clearly, an emergency room will employ doctors and staff who are "on call" and will have the flexibility to treat a high variety of cases rapidly. A general hospital, meanwhile, can afford more specialized labor resources, each geared to the treatment of a small set of cases. In Figure 2.5, the products of each PWP now share similar competitive priorities and thus occupy a smaller area. Each PWP process is more focused, and it is easier for each to perform effectively in its specific strategic direction.

Thus, companies that are not on the frontier can make simultaneous improvements on both dimensions by moving toward the frontier. In other words, *the purpose*

▪▪▪▪▪▪▪▪▪▪▪ **FIGURE 2.5** The Operations Frontier in the Health Care Sector

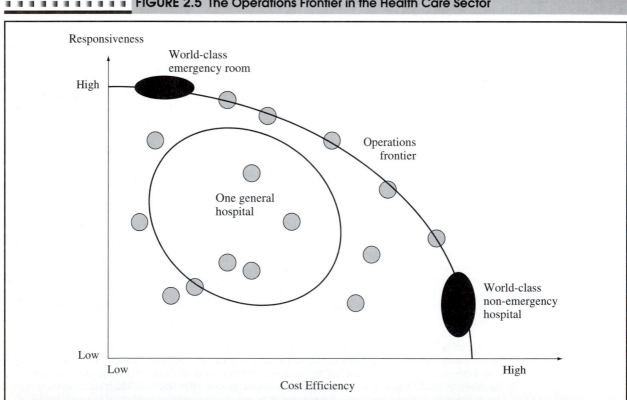

of improvements in operational effectiveness is to bring a company closer to the frontier or to move the frontier itself. The purpose of strategic positioning, on the other hand, is to specify a *direction of improvement and thus the position on the frontier* the company wants to occupy.

By including direction as part of effectiveness, we measure alignment between strategy and process competencies. (If effectiveness were defined in terms of horizontal distance to the frontier, where traditionally cost [price] efficiency is on the horizontal axis, then effectiveness would be equivalent to cost efficiency and would lose its alignment.) As such, operational effectiveness is at the core of superior performance. It is important to maintain alignment as we improve processes. This is illustrated by the success of Toyota: although the specifics of TPS are well documented and readily available, few competitors have managed to implement the strategy as well as Toyota has, which continues to raise the bar by improving its processes while keeping them aligned with its strategic priorities. In 2002, Toyota continued its quest for variety produced in a low-cost flow shop by unveiling its Global Body Line, a radical, company-wide overhaul of its already much-envied flexible manufacturing process (Visnic, 2002).

As technology and management practices advance, the operations frontier shifts outward, or away from the point of origin in the competitive space. World-class companies achieve either the same response time (or quality or variety) at a lower cost or better response time (or quality or variety) at the same cost. As the dynamics of competition keeps pushing the operations frontier outward, world-class firms must continuously improve operational effectiveness merely to maintain their positions.

The Internet is an example of a new technology with potential to shift the operations frontier outward. As Chopra and Van Mieghem (2001) point out, however, the value gained by adopting electronic commerce depends on the industry context. For example, the advent of Internet grocers such as Peapod in the United States and Tesco in the United Kingdom clearly enhances quality of service to customers, but the convenience of home-delivery service typically comes at an increased cost and reduced responsiveness and variety compared to a regular supermarket store. In 2003, Peapod offered about 10,000 items, whereas a regular U.S. supermarket carried about 40,000 items. Thus, while the adoption of the Internet in the grocery home-delivery business increases quality of service to consumers, it also increases cost and reduces responsiveness and variety. In this industry, the Internet thus pushes the frontier out along the quality-of-service dimension, but not along the other dimensions.

In the book industry, however, the impact of the Internet is quite different, as illustrated by Example 2.5, which compares a regular Wal-Mart Supercenter store with its Internet store. In the publishing industry, the adoption of Internet technology increases service and selection, and thus pushes the frontier out along the dimensions of service and variety.

Finally, in many business-to-business settings, the Internet allows improved responsiveness and accuracy of information exchange, which can translate into both cost savings and faster order fulfillment.

This book is about understanding how changes in process result in improvements in product value. Given that the Internet is "just" another channel for delivery of information, our general principles can be applied to determine the value impact of electronic commerce, as the remainder of the book will illustrate.

Example 2.5

As an example of the Internet's impact as a new channel for value creation on the operations frontier, consider Walmart.com, the Internet store of the well-known company introduced in Example 2.1. Walmart.com started selling online in July 1996, but replicating its off-line success was not easy. The online customer base is different from its traditional counterpart, and Internet

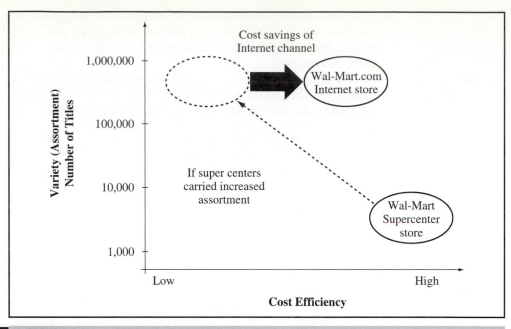

▪▪▪▪▪▪▪▪▪▪▪ **FIGURE 2.6** The Internet Channel versus Traditional Retail Stores

stores require different technology than regular stores. Seeking greater online expertise, Wal-Mart spun Walmart.com off as a separate company in January 2000.

Wal-Mart soon became convinced, however, that its true strength online is in bricks-and-clicks integration. So in July 2001, it bought back outside stakes and turned Walmart.com once again into a wholly owned subsidiary of Wal-Mart. Now, for example, a customer can choose replacement tires online and have them installed at a local Wal-Mart. By September 2002, Walmart.com had 6.5 million visitors, which put it in 13th position in terms of customer traffic in e-commerce. (According to Maguire [2002], eBay topped the list with 34.4 million visitors, followed closely by Amazon—the site most closely resembling Walmart.com—with 25.6 million visitors. Working down the list, Dell Computer had 11.4 million and Barnes & Noble 8.2 million.)

While a typical Wal-Mart Supercenter stocked about 100,000 items in 2003, Walmart.com stocked about 600,000. Most of that variety increase, however, is in the 500,000 book titles and 80,000 CDs that Walmart.com carries, compared to thousands stocked at regular stores. In addition, because of added transaction costs (order-sized pick, pack, and transportation) Walmart.com eliminated true low-cost items costing a few dollars or less. As illustrated in Figure 2.6, a single Internet channel for order taking together with a centralized warehouse for fulfillment allows greater variety in the book and CD segment at a lower cost than physical stores could provide. Compared to the fast-moving best-sellers offered in regular stores, increasing variety naturally requires stocking more slow-moving items that have less predictable sales. The Internet channel allows Walmart.com to centralize storage and fulfillment of those slow-moving items. Chapters 6 and 7 will show that the sources of those savings can be substantial and accrue because of increased scale economies and statistical pooling benefits on inventory. The end result is that adoption of Internet technology in this industry has the effect of pushing out the frontier along the variety and cost dimensions.

▪▪▪ 2.7 The Evolution of Strategy and Operations Management

Over time, strategies and processes will change in response to changes in the company's industry or in its technology. In particular, the historical evolution of operations and process management is linked intimately to technological changes and their role in the development of industrialization. Until 1765, the world of commerce and technology had changed very little from the one known to the Greeks and the Romans. Although advances had been made in the textile, printing, and construction industries, the commercial world of 1765 still faced the same physical limitations as ancient cultures. Transportation speed—whether of people, of goods, or of information—was limited on land by the speed of the fastest horse and on water by the most favorable winds. At the end of the 16th century, for example, the trip from New York to Boston—a distance of 288 kilometers, or 175 miles—took three days (Ambrose, 1996).

The Factory System and Specialization   This situation was destined to change dramatically in 1765, when the factory system heralded the start of the industrial revolution and the end of the "artisan" system consisting of craft guilds and decentralized cottage industries. The factory system was the result of three innovations:

1. Scottish economist Adam Smith proposed that the **division of labor** and **functional specialization**—a process and organizational structure where people are specialized by function, meaning each individual is dedicated to a specific task—would lead to vast improvements in cost and quality, albeit at the expense of flexibility. (The other organizational structure is **product specialization**— *wherein people are specialized by product, meaning each individual is dedicated to a specific product line.*)
2. Scottish engineer James Watt's invention of the steam engine made it possible for powered machinery to replace human labor. Powered by steam, the transportation speeds of goods carriers soon increased by a factor of 20. (Meanwhile, the telegraph removed virtually all limits on the transmission speed of information.)
3. The practice of centralizing work in one facility.

From Standardization to Mass Production   In 1810, based on the practices of Eli Whitney and Samuel Colt at the national armory at Springfield, Massachusetts, the **American system of manufacturing** *introduced the use of interchangeable parts, thereby eliminating the need to custom-fit parts during assembly.* Standardization had begun. The end of the 19th century brought technological advances that were prominent in such commercial phenomena as the "bicycle boom" of the 1890s—sheet-metal stamping and electrical-resistance welding allowed for both new designs and assembly methods. Another fundamental change occurred on April 1, 1913, when Henry Ford introduced the moving assembly line—the first machine-paced flow shop in manufacturing—at his plant in Highland Park, Michigan, and thus dawned the era of **mass production** or *the production of goods in quantity.* "Armory practice and sheet steel work," reports one survey of U.S. business history, "equipped Ford with the ability to turn out virtually unlimited numbers of components. It remained for the assembly line to eliminate the remaining bottleneck—how to put these parts together" (Hounshell, 1991). ("Disassembly lines" appeared earlier in the cow meat stockyards of Chicago at the end of the 19th century.)

Ford's primary mode of competition soon became low cost. Scale economies and the virtual elimination of all product flexibility made cars available in high volume for a mass market. Prior to the development of the assembly line, for instance, a Ford Model T required 12.5 hours of assembly-worker time—a limitation that the assembly line reduced to only 1.5 hours. Soon, Ford's plant in Rouge, Michigan, was a totally integrated facility with the best furnaces, operational equipment, and electrical systems efficiently converting raw materials into cash in 36 hours. It was also a highly focused plant serving a competitive strategy of low cost and zero flexibility. It produced one product, the Model T, and Henry Ford's attitude toward the higher costs entailed by product flexibility was uncompromising. Of the Model T, he said, "You can have any color as long as it's black."

Flexibility and the Productivity Dilemma   The changeover from Model T to Model A in 1927 was the end of Ford's competitive advantage. Alfred Sloan of General Motors had introduced the concept of "annual models" and the slogan "a car for every purpose and every price." The practice of **flexible mass production**—*a method of high-volume production that allows differences in products*—introduced product variety as a second mode of competition in the automobile industry. It was accompanied by one of the most significant trade-offs in the history of strategic positioning: faced with the so-called **productivity dilemma**, manufacturers were obliged to *choose between the lower productivity entailed by frequent product changes or the higher productivity that was possible only if they declined to introduce variety into their product lines* (Hounshell, 1991).

From Scientific Management to Employee Involvement   The first few decades of the 1900s also witnessed the rise of scientific management, which was based on the time and motion studies conducted by Frederick W. Taylor at the turn of the 20th century. Taylor's philosophy centered on three ideas (Hounshell, 1991):

1. Scientific laws govern how much a worker can produce per day.
2. It is management's function to discover and apply these laws to productive operations systems.
3. It is the worker's function to carry out management decisions without question.

Taylor's "ceaseless quest for the 'one best way' and efficiency changed the very texture of modern manufacturing. Taylor influenced Ford's assembly line" (Kanigel, 1997) and led universities to start new "industrial engineering" departments. His ideas of industrial organization and scientific observation inspired the **statistical quality control** studies—*a management approach that relies on sampling of flow units and statistical theory to ensure the quality of the process*—of Shewhart at Bell Laboratories in the 1930s and Elton Mayo's celebrated Hawthorne studies of worker motivation at Western Electric, which highlighted the importance of employee involvement and incentive systems in increasing productivity.

Competitive Dimensions after World War II   The period after World War II found the United States with a virtual monopoly over worldwide productivity. With most of Europe and Japan practically destroyed, there was no competition for meeting pent-up consumer demand. Thus, volume and scale economies rose to the top of the American strategic agenda. The 1960s witnessed the rise of enormous integrated economic structures and the emergence of huge capital investments as the main barrier to entry in many industries.

During the 1970s, Japanese manufacturers began to incorporate *quality* into their cost-focused strategy. Toyota began developing what, in Example 2.3, we described as the *Toyota Production System* (*TPS*). Among other things, TPS gave rise to a fourth competitive dimension: the use of *time* in product development, production, and distribution. The emergence of Japanese manufacturing as a global force in the 1980s led to a renewed interest in manufacturing as a competitive weapon in the rest of the industrialized world. It gave rise to a variety of new management philosophies and practices, including total quality management (TQM), just-in-time (JIT) manufacturing, time-based competition, and business process reengineering. In addition, new technologies like computer-aided design and manufacturing (CAD/CAM), flexible manufacturing systems, robotics, and Internet-based processes now play important roles in modernizing business activities.

SUMMARY

Chapter 1 stated that the effectiveness of any process depends on its current and past performance and on the future goals as expressed by the firm's strategy. In this chapter, we focused on the relationship between strategy and process.

Strategic positioning means deliberately performing activities different from those of the competition. *Operations strategy* consists of plans to develop the desired process competencies. *Operational effectiveness* requires developing processes and operating policies that support the strategic position better than the competitors'. Both strategic positioning and operational effectiveness are necessary for competitive advantage.

The key insight is that an effective business process is tailored to business strategy—process structure and operating policy work together to support the organization's overall strategic objectives. To ensure such strategic fit, a three-step approach can be adopted. First, determine the strategic positioning by prioritizing the targeted customer needs of product cost, quality, variety, and response time. Second, determine what the process should be good at to support that strategic position: in other words, infer the priorities among the process competencies of process cost, quality, flexibility, and flow time. Finally, given that different processes have different competencies, select the process whose competencies best support the strategy.

Focusing operations and matching products with processes are means of facilitating an effective *fit* between strategy and processes. Because the best operational practices improve constantly in competitive industries, firms must make continuous improvements in operational effectiveness.

KEY TERMS

- American system of manufacturing
- Business strategy
- Corporate strategy
- Competitive product space
- Cost efficiency
- Division of labor
- Flexible mass production
- Focused process

- Focused strategy
- Functional specialization
- Functional strategies
- Market-driven strategy
- Mass production
- Operational effectiveness
- Operations frontier
- Operations strategy
- Plant-within-a-plant (PWP)

- Process-driven strategy
- Productivity dilemma
- Product–process matrix
- Product specialization
- Statistical quality control
- Strategic fit
- Strategic positioning
- Trade-off

DISCUSSION QUESTIONS

2.1 How do the strategies of your neighborhood supermarket differ from those of Wal-Mart? How do their business processes support those strategies?

2.2 Compare and contrast the strategies and supporting business processes of Southwest Airlines and Singapore Airlines. That is, do some research (e.g., read their corporate Web sites) and compare their business strategy in terms of the four product dimensions, targeted market segments, and their process architectures.

2.3 Consider the life cycle of a product from introduction to maturity to decline. What kind of process (job shop, batch process, or line flow) would be appropriate at each stage, and why?

2.4 A small printed circuit board manufacturer has established itself based on the ability to supply a large variety of small orders in a timely manner. A firm approaches the manufacturer to place a large order (equal to the current volume from all other orders) but asks for a 30% discount. Do you think the circuit board manufacturer should accept the order? Justify your answer.

2.5 Compare the differences in patient needs at an emergency room in a hospital with that of a department doing knee replacements in terms of price, quality, time, and variety. Which of these departments should follow the approach taken by Shouldice? Why?

2.6 Briefly give an argument supporting the claim that "the essence of strategy is choosing what not to do."

2.7 MDVIP is a group of primary care physicians in Florida that offers a unique pricing structure. They charge patients a fixed fee of $1,500 per year on top of fees per visit over the year. That is, patients pay $1,500 even if they do not see a doctor during the year and still pay per consultation despite having paid the annual fee. The per-visit fees are comparable to industry averages and are covered by patients' health insurance. The fixed fee is not covered by standard health insurance. Since introducing the pricing format, the size of MDVIP's practice has shrunk from 6,000 patients to 300. Doctor's schedules are consequently more open, making it easier for patients to schedule appointments. In addition, doctor–patient consultations are well above the industry average of just under 10 minutes.

Using the four competitive dimensions, how would you describe MDVIP's strategic position relative to a comparable, traditional practice? What are the implications for how MDVIP must manage its resources?

2.8 There are a surprising number of styles of baby strollers and carriages available in the marketplace. One style is the jogging stroller, which features oversize wheels that make the stroller easy to push on rough surfaces as the parent jogs. One maker of jogging strollers is Baby Trend. Baby Trend makes a full line of baby products—from diaper pails to high chairs to a variety of strollers. Their jogging strollers consist of a cloth seat stretched over a metal frame, a fairly standard design in the industry. They make a limited number of styles of single joggers meant to carry one baby (mostly differentiated by the color of the cloth) and one style of double stroller meant to carry two children. In the Baby Trend double stroller, the children sit next to each other (again a standard industry design). Baby Trend sells through independent Web sites (e.g., www.strollers4less.com), specialty stores (e.g., The Right Start), and "big box" retailers (e.g., Toys "R" Us). Their prices range from under $100 for a simple single jogger to $299 for their double stroller.

Another competitor is Berg Design. Jogging strollers are the only baby products Berg Design makes, although it produces other products that involve metalworking. Berg Design's joggers offer a unique design in which the child sits in a molded plastic seat bolted to a metal frame. With a single seat, the child can face forward or backward (i.e., looking at mom or dad). For their multiple-seat strollers, the children sit in tandem as opposed to side by side. On the two-seat model, the children can both face forward or can face each other. They make models that can handle up to four children that are popular with day care centers. Berg Design's Web site emphasizes that each jogger "is made one at a time, no shortcuts; hand welded, powder painted and assembled with the utmost attention to craftsmanship." Berg Design sells direct to customer through the Web and an 800 number. Their prices range from $255 for their cheapest single jogger to $745 for a four-seat model.

a. How would you describe the strategic positions of Baby Trend and Berg Design?

b. How would you expect Baby Trend and Berg Design to have structured their respective processes for building strollers?

2.9 Give two main benefits of focus. Provide at least two reasons all organizations do not employ focused operations. (Note: Claiming a firm is ignorant of focus is not an option.)

SELECTED BIBLIOGRAPHY ▪▪▪▪▪▪▪

Ambrose, S. E. 1996. *Undaunted Courage: Meriwether Lewis Thomas Jefferson and the Opening of the American West.* New York: Simon & Schuster.

Brandes, D. 1998. *Konsequent Einfach: Die Aldi-Erfolgsstory.* Frankfurt: Campus Verlag.

Carpenter, M. 2003. "Dell Computers Founder Tells His Success Story." The Diamondback Online, April 7. Available at www.inform.umd.edu/ News/Diamondback/archives/2003/04/07/ news6.html.

Chopra, S., and J. A. Van Mieghem. 2000. "Which E-Business Is Right for Your Supply Chain?" *Supply Chain Management Review* 4, no. 3 (July–August): 32–40.

Collis, D. J., and C. A. Montgomery. 1995. "Competing on Resources: Strategy in the 1990s." *Harvard Business Review* 73, no. 4 (July–August): 118–29.

Harrison, J. M., and C. Loch. 1995. "Five Principles of Business Process Reengineering." Unpublished manuscript.

Hayes, R. H., and S. C. Wheelwright. 1979. "Link Manufacturing Process and Product Life Cycles." *Harvard Business Review* 57, no. 1 (January–February): 133–40.

Heskett, J. L. 1989. *Shouldice Hospital Limited*. Harvard Business School Case Study 9-683-068. Cambridge, Mass.: Harvard Business School, 1–16.

Hindle, T. 1994. *Field Guide to Strategy*. Cambridge, Mass.: Harvard Business School Press.

Hounshell, D. A. 1991. *From the American System to Mass Production 1800–1932: The Development of Manufacturing Technology in the United States*. Baltimore: Johns Hopkins University Press.

Jaikumar, R. 1986. "Postindustrial Manufacturing." *Harvard Business Review* 64, no. 6 (November–December): 69–75.

Kanigel, R. 1997. "The One Best Way: Frederick Winslow Taylor and the Enigma of Efficiency." Viking, New York, New York.

Maguire, J. 2002. "Insights-Trends: Case Study: Walmart.com." November 15. Available at http://www.ecommerce-guide.com/news/trends/article.php/10417_1501651.

Porter, M. E. 1996. "What Is Strategy?" *Harvard Business Review* 74, no. 6 (November–December): 61–78.

Rubin, H. 2001. "The Perfect Vision Dr. V." *Fast Company*, no. 43, February: 146.

Skinner, W. 1969. "Manufacturing—Missing Link in Corporate Strategy." *Harvard Business Review* 47, no. 3 (May–June): 136–45.

Skinner, W. 1974. "The Focused Factory." *Harvard Business Review* 52, no. 3 (May–June): 113–21.

Stalk, G., P. Evans, and L. E. Shulman. 1992. "Competing on Capabilities: The New Rules of Corporate Strategy." *Harvard Business Review* 70, no. 2 (March–April): 54–69.

Stalk, G., and A. M. Webber. 1993. "Japan's Dark Side of Time." *Harvard Business Review* 71, no. 4 (July–August): 93–101.

Treacy, M., and F. Wiersema. 1997. *The Discipline of Market Leaders*. Boston: Addison-Wesley.

Visnic, B. 2002. "Toyota Adopts New Flexible Assembly System." *Ward's Autoworld*, November, 30–31.

PART II

Process Flow Measurement

CHAPTER 3

Process Flow Measures

Introduction

Vancouver International Airport Authority manages and operates the Vancouver International Airport. According to Atkins et al. (2003), its focus on safety, security, and customer service has contributed to Vancouver International Airport's ranking among the top 10 airports in the world. In order to maintain its excellent customer service standards and in anticipation of new government regulations, airport management wanted to reduce the time customers spent in the airport security checkpoints. They wanted to improve the way that customers flowed through the process. In other words, they sought to better their *process flow*.

BellSouth International is a provider of wireless services in 11 Latin American countries. As a service provider, the company leases its network capacity on a monthly basis to two categories of customers: prepaid and postpaid. One of the most time-consuming processes for the company in the Latin American market is the service activation process: getting a wireless telephone into the hands of interested potential customers.

The various steps in the activation process include determination of the type of wireless service, credit check, selection of phone and service plan, assignment of the phone number, making a test call, and providing a short tutorial. At one of its largest activation centers, the company serves an average of 10,000 customers per week with 21% being activated with a postpaid account and the remaining with a prepaid account.

To manage and improve this activation process, the following questions must be answered: What operational measures should a manager track as leading indicators of the financial performance of the process? How does the time to process a customer and the number of customers that are being served at any point in time impact the total number of customers that can be served per week? How do these process measures impact the financial performance of the process? Which specific outcomes can be called "improvements?" How can we prioritize our improvements into an executable action plan?

This chapter aims to provide answers to these questions. We will define process flow in Section 3.1 of this chapter. Then, in Sections 3.2 through 3.4, we will introduce the three fundamental measures of process performance: inventory, throughput, and flow time. In Section 3.5, we will explore the basic relationship among these three measures, called Little's law. Section 3.6 shows how Little's law can be used to analyze financial statements. We will discuss the related concept of *inventory turns* in Section 3.7. Finally, Section 3.8 links these process flow measures to financial measures of performance to determine when a process change (e.g., reengineered process flows or allocation of additional resources) has been an improvement from both operational and financial perspectives.

▪▪▪ 3.1　The Essence of Process Flow

Thus far, we have learned that the objective of any process is to transform inputs into outputs (products) to satisfy customer needs. We also know that while an organization's strategic position establishes *what* product attributes it aims to provide, its operational effectiveness measures *how well* its processes perform this mission. We have seen that product attributes and process competencies are classified in terms of cost, time, variety, and quality. We noted that, to improve any process, we need internal measures of process performance that managers can control. We also saw that if chosen carefully, these internal measures can serve as leading indicators of customer satisfaction and financial performance as well.

In this chapter we focus on **process-flow measures**—*three key internal process performance measures that together capture the essence of process flow: flow time, flow rate, and inventory*. As we will see in subsequent chapters, these three process-flow measures directly affect process cost and response time, and they are affected by process flexibility (or lack thereof) and process quality.

Throughout this book, we examine processes from the perspective of *flow*. Specifically, we look at the process dynamics as inputs enter the process, flow through various activities performed (including such "passive activities" as waiting for activities to be performed), and finally exit the process as outputs. Recall from Chapter 1 that a flow unit is a unit flowing through a process. A flow unit may be a patient, a dollar, a pound of steel, a customer service request, a research-and-development project, or a bank transaction to be processed. In our study of process-flow performance, we look at three measures and answer three important questions:

1. On average, how much time does a typical flow unit spend within the process boundaries?
2. On average, how many flow units pass through the process per unit of time?

3. On average, how many flow units are within the process boundaries at any point in time?

The case of Vancouver International Airport, described in Example 3.1, is an example of a business situation in which examining process-flow performance is particularly useful. Later in this chapter, we will analyze this example to determine whether a process change leads to an improvement.

Example 3.1

Now, let us begin to look at how the Vancouver International Airport Authority went about improving its customer flow through its airport security checkpoints. To understand customer flow, managers began by analyzing a single security screening line, which is comprised of an X-ray scanner with an operator and screening officers. Arriving customers either queue up or, if there is no queue on arrival, directly put their bags on the scanner. While customers can have 0, 1, 2 or 3 carry-on bags, including purses, wallets, and so on, on average a typical customer has 1.5 bags. The X-ray scanner can handle 18 bags per minute. On average, about half the passengers arrive at the checkpoint about 40 minutes (± 10 minutes) before departure for domestic flights. The first passenger shows up about 80 minutes before departure, and the last passenger arrives 20 minutes before departure. For a flight with 200 passengers, this gives the following approximate arrival rate pattern: about 75 passengers arrive 80 to 50 minutes early, 100 arrive 50 to 30 minutes early, and the remaining 25 arrive between 30 to 20 minutes before scheduled departure.

To minimize layover time for passengers switching flights, many of Vancouver's flights depart around the same time. As we look at the three key process measures, we will assume for simplicity that exactly three flights, each carrying 200 passengers, are scheduled for departure each hour: that is, three flights depart at 10 a.m., three flights at 11 a.m., and so forth. With increased security procedures, however, the simultaneous departures of flights were overwhelming scanner capacity and creating long waiting times. The airport authority needed to know how staggering flight departures—for example, spreading out departures so that one flight would depart every 20 minutes—would affect the flow and waiting times of passengers through the security checkpoint.

▪▪▪ 3.2 Three Key Process Measures

Flow Time   Recall from Chapter 1 that processes transform flow units through networks of activities and buffers. Thus, as a flow unit moves through the process, one of two things happens to it:

1. It undergoes an activity.
2. It waits in a buffer to undergo an activity.

In the airport example, passengers and their luggage are either security scanned or wait in line before the X-ray machine. Let us follow a specific passenger or flow unit from the time it enters the process until the time it exits. *The total time spent by a flow unit within process boundaries is called* **flow time**. Some flow units move through the process without any wait; perhaps they require only resources that are available in abundance (there are several X-ray scanners and operators available), or they arrive at times when no other flow units are present (there are no other passengers checking through security when they arrive), or they are artificially expedited (a first-class passenger conceivably could be given priority over economy-class passengers). Others, meanwhile, may spend a long time in the process, typically waiting for resources to become available. In general, therefore, flow time varies—sometimes considerably— from one flow unit to another.

As a measure of process performance, flow time indicates the time needed to convert inputs into outputs and includes any time spent by a flow unit waiting for processing activities to be performed. It is thus useful information for a manager who must promise a delivery date to a customer. It also indicates how long working capital, in the form of inventory, is tied up in the process.

Flow Rate   An important measure of process flow dynamics is *the number of flow units that flow through a specific point in the process per unit of time*, which is called **flow rate**. In many settings, flow rates may change over time so that in addition to the specific point in the process, we also must specify the time when the measurement was taken. In Example 3.1, the inflow rate of passengers at a security checkpoint at Vancouver International Airport changes over time. Recall that for each of the three flights, about half the 200 passengers for each flight arrive between 50 and 30 minutes before flight departure. So for each of the three flights departing at 10 a.m., about 100 passengers arrive between 9:10 and 9:30 a.m., a 20-minute interval. This means that a *total* of 300 passengers arrive during this time period for the *three* flights, giving an inflow rate of roughly 15 passengers per minute. The remaining 300 passengers for the three flights arrive between 8:40 and 9:10 a.m. (about 80 to 50 minutes before departure) and between 9:30 and 9:40 a.m. (about 30 to 20 minutes before departure). That is, the remaining 300 passengers arrive during a total time period of 40 minutes, giving an inflow rate of 7.5 passengers per minute, which is half the inflow rate during the peak time period from 9:10 to 9:30 a.m. The outflow rate of the checkpoint, however, is limited by the X-ray scanner, which cannot process more than 18 bags per minute or, with an average of 1.5 bags per passenger, 12 passengers per minute.

When we consider the flow rate at a specific point in time t, we call it the *instantaneous* flow rate and denote it by $R(t)$. For example, if we focus on the flow through entry and exit points of the process at time t, we can denote the instantaneous total inflow and outflow rates through all entry and exit points, respectively, as $R_i(t)$ and $R_o(t)$.

The process that is shown graphically in Figure 3.1 features two entry points and one exit point. Total inflow rate $R_i(t)$, then, is the sum of the two inflow rates, one each from the two entry points. Remember that inputs may enter a process from multiple points and that outputs may leave it from multiple points.

Inventory   When the inflow rate exceeds the outflow rate, the number of flow units inside the process increases. **Inventory** is *the total number of flow units present within process boundaries*. In the airport example, during the peak period of 9:10 to 9:30 a.m., the inflow rate is 15 passengers per minute, while the outflow rate is 12 passengers per minute. Hence, an inventory of passengers will build in the form of a queue. We define the total number of flow units present within process boundaries at time t as the *process inventory at time t* and denote it by $I(t)$. To measure the process inventory at time t, we take a snapshot of the process at that time and count all the flow units within process boundaries at that moment. Current inventory thus represents all flow units that have entered the process but have not yet exited.

■ ■ ■ ■ ■ ■ ■ ■ ■ ■ ■ ■   **FIGURE 3.1 Input and Output Flow Rates for a Process with Two Entry Points**

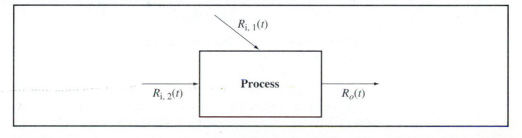

Inventory has traditionally been defined in a manufacturing context as material waiting to be processed or products waiting to be sold. Our definition considers a general flow unit and thus takes a much broader view that applies to *any* process, whether it is a manufacturing, a service, a financial, or even an information process. Inventory can thus encompass products, customers, cash, and orders. Our definition of inventory includes all flow units within process boundaries—whether they are being processed or waiting to be processed. Thus, raw materials, work in process (partially completed products), and finished goods inventories are included. This broader definition of inventory allows us to provide a unified framework for analyzing flows in all business processes.

What constitutes a *flow unit* depends on the problem under consideration. By defining the flow unit as money—such as a dollar, a euro, or a rupee—we can analyze financial flows. Adopting money as the flow unit and our broader view of inventory, we can use inventory to identify the working capital requirements. A key financial measure for any process is *investment in working capital*. Accountants define working capital as *current assets minus current liabilities*. Current assets include the number of dollars within process boundaries in the form of inventory as well as in the form of cash and any accounts receivable. Thus, inventory is like money that is tied up: a reduction in inventory reduces working capital requirements. Reduced working capital requirements reduce the firm's interest expense or can make extra cash available for investment in other profitable ventures. (Reducing inventory also reduces flow time and improves responsiveness, as we shall see later in this chapter.)

▪▪▪ 3.3 Flow Time, Flow Rate, and Inventory Dynamics

Generally, both inflow and outflow rates fluctuate over time. When the inflow rate exceeds the outflow rate in the short term, the inventory increases, or builds up. In contrast, if outflow rate exceeds inflow rate in the short term, the inventory decreases. Thus, inventory dynamics are driven by the difference between inflow and outflow rates. We define the **instantaneous inventory accumulation (buildup) rate**, $\Delta R(t)$, as *the difference between instantaneous inflow rate and outflow rate:*

Instantaneous inventory accumulation (or buildup) rate $\Delta R(t)$ = Instantaneous inflow rate $R_i(t)$ − Instantaneous outflow rate $R_o(t)$

or

$$\Delta R(t) = R_i(t) - R_o(t) \tag{3.1}$$

Thus, the following holds:

- If instantaneous inflow rate $R_i(t)$ > instantaneous outflow rate $R_o(t)$, then inventory is accumulated at a rate $\Delta R(t) > 0$.
- If instantaneous inflow rate $R_i(t)$ = instantaneous outflow rate $R_o(t)$, then inventory remains unchanged.
- If instantaneous inflow rate $R_i(t)$ < instantaneous outflow rate $R_o(t)$, then inventory is depleted at a rate $\Delta R(t) < 0$.

For example, if we pick a time interval (t_1, t_2) during which the inventory buildup rate ΔR is constant, the associated change in inventory during that period is

Inventory change = Buildup rate × Length of time interval

or

$$I(t_2) - I(t_1) = \Delta R \times (t_2 - t_1) \tag{3.2}$$

Given an initial inventory position and dividing time into intervals with constant accumulation rates, we can construct an **inventory buildup diagram** that depicts *inventory fluctuation over time*. On the horizontal axis we plot time, and on the vertical axis we plot the inventory of flow units at each point in time. Assuming that we start with zero inventory, the inventory at time *t* is the difference between the cumulative inflow and outflow up to time *t*. Example 3.2 provides an illustration of an inventory buildup diagram.

Example 3.2

MBPF Inc. manufactures prefabricated garages. The manufacturing facility purchases sheet metal that is formed and assembled into finished products—garages. Each garage needs a roof and a base, and both components are punched out of separate metal sheets prior to assembly. Production and demand data for the past eight weeks are shown in Table 3.1. Observe that both production and demand vary from week to week.

We regard the finished goods inventory warehouse of MBPF Inc. as a *process* and each garage as a *flow unit*. The production rate is then the inflow rate, while demand (sales) is the outflow rate. Clearly, both have fluctuated from week to week.

MBPF Inc. tracks inventory at the end of each week, measured in number of finished garages. Let $I(t)$ denote the inventory at the end of week *t*. Now suppose that starting inventory at the beginning of week 1 (or the end of week 0) is 2,200 units, so that

$$I(0) = 2,200$$

Now, subtracting week 1's production or inflow rate $R_i(1) = 800$ from its demand or outflow rate $R_o(1) = 1,200$ yields an inventory buildup rate:

$$\Delta R(1) = 800 - 1,200 = -400 \text{ for week 1}$$

So the ending inventory at week 1 is

$$I(1) = I(0) + \Delta R(1) = 2,200 + -400 = 1,800$$

We can similarly evaluate buildup rates and inventory for each week, as shown in Table 3.1. Clearly, the inventory of flow units varies over time around its average of 2,000 garages.

With these data, we can construct an inventory buildup diagram that depicts how inventory fluctuates over time. Figure 3.2 shows the inventory buildup diagram for MBPF over the eight weeks considered, where we have assumed, for simplicity, that inventory remains constant *during* the week and changes only *at the end of* the week when sales take place.

We can also analyze the airport security process of Example 3.1 by deriving the build-up of an inventory of passengers (and their associated waiting times) from the flow accumulation rate. We will define the X-ray scanner as our process and consider the representative example of three flights that are scheduled to depart at 10 a.m. Assume that we start at 8:40 a.m., when no passengers are waiting in line.

TABLE 3.1 Production, Demand, Buildup Rate, and Ending Inventory for MBPF Inc.

Week	0	1	2	3	4	5	6	7	8	Average
Production		800	1,100	1,000	900	1,200	1,100	950	950	1,000
Demand		1,200	800	900	1,100	1,300	1,300	550	850	1,000
Buildup rate ΔR		−400	300	100	−200	−100	−200	400	100	0
Ending inventory	2,200	1,800	2,100	2,200	2,000	1,900	1,700	2,100	2,200	2,000

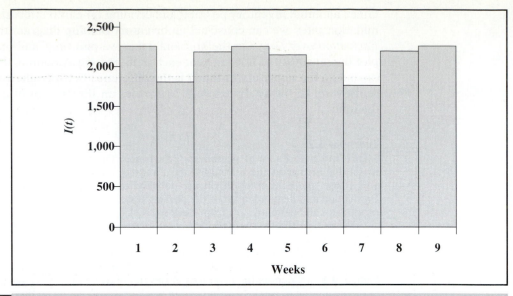

▪▪▪▪▪▪▪▪▪▪▪▪ **FIGURE 3.2** Inventory Buildup Diagram for MBPF Inc.

As derived earlier, the inflow rate during 8:40 to 9:10 a.m. is 7.5 passengers per minute. The outflow rate from the queue is the rate at which baggage is scanned. While the X-ray scanner can process up to 12 passengers per minute, it cannot process more passengers than are arriving, so the outflow rate also is 7.5 per minute. Thus, as summarized in Table 3.2, from 8:40 to 9:10 a.m., the buildup rate in the queue is zero: the X-ray scanner can easily keep up with the inflow, and no passengers have to wait in line. During the peak arrival period of 9:10 to 9:30 a.m., however, the inflow rate of 15 passengers per minute exceeds the maximal scanner outflow rate of 12 passengers per minute, so that a queue (inventory) starts building at $\Delta R = 3$ passengers per minute. At 9:30 a.m., the line for the scanner has grown to $\Delta R \times (9{:}30 - 9{:}10) = 3$ passengers per minute $\times$ 20 minutes = 60 passengers! After 9:30 a.m., the X-ray scanner keeps processing at the full rate of 12 passengers per minute, while the inflow rate has slowed to the earlier lower rate of 7.5 passengers per minute, so that the passenger queue is being depleted at a rate of 4.5 passengers per minute. Thus, the 60-passenger queue is eliminated after 60/4.5 = 13.33 minutes. In other words, at 9:43 and 20 seconds, the queue is empty again, and the X-ray scanner can keep up with the inflow.

Observe that while the lower inflow rate of 7.5 passengers per minute for the 10 a.m. flights ends at 9:40 a.m., the first set of passengers start arriving for the 11 a.m. flights

TABLE 3.2 Buildup Rates and Ending Inventory Data: Vancouver Airport Security Checkpoint of Example 3.1

Time	*8:40 a.m.*	*8:40–9:10 a.m.*	*9:10–9:30 a.m.*	*9:30–9:43:20 a.m.*	*9:43:20–10:10 a.m.*
Inflow rate R_i		7.5/min.	15/min.	7.5/min.	7.5/min.
Outflow rate R_o		7.5/min.	12/min.	12/min.	7.5/min.
Buildup rate ΔR		0	3/min.	4.5/min.	0
Ending inventory (number of passengers in line)	0	0			0

▪▪▪▪▪▪▪▪▪

at 9:40 a.m. Just as the queue starts building up at 9:10 a.m. for the 10 a.m. flight, it will start building up again at 10:10 a.m. for the 11 a.m. flights. Thus, the cycle repeats itself for the next set of flight departures. Figure 3.3 shows the inventory buildup diagram together with the associated cumulative number of passengers arriving to and departing from the checkpoint process and clearly indicates that the difference between cumulative inflows and outflows is inventory.

Now, if flight departures are staggered, the peaks and valleys in arrival rates for different flights cancel each other out, as illustrated in Table 3.3. (The shaded time buckets correspond to the passenger arrivals for a particular flight.) Spreading out flight departures thus gives a constant arrival rate of 600 passengers per hour, which equals 10 passengers per minute *at any point in time throughout the day.* This is well below the process capacity of the X-ray scanner, so that the buildup rate would be zero. In short, by staggering the flights, no queues would develop at the security checkpoint. (The previous analysis is approximate because it ignores the short-time variability of

---

FIGURE 3.3 Inventory Buildup Diagram for Vancouver Airport Security Checkpoint

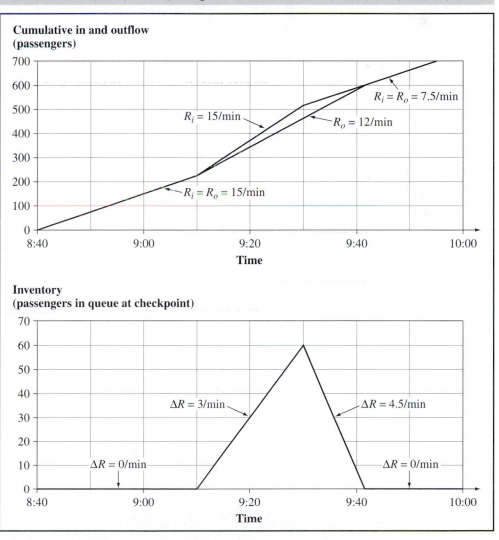

TABLE 3.3 Inflow Rates with Staggered Departures for Vancouver Airport Security Checkpoint of Example 3.1

Time (start of period)	8:40	8:50	9:00	9:10	9:20	9:30	9:40	9:50	10:00	10:10	10:20	10:30
Inflow rate for flights arriving on the hour, $R_{i,1}$	2.5/min.	2.5/min.	2.5/min.	5/min.	5/min.	2.5/min.	2.5/min.	2.5/min.	2.5/min.	5/min.	5/min.	2.5/min.
Inflow rate for flights arriving 20 minutes past the hour, $R_{i,2}$	5/min.	2.5/min.	2.5/min.	2.5/min.	2.5/min.	5/min.	5/min.	2.5/min.	2.5/min.	2.5/min.	2.5/min.	5/min.
Inflow rate for flights arriving 40 minutes past the hour, $R_{i,3}$	2.5/min.	5/min.	5/min.	2.5/min.	2.5/min.	2.5/min.	2.5/min.	5/min.	2.5/min.	2.5/min.	2.5/min.	2.5/min.
Total inflow rate R_i	10/min.	10/min.	10/min.	10/min.	10/min.	10/min.	10/min.	10/min.	10/min.	10/min.	10/min.	10/min.

passenger arrivals within any small time interval. This impact of short-time variability on process performance will be discussed in Chapter 8.)

3.4   Throughput in a Stable Process

A **stable process** *is one in which, in the long run, the average inflow rate is the same as the average outflow rate.* In the airline checkpoint example, while inflow and outflow rates change over time, the *average* inflow rate is 600 passengers per hour. Because the X-ray scanner can process up to 12 passengers per minute, equaling 720 passengers per hour, it can easily handle the inflow over the long run so that the *average* outflow rate also is 600 passengers per hour. The security checkpoint thus is a stable process.

When we have a stable process, we refer to average inflow or outflow rate as **average flow rate**, or **throughput**, which is *the average number of flow units that flow through (into and out of) the process per unit of time.* We will denote the throughput simply as R. As a measure of process performance, throughput rate tells us the average rate at which the process produces and delivers output. Ideally, we would like process throughput rate to match the rate of customer demand. (If throughput is less than the demand rate, some customers are not served. If the converse is true, the process produces more than what is sold.)

Even though inventory fluctuates over time, in a stable process we can define the *average inventory over time* and denote this by I. For example, let us find the average inventory at the Vancouver International Airport. Consider the inventory dynamics as shown in the bottom picture of Figure 3.3. From 8:40 to 9:10 a.m., the inventory or queue before the airline checkpoint is zero. From 9:10 through 9:43 a.m., the inventory builds up linearly to a maximum size of 60 and then depletes linearly to zero. Thus, the average inventory during that period is 60/2 = 30. (Recall that the average height of a triangle is half its maximum height.) Finally, the inventory is zero again from 9:43 to 10:10 a.m., when the cycle repeats with the next inventory buildup. To estimate the average queue size, it is then sufficient to consider the 60-minute interval between the start of two consecutive inventory buildups; for example, from 9:10 a.m. (when inventory builds up for the 10 a.m. flights) to 10:10 a.m. (when inventory starts to build up for 11 a.m. flights). As we have seen, during this interval there is an average of 30 passengers between 9:10 and 9:43 a.m. and zero passengers between 9:43 and 10:10 a.m. Thus, the average queue size is the time-weighted average:

$$I = \frac{33 \text{ min} \times 30 \text{ passengers} + 27 \text{ min} \times 0 \text{ passengers}}{60 \text{ min}}$$

$$= 17.5 \text{ passengers}$$

While the average inventory accumulation rate ΔR must be zero in a stable process (remember, average inflow rate equals average outflow rate), the average *inventory* typically is not.

Now let us look at **average flow time**. While the actual flow time varies across flow units, we can define the average flow time as *the average (of the flow times) across all flow units that exit the process during a specific span of time.* We denote the average flow time by T. One method to measure the average flow time is to track the flow time of each flow unit over a long time period and then compute its average. Another method is to compute it from the throughput and the average inventory, which we will explain next.

▪▪▪ 3.5 Little's Law: Relating Average Flow Time, Throughput, and Average Inventory

The three performance measures that we have discussed answer the three questions about process flows that we raised earlier:

1. On average, how much time does a typical flow unit spend within process boundaries? The answer is the *average flow time* T.
2. On average, how many flow units pass through the process per unit of time? The answer is the *throughput* R.
3. On average, how many flow units are within process boundaries at any point in time? The answer is the *average inventory* I.

Little's Law We can now show that in a stable process, there is a fundamental relationship among these three performance measures. This relationship is known as **Little's law**, which states that *average inventory equals throughput times average flow time:*

$$\text{Average Inventory } (I) = \text{Throughput } (R) \times \text{Average Flow Time } (T)$$

or

$$I = R \times T \tag{3.3}$$

To see why Little's law must hold, let us mark and track an arbitrary flow unit. After the marked flow unit enters the process boundaries, it spends T time units before departing. During this time, new flow units enter the process at rate R. Thus, during the time T that our marked flow unit spends in the system, $R \times T$ new flow units arrive. Thus, at the time our marked flow unit exits the system, the inventory is $R \times T$. Because our marked flow unit was chosen at random and because the process is stable, the average inventory within process boundaries that a randomly picked flow unit sees, I, must be the same as $R \times T$.

Little's law allows us to derive the flow time averages of all flow units from the average throughput and inventory (which are averages over time and typically easier to calculate than average over flow units). In the airport security checkpoint example, we found that average queue size $I = 17.5$ passengers, while throughput was $R = 600$ passengers per hour = 10 passengers per minute. To determine the average time spent by a passenger in the checkpoint queue, we use Little's law, $I = R \times T$ and solve for T so that

$$T = I/R = 17.5 \text{ passengers}/10 \text{ passengers per minute} = 1.75 \text{ minutes}$$

Recall that many passengers do not wait at all, while the passenger who waits longest is the one who arrives when the queue is longest at 60 passengers. That unfortunate passenger must wait for all 60 passengers to be processed, so that her waiting time is 60/12 minutes = 5 minutes. Example 3.3 illustrates Little's law for the MBPF Inc. example.

Example 3.3

Recall that average inventory at MBPF Inc. in Example 3.2 was $I = 2000$ garages. Computing the average production over the eight weeks charted in Table 3.1 yields an average production rate of 1,000 garages per week. Average demand experienced by MBPF Inc. over the eight weeks considered in Table 3.1 is also 1,000 garages. Over the eight weeks considered, therefore, average production at MBPF has matched average demand. *Because these rates are equal, we conclude that MBPF Inc. is a stable process with a throughput of 1,000 garages per week.*

Now suppose that in terms of material and labor, each garage costs $3,300 to produce. If we consider each dollar spent as our flow unit, MBPF Inc. has a throughput of $R = \$3,300 \times 1,000$

garages = \$3,300,000 per week. Thus, we have evaluated the throughput rate of MBPF Inc. using two different flow units: garages and dollars. Similarly, inventory can be evaluated as 2,000 garages, or 2,000 × \$3,300 (the cost of each garage) = \$6,600,000.

Because this is a stable process, we can apply Little's law to yield the average flow time of a garage, or of a dollar tied up in each garage, as

$$T = I/R = \$6,600,000/\$3,300,000 = 2 \text{ weeks}$$

Two immediate but far-reaching implications of Little's law are the following:

1. Of the three operational measures of performance—average flow time, throughput, and average inventory—*a process manager need only focus on two measures because they directly determine the third measure via Little's law.* It is then up to the manager to decide which two measures should be managed.
2. For a given level of throughput in any process, the only way to reduce flow time is to reduce inventory and vice versa.

Now let us look at some brief examples that well illustrate the wide range of applications of Little's law in both manufacturing and service operations. It will be helpful to remember the following:

> Average inventory is denoted by I.
> Throughput is denoted by R.
> Average flow time is denoted by T.

3.5.1   Material Flow

A fast-food restaurant processes an average of 5,000 kilograms (kg) of hamburgers per week. Typical inventory of raw meat in cold storage is 2,500 kg. The process in this case is the restaurant and the flow unit is a kilogram of meat. We know, therefore, that

$$\text{Throughput } R = 5,000 \text{ kg/week}$$
$$\text{and}$$
$$\text{Average inventory } I = 2,500 \text{ kg}$$

Therefore, by Little's law,

$$\text{Average flow time } T = I/R = 2,500/5,000 = 0.5 \text{ weeks}$$

In other words, an average kilogram of meat spends only half a week in cold storage. The restaurant may use this information to verify that it is serving fresh meat in its hamburgers.

3.5.2   Customer Flow

The café Den Drippel in Ninove, Belgium, serves on average 60 customers per night. A typical night at Den Drippel is long, about 10 hours. At any point in time, there are on average 18 customers in the café. These customers are either enjoying their food and drinks, waiting to order, or waiting for their order to arrive. Since we would like to know how long a customer spends inside the restaurant, we are interested in the average flow time for each customer. In this example, the process is the café, the flow unit is a customer, and we know that

$$\text{Throughput } R = 60 \text{ customers/night}$$
$$\text{Since nights are 10 hours long, } R = 6 \text{ customers/hour}$$
$$\text{and}$$
$$\text{Average inventory } I = 18 \text{ customers}$$

Thus, Little's law yields the following information:

$$\text{Average flow time } T = I/R = 18/6 = 3 \text{ hours}$$

In other words, the average customer spends three hours at Den Drippel.

3.5.3 Job Flow

A branch office of an insurance company processes 10,000 claims per year. Average processing time is three weeks. We want to know how many claims are being processed at any given point. Assume that the office works 50 weeks per year. The process is a branch of the insurance company, and the flow unit is a claim. We know, therefore, that

$$\text{Throughput } R = 10,000 \text{ claims/year}$$
$$\text{and}$$
$$\text{Average flow time } T = 3/50 \text{ year}$$

Thus, Little's law implies that

$$\text{Average inventory } I = R \times T = 10,000 \times 3/50 = 600 \text{ claims}$$

On average, then, scattered in the branch are 600 claims in various phases of processing— waiting to be assigned, being processed, waiting to be sent out, waiting for additional data, and so forth.

3.5.4 Cash Flow

A steel company processes $400 million of iron ore per year. The cost of processing ore is $200 million per year. The average inventory is $100 million. We want to know how long a dollar spends in the process. The value of inventory includes both ore and processing cost. The process in this case is the steel company, and the flow unit is a cost dollar. A total of $400 million + $200 million = $600 million flows through the process each year. We know, therefore, that

$$\text{Throughput } R = \$600 \text{ million/year}$$
$$\text{and}$$
$$\text{Average inventory } I = \$100 \text{ million}$$

We can thus deduce the following information:

$$\text{Average flow time } T = I/R = 100/600 = 1/6 \text{ year} = 2 \text{ months}$$

On average, then, a dollar spends two months in the process. In other words, there is an average lag of two months between the time a dollar enters the process (in the form of either raw materials or processing cost) and the time it leaves (in the form of finished goods). Thus, each dollar is tied up in working capital at the factory for an average of two months.

3.5.5 Cash Flow (Accounts Receivable)

A major manufacturer sells $300 million worth of cellular equipment per year. The average amount in accounts receivable is $45 million. We want to determine how much time elapses from the time a customer is billed to the time payment is received. In this case, the process is the manufacturer's accounts-receivable department, and the flow unit is a dollar. We know, therefore, that

$$\text{Throughput } R = \$300 \text{ million/year}$$
and
$$\text{Average inventory } I = \$45 \text{ million}$$

Thus, Little's law implies that

$$\text{Average flow time } T = I/R = 45/300 \text{ year} = 0.15 \text{ years} = 1.8 \text{ months}$$

On average, therefore, 1.8 months elapse from the time a customer is billed to the time payment is received. Any reduction in this time will result in revenues reaching the manufacturer more quickly.

3.5.6 Service Flow (Financing Applications at Auto-Moto)

Auto-Moto Financial Services provides financing to qualified buyers of new cars and motorcycles. Having just revamped its application-processing operations, Auto-Moto Financial Services is now evaluating the effect of its changes on service performance. Auto-Moto receives about 1,000 loan applications per month and makes accept/reject decisions based on an extensive review of each application. Assume a 30-day working month.

Until last year (under what we will call "Process I"), Auto-Moto Financial Services processed each application individually. On average, 20% of all applications received approval. An internal audit showed that, on average, Auto-Moto had about 500 applications in process at various stages of the approval/rejection procedure. In response to customer complaints about the time taken to process each application, Auto-Moto called in Kellogg Consultants (KC) to help streamline its decision-making process. KC quickly identified a key problem with the current process: although most applications could be processed fairly quickly, some—because of insufficient and/or unclear documentation—took a disproportionate amount of time. KC thus suggested the following changes to the process (thereby creating what we will call "Process II"):

1. Because the percentage of approved applications is fairly low, an Initial Review Team should be set up to preprocess all applications according to strict but fairly mechanical guidelines.
2. Each application would fall into one of three categories: *A* (looks excellent), *B* (needs more detailed evaluation), and *C* (reject summarily). *A* and *B* applications would be forwarded to different specialist subgroups.
3. Each subgroup would then evaluate the applications in its domain and make accept/reject decisions.

Process II was implemented on an experimental basis. The company found that, on average, 25% of all applications were *A*s, 25% *B*s, and 50% *C*s. Typically, about 70% of all *A*s and 10% of all *B*s were approved on review. (Recall that all *C*s were rejected.) Internal audit checks further revealed that, on average, 200 applications were with the Initial Review Team undergoing preprocessing. Just 25, however, were with the Subgroup A Team undergoing the next stage of processing and about 150 with the Subgroup B Team.

Auto-Moto Financial Services wants to determine whether the implemented changes have improved service performance.

Observe that the flow unit is a loan application. On average, Auto-Moto Financial Services receives and processes 1,000 loan applications per month. Let us determine the impact of the implemented changes on customer service.

Under Process I, we know the following:

$$\text{Throughput } R = 1{,}000 \text{ applications/month}$$
$$\text{and}$$
$$\text{Average inventory } I = 500 \text{ applications}$$

Thus, we can conclude that

$$\text{Average flow time } T = I/R$$
$$T = 500/1{,}000 \text{ months} = 0.5 \text{ months} = 15 \text{ days}$$

In Process I, therefore, each application spent on average 15 days with Auto-Moto before receiving an accept/reject decision.

Now let us consider Process II. Because this process involves multiple steps, it is better to start with the process flowchart in Figure 3.4. (We will discuss process flowcharts more fully in Chapter 4.) Note that, on average, 1,000 applications arrive per month for initial review. After initial review, 50% of these are rejected, 25% are categorized as Type A (looks excellent) and 25% are categorized as Type B (needs more detailed evaluation). On detailed evaluation by Subgroup A Team, 70% of Type A applications are accepted and 30% rejected. On evaluation by Subgroup B Team, 10% of Type B applications are accepted and 90% rejected. Thus, each month, an average of 200 applications are accepted and 800 rejected.

Furthermore, on average, 200 applications are with the Initial Review Team, 25 with the Subgroup A Team, and 150 with the Subgroup B Team. Thus we can conclude that for Process II

$$\text{Throughput } R = 1{,}000 \text{ applications/month}$$
$$\text{and}$$
$$\text{Average inventory } I = 200 + 150 + 25 = 375 \text{ applications}$$

▪▪▪▪▪▪▪▪▪▪▪ **FIGURE 3.4 Flowchart for Auto-Moto Financial Services**

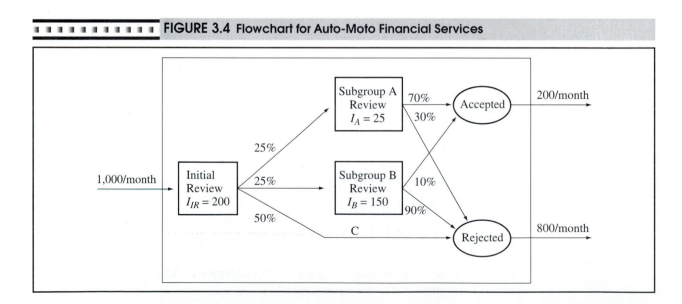

Thus, we can deduce that

$$\text{Average flow time } T = I/R$$
$$T = 375/1{,}000 \text{ month} = 0.375 \text{ months} = 11.25 \text{ days}$$

Under Process II, therefore, each application spends, on average, 11.25 days with Auto-Moto before an accept/reject decision is made. Compared to the 15 days taken, on average, under Process I, this is a significant reduction.

Another way to reach the same conclusion that $T = 11.25$ days is to do a more detailed analysis and calculate the average flow time of each *type* of application. (Recall that the Initial Review Team at Auto-Moto Financial Services categorizes each application received as Type A, B, or C.) To find the average flow time over *all* applications, we can then take the weighted average of the flow times for each type—in other words, break down Process II into its three subprocesses, initial review, Subgroup A review, and Subgroup B review, and find out how much time applications spend in each of these subprocesses. From that knowledge we can then compute the flow time of each type of application. The remainder of this section illustrates the detailed computations behind this argument.

As we can see in Figure 3.4, each application starts out in initial review. On average, there are 200 applications with the Initial Review Team. For initial review, the performance measures are denoted with subscript *IR* and are as follows:

$$\text{Throughput } R_{IR} = 1{,}000 \text{ applications/month}$$
$$\text{and}$$
$$\text{Average inventory } I_{IR} = 200 \text{ applications}$$

From this information we can deduce that for initial review,

$$\text{Average flow time } T_{IR} = I_{IR}/R_{IR}$$
$$T_{IR} = 200/1{,}000 \text{ months} = 0.2 \text{ months} = 6 \text{ days}$$

Thus, each application spends, on average, six days in initial review.

Now consider the applications classified as Type A by initial review. Recall that, on average, there are 25 applications with the Subgroup A Review Team. Because 25% of all incoming applications are categorized as Type A, on average, 250 of the 1,000 applications received per month are categorized as Type A. We will denote this group with a subscript *A*. So we have

$$\text{Throughput } R_A = 250 \text{ applications/month}$$
$$\text{Average inventory } I_A = 25 \text{ applications}$$

We can thus deduce that

$$\text{Average flow time } T_A = I_A/R_A$$
$$T_A = 25/250 \text{ months} = 0.1 \text{ months} = 3 \text{ days}$$

Type A applications spend, on average, another three days in the process with the Subgroup A Review Team.

Similarly, the Subgroup B Review Team receives 25% of incoming applications, or 250 applications per month. It is also given that there are 150 applications with subgroup B. That is,

$$\text{Throughput } R_B = 250 \text{ applications/month}$$
$$\text{Average inventory } I_B = 150 \text{ applications}$$

We can thus deduce that

$$\text{Average flow time } T_B = I_B / R_B$$
$$= 150/250 \text{ months} = 0.6 \text{ months} = 18 \text{ days}$$

Thus, Type B applications spend, on average, another 18 days in the process with the Subgroup B Review Team.

Recall that 50% of all incoming applications, or 500 applications per month, are rejected by the Initial Review Team itself. These applications are classified as Type C applications and leave the process immediately. (For sake of consistency, one could say that their additional time spent after IR is $T_C = 0$ so that their inventory $I_C = T_C \times R_C = 0$.)

Recall that the Initial Review Team at Auto-Moto Financial Services categorizes each application received as Type A, B, or C. Each application spends, on average, six days with the Initial Review Team. Type A applications are then reviewed by the Subgroup A Review Team, where they spend an additional three days. Type B applications are reviewed by the Subgroup B Review Team, where they spend, on average, another 18 days. Type C applications are rejected by the Initial Review Team itself.

Summarizing, we now have computed the average flow time of each *type* of application under Process II:

- Type A applications spend, on average, 9 days in the process.
- Type B applications spend, on average, 24 days in the process.
- Type C applications spend, on average, 6 days in the process.

Finally, we can now find the *average flow time* across all applications under Process II using this more detailed analysis by taking the *weighted average* across the three application types. Average flow time across all application types, therefore, is given as follows:

$$T = \frac{R_A}{R_A + R_B + R_C}(T_{IR} + T_A) + \frac{R_B}{R_A + R_B + R_C}(T_{IR} + T_B) + \frac{R_C}{R_A + R_B + R_C}(T_{IR})$$

So,

$$T = \frac{250}{250 + 250 + 500}(6 + 3) + \frac{250}{250 + 250 + 500}(6 + 18) + \frac{500}{250 + 250 + 500}(6)$$

$$T = \frac{250}{1,000}(9) + \frac{250}{1,000}(24) + \frac{500}{1,000}(6) = 11.25 \text{ days}$$

This indeed agrees with our earlier (shorter) computation of the average flow time of 11.25 days.

In the analysis so far, we defined flow units according to categories of applications. When evaluating service performance, however, Auto-Moto Financial Services may want to define flow units differently—as applications, approved applications, or rejected applications. Indeed, only approved applications represent customers who provide revenue, and Auto-Moto Financial Services would probably benefit more from reducing their flow time to less than 11.25 days.

Under Process I, the average time spent by an application in the process is 15 days—regardless of whether it is finally approved. Let us now determine how much time *approved* applications spend with Auto-Moto under Process II. Under Process II, 70% of Type A applications (175 out of 250 per month, on average) are approved, as are 10% of Type B applications (25 out of 250 per month, on average). Thus, the aggregate rate at which all applications are approved equals $175 + 25 = 200$ applications per month. The average flow time for *approved* applications, denoted by $T_{approved}$, is again a weighted average of the flow times of each type of approved application:

Average flow time for approved applications =

$$T_{approved} = \frac{175}{175+25}(T_{IR}+T_A)+\frac{25}{175+25}(T_{IR}+T_B)$$
$$= \frac{175}{200}(6+3)+\frac{25}{200}(6+18)$$
$$= 10.875 \text{ days}$$

Similarly, let us now determine the average time an eventually *rejected* application spends with Auto-Moto under Process II, denoted by T_{reject}. Under Process II, 30% of Type A applications (75 out of 250 per month, on average) are rejected, as are 90% of Type B applications (225 out of 250 per month, on average), as are 100% of Type C applications (500 per month, on average).

Average flow time for rejected applications, T_{reject}, is then the weighted average across each of these three types and is given by

$$T_{reject} = \frac{75}{75+225+500}(T_{IR}+T_A)+\frac{225}{75+225+500}(T_{IR}+T_B)+\frac{500}{75+225+500}(T_{IR})$$
$$= \frac{75}{800}(6+3)+\frac{225}{800}(6+18)+\frac{500}{800}(6)$$
$$= 11.343 \text{ days}$$

Process II, therefore, has not only reduced the average overall application flow time but also reduced it *more* for approved customers than for rejected customers. However, 12.5% of all approved applications (25 that are categorized as Type B, out of 200 approved each month) spend a lot longer in Process II than in Process I (an average of 24 instead of 15 days). This delay may be a problem for Auto-Moto Financial Services in terms of service performance. Since approved applications represent potential customers, a delay in the approval process may cause some of these applicants to go elsewhere for financing, resulting in a loss of revenue for Auto-Moto.

▪ ▪ ▪ 3.6   Analyzing Financial Flows through Financial Statements

Our business process-flow paradigm can also be used to analyze financial statements by considering the flow of a financial unit (say, a dollar) through the corporation. Let us return to MBPF Inc. of Example 3.2 and analyze its three financial statements: the firm's *income statement*, *balance sheet*, and the more detailed *cost of goods sold* (*COGS*) statement for 2004. With an appropriate use of Little's law, this analysis will not only help us understand the current performance of the process but also highlight areas for improvement.

Recall that a key financial measure for any process such as MBPF Inc. is the working capital, which includes the value of process inventories and accounts receivables. The following analysis shows us how to find areas within MBPF Inc. in which a reduction in flow time will result in a significant reduction in inventories and, therefore, the working capital.

In 2004, MBPF operations called for the purchase of both sheet metal (raw materials) and prefabricated bases (purchased parts). Roofs were made in the fabrication area from sheet metal and then assembled with prefabricated bases in the assembly area. Completed garages were stored in the finished goods warehouse until shipped to customers.

In order to conduct our analysis, we need the data contained in the following tables:

- Table 3.4: MBPF's 2004 income statement
- Table 3.5: MBPF's consolidated balance sheet as of December 31, 2004
- Table 3.6: Details concerning process inventories as of December 31, 2004, as well as production costs for 2004

Note in these tables that all values are in millions of dollars and that all data represent end-of-the-year numbers, although we will assume that inventory figures represent average inventory in the process.

3.6.1 Assessing Financial Flow Performance

Our objective is to study *cash flows* at MBPF in order to determine *how long it takes for a cost dollar to be converted into recovered revenue.* For that, we need a picture of process-wide cash flows. (Later, to identify more specific areas of improvement within the corporation, we will need a more detailed picture.) The flow unit here is a cost dollar, and the process is the entire factory, including the finished-goods warehouse. Incorporating inventory and cash-flow numbers obtained from Table 3.6, a process view of the financial flows through the entire process (factory + finished-goods warehouse) is shown in Figure 3.5. From Table 3.6, we see that raw materials (for roofs) worth $50.1 million and purchased parts (finished bases) worth $40.2 million are purchased each year. Labor and overhead costs in roof fabrication total $60.2 million per year and in final assembly total $25.3 million per year. Adding all costs, we obtain the

TABLE 3.4 MBPF Inc. Consolidated Statements of Income and Retained Earnings for 2004	
Net sales	250.0
Costs and expenses	
Cost of goods sold	175.8
Selling, general and administrative expenses	47.2
Interest expense	4.0
Depreciation	5.6
Other (income) expenses	2.1
Total costs and expenses	234.7
Income before income taxes	15.3
Provision for income taxes	7.0
Net income	8.3
Retained earnings, beginning of year	31.0
Less cash dividends declared	2.1
Retained earnings at end of year	37.2
Net income per common share	0.83
Dividend per common share	0.21

TABLE 3.5 MBPF Inc. Consolidated Balance Sheet as of December 31, 2004

Current assets
Cash	2.1
Short-term investments at cost (approximate market)	3.0
Receivables, less allowances of $0.7 million	27.9
Inventories	50.6
Other current assets	4.1
Total current assets	87.7

Property, plant, and equipment (at cost)
Land	2.1
Buildings	15.3
Machinery and equipment	50.1
Construction in progress	6.7
Subtotal	74.2
Less accumulated depreciation	25.0
Net property, plant, and equipment	49.2

Investments	4.1
Prepaid expenses and other deferred charges	1.9
Other assets	4.0
Total assets	146.9

(Selected) current liabilities
Payables	11.9

TABLE 3.6 MBPF Inc. Inventories and Cost of Goods Details

Cost of goods sold
Raw materials	50.1
Fabrication (L&OH)	60.2
Purchased parts	40.2
Assembly (L&OH)	25.3
Total	175.8

Inventory
Raw materials (roof)	6.5
Fabrication WIP (roof)	15.1
Purchased parts (base)	8.6
Assembly WIP	10.6
Finished goods	9.8
Total	50.6

annual cost of goods sold, which is $175.8 million (as shown in Table 3.4). From Table 3.5, we find that inventories at MBPF Inc. total $50.6 million.

On analyzing the cash flows, we arrive at the following information:

Throughput R = $175.8 million/year [Cost of Goods Sold, Table 3.4]

Average inventory I = $50.6 million [Inventories, Table 3.5]

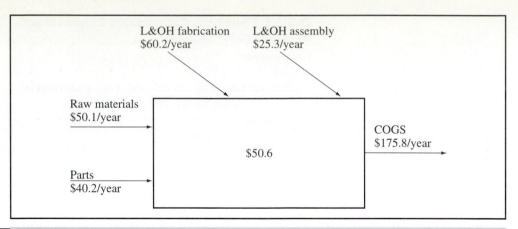

FIGURE 3.5 Financial Flows of MBPF Inc.

Thus, we can deduce *average flow time* as follows:

$$\text{Average flow time } T = I/R$$
$$= 50.6/175.8 \text{ year}$$
$$= 0.288 \text{ years} = 14.97 \text{ weeks}$$

Alternatively, if we replace the *annual* throughput figure, $175.8 million per year, by a *weekly* figure, $3.381 million per week, we can then obtain T in weeks directly as follows:

$$\text{Average flow time } T = I/R$$
$$= 50.6/3.381 \text{ weeks}$$
$$= 14.97 \text{ weeks}$$

So the average dollar invested in the factory spends roughly 15 weeks before it leaves the process through the door of the finished-goods inventory warehouse. In other words, it takes on average 14.97 weeks for a dollar invested in the factory to be billed to a customer.

A similar analysis can be performed for the accounts-receivable (AR) department. Let us find out *how long it takes, on average, between the time a dollar is billed to a customer and enters AR to the time it is collected as cash from the customer's payment.* In this case, process boundaries are defined by the AR department, and the flow unit is a dollar of accounts receivable. From Table 3.4, note that MBPF has annual sales (and thus an annual flow rate through AR) of $250 million. From Table 3.5, note that accounts receivable in AR total $27.9 million. Incorporating these numbers, Figure 3.6 presents the process flow view of MBPF's AR department.

When we analyze flows through AR, we arrive at the following information:

$$\text{Throughput } R_{AR} = \$250 \text{ million/year [Net Sales, Table 3.4]}$$
$$\text{Average inventory } I_{AR} = \$27.9 \text{ million [Receivables, Table 3.5]}$$

Accordingly, the *average flow time through AR* is

$$\text{Average flow time } T_{AR} = I_{AR}/R_{AR}$$
$$= 27.9/250 \text{ years}$$
$$= 0.112 \text{ years} = 5.80 \text{ weeks}$$

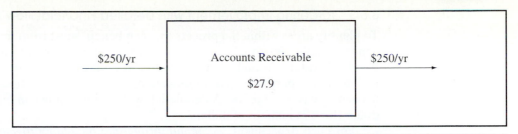

FIGURE 3.6 Accounts-Receivable Flows at MBPF Inc.

In other words, after a sale is made, MBPF must wait on average nearly six weeks before sales dollars are collected from the customer.

Finally, the same analysis can be done for the accounts-payable (AP)—or purchasing—process at MBPF Inc. Recall that MBPF purchases both raw materials and parts. Let us find out *how long it takes, on average, between the time raw material or parts are received and the supplier bills MBPF (and the bill enters AP) to the time MBPF pays the supplier.* In this case, process boundaries are defined by the AP department, and the flow unit is a dollar of accounts payable. From Table 3.6, note that MBPF spends $50.1 million on raw materials and $40.2 million on purchased parts per year. The annual flow rate through AP is therefore $50.1 + 40.2 = $90.3 million. The balance sheet in Table 3.5 shows that the average inventory in purchasing (accounts payables) is $11.9 million. Letting the subscript AP denote accounts payable, we can use Little's law to determine the *average flow time through AP* department:

$$T_{AP} = I_{AP}/R_{AP}$$
$$= 11.9/90.3$$
$$= 0.13 \text{ years} = 6.9 \text{ weeks}$$

In other words, it takes MBPF on average 6.9 weeks to pay a bill.

3.6.2 Cash-to-Cash Cycle Performance

Overall, there is an average lag of about 21 weeks (15 weeks in production and 5.8 weeks in AR) between the point at which cost dollars are invested and the point at which sales dollars are received by MBPF. We call this time of converting cost dollars into sales (21 weeks for MBPF) the *cost-to-cash* cycle for this process. Yet MBPF only pays for the cost dollars it invests in the form of purchased parts and raw materials after 6.9 weeks. Its total "cash-to-cash" cycle therefore is

$$21 - 6.9 = 14.1 \text{ weeks}$$

It is important to realize that flow rates can be expressed in either cost dollars or sales dollars. From Table 3.4, we see that 175.8 million cost dollars result in 250 million in sales dollars. When considering inventories, MBPF must use cost dollars. In contrast, when considering receivables or revenue, MBPF must consider sales dollars. When converting the appropriate rates into flow times, however, all flows are in time units and can be compared.

3.6.3 Targeting Improvement with Detailed Financial Flow Analysis

To identify areas within the process that can benefit most from improvement, we need a more detailed flow analysis. We now consider detailed operations by analyzing dollar flows separately through each of the following areas or departments of the process: raw materials, purchased parts, fabrication, assembly, and finished goods. The flow unit in each case is a cost dollar. A detailed flow diagram is shown in Figure 3.7, with all cost dollar flows in millions of dollars.

For each department, *we obtain throughput by adding together the cost of inputs and any labor and overhead (L&OH) incurred in the department.* So, the throughput rate through fabrication is

$$\begin{array}{r} \$50.1 \text{ million/year in raw materials} \\ + \ \ \$60.2 \text{ million in labor and overhead} \\ \hline = \$110.3 \text{ million/year} \end{array}$$

The throughput through the assembly area is

$$\begin{array}{r} \$110.3 \text{ million/year in roofs} \\ + \ \ \$40.2 \text{ million/year in bases} \\ + \ \ \$25.3 \text{ million/year in labor and overhead} \\ \hline = \$175.8 \text{ million/year} \end{array}$$

By analyzing the various flows through these four stages, we find the flow times for a cost dollar through each department shown in Table 3.7. (All data originate from Table 3.6.)

Working capital in each department includes the amount of inventory in it. Flow time in each department represents the amount of time a cost dollar spends, on average, in that department. Reducing flow time, therefore, reduces MBPF's required working capital. Knowing this principle, we are prompted to ask, *In which department*

▪▪▪▪▪▪▪▪▪▪▪ **FIGURE 3.7** Detailed Financial Flows at MBPF Inc.

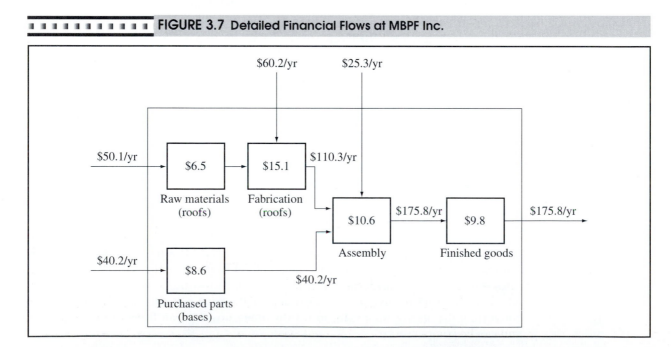

TABLE 3.7 Flow Times through MBPF Inc.

	Raw Materials	Fabrication	Purchased Parts	Assembly	Finished Goods
Throughput *R*					
$/year	50.1	110.3	40.2	175.8	175.8
$/week*	0.96	2.12	0.77	3.38	3.38
Inventory *I* ($)	6.5	15.1	8.6	10.6	9.8
Flow time *T = I/R* (weeks)*	6.75	7.12	11.12	3.14	2.90

* Rounding of numbers is done after working through with the initial data.

does a reduction of flow time have the greatest *impact on working capital?* Because *inventory equals the product of flow time and throughput,* the value of reducing flow time, say, by one week in any department is proportional to its throughput rate. For example, because throughput through the finished-goods warehouse is $3.38 million per week, reducing flow time here by one week saves $3.38 million in working capital (inventory). But because the throughput rate through purchased parts is only $0.77 million per week, a one-week reduction in flow time saves only $0.77 million in working capital. Naturally, the *current flow time of an activity represents the maximum potential reduction in flow time.*

Both current flow times and the value of reducing them are represented graphically in Figure 3.8. For each department, we plot throughput on the vertical axis and flow time on the horizontal axis. Each department corresponds to a rectangle whose area represents the inventory in the department. Typically, the throughput increases as

FIGURE 3.8 Representation of Inventory Value at MBPF Inc.

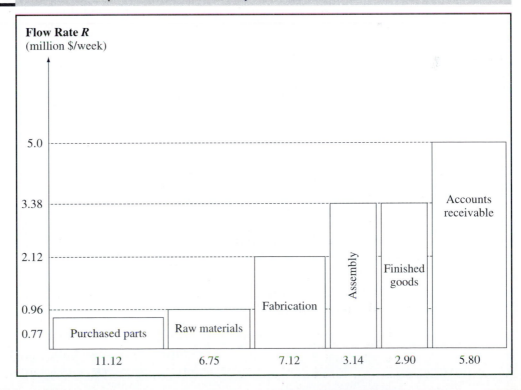

we go from inflows through the process and end with accounts receivable because it reflects value added.

Observe in Figure 3.8 that a one-week reduction flow time has the largest impact in the AR department because the rectangle for AR represents a flow rate of $5 million per week, which is highest. Thus, reducing the flow time in AR by one week would free up $5 million! (Example 3.4 illustrates typical actions to reduce the flow time in AR and free up cash.)

The smallest possible impact of a one-week reduction would be in the purchased parts department; the rectangle in Figure 3.8 that represents it is the shortest and has a flow rate of only $0.77 million. With a flow time of 11.12 weeks, however, the purchased parts department offers the greatest potential to decrease flow time itself.

Example 3.4

A portfolio company that provides custodial and security services to business customers needs to reduce its working capital to improve liquidity. The management team is focused on day-to-day operations and has not yet made significant progress in reducing accounts receivable (AR).

One of the board members of the firm, Jeb Bentley, an engineer and former operating manager in the automotive and industrial products industries, suggests applying flow concepts to help management create significant reductions in AR. This will free up about $10 million in cash to pay down debt and increase the value of the firm's investment.

Bentley suggests the following actions:

- The firm will draw a very basic process diagram outlining the length of time that cash is tied up in each stage of the collection process, enabling easier identification of target areas for improvement.
- Inventory of outstanding receivables will be reduced by decreasing the flow time of sending bills. Presently, typically between $2 million and $3 million in bills are in the mail at any given time. By using e-mail to send bills, this inventory will be cut by about 75%.
- A policy of ensuring quality at each point in the process ("quality at source") will be implemented to decrease processing time and avoid unnecessary delays. At present, billings to clients are sent by branch offices to headquarters for review to ensure that they are error free. By pushing this responsibility back onto branch offices, both billing errors and review time will be decreased, as the branches better know their typical billings and the reviewer at headquarters will no longer be a bottleneck. This will result in a further reduction of inventory.

⸎ ⸎ ⸎ 3.7 Inventory Turns (Turnover Ratio)

In addition to the average level of inventory and the average flow time, practicing operations managers, accountants, and financial analysts often use the concept of *inventory turns* or *turnover ratio* to show how many times the inventory is sold and replaced during a specific period. In the accounting literature, inventory turns is defined as the cost of goods sold divided by average inventory. The cost of goods sold during a given period is nothing other than throughput, expressed in monetary units. Therefore, in our broader view of inventory, **inventory turns**, or **turnover ratio**, is defined as *the ratio of throughput to average inventory*. It is expressed as

$$\text{Inventory turns} = R/I \tag{3.4}$$

But we can use Little's law, $I = R \times T$, to come up with an equivalent definition of inventory turns as follows:

$$
\begin{aligned}
\text{Inventory turns} &= R/I && \text{(by definition)} \\
&= R/(R \times T) && \text{(use Little's law)} \\
&= 1/T && \text{(R cancels out)}
\end{aligned}
$$

In other words, *inventory turns is the reciprocal of average flow time* and thus is a direct operational measure. This directly shows why high turns are attractive: a company with high inventory turns has small flow times and thus is quicker at turning its inputs into sold outputs.

To derive a meaningful turnover ratio, *we must specify the flow unit and measure inventory and throughput in the same units.* Some organizations measure turns as the ratio of sales to inventory. This measure has a drawback in that sales (a measure of throughput) are expressed in sales dollars but inventory is measured in cost dollars. A better way to calculate turns is the ratio of *cost of goods sold (COGS)*—labor, materials, and overhead expenses allocated to the products in question—to inventory because both are measured in cost dollars. Example 3.5 illustrates this calculation. Measuring turns as the ratio of sales to inventory can lead to erroneous conclusions when measuring process performance.

Example 3.5

Let us return to the MBPF financial statements in Tables 3.4 and 3.5 to analyze inventory turns. We will use cost dollar as the flow unit and designate the factory and the finished-goods warehouse as the process:

$$Turns = Throughput/Inventory$$
$$= (\$175.8/year)/\$50.6 = 3.47/year$$

In other words, during one year MBPF Inc. sells and thus replenishes its average inventory about three times.

▪▪▪ 3.8 Using Operational Measures to Improve Financial Measures: What Do We Mean by "an Improvement"?

Thus far, we have defined three operational process-performance measures: *flow rate, flow time,* and *inventory.* (Recall that inventory turns is equivalent to average flow time.) We have also seen how each can be evaluated for a variety of business process flows. Because Little's law relates these measures through one equation, we can manage only two of them independently; the third measure is then automatically determined. Now let us relate these operational measures to financial measures of process performance. Our goal is *to determine when a process change generates an improvement from both operational and financial perspectives.*

Net Present Value The financial performance of any business process may be measured by the **net present value (NPV)** of its current and future cash flows. *NPV is a measure of expected aggregate monetary gain or loss that is computed by discounting all expected future cash inflows and outflows to their present value.* Given a sequence of cash flows over a period of future time, a firm's NPV is equivalent to a single present sum such that any risk-neutral investor who is in a position to choose between accepting a future sequence of cash flows on the one hand or the single sum today values both the same. NPV is calculated by adjusting future cash flows by a discount factor to reflect the *time value of money*—that is, the principle that a dollar you hold today will be worth more than a dollar you expect to receive in the future. (The discount factor can also be adjusted to account for the investor's risk preferences but we will focus on the time value of money.) The discount factor is based on **rate of return** (r): *the reward that an investor demands for accepting payment delayed by one period of time.*

Let C_t represent the cash flow in period t, starting from period $t = 0$ and ending at period $t = n$. The NPV of these cash flows is found by first discounting each cash flow C_t—that is, multiply it by the discount factor of $1/(1 + r)^t$—and then summing all those discounted cash flows:

$$\text{NPV} = C_o + \sum_{t=1}^{n} \frac{C_t}{(1+r)^t}$$

(Net present value can also be directly computed using built-in spreadsheet functions, such as "NPV" in Microsoft Excel.)

Sales Volume and Cash Flows   The true throughput for any business process is measured by *sales volume*—the number of units sold. If MBPF Inc. produces 2,200 garages per week while market demand is for 1,000 garages per week, the throughput as measured by sales would be 1,000 garages per week, while the remaining 1,200 garages per week would simply build up as inventory. If, however, production is only 800 garages per week and demand is 1,000 per week, then finished-goods inventory will soon be depleted, after which actual sales—and thus throughput—will be only 800 garages per week. *True throughput, as measured by long-term average sales rate, therefore, is the minimum of its output and market demand.* Note that *positive cash flows* result from the revenue received from product sales (there may be other revenue sources, but product sales will be a major contributor). Thus, we can assume that positive cash flows are correlated with throughput. An increase in throughput (sales) thus increases positive cash flows.

Negative cash flows typically result from investment in resources, interest expense, and operating expense (labor + overhead). Interest expense is correlated with the amount of inventory in the process. Reducing inventory in the process reduces the company's working capital requirement. In turn, this reduction lowers its interest expense, thereby reducing negative cash flows. As we noted in Chapter 1, we define process cost as the total cost incurred in producing and delivering outputs. Negative cash flows, therefore, can also be reduced by reducing process cost because negative cash flows decrease when the process entails lower cost to produce the outputs.

Now we can assess when a change in the process can be called an improvement. From the financial perspective, a change is an improvement *if and only if it increases NPV*. A change may increase both positive and negative cash flows, which is an improvement only if the NPV of the increase in positive cash flows exceeds the NPV of the increase in negative cash flows. A change can certainly be called an improvement if it either increases positive cash flows without increasing negative cash flows or decreases negative cash flows without decreasing positive cash flows. This situation is equivalent to addressing the following three questions:

1. Has true process throughput (as measured by sales) risen without any increase in inventories or process cost?
2. Has process inventory declined without any reduction in throughput or increase in process cost?
3. Has process cost declined without any reduction in throughput or increase in inventory?

The first two questions really ask whether flow time has been reduced without any increase in process cost. All three questions are quite similar to those raised by E. M. Goldratt in his efforts to identify and characterize process improvement (Goldratt, 1992). All three questions address only simple instances in which we know that NPV will go up because of the change. In more complicated scenarios in which both positive and negative cash flows change, we must *evaluate* NPV before characterizing a change as an improvement.

Another common financial measure is **return on total assets**, *which shows how well a firm uses its assets to earn income for the stakeholders who are financing it.* We can express this measure as follows:

$$\text{Return on total assets} = \frac{\text{EBIT} - \text{Taxes}}{\text{Average total assets}}$$

where EBIT is *earnings before interest and taxes.* EBIT is also known as *operating income* and compares gross profit against operating expenses. It increases with an increase of annual unit sales and income per unit (assuming a positive income per unit). Average total assets include *fixed assets* (typically those invested in resources) and assets in the form of *working capital* (typically those invested in inventory). An affirmative answer to any of the three questions posed previously also means there is an increase in return on total assets.

In this chapter, we have established a relationship between three key operational measures and some common financial measures. Our discussion indicates that improvements in the three key operational measures translate into improvements in financial measures as well. Therefore, the operational measures of throughput, inventory, and flow time are *leading* indicators of financial performance.

SUMMARY ▮▮▮▮▮▮▮

The first chapter in this book discussed the importance of identifying operational measures that are good leading indicators of customer satisfaction and the financial performance of a process. This chapter introduces three key operational measures that characterize the *flow* of units through the process: throughput, inventory, and flow time. Throughput is the rate at which units flow through the process. Inventory is the number of flow units within the process boundaries at a given point in time. Flow time is the time it takes for a specific flow unit to be transformed from input to output. The three operational measures can be applied to processes with a variety of flow units, including money, customers, data, material, and orders.

For a stable process, the three operational measures are related through Little's law, which states that average inventory is the product of average throughput and average flow time. In other words, managers need to track and control only two of the three measures—average throughput and average inventory, typically, which then determine average flow time.

These operational measures are leading indicators of financial performance. Inventory is a measure of tied-up capital (for manufacturing) or customers who are waiting (for services). For a manufacturing firm, a decrease in inventory indicates a drop in working capital requirements. Throughput measures the rate at which the output of the process is being sold. An increase in throughput indicates increased revenues and also increased profits if the product has positive margin. Flow time measures how long it takes to transform orders and invested cash into products. A faster flow time means higher inventory turns and relatively lower working capital requirements. An improvement in the three operational measures thus leads to an improvement in long-term financial measures, such as net present value and return on investment.

KEY EQUATIONS AND SYMBOLS ▪▪▪▪▪▪▪

(3.1) $\Delta R(t) = R_i(t) - R_o(t)$
(3.2) $I(t_2) - I(t_1) = \Delta R \times (t_2 - t_1)$
(3.3) Little's law: $I = R \times T$
(3.4) Inventory turns $= R/I$
where
$R_i(t)$: Instantaneous inflow rate
$R_o(t)$: Instantaneous outflow rate

$\Delta R(t)$: Instantaneous inventory accumulation (or buildup) rate
$I(t)$: Inventory at time t
I: Average inventory
R: Throughput or average flow rate
T: Average flow time

KEY TERMS ▪▪▪▪▪▪▪

- Average flow rate
- Average flow time
- Flow rate
- Flow time
- Instantaneous inventory accumulation (buildup) rate

- Inventory buildup diagram
- Inventory turns
- Little's law
- Net present value (NPV)
- Process flow measures
- Rate of return

- Return on total assets
- Stable process
- Throughput
- Turnover ratio

DISCUSSION QUESTIONS ▪▪▪▪▪▪▪

3.1 Why is it important to look at *aggregate* flow performance, as measured by average inventory, average flow time, and average throughput?

3.2 Discuss why it is often easier to measure average inventory and average throughput rather than average flow time.

3.3 How can a manager determine the minimal set of operational measures that she should track on a daily basis to predict the financial performances of a process?

3.4 The Internal Revenue's Department of Tax Regulations writes regulations in accordance with laws passed by Congress. On average, the department completes 300 projects per year. The *Wall Street Journal* reports that, as of October 11, 2004, the number of projects currently "on the department's plate" is 588. Nevertheless, the department head claims that average time to complete a project is less than six months. Do you have any reason to disagree? Why or why not?

3.5 The *Wall Street Journal* reported that "although GM and Toyota are operating with the same number of inventory turns, Toyota's throughput is twice that of GM." The discrepancy, concluded the writer, "could be due to much faster flow times and lower inventories by virtue of Toyota's production system." With which of the following deductions do you agree?
   a. The two statements are consistent.
   b. The two statements are inconsistent: if both have the same inventory turns, they have the same flow time, but Toyota has higher average inventory than GM.
   c. The two statements are inconsistent: if both have the same inventory turns, they have the same flow time, but Toyota has lower average inventory than GM.
   d. The two statements are inconsistent: if both have the same inventory turns, they have the same average inventory, but Toyota has higher flow time than GM.
   e. The two statements are inconsistent: if both have the same inventory turns, they have the same average inventory, but Toyota has lower flow time than GM.

3.6 Is there a difference between low inventories and fast inventory turnover?

3.7 Why is it preferable to have a short cost-to-cash cycle, and how can that be achieved?

EXERCISES ▪▪▪▪▪▪▪

3.1 A bank finds that the average number of people waiting in line during lunch hour is 10. On average, during this period, 2 people per minute leave the bank after receiving service. On average, how long do bank customers wait in line?

3.2 At the drive-through counter of a fast-food outlet, an average of 10 cars waits in line. The manager wants to determine if the length of the line is having any impact on potential sales. Her study reveals that, on average, 2 cars per minute try to enter the drive-through area, but 25% of the drivers of these cars are dismayed by the long line and simply move on without placing orders. Assume that no car that enters the line leaves without service. On average, how long does a car spend in the drive-through line?

3.3 Checking accounts at a local bank carry an average balance of $3,000. The bank turns over its balance 6 times a year. On average, how many dollars flow through the bank each month?

3.4 A hospital emergency room (ER) is currently organized so that all patients register through an initial check-in process. At his or her turn, each patient is seen by a doctor and then exits the process, either with a prescription or with admission to the hospital. Currently, 55 people per hour arrive at the ER, 10% of who are admitted to the hospital. On average, 7 people are waiting to be registered and 34 are registered and waiting to see a doctor. The registration process takes, on average, 2 minutes per patient. Among patients who receive prescriptions, average time spent with a doctor is 5 minutes. Among those admitted to the hospital, average time is 30 minutes. On average, how long does a patient spend in the ER? On average, how many patients are being examined by doctors? On average, how many patients are there in the ER? Assume the process to be stable; that is, average inflow rate equals average outflow rate.

3.5 A triage system has been proposed for the ER described in Exercise 3.4. As mentioned earlier, 50 patients per hour arrive at the ER. Under the proposed triage plan, entering patients will be registered as before. They will then be quickly examined by a nurse practitioner who will classify them as Simple Prescriptions or Potential Admits. While Simple Prescriptions will move on to an area staffed for regular care, Potential Admits will be taken to the emergency area. Planners anticipate that the initial examination will take 3 minutes. They expect that, on average, 20 patients will be waiting to register and 5 will be waiting to be seen by the triage nurse. Recall that registration takes an average of 2 minutes per patient. The triage nurse is expected to take an average of 1 minute per patient. Planners expect the Simple Prescriptions area to have, on average, 15 patients waiting to be seen. As before, once a patient's turn comes, each will take 5 minutes of a doctor's time. The hospital anticipates that, on average, the emergency area will have only 1 patient waiting to be seen. As before, once that patient's turn comes, he or she will take 30 minutes of a doctor's time. Assume that, as before, 90% of all patients are Simple Prescriptions. Assume, too, that the triage nurse is 100% accurate in making classifications. Under the proposed plan, how long, on average, will a patient spend in the ER? On average, how long will a Potential Admit spend in the ER? On average, how many patients will be in the ER? Assume the process to be stable; that is, average inflow rate equals average outflow rate.

3.6 Refer again to Exercise 3.5. Once the triage system is put in place, it performs quite close to expectations. All data conform to planners' expectations except for one set—the classifications made by the nurse practitioner. Assume that the triage nurse has been sending 91% of all patients to the Simple Prescription area when in fact only 90% should have been so classified. The remaining 1% is discovered when transferred to the emergency area by a doctor. Assume all other information from Exercise 3.5 to be valid. On average, how long does a patient spend in the ER? On average, how long does a Potential Admit spend in the ER? On average, how many patients are in the ER? Assume the process to be stable; that is, average inflow rate equals average outflow rate.

3.7 Orange Juice Inc. produces and markets fruit juice. During the orange harvest season, trucks bring oranges from the fields to the processing plant during a workday that runs from 7 a.m. to 6 p.m. On peak days, approximately 10,000 kilograms of oranges are trucked in per hour. Trucks dump their contents in a holding bin with a storage capacity of 6,000 kilograms. When the bin is full, incoming trucks must wait until it has sufficient available space. A conveyor moves oranges from the bins to the processing plant. The plant is configured to deal with an average harvesting day, and maximum throughput (flow rate) is 8,000 kilograms per hour.

Assuming that oranges arrive continuously over time, construct an inventory buildup diagram for Orange Juice Inc. In order to process all the oranges delivered during the day, how long must the plant operate on peak days? (Assume, too, that because Orange Juice Inc. makes fresh juice, it cannot store oranges.) Assuming, finally, that each truck holds about 1,000 kilograms of oranges, at what point during the day must a truck first wait before unloading into the storage bin? What is the maximum amount of time that a truck must wait? How long will trucks wait on average? Among trucks that do wait, how long is the average wait?

3.8 Jasper Valley Motors (JVM) is a family-run auto dealership selling both new and used vehicles. In an average month, JVM sells a total of 160 vehicles. New vehicles represent 60% of sales, and used vehicles represent 40% of sales. Max has recently taken over the business from his father. His father always emphasized the importance of carefully managing the dealership's inventory. Inventory financing was a significant expense for JVM. Max's father consequently taught him to keep inventory turns as high as possible.

a. Examining the dealership's performance over recent years, Max discovered that JVM had been turning its inventory (including both new and used vehicles) at a rate of 8 times per year. What is JVM's average inventory (including both new and used vehicles)?

b. Drilling down into the numbers, Max has determined that the dealership's new and used businesses appear to behave differently. He has determined that turns of new vehicles are 7.2 per year, while turns of used vehicles are 9.6 per year. Holding a new vehicle in inventory for a month costs JVM roughly $175. Holding the average used vehicle in inventory for a month costs roughly $145. What are JVM's average monthly financing costs per vehicle?

c. A consulting firm has suggested that JVM subscribe to its monthly market analysis service. They claim that their program will allow JVM to maintain its current sales rate of new cars while reducing the amount of time a new car sits in inventory before being sold by 20%. Assuming the consulting firm's claim is true, how much should Max be willing to pay for the service?

3.9 Cheapest Car Rental rents cars at the Chicago airport. The car rental market consists of two segments: the short-term segment, which rents for an average of 0.5 weeks, and the medium-term segment, which rents for an average of 2 weeks. Cheapest currently rents an average of 200 cars a week to the short-term segment and 100 cars a week to the medium-term segment.

Approximately 20% of the cars returned (evenly distributed across both segments) are found to be defective and in need of repairs before they can be made available for rent again. The remaining cars not needing repairs are cleaned, filled with gas, and made available for rent. On average, there are 100 cars waiting to be cleaned. The average cost of this operation is $5 per car. Cars needing repairs spend an average of 2 weeks in the repair shop and incur an average cost of $150 per car. Assume that cars are rented as soon as they are available for rent, that is, as soon as they have been cleaned or repaired.

Short-term renters pay $200 per week, while medium-term renters pay $120 per week. The flow of cars is shown in Figure 3.9.

a. Identify throughput, inventory, and flow time at each stage.

b. What profit does Cheapest earn per week with the current system? Assume that each car loses $40 in value per week because of depreciation.

▮▮▮▮▮▮▮▮▮▮▮▮ **FIGURE 3.9** Flowchart for Cheapest Car Rentals

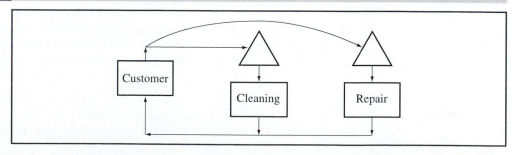

TABLE 3.8 Selected Income Statement and Balance Sheet Figures for ABC Corporation

	2004	2005
Net revenues	99,621	110,644
Cost of goods sold	97,380	98,350
Current assets		
Cash	13,491	8,079
Inventories	20,880	25,200
Accounts receivable	$21,596	$22,872

c. Cheapest is comparing two possible improvements:
   1. Decrease time in repairs from 2 weeks to 1 week.
   2. Decrease cost per repair from $150 per car to $120 per car while keeping flow time in repairs at 2 weeks.
   Assume that the effort that is required in each case is the same. Which change do you think will be more effective? Why?

3.10 The Evanstonian is an upscale independent hotel that caters to both business and leisure travelers. On average, one-third of the guests checking in each day are leisure travelers. Leisure travelers generally stay for 3.6 nights—twice as long as the average business customer.
   a. On an average day, 135 guests check into The Evanstonian. On average, how many guests of each type are in the hotel on any given day?
   b. How many times per month does the hotel turn over its inventory of guests (assume 30 days per month)?
   c. The average business traveler pays a rate of $250 per night, while leisure travelers pay an average rate of $210 per night. What is the average revenue The Evanstonian receives per night per occupied room?

3.11 ABC Corporation's consolidated income statement and balance sheet for the years 2004 and 2005 is shown in Table 3.8 (in thousands of dollars).
   How do you think cash flow performance in 2004 compares with that of 2005 in the factory as well as accounts receivable? Do you think 2005 is an improvement over 2004? Why?

MODELING EXERCISE ▪▪▪▪▪▪▪

www.prenhall.com/anupindi

For exercises and models using the evaluation software of iGrafx Process, insert the CD-ROM that is packaged with this book. An electronic copy of the User Guide is included on the CD. For more information on iGrafx, visit www.iGrafx.com. Detailed descriptions of the models may also be found at www.prenhall.com/anupindi.

Model

In Exercise 3.4, you were asked to analyze patient flow at an emergency room (ER) to estimate the average time it took various types of patients to flow through the ER and the average number of patients in ER. You used Little's law to estimate these performance metrics. In this modeling exercise, the ER of Exercise 3.4 is simulated using iGrafx Process. You may use the model to simulate patient flow in the ER. The simulation output, which gives estimates for average flow times, flow rates, and inventory at each stage of the process, can be used to experimentally verify that Little's law indeed holds.

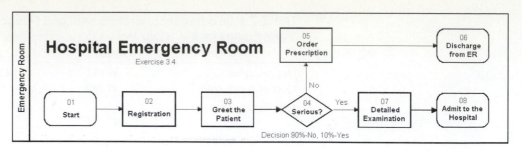

Simulation

To simulate the patient flow in the ER, double-click on iGrafx document CH3EX4. This loads the simulation model within iGrafx process. The main screen should have two panes. The left pane shows the Explorer bar with the following contents: Processes, Scenarios, and Reports. (If you do not see this, click on View and the Explorer bar from the menu item and ensure that the All Components view is chosen at the top of the Explorer bar.) You may view the model for this exercise by double-clicking on CH3EX4 under Processes. The Scenario1 tab gives details of the various parameters used in the simulation model. Finally, results of a simulation run may be viewed by double-clicking on Report 1 under the Reports tab in the Explorer bar.

To simulate the model, from the Model menu, point to Run and choose Start. A Simulation Progress window pops up at the right end of the screen. As soon as the simulation ends, the results of the simulation are displayed as a report. There are five tabs in a report. Select the Custom tab to see the customized report for this exercise.

Implementation

The process flow diagram is illustrated at the beginning of this section. The Start activity generates patient inflow into ER. Patients waiting to register are included in the Registration activity. However, the Greet the Patient activity represents the buffer where patients wait to see a doctor. Patients needing ordinary prescriptions go to the Order Prescription activity and exit through Discharge from ER, whereas patients needing more detailed examination go through the Detailed Examination and exit through Admit to Hospital.

While we have kept the same average parameter values (as in Exercise 3.4), the simulation model specifies more details on the times taken at each step, the arrival pattern, and the number of resources. These parameter values will result in average queue lengths similar to those specified in Exercise 3.4.

Specifically, in the simulation model, we assume that the patients arrive at an average rate of 55 per hour. In particular, the model specifies that the time between consecutive patient arrivals is *exponentially distributed* (see Appendix II) with a mean of 1.09 minutes. We assume that there are 2 nurses at the registration desk and 7 doctors examining patients. The registration activity takes between 1.5 to 2.5 minutes (with equal probability) averaging at 2 minutes. The examination time for a patient needing a simple prescription is between 4 and 6 minutes with an average of 5 minutes, and a patient needing hospital admission requires a detailed examination for 20 to 40 minutes with an average of 30 minutes.

Refer to the document in the CD for detailed explanations on the modeling approach for this exercise.

Performance Interpretation

The performance of the process is illustrated in the custom report and consists of the following:

- *Average flow time* of the process
- *Average inventory at each activity,* which includes patients waiting and in process
- *Overall transaction (patient) completion count,* which gives the total number of patients who complete the process
- *Elapsed time,* which measures the total elapsed time (in hours) in the simulation
- *Average flow rate,* which is the total number of patients processed per hour
- *Average flow times and inventory at each activity,* which gives the average flow time, waiting time, number of patients waiting, and the total number of patients (waiting + in process) at each stage of the process and finally the total number of patients processed at each of the stages. (This last count, when divided by the elapsed time, will give an estimate of the flow rate through each of the activities.)
- *Average flow time of each type of patient*

SELECTED BIBLIOGRAPHY ▪▪▪▪▪▪▪

Atkins, D., M. A. Begen, B. Kluczny, A. Parkinson, and M. L. Puterman. 2003. "Right on Queue: OR Models Improve Passenger Flows and Customer Service at Vancouver International Airport." *OR/MS Today,* April 2003, 26–29.

Goldratt, E. M. 1992. *The Goal.* 2nd ed. Great Barrington, Mass.: North River Press.

Hopp, W. J., and M. L. Spearman. 1996. *Factory Physics.* Chicago: Irwin.

CHAPTER 4

Flow-Time Analysis

Introduction

Zhang & Associates,[1] a financial advisory branch of American Express, provides comprehensive financial advisory and asset management services to individuals with high net worth. Zhang & Associates' new client process is typical of the industry. It entails a sequence of meetings with the new customer that continues until a mutually acceptable plan of action is identified and implemented. A major weakness of the process is the amount of time required for each customer—a new client with a simple portfolio is processed in four to six weeks; individuals with more complex financial services needs take much longer to process. In addition, management felt that the process was inefficient in the use of the company's resources.

Recently, the company has redesigned the process so that it can be completed in two weeks. Zhang & Associates' customers are delighted with the faster service. In addition, the company was able to better utilize its resources and improve its relation with *existing* customers.

How do companies such as Zhang and Associates manage their processes to reduce flow time? We discuss this question in the next few chapters.

---

[1]We are grateful to Ms. Lynn L. Chen-Zhang for bringing this example to our attention.

In the previous chapter, we introduced three important measures of process performance, namely, flow time, flow rate, and inventory. We also showed how Little's law establishes a fundamental relationship among the averages of these three measures. We stressed the importance of these measures and applied Little's law to a macro-level performance evaluation of a business process. In this chapter and in Chapter 5, we lay the foundation for more detailed process analysis. Our goal is to understand what factors affect the three key performance measures and the levers that can be manipulated to improve process performance.

We begin with the concept of flow time. Recall from Chapter 3 that the flow time of a given flow unit is the total amount of time required by that unit to flow through the process from entry to exit. For any given process, the flow time of different flow units varies substantially. We determine the average flow time of a process by looking at all flow units that flow through the process during a specific span of time and taking their average.

Process flow time is a valuable measure of process performance for several reasons. Consider the following advantages of shorter flow time:

1. Flow time affects delivery response time, a key product attribute that customers value, as discussed in Chapter 1. The less time customers must wait for a good or a service, the better the value for the customer. Also, the shorter the delivery response time, the more quickly a firm can collect revenues, thus improving its financial performance.

2. Short flow times in the production and delivery process reduce the inventory (by Little's law) and associated costs.

3. A shorter flow time in a firm's new product development process enables the firm to more quickly introduce the product to the market, which is a major source of competitive advantage. Likewise, it enables the firm to bring more generations of a product to market within a given amount of time.

4. In markets featuring short product life cycles, shorter manufacturing-process flow times allow firms to delay production closer to the time of sale and thus gain valuable market information, avoid product obsolescence, and minimize the inventory required.

5. Short flow times result in fast feedback and correction of quality problems, as we see in Chapters 9 and 10.

6. Finally, flow time is important because it is an integrative measure of overall process performance—short flow time frequently requires a high level of overall operational excellence. For instance, a process rife with quality problems would typically display the longer flow times required for inspections, rework (fixing defective products so that they conform to specifications), and so forth.

In this chapter, we study the factors that determine process flow time and specify some ways that managers can reduce it. Our first step in analyzing any process is to develop the process flowchart presented in the next section. In Section 4.2, we discuss flow-time measurement. In Section 4.3, we introduce the concept of *theoretical flow time* and show how it relates to the concept of a *critical path* in the process flowchart. We also examine the roles of activity time and waiting time as they relate to total flow time, and we introduce the concept of *flow-time efficiency*. In Section 4.4, we identify some key managerial levers for reducing theoretical flow time. (The levers for reducing *wait* time are discussed later in Chapters 6 to 8). Finally, in the Appendix, we present a formal version of the critical path method for determining both theoretical flow time and critical paths in complex processes.

▯▯▯ 4.1 The Process Flowchart

In Chapter 1, we described a process as having five elements, namely, inputs and outputs, flow units, network of activities and buffers, resources allocated to activities, and information structure. A **process flowchart** is a graphical representation of these five elements.

For the purpose of representation, it is useful to separate activities that require a decision (which we call *decisions*) from other types of activities. Decisions route a flow unit to one of two or more continuing routes, resulting in a "splitting" of flows. In a process flowchart, various elements are represented by different geometric shapes:

- Decisions are represented by diamonds.
- The remaining activities are represented by rectangles.
- Precedence relationships between any two activities are represented by solid arrows. (A precedence relation between two activities, A and B, is the requirement that A must be completed before B can start.)
- Buffers are represented by triangles.
- Information flows are represented by dashed arrows.

In addition, it is useful to identify events (e.g., the start and end of a process) in a business process. Events are represented by ovals.

Process flowcharts were originally developed to coordinate large projects involving complex sets of activities and considerable resources. They are also useful, however, for understanding, documenting, and analyzing almost any business process (see Example 4.1). Breaking down a process into its component activities, identifying their interrelationships, and viewing them graphically help to enhance our understanding of the total process. Studying the process also highlights non-value-adding activities and areas for possible improvements.

Example 4.1

To illustrate the function of a process flowchart, consider the manufacturing process at Wonder Shed Inc., a manufacturer of storage sheds. The manufacturing process involves the procurement of sheets of steel that will be used to form both the roof and the base of each shed.

The first step involves separating the material needed for the roof from that needed for the base. Then the roof and the base can be fabricated "in parallel," or simultaneously. Roof fabrication involves punching and forming the roof to shape. Base fabrication entails punching and forming plus a subassembly operation. Fabricated roofs and bases are then assembled into finished sheds that are subsequently inspected for quality assurance. A list of activities needed to fabricate a roof, fabricate a base, and assemble a shed is given in Table 4.1. The entire shed-making process is shown in Figure 4.1.

TABLE 4.1 Activity List for Wonder Shed Inc.

	Activity
1	Separate the roof and base modules
2	Punch the base
3	Punch the roof
4	Form the base
5	Form the roof
6	Subassemble the base
7	Assemble
8	Inspect

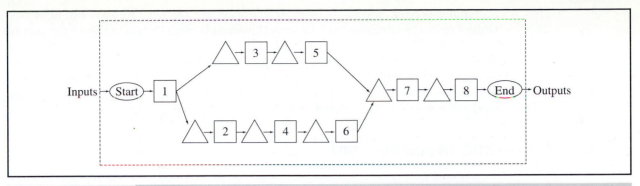

▪▪▪▪▪▪▪▪▪▪▪ **FIGURE 4.1** Process Flowchart for Wonder Shed Inc.

Subprocesses and Cascading   In any given representation of a process, such as the flowchart in Figure 4.1, activities are typically treated as indivisible parts of the process. However, *any activity may be broken down further (or "exploded") into a set of sub-activities;* we then refer to it as a **subprocess** of the original process. When we do this, the activity can be considered as a process in its own right, with its own set of inputs, outputs, activities, suppliers, customers, and so forth. How do we decide which parts to treat as indivisible activities, and which may be further subdivided into more elementary subprocesses? The answer depends on two factors: the parts of the process on which we want to focus and the level of detail that we need. If we want *to represent a given process at several levels of detail simultaneously,* we can use a technique called **cascading** the process. In Figure 4.2, we show how to cascade a process by depicting a process flowchart for a simple generic process and exploding activity "d" into a complete subprocess.

▪▪▪▪▪▪▪▪▪▪▪ **FIGURE 4.2** Cascading a Process

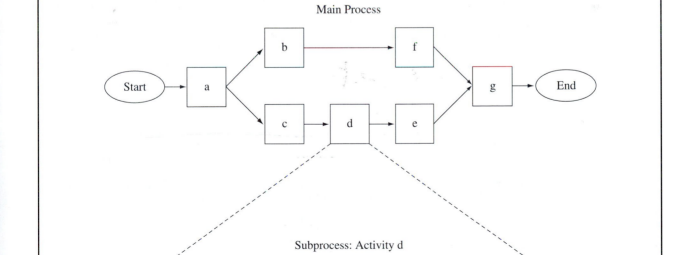

Finally, process flowcharts often depict resources required to carry out activities. Adding resource allocation to a process flowchart is useful when studying the sort of throughput and capacity issues that we consider in Chapter 5. One way to incorporate resource allocation is to partition the process flowchart into several horizontally distinct colors or bands, one for each resource. The decision as to which elements of the process should be represented on a given flowchart depends on the application and the degree of representational detail that is needed.

▪▪▪▪ 4.2   Flow-Time Measurement

The average flow time of a given process can be determined in two independent ways: directly or by measuring time indirectly by application of Little's law. A direct measurement can be made as follows:

1. Observe the process over a specified, extended period of time.
2. Take a random sample of flow units over the specified period.
3. For each flow unit in the sample, measure its flow time from entry to exit.
4. Compute the average of flow times measured.

To use the indirect approach as we discussed in Chapter 3, we measure average throughput or flow rate (R) and average inventory (I) and then compute average flow time (T) by using Little's law:

$$I = R \times T$$

Thus, the indirect method requires the following steps:

1. Observe the process over a specified, extended period of time.
2. Measure the number of units produced during the period and compute the throughput (R) by dividing the number of units produced by the duration of the observation time period.
3. At random points of time during the period, count the number of units of inventory (units in the process) and compute the average of these measurements giving average inventory (I).
4. Compute the average flow time (T) using Little's law.

The direct and indirect approaches are demonstrated in Example 4.2.

Example 4.2

Consider the process of credit approval at a small bank. During a given month, a sample of 50 applications was taken, and the average flow time was determined to be 20.85 working days. This is an estimate of the average flow time of the process using the direct approach. To see how the indirect approach could be used, assume that during that month 200 applications were processed and that the number of days of operations was 20. Thus, the flow rate (R) during the period was 10 applications per day. Now assume that the number of applications in process was counted four times during the month and that the average inventory (I) was found to be 215. We can compute the average flow time using Little's law, which can be rewritten as

$$T = I/R$$

Substituting for values of I and R, we get

$$T = 215/10$$

giving

$$T = 21.5 \text{ days}$$

This provides us with an alternative estimate of the average flow time. Naturally, we expect the two estimates to be close but not identical because of the randomness of sampling.

Both approaches require that flow units and entry and exit points are carefully specified. If we use the indirect method, we must also ensure that flow time, inventory, and throughput are defined *consistently*. Although flow-time theory allows us extremely wide latitude in selecting the appropriate specifications for each of these concepts and in most cases the rough specifications follow quite naturally from the context of the application, we must nevertheless be precise and consistent.

To illustrate some of the subtleties involved in the specification of flow units, consider the production process of a manufacturer such as Wonder Shed. Such a process typically handles a "mix" of distinct models that vary, for example, in size, cost, quality level, and routing. In addition, quality problems may cause a certain fraction of all products to be reworked or scrapped at various points along the process. Finally, each product may consist of several parts or modules that arrive at different times and travel separately through the factory. In cases like this, what is the appropriate definition of a flow unit?

Defining the Flow Unit   When defining the flow unit, we have many options, and the "right" choice depends on the nature and purpose of the analysis. For instance, consider a product manager in a multiproduct company who is concerned with the performance of her own relatively narrow line of products. In this case, it makes sense for her to define the flow as consisting of the products in the relevant line only. However, if we conduct the analysis from the perspective of the entire company, we must broaden our definition of flow unit to encompass the entire product mix. In *this* case, we need to consider how to aggregate the units of the various products that make up the product mix. Here we have several options.

If the units are relatively similar (e.g., if units correspond to customers of a restaurant), the best approach may be to weigh these units (customers) equally. On the other hand, if units vary significantly in terms of size, cost, price, profitability, and so forth, we may decide to account for their differences by weighing them according to the emphasis we place on certain attributes. For example, a law firm that handles individuals as well as corporate customers may wish to weigh cases by the size of their revenues. We illustrate some of this complexity in Example 4.3.

Example 4.3

The research department of Golden Touch Securities is charged with releasing research reports for the benefit of Golden's customers and brokers. The firm's reports can be classified into two types: major reports, which require a significant investment of research effort, and minor updates, which are much smaller in scope. In a typical month, the department releases 20 major reports and 40 updates. The average flow times for reports and updates, respectively, are 10 and 6 working days. What is the average flow time of the department?

A naive approach is to count each report, no matter the type, as a single flow unit. In that case, the flow rate for the month will be 60 units (reports and updates), and the average flow time is

$$\text{Reports} = 10 \text{ days} \times 20 \text{ reports}/60 \text{ total or } 200/60 = 3.33$$
$$\underline{+ \text{ Updates} = 6 \text{ days} \times 40 \text{ updates}/60 \text{ total or } 240/60 = 4.00}$$
$$\text{Average flow time} = 7.33 \text{ days}$$

or

$$10 \times 20/60 + 6 \times 40/60 = 7.33 \text{ days}$$

To complete a more refined analysis, we could assign different weights to the two types of reports. For instance, Golden could decide—based on the prices it charges—to treat each update report as the equivalent of *one-half* of a major report. In that case, the flow rate for the month amounts to 40 units (20 major reports plus 20 updates [40 updates/2]). In this way, the average flow time is

$$10 \times 20/40 + 6 \times 20/40 = 8 \text{ days}$$

We emphasize that both approaches are correct, and we are free to select the one that better matches the objectives of the study. However, once we select one approach, we must define inventory and throughput in a consistent way.

Defining the Process Boundaries   We also have choices to make about the process boundaries. When is a flow unit completed? Is it at the moment its construction is completed, when it enters finished goods inventory, when it is shipped to the customer, or when we get paid for it? What is the exit point for a scrapped unit (in case we decide to include it in our study)? Similar latitude exists in defining the starting point of the process. In some scenarios, the starting point can be defined as the moment at which all required parts or modules are available for production; in other cases, the proper choice is the time at which work starts on any part of the flow unit. Similar choices are present in a service situation. For instance, consider a passenger taking a flight. When does the process begin? When the passenger checks in, when she boards the plane, when she arrives at the airport, or maybe when she leaves her house to go to the airport? Depending on the situation under study, each one of these definitions could be the appropriate choice. Again, once we select one of these possibilities, then the definition of inventory must be consistent with that choice. (Recall that inventory is defined as the number of units of flow within the process boundaries.)

To summarize, the important point is that each valid set of specifications for the flow units and the process boundaries results in a different interpretation of—and a different numeric value for—flow time, inventory, and throughput.

▪▪▪ 4.3 Theoretical Flow Time

As a flow unit travels through the process from entry to exit, it typically undergoes a sequence of activities interspersed with periods of waiting in buffers. The unit's total flow time is made up of both the time during which activities are performed on it and the time the flow unit spends waiting in buffers. Because waiting time is usually a large part of total flow time in most business processes, it is an important aspect of flow-time management. In Section 4.3.5, we illustrate the importance of waiting time in flow-time management and define an efficiency measure to capture it. At this point, however, we focus on the *activity* component of flow time.

The **theoretical flow time** of a process *is the minimum amount of time required for processing a typical flow unit without any waiting.* Thus, it includes only the activity-time component of the process, ignoring completely the impact of waiting (which is typically significant). For this reason, theoretical flow time represents an idealized target for an actual flow time that can only rarely be achieved in practice. In this section, we show how theoretical flow time can be computed by combining a process flowchart with information about the time taken by the various activities represented on it.

4.3.1 Activity Time and Critical Paths

Activity time is *the time required by a typical flow unit to complete the activity once.* The activity times of a flow unit at various activities, coupled with the sequence in the various activities performed, allow us to compute the theoretical flow time.

Consider, first, a simple process in which all activities are carried out sequentially, one following the other. In this case, the process flowchart consists of a single *path* (or *route*) of activities connecting the entry and exit points of the process. Because all activities along this path must be completed sequentially, the total time required to complete all of them equals the sum of their individual activity times. For instance, if a process consists of three activities, A, B, and C, that must be performed sequentially and if each activity requires 10 minutes, then the total time required to process a flow unit is the sum of the three activity times, that is, $10 + 10 + 10 = 30$ minutes.

However, most processes consist of a combination of sequential and parallel activities, resulting in a process chart that contains several paths running from start to finish. *For each path,* theoretical flow time of that path is *the sum of the activity times of the activities that constitute the path.* Now, a flow unit can exit the process only after all the activities along *all* the paths are completed. Theoretical flow time of the process, therefore, must be the same as the theoretical flow time of the **critical path**—*the longest path in the process flowchart. Activities that lie on a critical path* are called **critical activities**. We illustrate these concepts in Example 4.4.

Example 4.4

To demonstrate the computation of theoretical flow time, consider again the Wonder Shed illustration begun in Example 4.1. Table 4.2 complements the information in Table 4.1 by adding the *activity time* of each activity.

Note that our flowchart in Figure 4.1 shows two paths connecting the beginning and end of the process:

Path 1 (roof): Start → 1 → 3 → 5 → 7 → 8 → End
Path 2 (base): Start → 1 → 2 → 4 → 6 → 7 → 8 → End

The theoretical flow time of path 1, followed by the roofs, is 80 minutes:

	Activity	Activity Time
1	Separate	10
3	Punch the roof	20
5	Form the roof	10
7	Assemble	10
8	Inspect	30
	Total	80 minutes

TABLE 4.2 Activity Times at Wonder Shed Inc. (in minutes)

	Activity	*Activity Time (minutes)*
1	Separate	10
2	Punch the base	25
3	Punch the roof	20
4	Form the base	5
5	Form the roof	10
6	Subassemble the base	10
7	Assemble	10
8	Inspect	30

The theoretical flow time of path 2, followed by the bases, is 90 minutes:

	Activity	Activity Time
1	Separate	10
2	Punch the base	25
4	Form the base	5
6	Subassemble the base	10
7	Assemble	10
8	Inspect	30
	Total	90 minutes

Thus, the theoretical flow time of the process is 90 minutes, and path 2 for making the bases is the critical path.

For simple processes, the critical path can often be determined by computing the theoretical flow time of each path. For complex processes, there may be too many paths. Consequently, we may sometimes need a more computationally efficient approach, like the one outlined in the Appendix, to identify the critical path.

The critical activities of a process are extremely important for managing flow time since they determine the flow time of the entire process. Thus, a delay in completing any critical activity results directly in a corresponding delay in processing the flow unit. As a result, management of the critical path is of paramount significance. In contrast, activities that are not critical can be delayed, to a degree, without affecting the flow time. Thus, they require a reduced level of monitoring by management.

In realistic settings, the activity time of any activity in a process may vary across flow units because of factors such as breakdown, interruptions, rework, and so on. As a result, the theoretical flow time will also vary across flow units. In such cases, we define an *average theoretical time* by taking an *average over all flow units*. In the rest of this book, we use the term *theoretical flow time* to mean the average theoretical time, when appropriate.

4.3.2 Computing Flow Time

Recall that as a flow unit travels through the process from entry to exit, it typically undergoes a sequence of activities interspersed with periods of waiting in buffers. Thus, the flow time of a particular unit can be written as

$$\text{Flow time} = \text{Theoretical flow time} + \text{Waiting time} \tag{4.1}$$

In the previous section, we examined how looking at the critical path can be used to combine information about activity time and the process flowchart in order to compute the theoretical flow time of the process. By adding information about waiting, we can use the same approach to study the flow time of a given process. The following simple three-step procedure can be used:

1. We treat waiting in each buffer as an additional (passive) activity with activity time equal to the amount of time in that buffer.
2. We add waiting times in buffers to the theoretical flow time of the appropriate path.
3. We obtain the average flow time of the process by finding the path whose overall length (activity plus waiting) is longest.

The amount of waiting along different paths may vary. Thus, when waiting times are added to the analysis, the relative lengths of the various paths—and the identity of the critical path—may change. In some instances, it may not be convenient to separate activity and waiting times. In such cases, we may prefer to combine the two into a single measurement. Remember, rather than measuring them directly, we can also use Little's law to compute both the average time spent in a given buffer and the total of waiting-plus-activity time associated with a given activity. We demonstrate these ideas in Example 4.5.

Example 4.5

Let us return to the Wonder Shed Inc. example. To calculate the average flow time using Little's law, we need information about the average flow rate and the average inventory in various buffers over the time period that we are interested in. Assume that the average flow rate has been measured at 16.5 sheds per hour. Assume, also, that average inventories of roofs and bases at relevant buffers were measured and reported as in Table 4.3. For notational purposes, we have numbered each buffer according to the activity that follows it. (Table 4.1 lists the activities and their numbers.) Because we have two types of flow units—roofs and bases, either of which could be in a buffer—we designate how much of each unit is in each buffer.

On analyzing the flow time for roofs, we note that the average number of roofs waiting in various buffers is 80. Thus, inventory (I) of roofs equals 80. Because the average flow rate (R) for roofs is 16.5 per hour (the same as the flow rate for sheds), we conclude that the average amount of waiting for a typical roof is

$$T = I/R = 80/16.5$$

giving

$$T = 4.85 \text{ hours, or } 291 \text{ minutes}$$

Adding to this figure the theoretical flow time of a roof, which is 80 minutes (from Example 4.4),

$$291 \text{ minutes} + 80 \text{ minutes} = 371 \text{ minutes}$$

we obtain the average flow time for a roof as 371 minutes. (We could also calculate the waiting time spent separately in each buffer and then add those figures, and the result would be the same). Similarly, the average number of bases waiting in various buffers (I) is 90, and then the average waiting time for a base is

$$T = I/R = 90/16.5$$

giving

$$T = 5.45 \text{ hours, or } 327 \text{ minutes}$$

Adding this figure to the theoretical flow time of 90 minutes for a base from Example 4.4,

$$327 \text{ minutes} + 90 \text{ minutes} = 417 \text{ minutes}$$

we obtain an average flow time of 417 minutes for the bases. The path traversed by a base remains the critical path.

TABLE 4.3 Average Inventories of Roofs and Bases in Buffers at Wonder Shed Inc.

Buffer	Average Number of Bases	Average Number of Roofs
2	30	—
3	—	25
4	10	—
5	—	20
6	20	—
7	10	15
8	20	20
Total	90	80

In Example 4.5, we computed average flow time for two types of flow units—roofs and bases. Because both parts are required for assembling a shed, average flow time for a shed is given by the average flow time of the longest path traversed by the bases, which is equal to 417 minutes. Such a flow-time measurement is useful for quoting due dates to customers. We note that under different scenarios (i.e., with different buffer sizes), the relative lengths of these two paths could be identical or even reversed.

4.3.3 Value-Adding and Non-Value-Adding Activities

The activities of a given process can be further divided into value-adding and non-value-adding activities.

Value-adding activities *are those activities that increase the economic value of a flow unit because the customer values them.* Performing surgery, piloting an airplane, serving meals in a hospital, manufacturing an item in a factory, and dispensing a loan are examples of value-adding activities.

Non-value-adding activities *are activities that, while required by a firm's process, do not directly increase the value of a flow unit.* The following are common non-value-adding activities:

- *Transport,* such as moving work (or workers) among various locations
- *Support,* such as setting up a machine, filling out a form, maintaining equipment, or scheduling work
- *Testing,* such as auditing and inspection

It may be useful to break the flow time of a process into two components as follows:

$$\text{Flow time} = \text{Value-adding flow time} + \text{Non-value-adding flow time}$$

Waiting is usually non-value-adding. (Of course, in some processes, such as wine or cheese making, aging is clearly a value-adding activity. However, in such cases, we should classify aging as *an activity* rather than as *waiting.*) The process itself, however, may have other non-value-adding activities that could further be eliminated in an improved process. For example, if the current process involves rework of some flow units at certain activities, a reduction in the amount of rework clearly decreases the process flow time. We examine the impact of rework reduction in Example 4.6.

If careful analysis reveals that all activities, except waiting, add value, then theoretical flow time is in fact the same as the value-adding flow time. Processes whose average flow time is close to their value-adding time are very rare!

4.3.4 Extensions: Rework, Visits, and Work Content

Recall that activity time was defined as the time required by a typical flow unit to complete the activity (once). Rework may require that activities be repeated several times before a unit is completed. We refer to these repetitions as *visits* to an activity. Conversely, in some situations, such as inspections, activities are not repeated for every flow unit. In these cases, the average number of visits over all flow units is *less than one.* The **work content of an activity** is *activity time multiplied by average number of visits at that activity. It measures the total amount of time required to perform an activity during the transformation of a flow unit.* Using the work content—rather than the activity time—in the computations of the critical path gives us a more accurate estimate of the theoretical flow time of a process, as illustrated in Example 4.6.

TABLE 4.4 Activity Times and Work Content at Wonder Shed

Activity	Activity Time (minutes)	Number of Visits	Work Content (minutes)
1. Separate	10	1	10
2. Punch the base	25	1.2	30
3. Punch the roof	20	1.1	22
4. Form the base	5	1.2	6
5. Form the roof	10	1.2	12
6. Subassemble	10	1.3	13
7. Assemble	10	1	10
8. Inspect	30	1.2	36

Example 4.6

To demonstrate the computation of theoretical flow time using the work content, reconsider Wonder Shed and the computations of Example 4.4. Table 4.4 complements the information in Table 4.2 by adding the *number of visits* for each activity. The last column, labeled "Work Content," is computed as *the product of activity time and number of visits*.

The two paths in the network are as in Example 4.4:

$$\text{Path 1 (roof): Start} \rightarrow 1 \rightarrow 3 \rightarrow 5 \rightarrow 7 \rightarrow 8 \rightarrow \text{End}$$
$$\text{Path 2 (base): Start} \rightarrow 1 \rightarrow 2 \rightarrow 4 \rightarrow 6 \rightarrow 7 \rightarrow 8 \rightarrow \text{End}$$

Using the work content, the theoretical flow time of path 1 is 90 minutes:

Activity	Activity Time (minutes)	Number of Visits	Work Content
1. Separate	10	1	10
3. Punch the roof	20	1.1	22
5. Form the roof	10	1.2	12
7. Assemble	10	1	10
8. Inspect	30	1.2	36
Total			90 minutes

The theoretical flow time of Path 2 is 105 minutes:

Activity	Activity Time (minutes)	Number of Visits	Work Content
1. Separate	10	1	10
2. Punch the base	25	1.2	30
4. Form the base	5	1.2	6
6. Subassemble	10	1.3	13
7. Assemble	10	1	10
8. Inspect	30	1.2	36
Total			105 minutes

What is the impact of rework on the theoretical flow time of the process? We can find out by comparing the calculations of Examples 4.4 and 4.6. The figure of 105 minutes computed in Example 4.6 includes units that both do and do not require some rework at some activity. In contrast, in Example 4.4 we concentrate only on units that flow through the process without any rework. Thus, in Example 4.4, the number of visits for each activity equals one, and the work content is the same as the activity time. In this

TABLE 4.5 Flow-Time Efficiency of Business Processes

Industry	Process	Flow Time	Theoretical Flow Time	Flow-Time Efficiency
Life insurance	New policy application	72 hours	7 minutes	0.16%
Consumer packaging	New graphic design	18 days	2 hours	0.14%
Commercial bank	Consumer loan	24 hours	34 minutes	2.36%
Hospital	Patient billing	10 days	3 hours	3.75%
Auto manufacture	Financial closing	11 days	5 hours	5.60%

case, the theoretical flow time of the process is 90 minutes. Thus, rework increases the theoretical flow time from 90 minutes to 105 minutes, an increase of more than 15%.

4.3.5 Flow-Time Efficiency

By comparing the average flow time with the theoretical value, we can get an indication of **flow-time efficiency**—the ratio between theoretical flow time and the average flow time that indicates the amount of waiting time associated with the process. The relationship between these two measures is defined as follows:

$$\text{Flow-time efficiency} = \text{Theoretical flow time}/\text{Average flow time} \qquad (4.2)$$

The values of the flow-time efficiency for a variety of processes were studied by Blackburn (1992) and are excerpted in Table 4.5. Their surprisingly low values underscore how significantly reducing waiting improves flow-time performance.

Let us now look at Example 4.7, which demonstrates the main concepts we have covered so far in this chapter.

Example 4.7

Valley of Hope Hospital has been under recent pressure from stakeholders to improve cost efficiency and customer service. In response, the hospital has undertaken a series of process-improvement initiatives. One of the first processes targeted for improvement was the X-ray service. A major concern identified by both physicians and patients has been the amount of time required to obtain an X-ray. In addition, management would like to make sure that available resources are utilized efficiently.

A process-improvement team was set up to study the X-ray service process and recommend improvements. The team identified the point of entry into the process as the instant that a patient leaves the physician's office to walk to the X-ray lab. The point of exit was defined as the instant that both the patient and the completed X-ray film are ready to enter the physician's office for diagnosis. The unit of flow is a patient.

To determine the flow time of the existing process, a random sample of 50 patients was observed over a two-week period. For each patient, the team recorded times of entry and exit from the X-ray service process. The difference between these two times was then used as a measure of flow time for each patient. The average of the 50 data points was 154 minutes. This figure, then, serves as an estimate of the average flow time for the X-ray service process.

To further study process flow time, the team examined the entire process in detail and broke it down into the constituent activities identified in Table 4.6.

The corresponding process flowchart is shown in Figure 4.3. It depicts all activities and the precedence relationships among them. For example, activity 2 must be completed before activity 3 can begin. Meanwhile, activity 1 can be carried out simultaneously with activities 2 and 3.

Next, another sample of 50 patients was studied over a two-week period. For each patient, the times required to perform each activity, as well as the number of visits to that activity, were recorded. Because activities 6 to 8 are repeated once for 25% of the patients, the average number of visits to these activities is 1.25. The average work content for each of these activities is obtained by multiplying their activity times by 1.25. The data and computations are summarized in Table 4.7.

TABLE 4.6 The X-Ray-Service Process at Valley of Hope Hospital

Activity/Event	Description	Type
Start	Patient leaves the physician's office.	Event: Start of process
1	Patient walks to the X-ray lab.	Activity: Transport
2	The X-ray request travels to the X-ray lab by a messenger.	Activity: Transport
3	An X-ray technician fills out a standard form based on the information supplied by the physician.	Activity: Support
4	The receptionist receives from the patient information concerning insurance, prepares and signs a claim form, and sends to the insurer.	Activity: Support
5	Patient undresses in preparation for X-ray.	Activity: Support
6	A lab technician takes X-rays.	Activity: Value added
7	A darkroom technician develops X-rays.	Activity: Value added
8	The lab technician checks X-rays for clarity.	Activity: Inspection and decision
9	Patient puts on clothes and gets ready to leave lab. If an X-ray is not satisfactory, activities 7 to 9 are repeated. (On average, 75% of X-rays are found satisfactory the first time around, while 25% require one retake; virtually no units require more than two takes.)	Activity: Support
10	Patient walks back to the physician's office.	Activity: Transport
11	The X-rays are transferred to the physician by a messenger.	Activity: Transport
End	Patient and the X-rays arrive at the physician's office.	Event: End of process

The team analyzing the process flowchart identified four activity paths:

Path 1: Start → 1 → 4 → 5 → 6 → 7 → 8 → 9 → 10 → End
Path 2: Start → 2 → 3 → 4 → 5 → 6 → 7 → 8 → 9 → 10 → End
Path 3: Start → 1 → 4 → 5 → 6 → 7 → 8 → 11 → End
Path 4: Start → 2 → 3 → 4 → 5 → 6 → 7 → 8 → 11 → End

The total work content of these four paths is

Path 1 = 50 minutes
Path 2 = 69 minutes
Path 3 = 60 minutes
Path 4 = 79 minutes

FIGURE 4.3 Flowchart for the X-Ray-Service Process at Valley of Hope Hospital

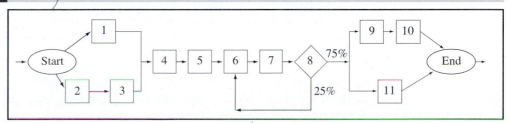

TABLE 4.7 Work Content in X-Ray-Service Process Activities

Activity	Activity Time (minutes)	Number of Visits per Flow Unit	Work Content per Flow Unit (minutes)
Start	—	1	—
1	7	1	7
2	20	1	20
3	6	1	6
4	5	1	5
5	3	1	3
6	6	1.25	7.5
7	12	1.25	15
8	2	1.25	2.5
9	3	1	3
10	7	1	7
11	20	1	20
End	—	1	—

Path 4, therefore, is the critical path, yielding a theoretical flow time of the process as 79 minutes. What is the flow-time efficiency of the process? Recall that flow-time efficiency is calculated as

Flow-time efficiency = Theoretical flow time/Average flow time

As actual flow time was measured at 154 minutes and theoretical flow time at 79 minutes, flow-time efficiency is expressed as follows:

79/154 = 51%

This means that waiting corresponds to roughly half the time in this process. Obviously, the challenge this poses to the management of Valley of Hope Hospital is whether some of this waiting can be eliminated.

4.4 Levers for Managing Theoretical Flow Time

How can managers reduce the flow time of a process? As we have seen, the flow time is the sum of two components—activity time (work content) and waiting time. Because these two components are so different, the levers available for managing each are naturally distinct. In this section, we examine the levers available for managing the activity part of the flow time—the *theoretical flow time*. However, since waiting time is often a significant part of the total flow time, it is critical to also examine ways to reduce waiting. Most of the wait-reducing actions aim to increase synchronicity between process flows by using levers such as reducing batch sizes, managing the effects of congestion, and reducing safety buffers, as examined in Chapters 6 to 8.

As we have seen, the theoretical flow time of a process is determined by the total work content of its critical path(s). Thus, the only way to reduce the theoretical flow time is to shorten the length of *every critical path*. There are three basic approaches to reducing the work content of a critical path:

1. **Eliminate:** Reduce the work content of a critical activity.
2. **Work in parallel:** Move some work content off the critical path.
3. **Select:** Modify the product mix.

There are significant differences between these three approaches. The first approach is one of *elimination*—it involves reducing the total amount of work required per unit. The second approach is one of *working in parallel*. It leaves the total amount of work per unit unaffected but manages the timing of the various activities in order to reduce the length of the critical path. The third approach is one of *selection,* or leaving the process as is but concentrating on selecting flow units that can be processed faster—to the extent allowed by the market. Let's examine each of these processes more fully.

4.4.1   Eliminate: Reducing the Work Content of Critical Activities

The idea that work should be "optimized" and some of its components eliminated is not new. It can be traced to the scientific management approach used by Frederic Taylor (1911), Frank Gilbreth (1911), and their followers discussed in Chapter 2. Originally, the approach was used for optimizing the speed of work by individual workers, typically in manual tasks such as laying bricks, loading coal, or typing a manuscript. However, the core ideas of this approach are still valid today in the much broader context of a general business process, both in service and in manufacturing.

The work content of any activity can be reduced by any combination of the following actions:

1. Eliminate non-value-adding aspects of the activity ("work smarter").
2. Reduce the number of repetitions of the activity ("do it right the first time").
3. Increase the speed at which the activity is performed ("work faster").

Consider the first item. It is a common observation that some of the work done by individuals and organizations is not essential for the product or service produced. Thus, it is natural for managers to examine the various processes under their control in order to identify and eliminate unnecessary steps. But which steps add value? The answer depends on what the *customers* of the process consider important. Typically, activities such as moving, inspecting, sorting, counting, filling out forms, and obtaining "approvals" are prime candidates for elimination. As an example, consider the accounts-payable process. The primary value-adding activity of this process is *paying the bills in an accurate and timely fashion.* However, the accounts-payable department typically spends much of its time performing other activities, such as reconciling contradictory information, verifying, matching documents, and investigating discrepancies. Such activities do not add value but are still necessary given the process utilized. They can be eliminated, however, if the process is modified. Hammer and Champy (1993), for instance, report that the accounts-payable department at Ford was reengineered to eliminate unnecessary steps with a dramatic reduction in flow time and cost. One of the innovations introduced was the elimination of issuing and processing invoices and the rejection of any shipment that does not conform exactly to the purchase order. For details, see Hammer and Champy (1993).

Decreasing the amount of repeat work reduces the average number of visits to an activity and thus decreases work content. Reductions are often achieved by process-improvement techniques such as statistical process control, design for manufacturability, process foolproofing, and workforce training. In data-rich environments, the key principle is to strive toward a process that "touches" any particular data input just once since the common custom of entering the same data over and over again adds time (as well as cost and errors).

The speed at which an activity is performed can be improved by acquiring faster equipment, increasing allocated resources, or offering incentives for faster work. Such steps often require either financial investment in faster equipment or modified incentives for labor resources. Consider, for instance, a manual checkout counter at a local grocery store. The speed of this operation can be increased by any of the following methods: using bar codes with a scanner, adding a second worker to bag products, or instituting proper incentives, coupled with training and better equipment so that checkout personnel work faster, without increasing error rates or jeopardizing service quality. In a research-and-development laboratory, so-called *dedicated teams* that concentrate fully on one activity rather than working on several projects simultaneously can increase the speed at which a particular research activity is carried out.

Finally, note that although reducing the work content of noncritical activities does *not* reduce the theoretical flow time, such reduction may still be useful for other reasons, such as decreasing total processing costs, increasing process capacity (see Chapter 5), and reducing the potential for errors and defects.

4.4.2 Work in Parallel: Moving Work Off the Critical Path

Another way to reduce the theoretical flow time is by moving work off the critical path and into paths that do not affect process flow time. This task can be accomplished in one of two ways:

1. Move work off the critical path to a noncritical activity.
2. Move work off the critical path to the "outer loop" (i.e., to some stage of pre- or postprocessing).

Moving work from a critical to a noncritical path means redesigning the process so that critical activities that are performed sequentially will be done in parallel. The scientific-management pioneer Frank Gilbreth mentioned earlier is reported to have trained himself to shave both sides of his face simultaneously, using both hands! (Gilbreth & Gilbreth, 1949). A prime—and somewhat more practical—example of this approach is the contemporary practice of *concurrent engineering*. Traditionally, activities such as product design, process planning, and manufacturing are performed sequentially. By permitting interfunctional coordination of such activities, concurrent engineering reduces the total time, cost, and rework necessary to design, produce, and deliver new products to market. (We describe the applications of concurrent engineering more fully in Chapter 10.)

For another example, consider the conventional approach to software development, which consists of five steps in sequence: specification, design, development, documentation (writing the user manual), and testing. Clearly, testing and documentation can be carried out in parallel. Moreover, it is often not necessary to complete the development of the software in order to start preparing the user manual. Thus, it is possible to perform some aspects of software design, development, testing, and documentation in parallel.

Moving activities to the so-called outer loop means *performing them either before the countdown for the process starts or after it ends,* as defined by the process boundary, an approach that is also called *pre-* or *postprocessing.* Note that although the work must still be done, the critical path is shortened. For example, in the case of hospital admission process, it is often possible to accomplish work such as verifying insurance, preparing and signing consent forms, and listing of allergies *before* the patient even shows up. As another example, consider the process of changing a "make-to-order" production system into a "make-to-stock" system. Instead of assembling a complete hamburger *after* receiving a customer order, it may be possible to precook beef patties and keep them ready *prior* to the lunchtime rush. As far as *customer flow* is concerned, theoretical flow time will be reduced because the production of the beef patty has been moved to the outer loop of the "order-fulfillment process." Note, however, that because it produces units prior to demand, this strategy affects the "material flow process" in the opposite fashion. In case of hamburgers, of course, it may also affect taste and quality.

4.4.3 Select: Modifying the Product Mix

Most processes involve a mix of products, characterized by different flow times for the various units of flow. If we modify the mix toward processing more of the products that require less processing time, the overall flow time of the process will decrease. Of course, product mix is often dictated by the market, and even when the organization has some control over it, there may be other relevant factors, such as profitability, market considerations, and resource utilization issues. Nevertheless, modifying the mix and serving more jobs or customers that could be handled faster is sometimes an effective way to reduce average flow time. We elaborate more on the product mix decision in Chapter 5.

We close with Example 4.8, a more detailed description of the process improvement activities undertaken by Zhang & Associates introduced earlier in the chapter.

Example 4.8

Zhang & Associates, mentioned in the introduction, provides comprehensive financial advisory and asset management services to high-net-worth individuals. Recently, the company has redesigned its new client process and cut the required time from four to six weeks (and in some cases considerably more) to two weeks. We now review how Zhang & Associates was able to achieve these results, utilizing some of the levers mentioned in Section 4.4.

The Old Process

The point of entry into the process is when a new client arrives to meet the adviser for the introductory meeting. During the meeting, the adviser took notes about the client's financial information and listed details such as the client's stocks, life insurance policies, and bank accounts. After the meeting, the adviser reviewed the notes with a staff member of the planning department, called a "paraplanner." The paraplanner typed the information into financial planning software and prepared a general financial plan. At this stage, the paraplanner often found that the adviser had neglected to obtain all the relevant information during the first meeting. In such cases, the paraplanner contacted the adviser, who in turn contacted the client to obtain the necessary information.

Some clients had advanced planning needs, such as estate planning, in which case the completed general financial plan was forwarded to the advanced planning department. The professionals in the advanced planning department, often attorneys or certified public accountants, reviewed the general financial plan and discussed the client situation with the adviser before providing recommendations. After the financial plan was completed, the adviser conducted a second meeting with the client to go over the plan. The client took the plan home for detailed review. If the plan was acceptable to the client, a third meeting was scheduled to finalize the plan and sign the necessary documents. If the client was not satisfied with the plan, another cycle of consultations with the staff of the advanced planning department was initiated. The process was completed when the plan was approved by the customer and implemented.

The process typically required one to one and a half months for completion. The time could be substantially longer if the client's situation was complicated, requiring a fourth or even a fifth meeting.

The New Process

Zhang & Associates has recently implemented a new process. The key differences from the old process can be summarized as follows.

A "homework" package is sent to the client and is completed by the client before the first meeting. This set of forms reveals critical personal and financial information. Clients can obtain assistance to complete the forms by calling the adviser's office.

The first meeting involves everyone required for devising the financial plan, including the adviser, the paraplanner, and all the relevant advanced planning professionals. By the end of the meeting, everyone understands all the issues involved and will be able to work on their parts of the plan simultaneously.

The paraplanner receives the various plans from the various participants and assembles them into a comprehensive plan. The competed plan is mailed to the client for reviewing prior to the second meeting. The customer reviews the plan and can resolve any remaining issues before the meeting, significantly reducing the possible need for a third or fourth meeting.

In preparation for the second meeting, the paraplanner prepares all the forms that are needed for the implementation of the plan. During that meeting, the adviser and the paraplanner go over the plan with the client and address all remaining questions or concerns. In most cases, the client approves the plan at this point and signs the necessary forms.

New Process Success

By adopting the new process, Zhang & Associates was able to reduce the time for completion of the process to two weeks! The improvement is achieved by a combination of the following levers:

1. Move work to the outer loop (premeeting "homework").
2. Work in parallel (after the first meeting, all professionals can work simultaneously since they are all on board).
3. Elimination of non-value-adding work (only two meetings instead of three or more).

The results of improving the process are quite dramatic: Clients are happy because they don't have to wait up to two months for their plan to be implemented. In addition, the company utilizes its personnel more effectively and saves costs because the advisers focus on activities that add value, such as investment portfolio design. Another bonus is that the new process builds a relationship of confidence between the customer and the paraplanner (in the old process, the customer never met the paraplanner). This increases customer satisfaction. Zhang & Associates further capitalized on this relationship in order to improve its meetings with the *exiting customers* along the same lines.

The new process imposes additional demands on the professional staff, especially the paraplanners and advanced planning staff. In the old process, the adviser was the only one meeting the customer, and all the other staff members were kept "behind the scenes." In contrast, in the new process, everyone is in the "front line."

SUMMARY

In the preceding chapters, we introduced three important measures of process performance—flow time, flow rate, and inventory—and discussed the relationship among them (Little's law). In this chapter, we focus on flow time, the first of those measures. Reducing the flow time of a given process is important to the organization and its customers since it increases responsiveness, customer satisfaction, and financial performance. In addition, reducing flow time often requires improvements in other aspects of the process, such as reduction in defects and rework, leading to improved quality.

The first step in analyzing any process is to develop the process flowchart, a graphical representation of a process that breaks it down into a set of activities and identifies these activities' interrelationships. Flow time of a given process can be measured either directly by observing the time taken by various flow units or indirectly by observing the throughput and inventory and then utilizing Little's law. Any flow unit, as it moves through the process, is either being worked on (i.e., undergoing an activity) or waiting to be worked on. Theoretical flow time measures the flow time of a unit without any waiting. The total flow time, then, is the sum of theoretical flow time and waiting time. Flow-time efficiency is a metric that gives an indication of the extent of waiting in a process.

Flow time can be reduced by affecting either of its components: theoretical flow time or waiting time. In this chapter, we have focused on theoretical flow time. To improve the (theoretical) flow time, we need to focus on the activities on the critical path. There are three key managerial levers for reducing theoretical flow time. First, theoretical flow time can be reduced by reducing the work content of a critical activity. This can be achieved in several ways, including elimination of non-value-adding aspects of the activity (i.e., working smarter), reducing the number of repetitions of the activity (i.e., doing it right the first time), and increasing the speed at which the activity is performed (i.e., working faster). Second, theoretical flow time can be reduced by moving some work content off the critical path. Two ways to achieve this include working in parallel rather than in sequence, thereby moving work to a noncritical activity, and moving work to the outer loop. Finally, theoretical flow time can be altered by selecting a suitable product mix.

Levers for reducing waiting time are discussed in Chapters 6 to 8.

KEY EQUATIONS AND SYMBOLS █ █ █ █ █ █ █

(4.1)   Flow time = Theoretical flow time + Waiting time

(4.2)   Flow-time efficiency = Theoretical flow time/ Average flow time

KEY TERMS █ █ █ █ █ █ █

- Activity time
- Cascading
- Critical activities
- Critical path
- Flow-time efficiency
- Non-value-adding activities
- Process flowchart
- Subprocess
- Theoretical flow time
- Value-adding activities
- Work content of an activity

DISCUSSION QUESTIONS █ █ █ █ █ █ █

4.1   Examine a service encounter such as a visit to a restaurant. Give a rough estimate of the average flow time, the theoretical flow time, and the flow-time efficiency.

4.2   Provide an example from your work environment of how flow time could be improved using the following levers:
  a. "Work smarter"
  b. "Do it right the first time"
  c. "Work faster"

4.3   Describe the process used by your bank for approving a home mortgage. In particular, highlight the activities that are done or could be done in parallel. What are the pros and cons of doing these activities in parallel?

4.4   A group of MBA students is preparing a business case for submission as a final project for their operation management course. Describe the process used by the group from the perspective of working in parallel versus working sequentially.

4.5   The speed at which pit crews replace flat tires at car races such as the Indy 500 is amazing. Discuss the effects of "moving work to the outer loop" in this context.

4.6   How long does it take your company to process a business expense form? What is your estimate of the theoretical time required for this process? What is the flow-time efficiency?

4.7   How long does it take your company to process a customer complaint? Draw a process map of the process utilized and discuss how some of the levers used in this chapter can be used to speed up this process.

4.8   Flow-time efficiency measures the extent of waiting in a process flow time. Should you design a process to aim for 100% flow-time efficiency? Explain.

4.9   Decreasing the activity time of an activity always improves the flow time. Explain.

4.1 Recall The Evanstonian, an upscale independent hotel that caters to both business and leisure travelers, introduced in Chapter 3 in Exercise 3.10. When a guest calls room service at The Evanstonian, the room-service manager takes down the order. She then submits an order ticket to the kitchen to begin preparing the food. She also gives an order to the sommelier (i.e., the wine waiter) to fetch wine from the cellar and to prepare any other alcoholic beverages. Eighty percent of room-service orders include wine or some other alcoholic beverage. Finally, she assigns the order to one of six waiters. Orders may be placed in a buffer if a resource (i.e., a waiter, a sommelier, or the kitchen) is not immediately available. Taking down the order and assigning work to the kitchen, sommelier, and waiter on average takes 4 minutes.

It takes the kitchen 18 minutes to prepare the typical order. There is a single sommelier. He fetches and readies the wine while the kitchen is preparing the meal. The sommelier takes 6 minutes to prepare an order. While the kitchen and the sommelier are doing their tasks, the waiter readies a cart (i.e., puts a tablecloth on the cart and gathers silverware). The waiter is also responsible for nonalcoholic drinks. In total, it takes the waiter 10 minutes to prepare the average order. Once the food, wine, and cart are ready, the waiter delivers it to the guest's room. If the waiter is not immediately available to deliver the order, the food, wine, and cart are held in buffers until he is. It takes the waiter on average 12 minutes to deliver the meal and return to the room-service station. At the room-service station, the waiter debits the guest's account. This takes 2 minutes. The waiter may wait to do the billing if he has another order to prepare or deliver.

   a. Draw a process map for the room-service process.
   b. What is the theoretical flow time of the process?
   c. The average flow time of the process was measured to be 60 minutes. What is the flow-time efficiency?

4.2 Kristen and her roommate are in the business of baking custom cookies. As soon as she receives an order by phone, Kristen washes the bowl and mixes dough according to the customer's order—activities that take a total of 6 minutes. She then spoons the dough onto a tray that holds one dozen cookies (2 minutes). Her roommate then takes 1 minute to set the oven and place the tray in it. Cookies are baked in the oven for 9 minutes and allowed to cool outside for 5 minutes. The roommate then boxes the cookies (2 minutes) and collects payment from the customer (1 minute).

   a. Draw a flowchart for the process described here and determine theoretical flow time from the time of order until the time of payment collection. Assume no waiting over the course of the process.
   b. Suppose that each order consists of two dozen cookies. Assume that although the mixing bowl can accommodate dough for two dozen cookies at a time, the oven can accommodate only one tray of one dozen cookies at a time. As before, spooning each tray takes 2 minutes, and both trays must be cooled prior to boxing the cookies for customer pickup. Draw a modified flowchart and determine theoretical flow time. Consider the effect on flow time of the following possible alternatives to the system:
      1. Buying a second oven that can bake one tray of one dozen cookies
      2. Buying a second oven that can hold two trays of one dozen cookies each
      3. Buying a faster convection oven that can bake one dozen cookies in 6 minutes instead of 9 minutes[2]

4.3 Wonder Shed Inc. produces steel sheds. The company produces two models, standard and deluxe. The production process for the two models is identical and is depicted in Figure 4.1. The activity times and number of visits for the two models are listed in Table 4.8.
   a. Compute the theoretical flow time for a deluxe shed.
   b. Compute the theoretical time for a mix of 75% standard and 25% deluxe sheds.

---

[2]This exercise is based on *Kristen's Cookie Company* (Harvard Business School, 1986).

TABLE 4.8 Activity Time and Number of Visits, Various Products, Wonder Shed

Activity	Activity Time, Standard (minutes)	Number of Visits, Standard	Activity Time, Deluxe (minutes)	Number of Visits, Deluxe
1	10	1	10	1.0
2	25	1.2	30	1.5
3	20	1.1	24	1.25
4	5	1.2	5	1.2
5	10	1.2	10	1.2
6	10	1.3	15	1.2
7	10	1.0	12	1.0
8	30	1.2	30	1.2

c. The company has determined that, for its current mix of 75% standard and 25% deluxe, the average flow time has been 10 working days (4,800 minutes). What is the flow-time efficiency?

4.4 Honda's 1,100-cc motorcycle, the "American Classic Edition" (ACE), is assembled in the United States from four major subassemblies. The first subassembly produces the engine from three activities: a left and right part of the engine block come out of the automatic mold every 2 minutes. These two parts are welded together, requiring 1 minute of the continuous welding machine. Finally, it takes the engine assembler 3 minutes to insert the two pistons and four valves. The second subassembly produces the frame in two steps: first, heavy metal bars are bent in the 10,000-pound press in 1 minute, then it takes 3 minutes to weld the multiple bars together with the continuous welding machine to produce the frame. The third subassembly consists of the front and rear fenders, both of which are formed using the same (as used for the metal bars) 10,000-pound press for 1 minute each. The fourth subassembly makes the seat. It takes an assembler 7 minutes to cut the padding, pit it on a preformed piece of sheet metal, and wrap the two with synthetic leather. In final assembly, first the four subassemblies are put together. Adding front- and tail-lights, wheels, driveshaft, brakes, and cables produces a new bike that is ready for test-drive. It takes 30 minutes to finish assembly of one motorcycle. Currently, Honda ACE staffing is as follows: there is 1 molding machine operator, 1 welder, 1 press operator, 1 engine assembler, 2 seat assemblers, and 10 final assemblers.
   a. Draw a process flowchart identifying resources, activity times, and any potential storage buffers.
   b. What is the theoretical flow time of the ACE production process?
   c. Knowing the benefits of flow-time reduction, Honda would like to decrease the theoretical flow time of the ACE process. Which specific action(s) do you recommend?

4.5 A home insurance application consists of two forms: F1, which relates to the home owner, and F2, which relates to the property. On receipt, each application is processed, recorded, and separated into F1 and F2. This operation is done by the data-entry clerk and requires 10 minutes. F1 is processed by professional A for 15 minutes per unit and then by professional B for 10 minutes per unit. F2 is processed by professional C for 20 minutes per unit. F1 and F2 are then combined and further processed by a loan officer for 15 minutes.
   a. Draw a process flowchart for the processes.
   b. What is the theoretical flow time?
   c. The average flow time of an application is seven working days. Assuming 480 minutes per day, compute the flow-time efficiency of the process.

4.6 The Vancouver International Airport Authority, described in Chapter 3, manages and operates the Vancouver International Airport (YVR). Its focus on safety, security, and customer service has contributed to YVR's ranking among the top 10 airports in the world. To maintain its excellent customer service standards and in anticipation of new government regulations, airport management sought to take leadership in improving customer flow through its airport security checkpoints.

TABLE 4.9 The Traffic Court

Defendant	Arrival	Departure	Time with Judge (minutes)	Time Paying Fine (minutes)
1	8:45	9:30	1	5
2	8:45	9:45	1.5	2
3	8:45	12:05	2	3
4	8:50	12:55	1.5	5
5	8:50	10:35	1	2
6	8:55	9:20	1	0
7	8:55	11:35	2	2
8	9:00	10:45	3	0
9	9:00	12:55	1	2
10	9:00	9:20	1.5	3

To understand flow, management started with a single security screening line comprised of an X-ray scanner with an operator and three screening officers. Arriving customers either queue up or, if there is no queue on arrival, directly put their bags on the scanner. Customers have 0, 1, 2, or 3 carry-on bags, including purses, wallets, and so forth. On average, a typical customer has 1.5 bags. The X-ray scanner can handle 18 bags per minute. After their bags are scanned, 80% of customers leave the security checkpoint and head for their gate, while 20% of customers are asked to undergo additional manual screening by one of three screening officers. A manual screening takes on average one minute per customer.

a. What is theoretical flow time through the security check for an average passenger?

b. A sample of 20 passengers was selected at random, and the time required for each to clear the security check was recorded. The average of the individual times was 135 seconds. What is the flow-time efficiency?

4.7 The Traffic Court of King James County operates between the hours of 9:00 a.m. and 1:00 p.m. Each morning, at roughly 9:00, 200 defendants show up for trial involving traffic violations such as speeding, illegal parking, and ignoring a stop sign. On Monday, June 10, 2003, a sample of 10 defendants was selected at random by a consultant. For each defendant, the consultant recorded the actual time spent in discussion with the judge and the time paying the fine (not including waiting). Also recorded were the times the defendant arrived and left the court. The data are summarized in Table 4.9.

a. Estimate the average theoretical flow time of the process.

b. Estimate the average flow time of the process.

c. What is the flow-time efficiency?

MODELING EXERCISE ▮▮▮▮▮▮▮

www.prenhall.com/anupindi

For exercises and models using the evaluation software of iGrafx Process, insert the CD-ROM that is packaged with this book. An electronic copy of the User Guide is included on the CD. For more information on iGrafx, visit www.iGrafx.com. Detailed descriptions of the models may also be found at www.prenhall.com/anupindi.

Model

In Exercise 4.3, you were asked to estimate the theoretical flow time of a mix of two models of sheds produced by Wonder Shed Inc. In this modeling exercise, Exercise 4.3 has been prebuilt using iGrafx Process. You can use the model to evaluate the theoretical flow times of various product mixes of sheds (also known as garages in the model).

Wonder Shed Inc.

Exercise 4.3

Simulation

To simulate the shed production process at Wonder Shed Inc., double-click on iGrafx document CH4EX3. This loads the simulation model within iGrafx Process. The main screen should have two panes. The left pane shows the Explorer bar with the following contents: Processes, Scenarios, and Reports. (If you do not see this, click on View and the Explorer bar from the menu item and ensure that the All Components view is chosen at the top of the Explorer bar.) You may view the model for this exercise by double-clicking on CH4EX3 under Processes. The Process Scenario tab gives details of the various parameters used in the simulation model. Finally, results of a simulation run may be viewed by double-clicking on Simulation Report under the Reports tab in the Explorer bar.

To simulate the model, from the Model menu, point to Run and choose Start. The default simulation length is set up for one work week (equal to five days). A Simulation Progress window pops up at the right end of the screen. As soon as the simulation ends, the results of the simulation are displayed as a report. There are five tabs in a report. Select the Custom tab to see the customized report for this exercise.

To change the product mix, from the Model menu, select Attributes. In the Define Attributes window, select S_Deluxe_Percent from the Initial Values pane to modify it.

Implementation

The process flow diagram of the simulation model is illustrated at the beginning of this section and is similar to the process flow diagram illustrated in Figure 4.1. Observe that buffers are not explicitly modeled, as we are interested only in theoretical flow times. There are several ways a simulation model can be used to estimate the theoretical flow time of a process. In this implementation, only one shed is produced at a time. That is, an order is generated (released into the process) only after the previous order is completed. Thus, no order (shed) will wait for any resources at any step of the process. To process a product mix, the appropriate type of shed is released on the basis of prespecified mix percentages.

Refer to the document in the CD for detailed explanations on the modeling approach for this exercise.

Performance Interpretation

The performance of the process is illustrated in the custom report. In this simulation, the garages are the same as sheds. The report consists of two tables. The first table shows the *Percent of Deluxe Garages*. The second table shows the *Theoretical Flow Time (in minutes)* for the standard and deluxe sheds as well as the average flow time for a given product mix. The report already has outcomes of two simulation runs—one for the case of 100% deluxe sheds and the other for a mix of 75% standard and 25% deluxe. Results of new simulation runs will be appended to these tables.

SELECTED BIBLIOGRAPHY ▪▪▪▪▪▪▪

Blackburn, J. D. 1992. "Time-Based Competition: White-Collar Activities." *Business Horizons* 35, no. 4: 96–101.

Chase, R. B., N. J. Aquilano, and F. R. Jacobs. 2004. *Production and Operations Management.* 10th ed. Chicago: Irwin McGraw-Hill.

Eppen, G. D., et al. 1998. *Introductory Management Science.* 5th ed. Upper Saddle River, N.J.: Prentice Hall.

Evans, J. R. 1994. *Applied Production and Operations Management.* 4th ed. Minneapolis: West Publishing.

Gilbreth, F. B. 1911. *Motions Study.* New York: Van Nostrand.

Gilbreth, F. B., Jr., and E. G. Gilbreth Carey. 1949. *Cheaper by the Dozen.* New York: T. Y. Crowell.

Hammer, M., and J. Champy. 1993. *Reengineering the Corporation.* New York: HarperBusiness.

Harvard Business School. 1986. *Kristen's Cookie Company.* Harvard Business School Case 9-686-093. Cambridge, Mass.: Harvard Business School Publishing.

Kaniegel, R. 1997. *The One Best Way: Fredrick Winslow Taylor and the Enigma of Efficiency.* New York: Penguin.

Kerzner, L. J. 1989. *Project Management.* Princeton, N.J.: Van Nostrand Reinhold.

Krajewski, L. J., and L. P. Ritzman. 1996. *Operations Management.* 4th ed. Reading, Mass.: Addison-Wesley.

McClain, J. O., L. J. Thomas, and J. B. Mazzola. 1992. *Operations Management.* 3rd ed. Upper Saddle River, N.J.: Prentice Hall.

Schroeder, R. J. 1993. *Operations Management.* 4th ed. New York: McGraw-Hill.

Schtub, J. F. Bard, and S. Globerson. 1994. *Project Management.* Upper Saddle River, N.J.: Prentice Hall.

Taylor, F. W. 1911. *The Principles of Scientific Management.* New York: Harper & Row.

Appendix: The Critical Path Method

In Section 4.3, we illustrated a method for finding the critical path of a process by computing the flow time of each path in the process flowchart and identifying the path with the longest flow time. However, more formal techniques have been developed for computing critical path and identifying critical activities. Here we outline one such approach, the critical path method (CPM), which is particularly useful for scheduling and controlling very large and complex projects.

Recall that all activities that lie along the critical path are labeled *critical activities* and that a delay in executing any of these activities will delay completion of the whole process. Noncritical activities, on the other hand, may be delayed (within limits) without affecting process flow time. We define the *slack time* of an activity as *the extent to which an activity could be delayed without affecting process flow time.* Thus, by definition, the slack time of a critical activity is zero. The critical path, therefore, is *a path consisting of activities, all of which have a slack time of zero.*

In order to compute slack time, we must calculate four time values for each activity in the processing network:

- **Early start time (EST):** The earliest possible time that we can begin an activity.
- **Early finish time (EFT):** EST plus the work content of the activity. It represents the earliest possible time we *can* finish that activity.
- **Late finish time (LFT):** The latest time at which an activity can end without delaying the process.
- **Late start time (LST):** LFT time minus the work content of the activity. It represents the latest we *must* start that activity in order not to delay its finish beyond its LFT.

Slack time may therefore be defined as follows:

$$\text{Slack time} = \text{LST} - \text{EST} = \text{LFT} - \text{EFT}$$

We now describe a systematic procedure for computing the various times. The procedure scans the process flowchart twice: forward from start to end and backward from end to start. We compute EST and EFT using *forward scheduling*—that is, we begin at the start of the process and schedule each activity in sequence as early as possible, taking into account that it cannot start before all its predecessor activities are completed. In contrast, LST and LFT are computed using *backward scheduling.* In that case, we start by specifying a given target date for completing the process. We then consider each activity, in reverse order (from end to start), and compute the latest time we can complete this activity without violating the desired completion time.

Computing EST and EFT

Start to scan forward at the event "Start." Set the EST and EFT of this event to zero. Then proceed *forward,* repeating the following steps:

1. Find an activity such that the EFT of all its immediate predecessors has been computed.
2. Set the EST of the activity as the maximum of the EFTs of its immediate predecessors.
3. Set the EFT of the activity as its EST plus its work content.

The rationale behind step 2 is that the activity can begin as soon as the last of its immediate predecessors has been completed. Once started, the EFT of the activity can be easily computed by step 3.

We repeat steps 1 to 3 until all the activities have been considered. The EST of the event "End" is then computed by one last iteration of step 2. The EFT of "End" is equal to its EST and signifies the earliest time the entire unit can be completed.

Computing LST and LFT

Start the backward scan at the event "End." Set the LFT of this event to equal its EFT (computed in the forward scan). Set the LST of the "End" event to equal its LFT. Then proceed *backward,* repeating the following steps:

1. Find an activity such that LST of all its immediate successors has been computed

TABLE 4.10 Slack Times for Activities at Wonder Shed Inc.

	Operation	Work Content	EST	EFT	LFT	LST	Slack Time
	"Start"	0	0	0	0	0	0
1	Separate	10	0	10	10	0	0
2	Punch the base	30	10	40	40	10	0
3	Punch the roof	22	10	32	47	25	15
4	Form the base	6	40	46	46	40	0
5	Form the roof	12	32	44	59	47	15
6	Subassemble	13	46	59	59	46	0
7	Assemble	10	59	69	69	59	0
8	Inspect	36	69	105	105	69	0
	"End"	0	105	105	105	105	0

2. Set the LFT of the activity as the minimum of the LSTs of its immediate successors

3. Set the LST of the activity as its LFT minus its work content

The rationale behind Step 2 is that the latest time by which an activity must be completed (without impeding the due date) is the time its successor activities must begin. In order to finish by this time, the activity must start no later than the LST computed in step 3.

We repeat steps 1 to 3 until all the activities have been considered. The LFT of the event "Start" is then computed (it will equal zero if the calculations were carried out correctly).

We demonstrate the forward and backward calculations in Example 4.9.

Example 4.9

Let's reconsider our computations of theoretical flow time and critical path at Wonder Shed. The first two columns of Table 4.10 list the activities (the number and its description) that must be performed in order to manufacture a shed. The third column gives the work content (equal to the activity time) corresponding to each activity, as derived in Table 4.2.

To see how the next four columns of Table 4.10 are computed, we first compute the early times, EST, and EFT using the forward scan. We start by setting the EST and EFT of the "Start" to 0. The first activity that could be analyzed is activity 1 since all the EFTs of its predecessors (namely, the event "Start") have been computed. Thus, for activity 1, we set its EST = 0 and EFT = 0 + 10 = 10. The next activity we can analyze is either 2 or 3 since for each of these activities the predecessor is activity 1. Choosing activity 2 first, we get EST = 10 (this is the EFT of activity 1). Continuing to step 3, we get EFT = 10 + 30 = 40 for activity 2. We continue similarly for the remaining activities.

Consider how step 2 works for an activity with more then one predecessor, such as activity 7. The predecessors of this activity are 5 and 6. By the time activity 7 is considered, the EFT of these two activities was already calculated at 44 and 59, respectively. The maximum is 59, and thus the EST of activity 7 is 59. The EFT is 59 + 10 = 69.

We continue this way for all activities, including activity 8, whose EFT is 105. This is also the EST and EFT of the event "End."

Consider now the backward scan and the calculation of the LST and LFT. We start by setting the LST and LFT of the event "End" at 105. The first activity to schedule is activity 8 since all its successors (namely, "End") have been scheduled. Thus, the LFT of activity 8 is 105. We calculate its LST (step 3) as 105 − 36 = 69. Continuing in this fashion, we ultimately reach activity 1. Its immediate successors are 2 and 3, whose LSTs are 10 and 25, respectively. Thus, using step 2, the LFT of activity 1 is 10 (the minimum of 10 and 25). Step 1 yields that the LST is 10 − 10 = 0, and this is also the LST and LFT for the event "Start."

The entire calculation of the theoretical flow time, the critical path, and the slacks is summarized in Table 4.10. We see, for instance, that activities 1, 2, 4, 6, 7, and 8 have slack times of zero and that the path connecting these activities is the critical path.

CHAPTER 5

Flow Rate and Capacity Analysis

Introduction

Southwest Airlines is the most successful airline in the history of the commercial airline industry and one of the most consistently profitable corporations in the United States. From its very modest beginning in 1972, with three Boeing 733 aircrafts serving three cities, the airline grew to 400 aircrafts serving 60 cities in 2001. Throughout these years, Southwest also maintained its leadership position in customer satisfaction, low prices, and efficient operations.

One of the most important metrics used by Southwest as well as other airlines is the number of passenger miles flown in a given year. Clearly, other things being equal, the more passenger miles an airline can fly, the higher its revenues and profit. A related measure is the load factor, which is the ratio of the actual passenger miles flown by a given airline and its capacity.

Southwest's strategy, which is based on high-frequency, point-to-point, short-distance flights, presents the airline with particular challenges with respect to its ability to generate a high level of passenger miles from its fleet. Short flights force an aircraft to spend a higher percentage of its time in takeoffs and landings and on the ground rather than flying passenger miles and generating revenues. To compensate for this handicap, the company relies on cutting-edge operations to accelerate the turnaround

101

process and get its planes back in the air as soon as possible. Southwest's goal is to turn flights around in just 15 minutes or less—an industry record. In addition, the company utilizes secondary, less congested airports, specifically selected in order to further reduce unproductive aircraft delays.

Every company strives to maximize its rate of producing goods or services, given its resources. In the case of Southwest Airlines, the critical factor for achieving this goal is to minimize the "setup" time—the wasted time between flights that cannot be used to produce output, that is, passenger miles.

As we have defined in earlier chapters, throughput, or average flow rate, of a stable process is *the average number of flow units that flow through the process per unit of time.* **Process capacity**, which we will discuss in this chapter, is *the maximum sustainable flow rate of a process.* The lean operations literature, started with the Toyota Production System (see Chapter 10), often describes throughput in terms of "takt time." Derived from the German word for pace, takt time is the reciprocal of throughput rate and is the average activity time at a workstation on the assembly line. (Current takt times for the assembly of mass-produced cars are on the order of 1 min.) Takt time is sometimes also called "cycle time," but some authors use "cycle time" as a synonym for "flow time." To avoid confusion, we do not use the term "cycle time" in this book. We discuss the relations among these concepts in section 5.2.1.

Throughput and capacity are important measures of process performance—they indicate a "scale" of a process: If the process earns an economic return for each processed flow unit, then it follows that the higher the throughput, the greater the return generated per unit of time. Capacity is also important from the perspective of managing process flow times since insufficient process capacity may lead to congestion and excessive waiting time. In this chapter, we study process flow rate and capacity and examine some key ways to increase them.

In Section 5.1, we identify the kinds of *resources* and *resource pools* available for performing processing activities. In Section 5.2, we define the *theoretical capacity of a resource pool*, show how the theoretical capacity *of the process* depends on that of its *bottleneck resources*, and introduce the concept of *capacity utilization*. In Section 5.3, we examine how product mix decisions impact the theoretical capacity of a process and its profitability. In Section 5.4, we discuss other factors that affect the process capacity and introduce the notion of *effective capacity*. Finally, in Section 5.5, we study some key ideas to improve the theoretical capacity of a process.

▪▪▪ 5.1 Resources and Resource Pools

As we discussed in Chapter 1, activities are performed by capital and labor resources. Each activity may require one or more resources, and each resource may be allocated to one or more activities. For example, in the process of making bread, input raw materials— flour, salt, butter, water, and so forth—are transformed into outputs of loaves of bread. The entire process requires performing such activities as mixing the ingredients, kneading the dough, forming the loaves, placing them in the oven(s), and baking them. In turn, these activities use such resources as mixers, bakers, and ovens. A given resource—for instance, a baker—may be used by several activities, such as mixing, kneading, and forming dough. Similarly, a given activity, such as loading the oven, may require multiple resources, such as a baker and an oven.

A **resource pool** is *a collection of interchangeable resources that can perform an identical set of activities.* Each unit in a resource pool is called a **resource unit**. For instance, in the case of bread making, three flexible bakers, each of whom can perform any baking activity, would be viewed collectively as *a single resource pool* containing three resource units. On the other hand, three individual bakers, each specialized in a separate activity (mixing, kneading, and forming dough, respectively), would be regarded as *three separate resource pools,* each consisting of a single resource unit. Through process investments, however, it is sometimes possible to make the separate resource pools flexible to handle tasks performed by each other. Such investments, called **resource pooling**, *involve the combining of separate resource pools into a single resource pool to perform several activities.* It is a powerful operational concept that can significantly affect not only process flow rate and process capacity but also flow time (as we will see in Chapter 8).

Unit Loads   As we learned in Chapter 4, the work content of each activity is the time required to complete the activity for one unit of flow. Since activities are performed by resources, we can extend this concept and define the **unit load of a resource unit** as *the total amount of time the resource works to process each flow unit.* It is measured in units of time per flow unit (e.g., minutes of oven time per loaf). It can be computed by taking the sum of the work contents of all activities that utilize that resource unit. We use T_p to denote the unit load of a resource unit in resource pool p. Example 5.1 demonstrates this concept.

Example 5.1

Health maintenance organizations (HMOs) provide their customers with all-inclusive medical service for a fixed monthly fee. To secure services, they contract with physicians and hospitals that provide their services on a fee-per-service basis. When members of an HMO receive medical service, the providing physician or hospital submits a claim to the HMO for reimbursement. NewLife Finance is a service provider to HMOs. For a small fee, it performs the entire claims processing operation on behalf of the HMO.

Processing a physician claim consists of the following operations:

1. Claims billed by physicians arrive by mail and are opened by the mailroom clerk and are date stamped. They are then placed into a data-entry bin.
2. Data entry clerks enter date-stamped applications—first in, first out—into NewLife's claims processing system. Data-entry clerks must check claims for proper formatting and completeness of data fields before they input claims into the system. If a claim is not legible, fully completed, or properly formatted, it must be sent back to the physician for resubmission. Once entered, claims are stored in a processing inventory called "suspended claims."
3. Claims are assigned to a claim processor for initial processing.
4. Processed claims are transferred by the system to a claim supervisor for inspection and possible alterations.
5. Claims are returned to their original claim processors who complete the transaction and issue instructions to accounts payable for settlement.

The resources required for each operation and the corresponding work contents are listed in Table 5.1.

TABLE 5.1 Activity Work Content at NewLife Finance

Activity	*Resource*	*Work Content (minutes per claim)*
Mailroom	Mailroom clerk	0.6
Data entry	Data-entry clerk	4.2
Initial processing	Claims processor	4.8
Inspection	Claims supervisor	2.2
Final processing	Claims processor	1.8

TABLE 5.2 Resource Unit Loads at NewLife Finance	
Resource Pool (p)	Unit Load (T_p) (minutes per claim)
Mailroom clerk	0.6
Data-entry clerk	4.2
Claims processor	6.6
Claims supervisor	2.2

Observe that the mailroom clerk only performs the mail room activity with a work content of 0.6 minutes per claim. Therefore, the unit load of the mail room clerk is 0.6 minutes. The claims processor, however, performs the two activities of initial processing and final processing. Consequently, the unit of load of claims processor is the sum of the work contents of these two activities given by 4.8 + 1.8 = 6.6 minutes. The unit loads of the various resources are listed in Table 5.2.

▪▪▪ 5.2 Flow Rate Measurement

Both flow rate and process capacity are expressed in terms of *number of flow units per unit of time*, such as customers per day, tons of steel per shift, cars per hour, dollars per month, and patients per year. Analogous to the estimation of average flow time outlined in Chapter 4, the average flow rate (throughput) of a stable process, *R*, can be determined by the following three-step procedure:

1. Observe the process over a given, extended period of time.
2. Measure the number of flow units that are processed by the process over the selected period of time.
3. Compute the average number of flow units per unit of time.

The capacity of the process is its maximum sustainable flow rate. In the sections that follow, we explore ways to estimate the capacity of a process.

5.2.1 Theoretical Capacity

If we observe a given resource unit during a length of time, we will see that it experiences periods in which it is utilized (or busy processing flow units), periods in which it is unavailable for processing units (for instance being out of service or occupied with other activities such as setups, interruptions, or maintenance), and periods during which it is idle (such as waiting for work to arrive from upstream activities). Obviously, an idle or unavailable resource does not process flow units. We will examine the impact of these factors on the flow rate in Section 5.5.

The **theoretical capacity of a resource unit** is *its maximum sustainable flow rate if it were fully utilized* (without interruptions, downtime, time wasted to setups, idle periods, and so on.) Likewise, the **theoretical capacity of a resource pool** is *the sum of the theoretical capacities of all the resource units in that pool*. Theoretical capacities of different resource pools may vary. Since all resource pools are required to process a flow unit, no process can produce output any faster than its **bottleneck**—the "slowest" resource pool of a process. A resource pool with minimum theoretical capacity is called a **theoretical bottleneck**. Therefore, we define the **theoretical capacity of a process** as *the theoretical capacity of the theoretical bottleneck*. Like theoretical flow time (studied in Chapter 4), theoretical capacity represents an idealized target that can rarely be achieved in practice.

5.2.2   Computing Theoretical Capacity

The theoretical capacities of various resource pools and of the entire process can be computed from the following data:

- Unit loads
- Number of units in the resource pool

As an illustration, consider a simple process requiring a single worker (resource) whose job is to file insurance claims. Assume, for example, that the unit load of the worker is 10 minutes per claim. Then the theoretical capacity of the resource unit is 1/10 claims per minute (60/10 = 6 claims per hour). If two workers were available to process claims, then the theoretical capacity of the resource pool would be $2 \times 6 = 12$ claims per hour.

Formally, we write

Theoretical capacity of a resource unit (in resource pool p) = 1/unit load = $1/T_p$

If all resource units of the resource pool are identical, then the theoretical capacity of a resource pool p, R_p, is then given by the number of resources in resource pool p (c_p) times the theoretical capacity of a resource unit in pool p. That is,

$$R_p = c_p/T_p$$

If the various resource units are nonidentical in terms of their theoretical capacities, then the theoretical capacity of the resource pool will be the sum of the theoretical capacities of each resource unit in the pool. For the rest of the chapter, however, we will assume that all units in a resource pool are identical.

Example 5.2

Consider the case of NewLife Finance introduced in Example 5.1. There are four resource pools required for processing a claim: mailroom clerks, data-entry clerks, claims processors, and claims supervisors. The unit loads for each of the resource pools were computed in Table 5.2.

In order to compute the theoretical capacity of the various *resource pools,* we need the number of resource units in each resource pool. Assume that NewLife employs 1 mailroom clerk, 8 data-entry clerks, 12 claims processors, and 5 claims supervisors. The theoretical capacities of each resource pool are calculated in Table 5.3. The theoretical bottleneck is the mailroom clerk resource pool. The theoretical capacity of the process is 1.66 claims per minute.

It is important to realize that T_p, the unit load utilized in the formula for the theoretical capacity, is usually not equal to the theoretical flow time of the process. For instance, consider a process that involves two operations in sequence. The first operation requires 6 minutes and the resource pool contains two resource units. The second operation requires 2 minutes and the resource pool contains one resource unit. Then,

TABLE 5.3 Theoretical Capacity for Physician Claims, NewLife Finance

Resource Pool (p)	Unit Load (minutes per claim) (T_p)	Theoretical Capacity of a Resource Unit (claims per minute) ($1/T_p$)	Number of Units in the Resource Pool (c_p)	Theoretical Capacity of a Resource Pool (claims per minute) ($R_p = c_p/T_p$)
Mailroom clerk	0.6	1/0.6 = 1.66	1	1.66
Data-entry clerk	4.2	1/4.2 = 0.24	8	1.90
Claims processor	6.6	1/6.6 = 0.15	12	1.82
Claims supervisor	2.2	1/ 2.2 = 0.45	5	2.27

the theoretical flow time is $6 + 2 = 8$ minutes, but the theoretical capacity is $2/6 = 1/3$ units per minute with the bottleneck being the first operation.

5.2.3 Extensions: Other Factors Affecting Theoretical Capacity

The calculations of theoretical capacity discussed in the previous section are based on the premise that all resources process units sequentially or one unit at a time and that they are available for the same amount of time. Often these assumptions do no hold. Next we discuss how one adjusts the calculation of the theoretical capacity to account for these differences.

Load Batching Often, resources can process several flow units simultaneously, a phenomenon referred to as **load batching.** For example, consider a given oven that can bake 10 loaves simultaneously. We say in that case that its load batch is 10. Naturally, the higher the load batch, the higher the capacity. (See Section 5.4 for other types of batching effects.)

Scheduled Availability Typically, each resource unit is scheduled for operation only a portion of the total time (e.g., eight hours per day, five days per week). *The amount of time that a resource is scheduled for operation is called the* **scheduled availability** *of the resource.* Scheduled availability of various resources in a process may differ. For example, in a manufacturing setting, it is not uncommon that some areas within a plant operate only one shift per day (8 hours) while others operate two (16 hours). Moreover, the choice of *one day* as the time period of measurement is based on the assumption that availability patterns repeat on a daily basis. However, more complicated patterns are possible. Some resource pools, for example, may be available only on Mondays and Thursdays, with the pattern repeating *every week*. In that case, we should measure scheduled availability in *number of hours a week*.

Taking into account the load batching and the scheduled availability of a given resource, we obtain a more general expression for the theoretical capacity of a resource unit:

$$\text{Theoretical capacity of a resource unit} = (1/T_p) \times \text{Load batch} \times \text{Scheduled availability}$$
$$\textbf{(5.1)}$$

Recall that the theoretical capacity of resource pool p, R_p, is given by the number of resources in resource pool p (c_p) times the theoretical capacity of a resource unit in the pool, which translates to

$$R_p = (c_p/T_p) \times \text{Load batch} \times \text{Scheduled availability} \qquad \textbf{(5.2)}$$

For example, consider a resource pool containing two ovens, each of which bakes 10 loaves of bread simultaneously. The baking time is 15 minutes. Finally, assume that the oven is scheduled for operations 7.5 hours per day (450 minutes per day). To calculate the theoretical capacity of the pool, we identify the following parameters:

$$c_p = \text{Number of resource units} = 2 \text{ ovens}$$
$$T_p = \text{Unit load} = 15 \text{ minutes}$$
$$\text{Load batch} = 10 \text{ loaves}$$
$$\text{Scheduled availability} = 450 \text{ minutes per day}$$

Using Formula 5.2, we estimate the theoretical capacity of the oven resource pool to be

$$R_p = (2/15) \times 10 \times 450 = 600 \text{ loaves per day}$$

TABLE 5.4 Theoretical Capacity for Physician Claims, NewLife Finance (Revised)

Resource Pool	Scheduled Availability (minutes per day)	Unit Load (minutes per claim) (T_p)	Theoretical Capacity of a Resource Unit (claims per day)	Number of Units in Resource Pool (c_p)	Theoretical Capacity of a Resource Pool (claims per day) (R_p)
Mailroom clerk	450	0.6	450/0.6 = 750	1	750 × 1 = 750
Data-entry clerk	450	4.2	450/4.2 = 107.1	8	107.1 × 8 = 857
Claims processor	360	6.6	360/6.6 = 54.5	12	54.5 × 12 = 655
Claims supervisor	240	2.2	240/2.2 = 109.1	5	109.1 × 5 = 545

We demonstrate these extensions in Example 5.3.

Example 5.3

Consider again NewLife Finance. In the previous examples, we have computed the theoretical capacity of the various resource pools in terms of claims per minute. Consider now the effects of scheduled availability.

Assume that mailroom and data-entry clerks report to work for 9 hours per day. They take 1 hour for lunch break and two 15-minute breaks—one mid-morning and one mid-afternoon. Thus, clerks are available to process claims for a total of 7.5 hours (450 minutes) per day. Similarly, assume that the claims processors are available 6 hours per day, with the rest of the time used on other activities, such as training. Claims supervisors are available for processing claims only 4 hours per day on average. They spend the remaining time on other administrative duties. Since the processing of claims by each resource pool is sequential, the load batch for each resource is equal to one.

The scheduled availability and theoretical capacity of each resource is computed in Table 5.4. The claims supervisors constitute the bottleneck, and the theoretical capacity is 545 claims per day. Note that the appropriate measure of capacity here is claims per day and not claims per hour.

5.2.4 Throughput and Capacity Utilization

The throughput of a process, *R*, is the average number of flow units processed over a given period of time. Throughput of a process is rarely equal to its theoretical capacity because of internal inefficiencies that lead to resource unavailability and idleness as well as external constraints such as low outflow rate (due to low demand rate) or low inflow rate (due to low supply rate).

Working from the notion of theoretical capacity of a resource pool, R_p, which is an idealized but easily computable measure of capacity, we can measure **capacity utilization of a resource pool** (denoted by ρ_p) which measures the degree to which resources are effectively utilized by a process. Capacity utilization is an important performance measure and is calculated as

$$\text{Capacity utilization of resource pool } p = \text{Throughput/theoretical capacity of resource pool } p$$

$$\rho_p = R/R_p \tag{5.3}$$

Capacity utilization indicates the extent to which resources—which represent invested capital—are utilized to generate outputs (flow units and ultimately profits). Capacity utilization is defined for each resource pool. Thus, the theoretical capacity (R_p) in the denominator is of the specific resource pool in consideration. The *capacity utilization of the process* is defined as the capacity utilization of the bottleneck resource pool. We illustrate the computation of utilizations in Example 5.4.

Example 5.4

Assume that the average number of claims processed by NewLife Finance during a given month was measured to be 480 per day. Thus, throughput, R, is 480 per day. Using the theoretical capacities of the various resource pools computed in Example 5.3 (see Table 5.4), we compute the capacity utilization of the various resources in Table 5.5.

TABLE 5.5 Capacity Utilization for NewLife Finance

Resource Pool (p)	Theoretical Capacity of a Resource Pool (claims per day) (R_p)	Capacity Utilization ($\rho_p = R/R_p$)
Mailroom clerk	750	480/750 = 64%
Data-entry clerk	857	480/857 = 56%
Claims processor	655	480/655 = 73%
Claims supervisor	545	480/545 = 88%

TABLE 5.6 Work Content and Resources, VOH Hospital

Activity/ Event	Description	Work Content (minutes per patient)	Resources Allocated
Start	Patient leaves the physician's office.	—	—
1	Patient walks to the X-ray lab.	7	—
2	The X-ray request travels to the X-ray lab by a messenger.	20	Messenger
3	An X-ray technician fills out a standard form based on the information supplied by the physician.	6	X-ray technician
4	The receptionist receives from the patient information concerning insurance, prepares and signs a claim form, and sends to the insurer.	5	Receptionist
5	Patient undresses in preparation for X-ray.	3	Changing room
6	A lab technician takes X-rays.	7.5	X-ray technician, X-ray lab
7	A darkroom technician develops X-rays.	15	Darkroom technician, darkroom
8	The lab technician checks X-rays for clarity. If an X-ray is not satisfactory, activities 7 to 9 are repeated. (On average, 75% of X-rays are found satisfactory the first time around, while 25% require one retake; virtually no units require more than two takes.)	2.5	X-ray technician
9	Patient puts on clothes and gets ready to leave lab.	3	Changing room
10	Patient walks back to the physician's office.	7	—
11	The X-rays are transferred to the physician by a messenger.	20	Messenger
End	Patient and the X-rays arrive at the physician's office.	—	—

TABLE 5.7 Theoretical Capacity, VOH Hospital

Resource Pool (p)	Unit Load (minutes per patient) (T_p)	Theoretical Capacity of Resource Unit (patients per hour) ($1/T_p$)	Number of Units in Resource Pool (c_p)	Theoretical Capacity of Resource Pool (patients per hour) (R_p)
Messenger	$20 + 20 = 40$	$60/40 = 1.5$	6	$1.5 \times 6 = 9$
Receptionist	5	$60/5 = 12$	1	$12 \times 1 = 12$
X-ray technician	$6 + 7.5 + 2.5 = 16$	$60/16 = 3.75$	4	$3.75 \times 4 = 15$
X-ray lab	7.5	$60/7.5 = 8$	2	$8 \times 2 = 16$
Darkroom technician	15	$60/15 = 4$	3	$4 \times 3 = 12$
Darkroom	15	$60/15 = 4$	2	$4 \times 2 = 8$
Changing room	$3 + 3 = 6$	$60/6 = 10$	2	$10 \times 2 = 20$

TABLE 5.8 Capacity Utilization, VOH Hospital

Resource Pool (p)	Theoretical Capacity of Resource Pool (patients per hour) (R_p)	Capacity Utilization (%) ($\rho_p = R/R_p$)
Messenger	9	$5.5/9 = 61.11\%$
Receptionist	12	$5.5/12 = 45.83\%$
X-ray technician	15	$5.5/15 = 36.67\%$
X-ray lab	16	$5.5/16 = 34.38\%$
Darkroom technician	12	$5.5/12 = 45.83\%$
Darkroom	8	$5.5/8 = 68.75\%$
Changing room	20	$5.5/20 = 27.50\%$

The theoretical capacity of the process is 545 claims per day. Thus, the capacity utilization of the entire process is 88%.

The concepts discussed thus far are demonstrated in Example 5.5 using the Valley of Hope Hospital example introduced in Chapter 4.

Example 5.5

Reconsider the situation at Valley of Hope (VOH) Hospital, first introduced in Chapter 4. Consolidating the data in Tables 4.6 and 4.7, the activities required for each X-ray, with corresponding work content and allocated resources, are restated in Table 5.6.

All resources are scheduled for operation from 9:00 a.m. to 5:00 p.m. each day, six days per week. Assume that the scheduled availability is 60 minutes per hour. Since all processing is sequential, load batch equals one. Using the information in Table 5.6, we can compute the unit loads and theoretical capacity of various resource units as given in Table 5.7. Further, with information on the number of resource units in each resource pool, we compute the theoretical capacity of the resource pools as shown in Table 5.7. Note that the theoretical bottleneck resource is the darkroom, with a capacity for processing only 8 patients per hour. The theoretical capacity of the process itself, therefore, is 8 patients per hour.

Finally, by observing the process over a three-week period, VOH Hospital found that its X-ray unit processes, on average, 5.5 patients per hour. Based on throughput, $R = 5.5$ patients per hour, we summarize the utilization of various resources in Table 5.8.

5.3 Effect of Product Mix on Theoretical Capacity and Profitability of a Process

Firms often produce several products simultaneously. In this section, we will first show that the theoretical capacity of a process is a function of the product mix that it produces. This observation has an important business implication. In most organizations, sales/marketing departments make product mix decisions. Since such decisions affect the process capacity (a major driver of profitability), input from the operations group, which is responsible for production, is required. We will also explore how the interaction between product mix and capacity affects the profitability of a firm.

5.3.1 Unit Load for Product Mix

For a process that produces several types of products, a flow unit may correspond to a given mix of the various products. We can calculate the unit load for a given product mix by averaging the unit loads of individual products, using weights determined by the mix, as illustrated in Example 5.6.

Example 5.6
In addition to processing *physician* claims, NewLife also handles claims submitted by hospitals. The process used to handle *hospital claims* is the same process used for physician claims. However, the unit loads required for the various operations are different. Currently, NewLife handles a product mix of 60% physician claims and 40% hospital claims. Table 5.9 lists the unit loads of the two types of claims. The third column, listing the unit loads of the 60%–40% mix, is computed by taking the weighted average of the previous two columns. For example, the unit load for the mailroom clerk equals 60% × 0.6 + 40% × 1.0 = 0.76.

5.3.2 Theoretical Capacity for Product Mix

Since different products may utilize various resources differently, the theoretical capacity of a resource pool—and thus the theoretical bottlenecks and capacity of the process—may depend on the products being produced and on the company's product mix. We can compute the theoretical capacity of a resource pool for a product mix directly from the unit loads of the product mix only when the load batch at the resource pool is identical across all products in the mix. For simplicity, we will assume this is the case. A more extensive procedure is necessary when the load batch is not identical.

Example 5.7
In Example 5.3, we found that the theoretical capacity for *physician claims* in NewLife Finance is 545 claims per hour. What is the theoretical capacity for *hospital claims*? We can find out by repeating the process we used in Example 5.3. As can be seen from Table 5.10, the theoretical process capacity is 375 (hospital) claims per day. The bottleneck resource remains the pool of claims supervisors.

TABLE 5.9 Unit Loads for Various Products, NewLife Finance

Resource Pool	Unit Load (Physician) (minutes per claim)	Unit Load (Hospital) (minutes per claim)	Unit Load (60%–40% mix) (minutes per claim)
Mailroom clerk	0.6	1.0	0.76
Data-entry clerk	4.2	5.2	4.60
Claims processor	6.6	7.5	6.96
Claims supervisor	2.2	3.2	2.60

TABLE 5.10 Theoretical Capacity for Hospital Claims, NewLife Finance

Resource	Scheduled Availability (minutes per day)	Unit Load (minutes per claim)	Theoretical Capacity of a Resource Unit (claims per day)	Number of Units in Resource Pool	Theoretical Capacity of a Resource Pool (claims per day)
Mailroom clerk	450	1.0	450/1.0 = 450	1	450 × 1 = 450
Data-entry clerk	450	5.2	450/5.2 = 86.5	8	86.5 × 8 = 692
Claims processor	360	7.5	360/7.5 = 48	12	48 × 12 = 576
Claims supervisor	240	3.2	240/3.2 = 75	5	75 × 5 = 375

TABLE 5.11 Theoretical Capacity for 60%/40% Mix, NewLife Finance

Resource	Scheduled Availability (minutes per day)	Unit Load (minutes per claim)	Theoretical Capacity of a Resource Unit (claims per day)	Number of Units in Resource Pool	Theoretical Capacity of a Resource Pool (claims per day)
Mailroom clerk	450	0.76	592	1	592
Data-entry clerk	450	4.60	98	8	784
Claims processor	360	6.96	51.7	12	621
Claims supervisor	240	2.60	92	5	460

Next, we compute the theoretical capacities of resources and process for a product mix of 60% physician claims and 40% hospital claims. As shown in Table 5.11, which is based on the unit load of the 60%/40% mix derived in Table 5.9, the theoretical capacity is 461 claims per day.

In the case of NewLife, the pool of claim supervisors is the bottleneck resource for every product mix. However, in general, a change in the product mix can affect not only the theoretical capacity but also the theoretical bottleneck.

In Example 5.8 we revisit the Wonder Shed Company, introduced in Chapter 4, and reexamine the concepts presented so far in this chapter. This example will also set the stage for discussing the profitability issues relating to product mix.

Example 5.8
Recall Wonder Shed Inc., producer of prefabricated storage sheds introduced in Chapter 4, Example 4.1. Table 5.12 lists some of the information related to the production process at Wonder Shed. In particular, the table lists the following:

- The *activities* required to complete a standard shed
- The *resources* (machines, tools, and workers) required to perform these activities
- The *work content* for each resource

Table 5.12 lists several types of workers. For example, worker-S is trained to perform the "Separate" activity; worker-PR operates punch press-R, worker PB operates punch press-B, and so on. We can use the data in Table 5.12 to compute the unit loads imposed by a standard shed on each resource pool as shown in Table 5.13.

We now compute the theoretical capacity for standard sheds. Table 5.14 summarizes the required data for each resource. The load batch for each resource is one. The scheduled availability is 60 minutes per hour. The number of units of each resource and the theoretical capacity are also listed in Table 5.14. It can be seen from this table that the theoretical capacity is 2.0 sheds per hour and that the theoretical bottleneck resources are punch press-B and worker-PB.

Assume that, in addition to standard sheds, Wonder Shed also manufactures another model, called fancy. Wonder Shed produces a product mix of 75% standard and 25% fancy (i.e., 3 standard sheds for each unit of fancy). Unit loads for the two products and the 75%–25% product

TABLE 5.12 Activities, Work Content, and Resource Pools for a Standard Shed, Wonder Shed Inc.

	Activity	*Work Content (minutes per unit)*	*Resource Allocated*
1	Separate	10	Worker-S
2	Punch the base	30	Punch press-B, worker-PB
3	Punch the roof	22	Punch press-R, worker-PR
4	Form the base	6	Forming machine-B, worker-FB
5	Form the roof	12	Forming machine-R, worker-FR
6	Subassemble	13	Welding gun, worker-SA
7	Assemble	10	Worker-FA
8	Inspect	36	Inspector

TABLE 5.13 Unit Loads for a Standard Shed, Wonder Shed Inc.

Resource Pool	*Unit Load (minutes per unit)*
Worker-S	10
Punch press-R	22
Punch press-B	30
Worker-PR	22
Worker-PB	30
Forming machine-R	12
Forming machine-B	6
Worker-FR	12
Worker-FB	6
Welding gun	13
Worker-SA	13
Worker-FA	10
Inspector	36

TABLE 5.14 Theoretical Capacity for a Standard Shed, Wonder Shed Inc.

Resource Pool	*Unit Load (minutes per unit)*	*Load Batch*	*Theoretical Capacity of a Resource Unit (sheds per hour)*	*Number of Units in the Resource Pool*	*Theoretical Capacity of the Resource Pool (sheds per hour)*
Worker-S	10	1	6.00	1	6.00
Punch press-R	22	1	2.73	1	2.73
Punch press-B	30	1	2.00	1	2.00
Worker-PR	22	1	2.73	1	2.73
Worker-PB	30	1	2.00	1	2.00
Forming machine-R	12	1	5.00	1	5.00
Forming machine-B	6	1	10.00	1	10.00
Worker-FR	12	1	5.00	1	5.00
Worker-FB	6	1	10.00	1	10.00
Welding gun	13	1	4.62	1	4.62
Worker-SA	13	1	4.62	1	4.62
Worker-FA	10	1	6.00	1	6.00
Inspector	36	1	1.67	2	3.33

TABLE 5.15 Unit Loads for a 75%–25% Product Mix at Wonder Shed Inc.

	Unit Load (minutes per shed)		
Resource Pool	*Standard*	*Fancy*	*75%–25% Mix*
Worker-S	10	10	10
Punch press-R	22	30	24
Punch press-B	30	50	35
Worker-PR	22	30	24
Worker-PB	30	50	35
Forming machine-R	12	15	12.75
Forming machine-B	6	10	7
Worker-FR	12	15	12.75
Worker-FB	6	10	7
Welding gun	13	20	14.75
Worker-SA	13	20	14.75
Worker-FA	10	15	11.25
Inspector	36	40	37

mix are listed in Table 5.15. Recall that to compute the unit load of a product mix, we take the weighted average of the respective unit loads. For example, given that the unit load of worker-S for standard and fancy sheds is 10 minutes each, its unit load for a 75%–25% product mix is equal to $.75 \times 10 + .25 \times 10 = 10$ minutes.

The theoretical capacity for the fancy shed is computed in Table 5.16. As the table indicates, the theoretical capacity is 1.2 fancy sheds per hour. The theoretical bottleneck resources are punch press-B and worker-PB, the same as for the standard model.

Finally, we compute the theoretical capacity for the product mix of 75%–25%, which is based on the unit load of the mix calculated in Table 5.15. The calculations are presented in Table 5.17. The bottleneck resources remain punch press-B and worker-PB. The theoretical capacity is 1.71 sheds per hour.

TABLE 5.16 Theoretical Capacity for Fancy Sheds, Wonder Shed Inc.

Resource Pool	*Unit Load (minutes per shed)*	*Load Batch*	*Theoretical Capacity of a Resource Unit (sheds per hour)*	*Number of Units in the Resource Pool*	*Theoretical Capacity of the Resource Pool (sheds per hour)*
Worker-S	10	1	6.00	1	6.00
Punch press-R	30	1	2.00	1	2.00
Punch press-B	50	1	1.20	1	1.20
Worker-PR	30	1	2.00	1	2.00
Worker-PB	50	1	1.20	1	1.20
Forming machine-R	15	1	4.00	1	4.00
Forming machine-B	10	1	6.00	1	6.00
Worker-FR	15	1	4.00	1	4.00
Worker-FB	10	1	6.00	1	6.00
Welding gun	20	1	3.00	1	3.00
Worker-SA	20	1	3.00	1	3.00
Worker-FA	15	1	4.00	1	4.00
Inspector	40	1	1.50	2	3.00

TABLE 5.17 Theoretical Capacity for 75%/25% Product Mix, Wonder Shed Inc.

Resource Pool	Unit Load (minutes per shed)	Load Batch	Theoretical Capacity of a Resource Unit (sheds per hour)	Number of Units in the Resource Pool	Theoretical Capacity of the Resource Pool (sheds per hour)
Worker-S	10	1	6.00	1	6.00
Punch press-R	24	1	2.50	1	2.50
Punch press-B	35	1	1.71	1	1.71
Worker-PR	24	1	2.50	1	2.50
Worker-PB	35	1	1.71	1	1.71
Forming machine-R	12.75	1	4.71	1	4.71
Forming machine-B	7	1	8.57	1	8.57
Worker-FR	12.75	1	4.71	1	4.71
Worker-FB	7	1	8.57	1	8.57
Welding gun	14.75	1	4.07	1	4.07
Worker-SA	14.75	1	4.07	1	4.07
Worker-FA	11.25	1	5.33	1	5.33
Inspector	37	1	1.62	2	3.24

5.3.3 Optimizing Profitability

Which of the two models made by Wonder Shed—standard or fancy—is the more profitable? To answer this question, it is useful to measure capacity and throughput *in terms of financial flows rather than in terms of physical unit flows*. We define the *contribution margin* of each flow unit as *its revenue less all of its variable costs*. Given the unit contribution margins of various products, what product mix should be produced to optimize profitability? It may seem logical to produce products with the highest unit contribution margins first. What roles, if any, do the concepts of unit load, resource capacity, and process capacity play in making the product mix decision? We illustrate these issues using Example 5.9.

Example 5.9

Let us say, for example, that the contribution margins of the standard and fancy sheds have been determined to be $200 and $260 per unit, respectively. Furthermore, market research suggests that the market potential (the maximum number that the firm could sell at its advertised prices) for standard and fancy sheds is 350 and 150 per month, respectively. Suppose Wonder Shed operates one shift of 8 hours per day and a working month of 25 days. The problem is to determine the optimal product mix: the number of sheds of each model to make and sell.

At first glance, it appears that the fancy shed is more profitable than the standard since it has a higher contribution margin ($260 per unit versus $200 per unit). However, this conclusion is false since it does not take into account the amount of time required to produce the various sheds. If the fancy shed were in fact the most profitable shed, the "best" plan for Wonder Shed would be to produce and sell as many fancy sheds as possible and then—only if spare capacity is available—produce standard models with the remaining capacity. From Table 5.16, we notice that theoretical capacity of fancy sheds is 1.2 units per hour. Multiplying by the duration of the shift (8 hours) and the number of days in a working month (25 days), we can express the theoretical capacity as $1.2 \times 8 \times 25 = 240$ fancy sheds per month. Since the market potential for fancy sheds is only 150 units per month, Wonder Shed has enough capacity to satisfy the demand. In fact, producing at the rate of 1.2 fancy sheds per hour, the total bottleneck resource (punch press-B and worker-PB) time required to produce 150 fancy sheds is $150/1.2 = 125$ hours.

Again, operating 8 hours per shift for 25 days each month, Wonder Shed has a total availability of 200 hours per month. Thus, after producing 150 fancy sheds—which requires 125 hours—Wonder Shed still has 75 hours of time remaining during the month at the bottlenecks, time that it could use to produce standard sheds. Recall from Table 5.14 that the theoretical capacity of Wonder Shed to produce the standard shed is 2 units per hour. In 75 hours, therefore, Wonder Shed can produce approximately $75 \times 2 = 150$ standard sheds per month. Thus, based on unit contribution margins alone, we determine that Wonder Shed should produce 150 fancy and 150 standard sheds per month, realizing a total monthly contribution of $69,000:

Fancy shed:	($260 × 150) = $39,000	
Standard shed:	($200 × 150) = $30,000	
Total monthly contribution	= $69,000	

Can Wonder Shed Inc. do better?

Note that while the contribution margin of a standard shed is $200, Wonder Shed's theoretical capacity to produce it is 2 units per hour. Its contribution per unit of time is therefore

$$2 \times 200 = \$400 \text{ per hour}$$

Similarly, the contribution margin per unit of time of the fancy shed is

$$1.2 \times \$260 = \$312 \text{ per hour}$$

Thus, based on contribution margin per unit of time, the standard shed is the more profitable product. Therefore, Wonder Shed should produce as many standard sheds as the market will bear and only then, if excess capacity is available, produce fancy sheds. Since two standard sheds are produced in an hour, the production of 350 standard sheds (to meet the product's full market potential) would require a total of 175 hours. In the remaining 25 hours of monthly availability, Wonder Shed can produce 30 fancy sheds. Based on contribution margin per unit of time, therefore, Wonder Shed should produce 175 standard sheds and 30 fancy sheds to realize a net profit of $77,800, which is a 13% increase in profits:

Standard shed:	($200 × 350) = $70,000	
Fancy shed:	($260 × 30) = $7,800	
Total monthly contribution	= $77,800	

As this example demonstrates, the criterion in determining which products are more profitable is *contribution per unit of time* on the bottleneck resource(s) rather than *contribution margin per unit.* In a simple setting involving few products with common bottleneck resources such as that of Example 5.9, it is fairly straightforward to derive the optimal product mix decision by simply comparing the contribution per unit of time of the various products. However, more complex settings that involve multiple products with multiple and different bottleneck resources involve more difficult trade-offs. In the Appendix, a generic approach to solving optimal product mix problems is briefly illustrated.

▪▪▪ 5.4 Other Factors Affecting Process Capacity

Earlier we have defined the flow rate of a process as the number of flow units processed per unit of time, throughput as the average flow rate, and capacity as the maximum sustainable flow rate. Also, the theoretical capacity is the maximum sustainable flow rate if the bottleneck resource(s) is fully utilized.

Process capacity is often less than the theoretical capacity of a process since resources are often not fully utilized during their scheduled availability period. Rather, resource units alternate between periods during which they are utilized and periods during which time is wasted. Wasted time may occur for several reasons, either planned or unforeseen, including **resource breakdown**, **preventive maintenance**, **starvation**, and **blockage**:

- **Resource breakdown**: *A resource may be unavailable for processing because of equipment malfunction or worker absenteeism.*
- **Preventive maintenance**: *When resources are undergoing scheduled maintenance activities, they are unavailable for processing.*
- **Starvation**: *Sometimes resources are forced to be idle because necessary inputs are unavailable. This circumstance is referred to as starvation.*
- **Blockage**: *Resources may be prevented from producing more flow units because there is no place to store the already processed flow units or additional processing has not been authorized.*

In the case of the first two items on this list, *the resource itself is not available for processing,* and we categorize these items as **resource availability loss**. In the case of the last two items, the problem lies elsewhere—*the resource is available but is not processing units.* These items are classified as **resource idleness**.

5.4.1   Net Availability

Scheduled availability defines the time period during which a resource unit is scheduled for processing. The **net availability of a resource** is *the actual time during which it is available for processing flow units.* Resource availability loss is *the difference between the scheduled availability and the net availability of a resource unit.* It represents a loss of resource unit capacity and thus of process capacity. **Availability loss factor** is *resource availability loss expressed as a fraction of scheduled availability,* as shown in the following equation:

$$\text{Availability loss factor} = 1 - (\text{Net availability/Scheduled availability}) \qquad \textbf{(5.4)}$$

Availability loss factor for a resource can be determined from the data that are available on events such as historical resource breakdowns, preventive maintenance schedules, and worker absenteeism.

Note that the concept of net availability does not take into account resource idleness. Thus, a resource will not necessarily be processing units during the entire period of net availability. An available resource may be idle because of starvation, blockage, or both.

5.4.2   Setups

In processes that involve multiple products, it may be necessary to set up the process each time the product is changed. This *cleaning, resetting, or retooling of equipment in order for it to process a different product is called* **setup** *or* **changeover**. For instance, the painting robots in a paint shop require draining the pipelines and cleaning of the painting heads each time the color is changed. Similarly, when researchers in a research-and-development organization switch often among several research projects, they are likely to waste time with every such switch.

While the time lost due to setups can be incorporated into our analysis through the concept of net availability introduced in the previous section, often a direct approach, as outlined in the following, leads to more accurate results. The basic idea is to amortize the setup time across the number of units produced and add that to the unit load.

We denote the average time required to set up a resource (at resource pool p) for a particular product by S_p (minutes per setup). Assume that once the setup is completed, we run a continuous batch of Q_p units of the same product before we change over and set up the resource for the next product. We refer to Q_p as the **setup batch** or the **lot size**—*the number of units processed consecutively after a setup.*

Since we utilize one setup for Q_p units, the average time for setup per unit is S_p/Q_p. This time should be added to the unit load of the product. We call the sum of the unit load and S_p/Q_p the *total unit load:*

$$\text{Total unit load} = T_p + S_p/Q_p \tag{5.5}$$

What is the "right" lot size or the size of the setup batch? On one hand, the higher we set the lot size, the lower will be the total unit load and thus the higher the capacity. On the other hand, the lower we set the lot size, the lower will be the inventory and consequently (using Little's law) the lower the flow time. Reducing the size of the setup batch is one of the most effective ways to reduce the waiting part of the flow time. We explore this relationship and also the determination of the optimal batch size in detail in Chapter 6.

Example 5.10

The Tile&Style company produces kitchen and bathroom tiles in two sizes: jumbo (12×12 inches) and regular (8×8 inches). Both types are cut out of larger tiles, 24.25×24.25 inches, which are called "plates." The tiles cut out of a single plate are packed into a bundle. A bundle contains 4 jumbo tiles or 9 regular tiles. The margins of 0.25 inches on each side of the plate are used for the cuts; the extra material is recycled.

Plates are cut into tiles by a cutting machine that is available 8 hours per day with a scheduled availability of 60 minutes per hour. The cutting time per jumbo plate is 1 minute. The regular plates, which involve more cutting, require 2 minutes per bundle. Typically, Tile&Style produces 300 bundles of regular tiles before it switches over and produces 100 bundles of jumbo. Thus, 75% of the bundles are regular, and 25% are jumbo. Furthermore, the switching time from one size to the other is 30 minutes and is independent of the sequence in which the products are produced. Thus, the setup time for each product, $S_p = 30$ minutes, and the lot sizes, Q_p, are 300 and 100 units, respectively, for regular and jumbo tiles. Table 5.18 lists the unit load for each type of tile, computes the setup per unit (S_p/Q_p), and adds these up for the total unit load for each product. The last column of the table combines the data for the individual products, using the weights 75% and 25%.

The difference between the *total unit load* (1.91 minutes per bundle) and the *unit load* (1.75 minutes per bundle) is due to the impact of setups. The *total unit load* is a more realistic estimate of the time required to process units than the *unit load*.

Note that the *setup batch* discussed in this section is an entirely different concept than the *load batch* introduced in Section 5.2.2. Whereas the load batch relates to the ability of the resource to handle units *simultaneously,* as in the case of baking bread, the setup batch indicates the number of units processed *sequentially,* between subsequent setups. The load batch is often constrained by the technological capabilities of the resource, such as the size of the oven. In contrast, the setup batch is determined managerially—it simply represents the number of flow units of a given type that are processed before we switch over to a different type. In the paint shop example discussed earlier, the setup batch represents the number of units of a particular color that are painted before we switch the process to another color.

TABLE 5.18 Tile&Style: Total Unit Load and Unit Load for Various Products

	Regular	*Jumbo*	*Mix*
Unit load (T_p)	2	1	$2 \times .75 + 1 \times .25 = 1.75$
S_p/Q_p	$30/300 = 0.1$	$30/100 = 0.33$	$.1 \times .75 + .33 \times .25 = 0.16$
Total unit load	$2 + 0.1 = 2.1$	$1 + 0.33 = 1.33$	$21. \times .75 + 1.33 \times .25 = 1.91$

5.4.3 Effective Capacity of a Process

Recall that the theoretical capacity of a resource unit is its maximum flow rate if it is fully utilized during its scheduled availability (i.e., if there are no periods of unavailability, time wasted on setups, or periods of idleness). We now define the **effective capacity of a resource unit** as its *maximum flow rate, if it were fully utilized during its net availability (if there were no periods of resource idleness).* Analogous to Formula 5.1, the effective capacity of a resource unit can be calculated using the following relation:

$$\text{Effective capacity of a resource unit} = (1/\text{total unit load}) \times \text{Load batch} \times \text{Net availability} \tag{5.6}$$

The effective capacity of a resource pool is the sum of the effective capacities of all the resource units in the pool:

$$\text{Effective capacity of a resource pool} = (c_p/\text{total unit load}) \times \text{Load batch} \times \text{Net availability} \tag{5.7}$$

The **effective capacity of a process** is *the effective capacity of its slowest resource pool(s),* called the **effective bottleneck(s)**. Finally, capacity utilization of resource, introduced earlier, may also be computed using its effective capacity instead of its theoretical capacity.

It is instructive to compare the notions of theoretical and effective capacity of a given resource unit. Recall from Formula 5.2 the definition of theoretical capacity of a resource pool:

$$(c_p/\text{unit load}) \times \text{Load batch} \times \text{Scheduled availability}$$

By definition, effective capacity of each resource pool—and of the process itself—is no more than its respective theoretical capacity since the *net availability* is less than the *scheduled availability* and the *total unit load* is more than the *unit load.* Thus, the effective capacity is a better (more conservative) estimate of overall process capacity.

Example 5.11

Suppose, for instance, that the Wonder Shed plant is scheduled to run 1 shift of 8 hours per day. Thus, scheduled availability of each resource pool is 8 hours per day. The available resources, with their scheduled availabilities and loss factors, are summarized in Table 5.19. The availability loss factors were estimated by observing each resource pool over a 3-week period. The net-availability column is computed by subtracting availability loss from scheduled availability. If, for example, the loss factor for worker-S is 6.25%, then that worker is available 93.75% of the scheduled time of 8 hours. Thus, the net availability of worker-S is equal to $8 \times .9375 = 7.5$ hours per day.

To compute the effective capacities, consider, for example, worker-S who has a unit load of 10 minutes per flow unit. With a load batch of 1 unit, we compute its effective capacity:

$$1/10 \text{ (batches/minute)} \times 1 \text{ (sheds/batch)} \times 7.5 \text{ (hours/day)} \times 60 \text{ (minutes/hour)}$$
$$= 45 \text{ sheds per day}$$

Likewise, the effective capacity of each resource pool at Wonder Shed can now be computed as displayed in Table 5.19. We see (1) that punch press-B and worker-PB remain the bottlenecks and (2) that effective capacity of the process is 15.2 sheds per day; the theoretical capacity of the process was 2.0 sheds per hour, or 16.0 sheds per day. The effective capacity is a more realistic approximation of the capacity of the process.

In the case of Wonder Shed, we see that incorporating loss factors into our availability computations left the bottleneck resource unchanged. In general, however, effective bottlenecks may differ from their theoretical counterparts.

TABLE 5.19 Resource Pools, Availabilities, and Effective Capacity for Standard Sheds, Wonder Shed Inc.

		Availability		
Resource Pool	Scheduled (hours/day)	Loss Factor (%)	Net (hours/day)	Effective Capacity of Resource Pool (flow units/day)
Worker-S	8.00	6.25	7.50	45.00
Punch press-R	8.00	5.00	7.60	20.73
Punch press-B	8.00	5.00	7.60	15.20
Worker-PR	8.00	5.00	7.60	20.73
Worker-PB	8.00	5.00	7.60	15.20
Forming machine-R	8.00	10.00	7.20	36.00
Forming machine-B	8.00	10.00	7.20	72.00
Worker-FR	8.00	6.25	7.50	36.00
Worker-FB	8.00	6.25	7.50	75.00
Welding gun	8.00	10.00	7.20	33.23
Worker-SA	8.00	6.25	7.50	34.62
Worker-FA	8.00	6.25	7.50	45.00
Inspector	8.00	6.25	7.50	25.00

▪▪▪ 5.5 Levers for Managing Throughput

Now let us examine some of the levers available for managing the throughput of a given process. As mentioned earlier, such levers have a powerful impact on profitability. Since a large fraction of the costs of operating a process are fixed, small changes in throughput could be translated into large changes in profits, as illustrated in Example 5.12.

Example 5.12

Consider a process with the following economics of operations. The fixed costs of owning and operating the resources amount to $90,000 per month. The contribution margin (revenue minus all variable costs) of the process is $10 per unit. In July 2002, the process throughput was 10,000 units. The profit for July was then $10,000:

$$\text{\$10 per unit} \times 10,000 \text{ units} - \$90,000 \text{ fixed costs} = \$10,000 \text{ profit}$$

A process improvement team was able to increase output in August to 11,000 units, without any increase in the fixed cost. The profit for August was then $20,000:

$$\text{\$10 per unit} \times 11,000 \text{ units} - \$90,000 \text{ fixed costs} = \$20,000 \text{ profit}$$

Thus, a 10% increase in throughput has resulted in a 100% increase in profits!

5.5.1 Comparisons

By definition, effective capacity of a process is less than its theoretical capacity. Moreover, because of various operational procedures, it is conceivable that resources would idle even during periods of their net availability. Thus, resource idleness reduces the capacity of the process even below its effective capacity. Finally, recall that throughput cannot exceed process capacity. We then have the following inequalities:

$$\text{Throughput} \leq \text{Process capacity} \leq \text{Effective capacity} \leq \text{Theoretical capacity} \quad (5.8)$$

On one hand, the inequalities between process, effective, and theoretical capacities are a result of internal inefficiencies and constraints. On the other hand, throughput may be lower than the process capacity because of external (to the process) constraints. In such cases, we say that the bottleneck is external to the process.

The separation between the effective capacity (affected by resource unavailability and time wasted by setups) and the process capacity (affected, in addition, by idleness) also allows us to see which of the two effects—resource unavailability and setup waste or resource idleness—dominates. That is, suppose we want to increase the process capacity that is observed to be less than the theoretical capacity. Where should we focus attention? If the effective capacity of a process happens to be close to its theoretical capacity, we need to look at reducing idleness. Otherwise, we need to work to increase the net availability of the bottleneck resource pools or reduce time wasted on setups. Finally, data on resource unavailability and setup waste (time lost due to machine breakdowns, preventive maintenance, time spent on changeovers, worker absenteeism, and so forth) are more readily available. The effective capacity of a process, therefore, is still relatively easy to compute, and it gives a tighter bound than the theoretical capacity on the throughput of the process.

5.5.2 Improving Theoretical Capacity

To improve theoretical capacity, we must increase the theoretical capacity of each (theoretical) bottleneck. Recall the following formula:

$$\text{Theoretical capacity of a resource unit} = (1/\text{unit load}) \times \text{Load batch} \times \text{Scheduled availability}$$

Since the theoretical capacity of the resource pool is the sum of the theoretical capacities of each resource in the pool, increasing the theoretical capacity of a resource pool requires taking at least one of the following actions:

1. Decrease unit load on the bottleneck resource pool (work faster, work smarter).
2. Increase the load batch of resources in the bottleneck resource pool (increase scale of resource).
3. Increase the number of units in the bottleneck resource pool (increase scale of process).
4. Increase scheduled availability of the bottleneck resource pool (work longer).

Decreasing Unit Load on the Bottleneck Resource Pool   In Chapter 4, we saw that the theoretical flow time is decreased by decreasing the work content of *each critical path*. Similarly, the theoretical capacity can be increased by decreasing the unit load of each *theoretical bottleneck resource pool*. We know that the unit load on a resource pool is the total work content of all activities that the resource is assigned to perform. Therefore, the principles that apply to reducing the work content of critical activities also apply to the work content of activities performed by the bottleneck resource pool, thereby increasing its theoretical capacity.

We can emphasize this symmetry with concepts in Chapter 4 even further by recalling the levers for managing the theoretical flow time described in Section 4.4—reducing the work content of critical paths by either (1) decreasing the work content of an activity on the critical path, (2) moving some of the work content off the critical path, or (3) modifying the product mix. Likewise, because the unit load on a resource pool consists of the total work content of all activities that the resource pool is assigned to perform, we can decrease the unit load on a bottleneck resource pool by taking one of the following actions:

1. Decreasing the work content of an activity performed by the bottleneck resource pool.

2. Moving some of the work content to nonbottleneck resources.

3. Modifying the product mix.

Essentially, then, these levers are similar to those we developed in Chapter 4 to decrease the theoretical flow time. The only difference is in our choice of focus on what to improve: for flow rate, we focus on activities performed by bottleneck resources, whereas in Chapter 4 we focused on activities along the critical path to reduce the flow time. In either case, we need to decrease the work content of an activity by working smarter, working faster, doing it right the first time, or changing the product mix.

Reducing the unit load of a *nonbottleneck* resource does not affect theoretical capacity. Such reduction may still be useful because it may decrease costs, flow time, and the potential for error and defects. Moving part of the unit load of bottleneck resources to nonbottleneck resources can also increase the theoretical capacity of a bottleneck resource pool. This, of course, is possible only if the nonbottleneck resources are flexible and can perform some of the activities currently performed by the bottleneck resources. If two resources are completely able to perform each others' tasks, then we can combine them into a single resource pool—a technique called resource pooling. Note, however, that flexibility of resources increases the theoretical process capacity only when this flexibility helps perform activities currently performed by bottleneck resources. Example 5.13 illustrates how flexibility of resources improves theoretical process capacity.

Example 5.13

In Table 5.14, we found that the theoretical capacity of Wonder Shed Inc. was limited to 2.0 standard sheds per hour by bottlenecks at punch press-B and worker-PB. Now suppose we make specific investments such that punch press-B and punch press-R are able to perform both the activities of punching a base and a roof. In addition, we cross-train worker-PB and worker-PR to be able to punch both bases and roofs. We rename these flexible resources punch press-RB and worker-PRB. Observe that we now have two units each of punch press-RB and worker-PRB. In Table 5.20, we summarize the computation of theoretical capacity when these flexible resources are used.

The theoretical capacity of the process increases to 2.3 standard sheds per hour. Observe that making flexible the resources currently performing the roof- and base-forming activities (forming machine-R and forming machine-B and worker-FR and worker-FB) will not impact the theoretical capacity of the process because these resources are not the bottlenecks.

TABLE 5.20 Theoretical Capacity, Standard Shed, Wonder Shed Inc., with Flexible Punch Resources

Resource	Unit Load (minutes per flow unit)	Load Batch (flow units per batch)	Theoretical Capacity of a Resource Unit (flow units per hour)	Number of Units	Theoretical Capacity of the Resource Pool (flow units per hour)
Worker-S	10	1	6.00	1	6.00
Punch press-RB	52	1	1.15	2	2.30
Worker-PRB	52	1	1.15	2	2.30
Forming machine-R	12	1	5.00	1	5.00
Forming machine-B	6	1	10.00	1	10.00
Worker-FR	12	1	5.00	1	5.00
Worker-FB	6	1	10.00	1	10.00
Welding gun	13	1	4.62	1	4.62
Worker-SA	13	1	4.62	1	4.62
Worker-FA	10	1	6.00	1	6.00
Inspector	36	1	1.67	2	3.33

The actions outlined to improve the theoretical capacity of the process have different prerequisites and consequences. Working smarter and doing it right the first time require process improvement. Working faster typically involves investments in faster resources or incentives to workers. Changing the product mix requires a tight coordination between the operations and marketing groups. Reassigning or shifting work from bottleneck to nonbottleneck resources requires greater flexibility on the part of nonbottleneck resources as well as financial investments in tooling, cross-training, and so forth. Finally, moving some (subcontracting) or all (outsourcing) work to a third party may involve swapping operating costs of lower labor and capital for higher costs of inputs (supplies).

Increasing the Load Batch of Bottleneck Resources Because resources can often process multiple units simultaneously—a phenomenon referred to as *load batching*—one simple way to increase resource capacity is to increase the load batch of the resource. For example, if we have an oven that constitutes a bottleneck because it can bake only 10 loaves at a time, we could increase its capacity by replacing it with an oven that can accommodate 15 loaves at a time.

Increasing the Number of Units of Bottleneck Resources Adding more units of the resource to the bottleneck resource pool will also increase its theoretical capacity. Because the "slowest" resource pool determines the theoretical capacity of the process, the addition of new units to the current bottleneck resource pool could create new bottleneck resource pools. If this happens, we say that *the bottleneck has shifted*. This phenomenon is illustrated in Example 5.14.

Example 5.14

In Table 5.14, for instance, we found that, limited by bottlenecks at punch press-B and worker-PB, the theoretical capacity of Wonder Shed Inc. for producing standard sheds was 2.0 units per hour. If we purchased another (identical) punch press and hired another worker to operate it, it would increase the capacities of the resources and hence the theoretical process capacity as well. At first glance, we might expect the theoretical capacity of the process to *double* because of this duplication. From the new resource capacities computed in Table 5.21, however, we see that this may not be the case. The reason is that the theoretical bottleneck has *shifted*, and our new

TABLE 5.21 Theoretical Capacity, Standard Shed, Wonder Shed Inc., with Additional Punch Resources

Resource	Unit Load (minutes per flow unit)	Theoretical Capacity of a Resource Unit (flow units per hour)	Number of Units	Theoretical Capacity of the Resource Pool (flow units per hour)
Worker-S	10	6.00	1	6.00
Punch press-R	22	2.73	1	2.73
Punch press-B	30	2.00	2	4.00
Worker-PR	22	2.73	1	2.73
Worker-PB	30	2.00	2	4.00
Forming machine-R	12	5.00	1	5.00
Forming machine-B	6	10.00	1	10.00
Worker-FR	12	5.00	1	5.00
Worker-FB	6	10.00	1	10.00
Welding gun	13	4.62	1	4.62
Worker-SA	13	4.62	1	4.62
Worker-FA	10	6.00	1	6.00
Inspector	36	1.67	2	3.33

theoretical process capacity is now constrained by the bottleneck resources of punch press-R and worker-PR to 2.73 units per hour.

Therefore, in selecting the level of financial investment in resources, we should look closely at the process capacity that we are trying to improve. As we relax bottlenecks by adding more resource units, new bottlenecks may appear, and the total process capacity may increase, but only at a decreasing rate.

Increasing Scheduled Availability of Bottleneck Resources Extending the time period during which the bottleneck resource operates (working longer) can increase its scheduled availability. If the oven is the bottleneck in our bread-making process, we could increase its daily capacity by operating it more than 8 hours a day. In both manufacturing and service operations, increasing the hours of operation and employee overtime are common methods to increase process output.

5.5.3 Other Improvements

Process capacity could also be increased by increasing the net availability of the bottleneck, by reducing the time wasted by setups, and by reducing resource idleness:

- **Increasing net availability**: The total loss due to breakdowns and maintenance can be reduced by improved maintenance policies, by scheduling preventive maintenance outside periods of availability, and by effective problem-solving measures that reduce the frequency and duration of breakdowns.
- **Reducing setup waste**: The unproductive time incurred in setups and changeovers can be reduced by decreasing the frequency of changeovers, working proactively to reduce the time required for setups (see the more detailed discussion in Chapter 10), and managing the product mix (see Section 5.4). When we decrease the frequency of changeovers, we need to produce a larger number of units of a product (batch size) before changing over to produce a different product. This increased batch size, however, may lead to higher inventories and longer flow times (we will discuss this in Chapter 6).
- **Decreasing resource idleness**: Resource idleness results from starvation, blockage, or both. These occur because of limited buffer sizes and the lack of synchronization among various flows within the process. For example, if components A and B are to be assembled into a product, unavailability of either component can result in idleness (starvation) of the resource performing the assembly. This can be minimized by allowing for larger buffers of A and B immediately before (upstream) from the assembly operation, or by synchronizing the flows of A and B. Similarly, a large buffer following (down stream from) a resource can help minimize the blockage of that resource. Proper buffer size selection is discussed in Chapter 7, and the impact of buffer size on flow rate is discussed in Chapter 8. Process flow synchronization issues are discussed in detail in Chapter 10.

5.5.4 Internal and External Bottlenecks

As we saw earlier, for every process, throughput is less than or equal to capacity:

$$\text{Throughput} \leq \text{Process capacity}$$

When this inequality is tight (when throughput equals process capacity), the output of the process is limited by the process's own constraints—its bottleneck resource. In this case, we say that the bottleneck is *internal* to the process. When the inequality holds as an *inequality* (throughput is less than process capacity), we say that the bottleneck is *external*—the process is limited by factors that lie *outside* its bounds, such as the demand for its outputs or the supply of its inputs. If the bottleneck is external, the only way to increase output is to increase the "capacity" of this external bottleneck. For instance, consider a process whose capacity to produce is larger than the demand for its products. The only way to increase the output of the process is to tackle this external bottleneck, that is, to stimulate the level of demand. This could be accomplished, for instance, by lowering prices, increasing sales efforts, or increasing the advertising budget.

5.5.5 The Improvement Spiral

As we have seen in Section 5.5.3, the only way to increase the throughput of a process is to identify its bottleneck (external or internal) and to increase its capacity. Once the capacity of the bottleneck is increased above a certain level, however, the bottleneck shifts—the original bottleneck is no longer the bottleneck but is replaced by some other resource whose capacity is now the lowest. Once this happens, it is futile to increase its capacity of the "old" bottleneck any further since it is no longer a bottleneck. The only way to increase the capacity further is to shift attention to the new bottleneck and increase its capacity. We examined this phenomenon in Example 5.12.

This observation leads to the following spiral of throughput improvement:

1. Identify the process bottleneck (internal or external).
2. Increase the capacity of this bottleneck until it is no longer a bottleneck.
3. Identify the new bottleneck and repeat step 2.

We note that the bottleneck can shift from internal to external several times as we spiral through these steps. For an extensive treatment of the throughput improvement spiral, see Goldratt (1990).

SUMMARY ▪▪▪▪▪▪▪

In Chapter 3, we introduced three measures of process performance, namely flow time, flow rate, and inventory, and discussed the relations among them (Little's law). In Chapter 4, we studied the first of these measures, namely, the flow time. In this chapter, we examined the flow rate of a process.

The throughput, or average flow rate of a stable process, is the average number of flow units that flow through the process per unit of time. Capacity is the maximum sustainable throughput of a process. The throughput is a key operational measure of performance since the process creates value via its stream of flow units, and thus the higher the throughput, the higher the value created in a given period. Capacity is also important from the perspective of flow times since insufficient process capacity may lead to excessive waiting time.

The capacity of a process depends on its resources and resource pools. The theoretical capacity of a process serves as a simple approximation for the capacity of a process and allows us to study the key drivers of capacity. The theoretical capacity can be obtained from data relating to the various resource pools. A key concept in computing the theoretical capacity is that of the bottleneck resource pool. The theoretical capacity represents an ideal aspiration level for the throughput of the process that can never be achieved in practice. Capacity utilization is a measure of how close a given process is to this ideal.

Several factors affect process capacity. These include internal inefficiencies due to equipment downtimes and absenteeism leading to unavailability of resources, waste due to setups or changeovers, and starvation or blockage due to unavailability of adequate inputs or space leading to resource idleness. Effective process capacity is a more realistic approximation for capacity that captures some of these inefficiencies. Finally, product mix decisions impact the capacity of a process and its profitability.

The throughput of a process is limited by either an internal (to the process) or an external bottleneck. When the bottleneck is internal, throughput can be increased by increasing process capacity. There are four broad ways to achieve this. First, process capacity can be increased by decreasing the level of resource idleness in the process. This can be achieved by synchronizing the flows to reduce starvation and setting appropriate buffers to reduce blockage. Second, process capacity can be increased by increasing the net availability of resources to increase effective process capacity. Net availability of resources can be increased, for example, by improving equipment maintenance policies, performing preventive maintenance outside of the scheduled availability, and instituting incentive and motivational programs to reduce employee absenteeism. Third, process capacity loss occurs because of setup waste. Reducing the setup or changeover times or reducing the frequency of setups decreases the unproductive time lost on setups, increasing throughput. Finally, process capacity can be impacted by managing theoretical capacity. Theoretical capacity can be improved by focusing on the bottleneck resource pool to decrease its unit load, increase the load batch, increase the number of units of the bottleneck resource, increase the scheduled availability, and modify the product mix.

Finally, when the bottleneck is external, throughput can be improved by increasing sales effort or improving the supply of inputs.

Key Equations and Symbols ▪▪▪▪▪▪▪

(5.1) Theoretical capacity of a resource unit = $(1/T_p) \times$ Load batch × Scheduled availability

(5.2) Theoretical capacity of resource pool, $R_p = (c_p/T_p) \times$ Load batch × Scheduled availability

(5.3) $\rho_p = R/R_p$

(5.4) Availability loss factor = $1 -$ (Net availability/ Scheduled availability)

(5.5) Total unit load = $T_p + S_p/Q_p$

(5.6) Effective capacity of a resource unit = (1/total unit load) × Load batch × Net availability

(5.7) Effective capacity of a resource pool = $(c_p/$total unit load) × Load batch × Net availability

(5.8) Throughput ≤ Process capacity ≤ Effective capacity ≤ Theoretical capacity

where

R_p = Theoretical capacity of resource pool p
T_p = Unit load at resource pool p
c_p = Number of resource units in resource pool p
ρ_p = Capacity utilization of resource pool p
R = Process throughput
S_p = Setup time at resource pool p
Q_p = Setup batch size (or lot size) at resource pool p

Key Terms ▪▪▪▪▪▪▪

- Availability loss factor
- Blockage
- Bottleneck
- Capacity utilization of a resource pool
- Changeover
- Effective bottleneck
- Effective capacity of a process
- Effective capacity of a resource unit
- Load batching

- Lot size
- Net availability of a resource
- Preventive maintenance
- Process capacity
- Resource availability loss
- Resource breakdown
- Resource idleness
- Resource pool
- Resource pooling
- Resource unit
- Scheduled availability

- Setup
- Setup batch
- Starvation
- Theoretical bottleneck
- Theoretical capacity of a process
- Theoretical capacity of a resource pool
- Theoretical capacity of a resource unit
- Unit load of a resource unit

DISCUSSION QUESTIONS ▪▪▪▪▪▪▪

5.1 While visiting your favorite restaurant, identify the major resource pools and the bottleneck and estimate the overall capacity utilization.

5.2 Explain the concepts of unit load and total unit load for an airline such as Southwest Airlines.

5.3 The theoretical capacity of a process is the reciprocal of the theoretical flow time of the process. Do you agree? Explain.

5.4 List examples of service organizations that rely mainly on setup reductions to improve their capacity and throughput.

5.5 List examples of organizations that rely on judicious product mix decisions in order to maximize their throughput and revenues.

5.6 Comment on the statement, "To maximize profitability, it is always better to give priority to produce products with the highest unit contribution margins."

5.7 Comment on the statement, "Doubling the number of units of a bottleneck resource will double the process capacity."

5.8 Comment on the statement, "Maximizing utilization of each resource pool is an exercise in futility."

EXERCISES ▪▪▪▪▪▪▪

5.1 Let us look again at the efficiency of room service at The Evanstonian introduced in Exercises 3.1 and 4.1. When a guest calls room service, the room service manager takes down the order. She then submits an order ticket to the kitchen to begin preparing the food. She also gives an order to the sommelier (i.e., the wine waiter) to fetch wine from the cellar and to prepare any other alcoholic beverages. Eighty percent of room service orders include wine or some other alcoholic beverage. Finally, she assigns the order to 1 of 6 waiters. The waiter readies a cart (i.e., putting on a table cloth, fetching silverware). The waiter is also responsible for nonalcoholic drinks.

Taking down the order and assigning work to the kitchen, sommelier, and waiter on average takes 4 minutes. It takes the kitchen 18 minutes to prepare the typical order. There is sufficient staff to process 5 room service orders simultaneously. There is a single sommelier. The sommelier takes 6 minutes to prepare an order (assuming that the order includes wine or other alcoholic beverage). It takes the waiter 10 minutes to prepare the average order. It takes the waiter on average 12 minutes to deliver the meal and return to the room-service station. At the room-service station, the waiter bills the guest's account. This takes 2 minutes.

a. What is the theoretical capacity of the process?

b. When the process operates at capacity, what is the utilization of the waiters?

5.2 Reconsider Kristen's cookie-baking enterprise from Exercise 4.2. Determine the unit load on the three resources in the process—Kristen, her roommate, and the oven. Assuming that all three resources are available 8 hours a day 100% of the time, determine the following:

a. The capacity of the cookie-making process

b. The capacity of the three resources

c. The cumulative effect of each of the following actions on the process capacity and flow rate:

1. Purchasing another oven

2. Training the roommate to perform the spooning operation

5.3 Wonder Shed Inc. (see Example 5.8) is considering a new product line, the super shed, which is projected to yield a per-unit profit contribution of $300. Unit loads for the various resources needed are estimated in Table 5.22.

a. Find the theoretical capacity of the super shed in terms of both units and profit contribution per hour.

b. Find the theoretical capacity of a product mix composed of 50% standard, 25% fancy, and 25% super sheds.

TABLE 5.22 Unit Loads, Super Shed, Wonder Shed Inc.

Resource Pool	Unit Load (Standard Shed) (minutes per unit)	Unit Load (Fancy Shed) (minutes per unit)	Unit Load (Super Shed) (minutes per unit)
Worker-S	10	10	10
Punch press-R	22	30	30
Punch press-B	30	50	50
Worker-PR	22	30	30
Worker-PB	30	50	50
Forming machine-R	12	15	15
Forming machine-B	6	10	15
Worker-FR	12	15	15
Worker-FB	6	10	15
Welding gun	13	20	20
Worker-SA	13	20	20
Worker-FA	10	15	26
Inspector	36	40	50

5.4 Reconsider the ACE production process introduced in Exercise 4.4.
   a. What is the theoretical capacity of the ACE production process?
   b. Unable to meet demand for this bike, Honda wants to increase throughput. A team member suggests cross training the engine and the seat assemblers. Should this suggestion be implemented? If so, why? If not, why not, and what do you suggest?

5.5 NewLife Finance handles two types of claims: hospital and physician. NewLife charges the HMOs $10 per hospital claim (HC) and $9 per physician claim (PC). The variable costs per claim are negligible. The theoretical capacity of the process is 375 claims per day in the case of HC and 545 claims per day for PC.
   a. Which of the two types of claims is more profitable for NewLife?
   b. Assume that the maximum number of PCs available for processing per day is 400. What is the best product mix for NewLife?

5.6 Recall from this chapter that the Tile&Style Company produces kitchen and bathroom tiles in two sizes: jumbo and regular. A bundle of tiles contains 4 jumbo tiles or 9 regular tiles and is cut out of a single, larger plate. The cutting time per bundle is 1 minute for jumbo and 2 minutes for regular. Currently, 75% of the bundles are regular, and 25% are jumbo. Typically, Tile&Style produces 300 bundles of regular tiles before it switches over and produces 100 bundles of jumbo. The switching time from one size to the other is 30 minutes in both directions. Plates are cut into tiles by a cutting machine that is available 8 hours per day. The availability loss factor is 20%.
   a. Compute the theoretical capacity of the process (bundles per hour).
   b. Compute the effective capacity of the process (bundles per hour).

5.7 Three hairstylists, François, Bernard, and Mimi, run Fast Service Hair Salon for busy professionals in the Gold Coast area of downtown Chicago (see Figure 5.1). They stay open from 6:45 a.m. to 9:00 p.m. in order to accommodate as many people's work schedules as possible.

▪▪▪▪▪▪▪▪▪▪▪▪ **FIGURE 5.1** Current Process at Fast Service Hair Salon

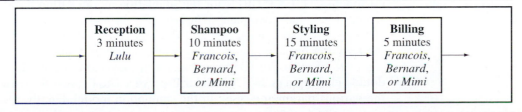

Reception	Shampoo	Styling	Billing
3 minutes	10 minutes	15 minutes	5 minutes
Lulu	Francois, Bernard, or Mimi	Francois, Bernard, or Mimi	Francois, Bernard, or Mimi

They perform only shampooing and hairstyling activities. On average, it takes 10 minutes to shampoo, 15 minutes to style the hair, and 5 minutes to bill the customer. When a customer arrives, he or she first checks in with the receptionist (Bernard's younger sister LuLu). This takes only 3 minutes. One of the three stylists then takes charge of the customer and performs all three activities—shampooing, styling, and billing—consecutively.

a. What is the number of customers that can be serviced *per hour* in this hair salon?

b. A customer of Fast Service Salon, an operations specialist, has suggested that the billing operation be transferred to LuLu. What would be the impact on the theoretical capacity?

MODELING EXERCISE ▪▪▪▪▪▪▪

www.prenhall.com/anupindi

For exercises and models using the evaluation software of iGrafx Process, insert the CD-ROM that is packaged with this book. An electronic copy of the User Guide is included on the CD. For more information on iGrafx, visit www.iGrafx.com. Detailed descriptions of the models may also be found at www.prenhall.com/anupindi.

Model

In Exercise 5.3, you were asked to estimate the theoretical capacity (in terms of units per hour as well as contribution margin per hour) of a mix of several models of sheds produced by Wonder Shed Inc. In this modeling exercise, Exercise 5.3 has been pre-built using iGrafx Process. You can use the model to evaluate the theoretical capacity of various product mixes of sheds (also known as garages in the model).

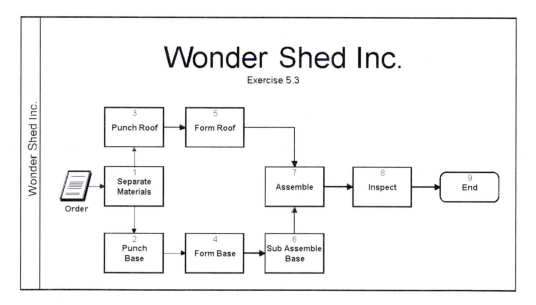

Simulation

To simulate the shed production process at Wonder Shed Inc., double-click on iGrafx document CH5EX3. This loads the simulation model within iGrafx Process. The main screen should have two panes. The left pane shows the Explorer bar with the following contents: Processes, Scenarios, and Reports. (If you do not see this, click on View and the Explorer bar from the menu item and ensure that the All Components view is chosen at the top of the Explorer bar.) You may view the model for this exercise by double-clicking on CH5EX3 under Processes. The Process Scenario tab gives details of the various parameters used in the simulation model. Finally, results of a simulation run may be viewed by double-clicking on Simulation Report under the Reports tab in the Explorer bar.

To simulate the model, from the Model menu, point to Run and choose Start. The default simulation length is set up for 31 days. A Simulation Progress window pops up at the right end of the screen. As soon as the simulation ends, the results of the simulation are displayed as a report. There are five tabs in a report. Select the Custom tab to see the customized report for this exercise.

To change the product mix, from the Model menu select Attributes. In the Define Attributes window, select S_Fancy_Percent or S_Super_Percent from the Initial Values pane to modify it.

Implementation

The process flow diagram of the simulation model is illustrated at the beginning of this section and is similar to the process flow diagram illustrated in Figure 4.4. Observe that buffers are not explicitly modeled, but they are part of the activities. The simulation is not designed to give the theoretical capacities of each resource pool but only gives the theoretical capacity of the process for a particular product mix. The model releases orders into the process only whenever the first activity, namely, "Separate Materials," is ready to process it. Thus, material is released into the process at the rate at which the first activity can process it. If the resource executing the first activity is the bottleneck, then it will determine the process capacity. If the bottleneck is somewhere downstream, that resource will determine the process capacity, and material will accumulate in front of the bottleneck. Resources for each activity are also modeled as specified in Exercise 5.3. The activity times are assumed to be deterministic. To process a product mix, the appropriate type of shed is released on the basis of specified mix percentages.

Refer to the document in the CD for detailed explanations on the modeling approach for this exercise.

Performance Interpretation

The performance of the process is illustrated in the custom report consisting of various tables. In this simulation, the garages are the same as sheds. The report already has outcomes of two simulation runs. The first run corresponds to Exercise 5.3(a) with 100% super sheds. The second run corresponds to Exercise 5.3(b) with a mix of 25% fancy, 25% super, and 50% standard. Results of new simulation runs are appended to these tables. Each table is explained here:

- **Percent of fancy and super garages**: This gives the percentage of the various types of models produced in a particular simulation.
- **Super garage capacity and profit contribution per hour**: This gives the theoretical capacity (both units per hour and profit contribution per hour) of super sheds in a particular simulation. Thus, column 5.3a corresponds to the case of 100% super sheds, and column 5.3b gives the theoretical capacity of super garages in a mix of 25% fancy, 25% super, and 50% standard.
- **Theoretical capacity**: This gives the theoretical capacity in units per hour of a given product mix.
- **Monitor statistics**: This table gives the number of units processed ("Count"), average flow time ("Avg. Cycle"), theoretical flow time ("Avg. Work"), and average waiting time ("Avg. Wait") for each of the different types of sheds processed for the *latest* simulation run.

SELECTED BIBLIOGRAPHY ▪▪▪▪▪▪▪

Eppen, G. D., F. J. Gould, C. P. Schmidt, J. H. Moore, and L. R. Weatherford. 1998. *Introductory Management Science.* 5th ed. Upper Saddle River, N.J.: Prentice Hall.

Goldratt, E. M. 1990. *Theory of Constraints.* Croton-on-Hudson, N.Y.: North River Press.

Goldratt, E. M., and J. Cox. 1992. *The Goal.* 2nd rev. ed. Barrington, Mass.: North River Press.

Winston, W. L. 1991. *Operations Research: Applications and Algorithms.* 2nd ed. Boston: PWS-Kent Publishing.

Appendix: Optimizing Product Mix with Linear Programming

Determining the optimal product mix can be stated as a problem of allocating resources to products in order to maximize profits. Suppose that a firm can produce two products, labeled 1 and 2, using three resources, labeled $E, F,$ and G. We need information regarding the contribution margin and market demand of each product, the scheduled availability of each resource pool, and the unit load imposed by each product on each resource pool. We could also determine the optimal product mix using net availability instead of the scheduled availability; we illustrate the approach using scheduled availability.

Let m_1 and m_2 represent the contribution margins of products 1 and 2, and D_1 and D_2 their respective market demand. Let the scheduled availability of resource pools $E, F,$ and G be denoted by $b_E, b_F,$ and b_G, respectively.

Let the unit load of product 1 on resource pools $E, F,$ and G be denoted by $a_{E1}, a_{F1},$ and a_{G1}, respectively. Similarly, let $a_{E2}, a_{F2},$ and a_{G2} denote the unit load of product 2 on resource pools $E, F,$ and G, respectively.

Given these data, we need to compute the quantity of products 1 and 2, denoted by x_1 and x_2, to be produced that will maximize profits while ensuring that we use the resources only during their scheduled availability (known as *resource constraints*) and that we do not produce more than is demanded (known as *demand constraints*).

The total contribution generated by producing x_1 units of product 1 and x_2 units of product 2 is given by

$$m_1 x_1 + m_2 x_2$$

Resource constraints entail that the total time required to produce the products on each resource pool is less than the scheduled availability of that resource pool.

The total unit load of resource pool E for producing x_1 and x_2 units of products 1 and 2 is given by

$$a_{E1} x_1 + a_{E2} x_2$$

which cannot exceed its scheduled availability, b_E. Similar constraints need to be enforced for resources F and G.

Demand constraints entail that the total production of a product is less than its market demand. That is, for each product 1,

$$x_1 \leq D_1$$

An analogous demand constraint applies for product 2. Therefore, the problem of determining the optimal product mix can be stated as the problem of finding appropriate values of x_1 and x_2 that maximize

$$m_1 x_1 + m_2 x_2$$

subject to

$$a_{E1} x_1 + a_{E2} x_2 \leq b_E$$
$$a_{F1} x_1 + a_{F2} x_2 \leq b_F$$
$$a_{G1} x_1 + a_{G2} x_2 \leq b_G$$
$$x_1 \leq D_1$$
$$x_2 \leq D_2$$

The first set of three constraints represents the resource constraints, and the next set of two constraints represents the demand constraints. The theoretical capacity of the process for a *given* mix of products is represented by a point on the boundary of the region defined by the three resource constraints. At the optimal product mix, the theoretical bottleneck resource pools are identified by the resource constraints of those resource pools that are satisfied with equality. If, however, one or more of the demand constraints are satisfied with equality, we say that the corresponding market demand is a bottleneck. The formal optimization technique of *linear programming* can be used for solving these generic optimal product mix problems. Such techniques are detailed in many operations research and management science textbooks such as those listed at the end of this chapter.

CHAPTER 6

Inventory Analysis

Introduction

The health care industry faces enormous pressures to improve quality of care and access to care in an environment of declining reimbursements and increasing costs. Surveys reveal that a typical hospital spends between 15% and 25% of its budget on medical, surgical, and pharmaceutical supplies. In U.S. hospitals, this represents between $113 billion and $188 billion annually. The procurement process has traditionally relied on phone and fax orders with the cost of cutting a purchase order often higher than the product being purchased. Different areas within a hospital appear to order their own supplies. This has led to bloated and costly inventory. There appears to be a tremendous opportunity to streamline the supply chain and improve procurement practices to reduce inventory.

In the past few years, several hospitals have begun to look at their materials management systems to improve efficiency. Phoebe Putney Health System in Georgia is expecting to save $3 million over five years. The Memorial Sloan Kettering Institute is using the Internet to control procurement costs. Centura Health, a nine-hospital integrated delivery

TABLE 6.1 Benchmarking Inventory Turns

Industry	Upper Quartile	Median	Lower Quartile
Dairy products	34.4	19.3	9.2
Electronic components	9.8	5.7	3.7
Computers	9.4	5.3	3.5
Book publishing	9.8	2.4	1.3
Consumer electronics	6.2	3.4	2.3
Appliances	8.0	5.0	3.8
Industrial chemical	10.3	6.6	4.4

network in Denver, is using e-commerce to trim and improve on its $100 million annually spent on supplies. Several of these initiatives require substantial investments in information technology and warehousing. Before making such investments, a hospital's materials management staff needs to understand the key drivers of inventory.

Health care is not the only industry plagued by inventory. While inventory is ubiquitous across all industries, the ability of companies to manage them varies dramatically within and across industry sectors. Inventory turnover, introduced in Chapter 3, is one measure of a firm's inventory management capability, with higher values indicating superior capability. Table 6.1 gives a comparison of inventory turns across some industry sectors in the United States.

Developing better inventory management capability can significantly affect the bottom line. Consider, for example, the retail book industry. Borders Group, Barnes & Noble, and Amazon are the three largest booksellers in the United States. In 2002, the Borders Group with annual sales of $3,513 million and gross margins of 30.03%, carried about 174 days of inventory in its network. In contrast, Barnes & Noble carried about 128 days of inventory in 2002. If the Borders Group could improve its inventory management capability to match the 128 days of inventory of Barnes & Noble, it would reduce its working capital requirement by approximately $310 million.

From a macroeconomic perspective, inventory-related costs accounted for approximately 2.5% of the gross domestic product of the United States in 2002. According to the U.S. Department of Commerce, which tracks the monthly sales and inventory for the U.S. economy, in 2002 the average monthly inventory in the U.S. economy was about $1.13 trillion on annual sales of $9.66 trillion. Of this, the inventory at the manufacturer, wholesaler, and retailer levels was $430 billion, $230 billion, and $411 billion, respectively, which shows that there is enormous opportunity to make significant impact by better inventory management.

What are the various reasons for carrying inventory? What is the impact of procurement transaction costs on inventory? What is the value of aggregating purchases across multiple entities? What are the right metrics? How does better inventory management affect the bottom line?

In this chapter and the next, we provide a framework to answer these questions. We begin with an analysis of different types of inventories, reasons for carrying them, and the associated costs. Then we analyze the key trade-offs in managing inventory under an economies-of-scale effect. In Chapter 7, we discuss the protective role of inventories against unforeseen changes in demand or supply.

We begin in Section 6.1 with a broad classification of inventory depending on its location in the process and introduce the concept of theoretical inventory. In Sections 6.2 and 6.3, we identify the reasons for carrying inventories and the various costs of holding inventories. Section 6.4 derives the inventory dynamics under batch purchasing and processing. Section 6.5 examines the optimal inventory level that balances costs and benefits. Section 6.6 studies the effect of lead times on ordering decisions. Section 6.7 discusses the effect of price promotions on inventory accumulation. Finally, in Section 6.8, we conclude the chapter by summarizing some key levers for managing various types of inventory.

▮▮▮6.1 Inventory Classification

In addition to flow time and flow rate (throughput), which we studied in Chapters 4 and 5, inventory is the third basic measure of process performance. As we did with the other two measures, we first identify the boundaries of the process under study. Then we define inventory as the number of flow units present within those boundaries. Because average inventory is related by Little's law to both average flow time and average flow rate, controlling inventory indirectly controls flow rate, flow time, or both. Inventory also directly affects cost—another important measure of process performance. Because it affects several dimensions of process performance, inventory is a key lever in managing business process flows.

Inventory includes all flow units within the process boundaries. Depending on the inventory's location or stage in the process, we can classify units of inventory as belonging to one of three categories:

1. *Flow units that are waiting to begin processing constitute* **inputs inventory**.
2. *Flow units that are being processed constitute* **in-process inventory**.
3. *Processed flow units that have not yet exited process boundaries accumulate in* **outputs inventory**.

Figure 6.1 shows the process flow and the three stages of inventory accumulation.

In-process inventory can further be classified as work-in-process or in-transit inventory. **Work-in-process inventory** *are the flow units being processed in a manufacturing or service operation.* **In-transit inventory** *or* **pipeline inventory** *refers to the flow units being transported.*

In a manufacturing process, inputs inventory consists of raw materials or components, in-process inventory includes all work being processed, and outputs inventory contains finished goods. The classification of inventory, however, will also depend on where the process boundaries are drawn. Outputs inventory for one process can be inputs inventory for the other, as illustrated in Figure 6.2.

In a service process, a flow unit is typically a customer. Inputs inventory here refers to customers waiting for service, and in-process inventory refers to customers being

▮▮▮▮▮▮▮▮▮▮▮ **FIGURE 6.1 Process Flows and Inventories**

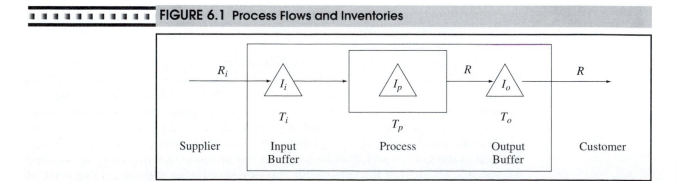

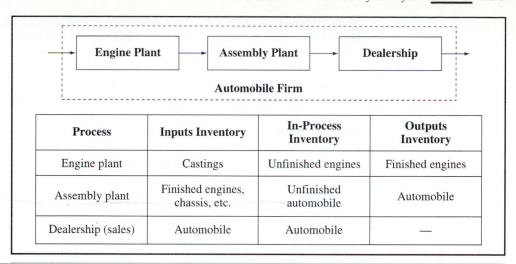

FIGURE 6.2 Inventory Classifications for an Automobile Firm

served. If served customers leave the process immediately, there is no outputs inventory. We will postpone the analysis of the special problems of managing inventory of customers in service processes to Chapter 8.

We begin by establishing the following notation:

$$\text{Average input inventory} = I_i$$
$$\text{Average in-process inventory} = I_p$$
$$\text{Average output inventory} = I_o$$

Thus, average total inventory, I, within process boundaries can be expressed as

$$I = I_i + I_p + I_o$$

A flow unit moving through the process will then spend some time in each of three classes of inventory. Average values of these waiting times are denoted as follows:

$$\text{Average time spent in input inventory} = T_i$$
$$\text{Average time spent in in-process inventory} = T_p$$
$$\text{Average time spent in output inventory} = T_o$$

Total average flow time, therefore, can be expressed as

$$T = T_i + T_p + T_o$$

If we denote average process flow rate in equilibrium as R, then flow units enter and leave each stage at this rate R. As we have seen in Chapter 3, Little's law applies to the aggregate values, giving the relationship $I = R \times T$. Little's law can also be applied to each of the stages to establish the relationship between the flow rate in equilibrium and the corresponding average inventory and average time at that stage.

Theoretical Inventory   Although Little's law determines average inventory, an imbalance between inflows and outflows that develops over time will cause actual inventory to fluctuate around this average. In Chapter 3, we discussed in detail the inventory dynamics and also introduced the concept of the inventory buildup diagram. Briefly, inventory accumulates at any stage in a process whenever inflow into that stage exceeds the outflow from that stage. Similarly, inventory depletes at any stage whenever the outflow from a stage exceeds the inflow into that stage.

However, even in an ideal situation with perfectly balanced flows—one in which inflow, processing, and outflow rates are all equal at every point in time—we still encounter work-in-process inventory. Recall from Chapter 4 the concept of theoretical flow time, which represents the minimal flow time in a process. Even if no flow unit ever waits in a buffer, it remains within the process boundaries as work in process until it exits the process. Therefore, if a process needs to produce some output, there will always be some inventory within its boundaries. To remain consistent with the concepts of theoretical flow time and theoretical capacity that we discussed earlier, we introduce the concept of *theoretical inventory* and denote it by I_{th}. Much like theoretical flow time, **theoretical inventory** is *the minimum amount of inventory necessary to maintain a process throughput* of R and can be expressed as

$$\text{Theoretical inventory} = \text{Throughput} \times \text{Theoretical flow time}$$

$$I_{th} = R \times T_{th} \tag{6.1}$$

Theoretical inventory is the average inventory for a given throughput if no flow unit ever had to wait in any buffer. It represents the minimal amount of flow units undergoing activities (without waiting) to sustain a given flow rate. Like theoretical flow time, theoretical inventory gives us an optimal target to aim for.

In reality, of course, flow units may wait in buffers before being processed at any stage, leading to a flow time (T_p) longer than the theoretical flow time (T_{th}). Consequently, in-process inventory will often be larger than the theoretical inventory. Indeed, it follows from Little's law and our definition of theoretical flow time that the in-process inventory is at least as large as the theoretical inventory, or

$$I_p = R \times T_p \geq R \times T_{th} = I_{th}$$

In-process inventory will be exactly equal to theoretical inventory whenever the process flow time equals the theoretical flow time. This occurs, for example, in a process consisting of a single activity.

Decoupling Processes   Input and output inventories form buffers that decouple the process from its environment, thereby permitting relatively independent operation. Input inventory permits the process manager to manage processing rates independently of material inflow (supply) rates; output inventory permits managing the processing rate independently of product outflow (demand) rate.

Input and output inventories may be viewed and analyzed in the same way—each has its supplier and customer, and each serves as a buffer between the two. If inflow (supply) into the buffer exceeds outflow (demand) from the buffer, the excess is added to the buffer; if outflow exceeds inflow, the buffer shrinks. If the buffer is emptied, the next stage in the process is "starved" of work. Such starvation, which we mentioned briefly in Chapter 5, typically deteriorates process performance. For example, starvation in outputs inventory results in stockouts and customer dissatisfaction, and starvation in in-process or inputs inventory results in lost production. Starvation occurs because of unpredictable events that affect the inflow to or outflow from the buffer. Management of buffer inventories to prevent starvation will be discussed in detail in Chapter 7. In general, several factors may affect the buildup and build-down of inventory in buffers, giving rise to various reasons for holding inventories, which we discuss next.

IIII 6.2   Inventory Benefits

Why do firms carry inventory? As we already observed, a minimum level of in-process inventory, called theoretical inventory, is necessary to maintain a given process throughput. Reducing inventories to less than the theoretical inventory will result in a loss of throughput. In transportation and logistics, flow units are transported from one location to another. As we mentioned, the units that are being transported (that are en route) at a given point in time constitute in-transit or pipeline inventory. Pipeline inventory is necessary to allow the functioning of a business process whose activities are distributed over many locations. In practice, however, firms plan and maintain far in excess of the theoretical and pipeline inventory. Therefore, the question is: Why do firms intentionally plan for such excesses? We now survey four possible answers to this question.

6.2.1   Economies of Scale

We say that a process exhibits **economies of scale** when *the average unit cost of output decreases with volume.* Economies of scale may arise from either external or internal causes in areas such as procurement, production, or transportation. One reason firms intentionally plan for such excess inventory is to take advantage of economies of scale, making it attractive to procure, produce, or transport in quantities more than immediately needed. If, for example, an external supplier offers price discounts, the buyer may find it economical to procure in quantities larger than those needed for immediate processing. Internally, perhaps the buyer finds it more economical to procure or process in large quantities because of a fixed cost that is incurred each time the activity is undertaken. For example, procuring inputs often involves a **fixed order cost**—*the administrative cost of processing the order, transporting the material, and receiving and inspecting the delivery.* Each of these costs may add a significant fraction to total cost that is *independent of order size.* For example, if a truck is dispatched each time an order must be picked up, a large fraction of the cost of the trip will not depend on the quantity ordered (up to the size limit of the truck). In producing outputs, the process of starting production runs may involve a **fixed setup cost**—*the time and materials required to set up a process* (e.g., clean equipment and change tools). An ice cream maker, for instance, must clean pots before changing from chocolate to vanilla. The time taken for changeovers is unavailable for production, thus decreasing throughput. Hence, the manager may decide to produce large quantities of an ice cream flavor before switching over to produce another flavor. Chapter 5 highlighted the impact of fixed setup times on flow rate and flow time. In this chapter, we will study its impact on inventory.

We often refer to *the order or production in response to the economies of scale effect as a* **batch**. Sometimes, more specific names are associated with it, depending on the type of activity being performed, such as a **production batch** *(or lot) in the case of production,* a **transfer batch** *for transportation or movement,* and **procurement batch** (or *order*). The number of units constituting a batch is called a *batch size,* also referred to as *lot size.* Faced with an economies-of-scale effect, a manager finds it more economical to procure (or produce) infrequently in large batches, thereby spreading the fixed cost over more units. Such practice of intermittent procurement or production leads to periodic buildup and build-down of inventory, as we will see in the next section. *The average inventory arising due to a batch activity is referred to as* **cycle inventory**.

6.2.2 Production and Capacity Smoothing

A related reason for planning inflows in excess of outflows is production and capacity smoothing. When demand fluctuates seasonally, it may be more economical to *maintain a constant processing rate* and build inventories in periods of low demand and deplete them when demand is high. This is often referred to as a **level-production strategy**. Examples of leveling include building toy inventories throughout the year for sales during the Christmas season or producing lawn mowers year-round for spring and summer sale. Demand fluctuations are then absorbed by inventories rather than by intermittent and expensive adjustments in processing capacity. Likewise, there could be seasonality in supply. For example, agricultural products are the key inputs to the food processing industry. The flow of agricultural inputs into a processing center will exhibit seasonality that is dependent on the timing of harvests. To maintain a level production, then, input inventories are allowed to accumulate and are then gradually depleted over time. *Inventories that serve as buffers to absorb seasonal fluctuations of supply and demand are called* **seasonal inventories**. Although the costs of holding of inventory increase, a level production strategy minimizes the cost of capacity changes.

An alternate strategy to deal with demand fluctuations is called **chase demand strategy**, *whereby a firm produces quantities exactly to match demand.* By matching demand and production, the firm, of course, carries no inventory. Unfortunately, it also transfers all demand fluctuations to its processing system. In particular, matching demand patterns would require constantly altering process capacity or its utilization with associated costs.

Which is the better strategy—level production or chase demand? The answer depends on the relative magnitudes of the fixed costs of altering capacity and the variable costs of holding inventory. It is better to level production if capacity changes are expensive and to chase demand if inventories are expensive to carry. Not surprisingly, the true optimum lies somewhere between these two extremes, employing a combination of capacity adjustments and inventory buffers. The problem of finding this optimal combination is called **aggregate production planning**. A detailed discussion of this topic is beyond the scope of this book, and we refer the reader to Chopra and Miendl (2002) or Nahmias (2000).

6.2.3 Stockout Protection

The third reason for holding inventories is to protect against stockouts due to unexpected supply disruptions or surges in demand. Any number of events—supplier strikes, fire, transportation delays, and foul weather—may reduce input availability. Potential consequences to the buyer include process starvation, downtime, and temporary reduction in throughput. Many producers, therefore, maintain inventories of inputs to insulate the process and continue operation despite supply shortages.

Likewise, because customer-demand forecasts are usually inaccurate, planning process output to meet only forecasted demand may result in stockouts, delayed deliveries, lost sales, and customer dissatisfaction. Thus, many producers maintain cushions of excess inventory to absorb excess demand and ensure product availability and customer service despite forecast errors. *Inventories maintained to insulate the process from unexpected supply disruptions or surges in demand are called* **safety inventories** or **safety stock**. In Chapter 7, we will discuss the degree of stockout protection provided by a given level of safety inventory and the level of safety inventory needed to provide a desired level of protection.

6.2.4   Price Speculation

The fourth reason for holding inventories is to profit from probable changes in the market prices of inputs or outputs. In addition to protecting against sudden price changes due to such crises as wars or oil shortages, speculative inventories of commodities (such as corn, wheat, gold, and silver) and financial assets (such as stocks, bonds, and currencies) can be held as investments. As prices fluctuate over time, investors can manage their inflows (purchases) and outflows (sales) to optimize the financial value of their inventories. In the semiconductor industry, for instance, a rapid price decline of chips over time gives computer manufacturers a very strong incentive to delay purchasing chips as inputs; rather, they can wait to enjoy the latest, and often lowest, purchase price. The process manager then holds some **speculative inventory**. Although speculative inventories are important in finance and economics, we will not study them in any detail in this book, as our focus is more on processing operations.

To illustrate the remaining concepts in this chapter, we will use the example of procurement decisions in a hospital network described in Example 6.1.

Example 6.1

Centura Health[1] is a nine-hospital integrated delivery network based in the Denver area in the United States. Presently each hospital orders its own supplies and manages the inventory. A common item used is a sterile Intravenous (IV) Starter Kit. The weekly demand for the IV Starter Kit is 600 units. The unit cost of an IV Starter Kit is $3. Centura has estimated that the physical holding cost (operating and storage costs) of one unit of medical supply is about 5% per year. In addition, the hospital network's annual cost of capital is 25%. Each hospital incurs a fixed order cost of $130 whenever it places an order, regardless of the order size. The supplier takes one week to deliver the order. Presently, each hospital places an order of 6,000 units of the IV Starter Kit whenever it orders. Centura has recently been concerned about the level of inventories held in each of the hospitals and is exploring strategies to reduce them. The director of materials management has been exploring the following options:

1. Increasing the frequency of ordering by reducing the current order size
2. Centralizing the order process across all nine hospitals and perhaps serving all the hospitals from a single warehouse

6.3   Inventory Costs

Carrying inventory is expensive both in operational and in financial terms. Assume that a firm is carrying a large inventory of work in process and outputs. If market demand shifts to new products, the firm is left with two choices. One is to empty the process by scrapping all current work in process and liquidating the obsolete outputs inventory at marked-down prices and then quickly introducing the new product. This option results in a significant loss on the old inventory. The other choice is to finish processing all in-process inventory and sell all output before introducing the new product. This option causes delay, which creates a reduced responsiveness to the market.

Large inventories also delay execution of design changes because current inventory must be processed and sold first. Moreover, the buildup of inventories between successive processing stages has other operational consequences. For example, it obstructs workers' view of the total process. It also decouples the operation of consecutive stages of processing such that each stage works independently of the other. Such decoupling, however, may discourage teamwork and coordination across a process. We will discuss these operational inefficiencies from holding inventories further in Chapter 10.

---

[1]All numbers are fictitious and are used only to illustrate the concepts.

Inventory Holding Cost   Carrying inventory entails a financial cost called **inventory holding cost**, *which has two components—the physical holding cost and the opportunity cost of capital tied up in inventory:*

1. **Physical holding cost** refers to *the cost of storing inventory.* It includes all operating costs (insurance, security, warehouse rental, lighting, and heating/cooling of the storage) plus all the costs that may be entailed before inventory can be sold (spoilage, obsolescence, pilferage, or necessary rework). Physical holding cost per unit of time (typically a year) is usually expressed as a fraction h of the variable cost C of acquiring (or producing) one flow unit of inventory. Thus, the physical holding cost of carrying a unit of inventory for one time unit is hC.

2. **Opportunity cost** *of holding inventory refers to the forgone return on the funds invested in inventory which could have been invested in alternate projects.* Indeed, inventory shows up as an asset on the balance sheet because it is an economic resource that is expected to be of future value. The firm could realize this value by liquidating it and investing the proceeds elsewhere. Or, even more to the point, the sooner inventory sells, the sooner it creates accounts receivable— and the sooner accounts receivable generates cash. The opportunity cost of holding one flow unit is usually expressed as rC, where r is the firm's rate of return (measured as annual percentage return on capital) and C is the variable cost of acquiring (or producing) one flow unit of inventory (measured as cost/ flow unit).

Together, the physical and opportunity costs of inventory give the total unit inventory holding cost per unit time, denoted by H, which is expressed as follows:

$$\text{Total unit inventory holding cost} = \text{Unit physical holding cost}$$
$$+ \text{ Unit opportunity cost of capital}$$

$$H = (h + r)C \tag{6.2}$$

For example, if the unit time period is a year, H represents the total cost of keeping one unit in inventory for one year. Example 6.2 illustrates the computation of H for Centura Health introduced in Example 6.1.

Example 6.2

Consider Centura Health introduced in Example 6.1. Recall the unit cost of the IV Starter Kit, $C = \$3$. Furthermore, the annual physical holding of 5% implies

$$hC = \$(0.05)(3) = \$0.15/\text{year}$$

Centura's annual cost of capital is $r = 25\%$. Thus, a dollar of inventory carries an opportunity cost of $\$0.25$ per year in terms of possible alternate uses of the funds. Since $\$3$ is tied up in each unit of the IV Starter Kit, the opportunity cost of keeping one unit in inventory for a year is

$$rC = \$(0.25)(3) = \$0.75/\text{year}$$

Hence, the total annual holding cost of a unit of IV Starter Kit is

$$H = (h + r)C = \$0.15 + \$0.75 = \$0.90$$

While H represents the unit inventory holding cost per unit time, the total inventory holding cost per unit time will be $H \times I$, where the average inventory level is I. Therefore, to decrease the holding cost of inventory, we have two levers:

1. Decrease unit inventory holding cost H (typically by getting concessions on h or C).
2. Decrease average inventory level I.

▪▪▪ 6.4   Inventory Dynamics of Batch Purchasing

In the rest of this chapter, we focus on the effect of economies of scale, discussed in Section 6.2.1, leading to what we call cycle inventory. We start with developing the inventory profile resulting from batch purchasing. We will rely on the basic methodology outlined in Chapter 3 to study the dynamics of flow rate and inventory. Subsequently, we will present a framework for decision making under economies of scale. While we focus our discussion on purchasing, the concepts apply equally well to other batch activities.

We illustrate these concepts as a means of answering two important managerial questions that arise at a hospital in Centura Health, introduced in Example 6.2, during the process of purchasing IV Starter Kits (inputs). Recall that Centura buys a batch of IV Starter Kits at a time even though the consumption of these kits has been quite steady for the past several months. The hospital materials manager at a Centura hospital must decide (1) *how much* to purchase at a time, and (2) *when* to purchase a new batch of IV Starter Kits. Both decisions will affect the hospital's balance sheet as they impact costs.

To answer these questions, we analyze the inventory dynamics of the process view of a Centura hospital (represented graphically in Figure 6.3). We must consider the following procedures that are valid in this purchasing scenario.

1. Inputs are procured in multiple units at a time—a system called batch purchasing.
2. Processing takes place continuously at a constant rate.

As an answer to the first question, *how much to purchase at a time,* we will assume that the manager buys the IV Starter Kit in batches of Q units at a time and analyze the financial consequences of such a decision. In the next section, we will determine the optimal quantity to purchase. The entry point into the process is the point at which a batch of Q units is delivered to a Centura hospital and added to its inputs inventory. Assume that Centura faces a steady consumption rate of R. Once a request for a Starter Kit comes in, it is fulfilled by pulling out the required number of kits from the local storage area and delivering to the point of use. This "order fulfillment process" maintains (approximately) constant in-process inventory I_p. Because the exit point is the point at which units ready to be consumed leave the process immediately, Centura has no outputs inventory, and $I_o = 0$ always. Therefore,

$$\text{Total average inventory} = \text{Average inputs inventory}$$
$$+ \text{Average in-process inventory}$$
$$I = I_i + I_p$$

▪▪▪▪▪▪▪▪▪▪▪ **FIGURE 6.3** The Purchase Order Fulfillment Process at Centura Health

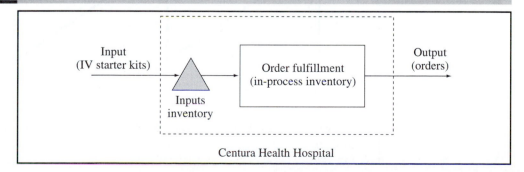

Centura Health Hospital

Finally, assume that initial input inventory, just before the first IV Starter Kit delivery arrives at time $t = 0$, is zero.

As inputs inventory will vary over time, we will denote its level at any time t with $I_i(t)$. Thus, just after the first batch is received at time 0, we have inputs inventory, $I_i(0) = Q$. Total process inventory level is the sum of input inventory and in-process inventory given by $Q + I_p$. After the first delivery, inflow rate remains at zero until the next shipment is received. Outflow rate due to consumption, meanwhile, remains constant at R. After the first delivery, therefore, the process inventory buffer is depleted at a rate R, so that change in flow rate, denoted by ΔR, is negative R, or $\Delta R = -R$. To sustain its throughput R, order fulfillment keeps in-process inventory level I_p constant. Consequently, only input inventory is depleted at rate R, whereby it will reach zero after, say, time t_z, so that $I_i(t_z) = 0$. Thus, we have

Input inventory at time t_z = Input inventory at time 0 – Total demand during time t_z
$$I_i(t_z) = Q - R \times t_z = 0$$

so that

$$t_z = Q/R$$

Simply stated, it takes Q/R time units to deplete input stock of size Q at rate R. If the process manager always orders in batches of size Q, the same cycle repeats itself every t_z time units. Over time, the resulting inventory buildup diagram displays the sawtooth pattern shown in Figure 6.4. It answers our second question, *when to order a new batch of IV Starter Kits:* a Centura hospital should order another batch of IV Starter Kits to arrive whenever the total inventory drops to I_p (and thus the input buffer is empty). As a result, Centura should place orders so that a batch arrives every t_z time units.

Under batch purchasing and a constant depletion rate, therefore, the input inventory profile is triangular with height Q. In a typical order cycle, average input inventory is one half the batch (or order) size or

$$I_i = Q/2$$

▪▪▪▪▪▪▪▪▪▪▪▪ **FIGURE 6.4** Inventory Profile with Batch Size Q

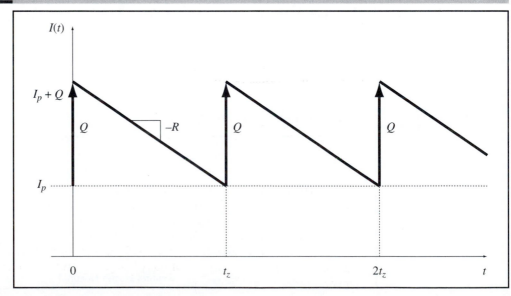

Average total inventory is then given by the sum of average inputs inventory and average in-process inventory

$$I = Q/2 + I_p$$

In terms of flow time, the first flow unit purchased in each batch goes into order fulfillment immediately, while the last unit spends all the $t_z = Q/R$ time units in input inventory buffer storage before its processing can begin. Thus, an average flow unit spends $t_z/2 = (Q/2)/R$ time units in input inventory storage. Alternately, we can apply Little's law to determine the average flow time spent in the input buffer as

$$T_i = (Q/2)/R$$

Similarly, Little's law applied to in-process inventory yields

$$T_p = I_p/R$$

Finally, the average total flow time in the purchase order fulfillment process is the sum of the average flow time in inputs buffer and the average in-process flow time and is

$$T = T_i + T_p = (Q/2)/R + I_p/R$$

Each flow unit, therefore, spends an average time of $Q/2R$ in the input buffer and additional time of I_p/R units in process.

To summarize, the cyclical pattern of inventory buildup and build-down with a batch size of Q gives us an average input inventory of $Q/2$. While we focused our discussion on inputs inventory, batching could lead to similar patterns in in-process or outputs inventory buffers. Thus, the average inventory of $Q/2$ is driven primarily by batching and is not particular to inputs, in-process, or output buffers. We label the average inventory arising due to batch size of Q as **cycle inventory** and denote it by

$$I_{cycle} = Q/2 \tag{6.3}$$

Example 6.3 illustrates the situation at Centura Health.

Example 6.3
Recall that one of the hospitals of Centura Health processes a demand of 600 units of the IV Starter Kit each week and places an order of 6,000 kits at a time. The hospital must then be ordering once every 10 weeks. Accordingly, average IV Starter Kit inventory will be $I_{cycle} = 6,000/2 = 3,000$ units, and a typical IV Starter Kit spends an average of five weeks in storage. Thus, the Centura hospital carries an average cycle inventory of 3,000 IV Starter Kits.

Whenever there are economies of scale, it is cost effective to order (or produce) in batches. Although our focus has been on a purchasing process with flow units of products, it equally applies to other processes and types of flow units, as illustrated in the following examples:

- Joe Smith goes to withdraw cash from an automated teller machine (ATM). Since he has to drive two miles to get to the closest ATM for his bank, he prefers to withdraw sufficient cash to meet his entire week's cash expenses. This practice of periodic withdrawal leaves a cycle inventory of cash in Joe's wallet.
- Office Assistants trains people for secretarial and office administrative tasks for placement with its clients. A team of experts conducts the program. The compensation paid to this team is usually independent of the size of the class. Hence, it is considered a fixed cost. Office Assistants decides to restrict the class size to 45 people who are absorbed in the workforce in about three months. The average inventory of the pool of trained but unemployed people constitutes cycle inventory.

- Big Blue runs a campus shuttle service at the University of Michigan. There are fixed costs of running a bus along a specific route. Therefore, the university finds it economical to traverse the route with a limited frequency. The number of people who arrive between two consecutive trips becomes the batch size. The average number of people waiting to board a bus is cycle inventory.
- The City of Pittsburgh collects trash from its residents' homes once every week. Meanwhile, trash accumulates in the garbage cans every day until it gets picked up on Monday. The average inventory of trash in the household constitutes that household's cycle inventory.

Like the purchasing process, the first two examples illustrate a situation where there is an instantaneous buildup of inventory followed by a gradual depletion of it. The next two examples, unlike the purchasing process, involve a situation with a gradual buildup of inventory followed by an instantaneous build-down. The resulting inventory profile will be different than that of Figure 6.4. Both situations, nevertheless, lead to cycle inventory because of the periodic nature of the respective activities.

▮▮▮ 6.5 Economies of Scale and Optimal Cycle Inventory

Process managers would like to determine inventory levels that optimally balance costs and benefits of carrying various inventories. In the remainder of this chapter, we will show how to determine the optimal level of cycle inventory that balances the costs of holding inventory with the benefits of economies of scale. In doing so, we will distinguish two causes of scale economies:

1. Economies arising from a *fixed-cost component of costs* in either procurement (e.g., order cost), production (e.g., setup cost), or transportation
2. Economies arising from *price discounts* offered by suppliers

In this section, we will concentrate on the former and postpone analysis of price discounts to Section 6.7.

Fixed Cost of Procurement: Economic Order Quantity   As mentioned earlier, our analysis applies equally to input and output buffers. Indeed, in batch procurement or purchasing, we analyze input buffers, while in batch processing we analyze in-process and output buffers. Suppose outflow from the buffer occurs at a constant rate of R flow units per unit of time (e.g., per year). Assume that the process manager can control inflow into the buffer. Each time the inflow is initiated by the procurement of material, a fixed cost of ordering, S, is incurred regardless of the quantity procured. It is therefore more economical to procure inputs infrequently in batches, even though outflow requirements remain steady over time. Let Q be the size of each order (batch) procured at a single time. The annual order frequency, which represents the number of times we need to order to satisfy an annual outflow rate of R, is

$$\text{Annual order frequency} = \text{Annual outflow rate/Order size}$$
$$= R/Q$$

Since each order incurs a fixed cost S, the total annual fixed order cost is

$$\text{Fixed cost per order} \times \text{Annual order frequency}$$

or

$$S \times R/Q$$

Observe that this annual order cost decreases as the order size Q increases because the more we order at a given time, the fewer orders we need to place over the course of a year.

Conversely, recall from Section 6.4 that average cycle inventory is $I_{cycle} = Q/2$ units. Consequently, total annual inventory holding cost is expressed as

$$\text{Unit holding cost per year} \times \text{Average inventory}$$

or

$$H \times I_{cycle} = H \times (Q/2)$$

Note that this cost increases when order size Q increases. *purchasing cost*

Finally, we must also consider total annual cost of materials procured, which is given by

$$\text{Unit cost} \times \text{Outflow rate}$$

or

$$C \times R$$

Observe that the annual cost of materials is independent of the choice of order size Q. We assume the unit variable cost to be constant; that is, we get no price discounts for purchasing in large quantities. We discuss price discounts in Section 6.7.

Thus, the total annual cost, denoted by *TC*, is given by the sum of the total annual fixed order cost, total annual inventory cost, and total annual cost of materials as follows:

$$TC = S \times \frac{R}{Q} + H \times \frac{Q}{2} + C \times R \qquad (6.4)$$

Example 6.4 illustrates the cost structure of the current operating policy at a Centura Health hospital.

Example 6.4

Recall that a Centura Health hospital incurs a cost of $130 regardless of the quantity purchased each time it places an order for and receives IV Starter Kits. Hence, fixed cost per order $S = \$130$. From Example 6.1, we also know that unit cost $C = \$3$, and the weekly outflow rate of 600 translates to an annual outflow of $R = 31,200$ per year, assuming 52 weeks per year.

In Example 6.2, we computed Centura's inventory holding cost as $H = \$0.90$ per unit per year. Recall that a Centura hospital currently procures 6,000 units in each order, so we have $Q = 6,000$. The components of the total annual cost can be computed as

$$\text{Total annual fixed order cost} = S \times R/Q$$
$$= 130 \times 31,200/6,000 = \$676$$
$$\text{Total annual holding cost} = H \times (Q/2)$$
$$= 0.90 \times 3,000 = \$2,700$$
$$\text{Total annual cost of materials} = C \times R$$
$$= 3 \times 31,200 = \$93,600$$

The total annual cost can thus be computed as

$$TC = S \times \frac{R}{Q} + H \times \frac{Q}{2} + C \times R$$
$$= 676 + 2,700 + 93,600$$
$$= \$96,976$$

TABLE 6.2 Total Cost as a Function of Order Size: Spreadsheet Approach

Batch Size (Q)	Number of Orders (R/Q)	Annual Order Cost (S × R/Q)	Average Cycle Inventory (Q/2)	Annual Holding Cost (H × Q/2)	Annual Procurement Cost (C × R)	Total Annual Costs (TC)
500	62.40	8,112.00	250	225.00	93,600	101,937.00
1000	31.20	4,056.00	500	450.00	93,600	98,106.00
1500	20.80	2,704.00	750	675.00	93,600	96,979.00
2000	15.60	2,028.00	1,000	900.00	93,600	96,528.00
2500	12.48	1,622.40	1,250	1,125.00	93,600	96,347.40
3000	10.40	1,352.00	1,500	1,350.00	93,600	96,302.00
3500	8.91	1,158.86	1,750	1,575.00	93,600	96,333.86
4000	7.80	1,014.00	2,000	1,800.00	93,600	96,414.00
4500	6.93	901.33	2,250	2,025.00	93,600	96,526.33
5000	6.24	811.20	2,500	2,250.00	93,600	96,661.20
5500	5.67	737.45	2,750	2,475.00	93,600	96,812.45
6000	5.20	676.00	3,000	2,700.00	93,600	96,976.00
6500	4.80	624.00	3,250	2,925.00	93,600	97,149.00

In fact, once we know the three components of the total annual cost, we can use a spreadsheet to determine the batch size that minimizes the total cost. Table 6.2 illustrates this for the data in Example 6.1 to 6.4.

Observe that of the total annual cost *TC*, the order cost component decreases when order size increases and the holding-cost component increases when order size increases. Figure 6.5 shows an optimal order size Q^* that minimizes total annual cost *TC. This optimal order quantity, Q^*, that minimizes total fixed and variable costs is called the* **economic order quantity (EOQ)**. From Table 6.2, we see that an order size of

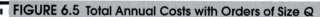

▪▪▪▪▪▪▪▪▪▪▪ **FIGURE 6.5** Total Annual Costs with Orders of Size Q

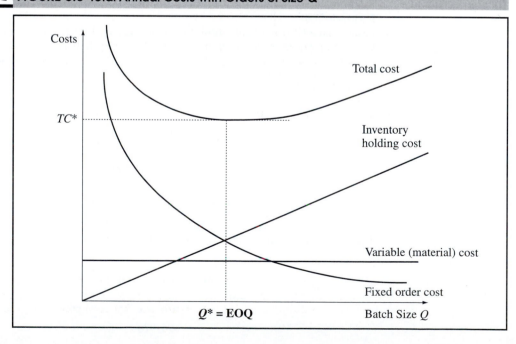

$Q = 3{,}000$ gives the total minimum cost. The EOQ can also be found analytically using calculus (see the Appendix for details) leading to a concise formula for the optimal order size, Q^*:

$$\text{Optimal order size} = \sqrt{\dfrac{2 \times Fixed\ cost\ per\ order \times Annual\ outflow\ rate}{Unit\ holding\ cost\ per\ year}}$$

$$Q^* = \sqrt{\dfrac{2SR}{H}}$$

(6.5)

also known as the **EOQ formula**.

Figure 6.5 shows all costs as functions of the order quantity as well as optimal order quantity and corresponding costs. Notice that the optimal order quantity exactly balances annual ordering and holding costs. Thus, we have, at optimality,

Total annual fixed costs per order = Total annual holding costs

$$S \times R/Q^* = H \times (Q^*/2)$$

If we substitute for the optimal order quantity in the total annual cost expression given by Formula 6.4 and simplify, we find that the minimum annual total cost, TC^*, is

$$TC^* = \sqrt{2SRH} + CR$$

(6.6)

where the first term ($\sqrt{2SRH}$) represents the total annual order and inventory holding cost at optimality and the second term (CR) is the total annual cost of materials.

Observe that to determine EOQ, we need to estimate three parameters, namely, the fixed cost per order S, the outflow rate R, and the unit holding cost per time H. In most practical settings, it is difficult to obtain accurate estimates of these parameters. A natural concern, then, is that the use of these parameter estimates in the EOQ formula will not result in the truly optimal order quantity. While this is true, does it matter from a total cost perspective? From Figure 6.5, we observe that the total cost curve is relatively flat around EOQ; that is, some deviation from EOQ will not significantly increase total annual costs. Thus, even if the parameter estimates are not quite accurate, the total costs of the resulting policy will not deviate too far from the true optimal cost. Therefore, we say that the model is robust and practically useful. Similarly, even when the parameter estimates are accurate, a manager may wish to deviate from the resulting EOQ for considerations not included in this model. The robustness of the EOQ model guarantees that the cost consequences of such deviations will not be dramatic. Thus, EOQ provides a ballpark estimate of the range in which we should operate. Example 6.5 illustrates inventory management at a Centura hospital.

Example 6.5
Using Examples 6.1 and 6.2, substituting known information into the EOQ formula yields

$$Q^* = \sqrt{\dfrac{2SR}{H}}$$
$$= \sqrt{\dfrac{2 \times \$130 \times 31{,}200}{\$0.90}} = 3{,}002$$

Thus, Centura should order IV Starter Kits in batches of 3,002 units whenever it places an order. The minor discrepancy with the spreadsheet approach of Table 6.2 arises as the spreadsheet approach evaluated costs for order quantities in steps of 500 instead of for each possible order quantity.

The resulting average cycle inventory will be

$$I_{cycle} = Q^*/2 = 1,501 \text{ units}$$

Using the formula 6.4 we can calculate the minimum annual total cost TC^* as

$$TC^* = 130 \times (31,200/3,002) + 0.9 \times (3,002/2) + 3 \times 31,200 = \$96,302$$

This total results from \$2,702 in ordering and inventory holding cost plus \$93,600 in material cost. Average time spent by an IV Starter Kit in the input buffer can be computed as

$$T_i = I_{cycle}/R = 1,501/600 \text{ weeks} = 2.5 \text{ weeks}$$

Now suppose that Centura's supplier prefers to ship in batch sizes of 3,500. It may be more convenient, therefore, to order 3,500 units at a time rather than the 3,002 specified by the EOQ formula. Deviating from the EOQ (in this case by 16.6%) increases total costs, but not much—if we substitute $Q = 3,500$ into the TC formula, we find that total annual cost would be only \$31.86 higher than the minimum. This figure reflects an increase of 0.03% in total cost and 1.18% in order and inventory holding cost.

Three managerial insights follow from the EOQ formula and are discussed in the following sections.

Fixed Order Cost Reduction   The optimal order size increases if the fixed order cost increases. The higher the fixed cost, the more we should order at a time in order to reduce the total number of orders per year. Conversely, lowering fixed cost would make ordering smaller quantities more economical which will reduce average inventory and flow time (see Example 6.6).

While discussion thus far has focused on decision making under economies of scale in procurement, it applies equally well when we have fixed costs in transportation or production. Fixed costs in procurement usually include administrative costs of creating a purchase order, activities of receiving the order, and so on. Technology can be used to significantly reduce these costs. For example, creating electronic purchase orders takes less time and costs less. Firms that have adopted Electronic Data Interchange and the Internet for electronic purchasing have benefited from reduced fixed order costs, making it economical for them to order smaller quantities more frequently.

Fixed costs in transportation can be directly reduced by changing the mode of transportation—from a ship to a large truck to a small truck to, perhaps, air. It can also be effectively reduced by sharing the fixed cost of a transportation mode across multiple supply or demand locations. These issues are discussed in more detail in supply chain management textbooks, such as Chopra and Meindl (2003).

Finally, reducing the setup or changeover costs can lower fixed costs in production. As we will see in Chapter 10, reducing setup times and hence costs has been a major factor in lean operations and just-in-time systems.

Example 6.6
In Example 6.5, we have already seen, for instance, that ordering in batches of 3,002 results in a cycle inventory of 1,501 and adds 2.5 weeks to the flow time of IV Starter Kits through a Centura hospital. Now suppose that Centura wants to reduce the cycle inventory by half. In order to do so, it must reduce order size to 1,501—a change that would reduce flow time by 1.25 weeks. Since the optimal order size of 3,002 yields minimum total cost, any deviation from it without changing other factors will only increase the total cost. Recall, however, that one key lever available to Centura is reducing the fixed order cost S. Using the EOQ formula, we can infer that in order for 1,501 to be its optimal order size, Centura should reduce S to \$32.50 (from the current value of \$130). Investment in information technology for procurement along with innovative ways to reduce fixed costs of transportation may be necessary to achieve this reduced level of fixed order costs.

Inventory versus Sales Growth   From the EOQ formula, we observe that the optimal batch is proportional to the square root of outflow rate. *Quadrupling* the outflow rate, therefore, will only *double* EOQ and thus average inventory and average flow time in the buffer. Therefore, a doubling of a company's annual sales does *not* require a doubling of cycle inventories. That is, inventory growth should not track sales growth. Indeed, optimal inventory management would entail ordering more frequently, so that the 100% growth in throughput can be sustained by a mere 41% (from the square root of 2) increase in cycle inventory.

Centralization and Economies of Scale   The fact that the optimal batch Q^* is proportional to the square root of the outflow rate R also leads to the idea of inventory centralization. For example, if a hospital network has multiple hospitals that order supplies independently, it can reduce its total cycle inventory by centralizing all the purchasing. For example, consider Centura Health introduced in Example 6.1. It has nine hospitals that ordered their supplies independently. Instead, Centura could centralize purchasing of all supplies and perhaps store these in a central warehouse. Under such a scenario, Centura will have to order for a total output flow rate that is nine times the output flow rate of each hospital. Assuming that the cost parameters remain unchanged in the central warehouse, we would expect the average inventory to be only three times (equal to the square root of 9) that of the decentralized hospital network. Example 6.7 illustrates the exact calculations.

Example 6.7

As described in Example 6.1, Centura Health operates a network of nine hospitals. Currently, each hospital places orders with suppliers independently. Assume that each hospital operates under identical cost parameters ($S = \$130$ per order, and $H = \$0.90$ per unit per year) and that each satisfies a flow rate of 600 units per week. In Example 6.5, we computed the optimal order quantity for one of the hospitals as 3,002 units—the EOQ. The average cycle inventory of each hospital is then $3,002/2 = 1,501$ units. Furthermore, the total annual order and holding cost for each hospital was \$2,702. If each hospital is assumed to be identical (in terms of the economics of placing orders and consumption of IV Starter Kits), the total cycle inventory across all nine hospitals is simply nine times the cycle inventory of each hospital operating independently and equals

$$9 \times 1501 = 13,509 \text{ units}$$

with total annual order and holding costs as

$$9 \times \$2,702 = \$24,318$$

If Centura were to switch to purchasing via a central warehouse, then the total flow rate to be met from the new order process will be the total flow rate across all nine hospitals:

$$9 \times 31,200/\text{year} = 280,800 \text{ units/year}$$

Assuming that the cost parameters remain the same, the new EOQ is given by

$$\sqrt{\frac{2 \times \$130 \times 280,800}{\$0.90}} = 9,006$$

Corresponding average cycle inventory in the central warehouse is equal to

$$\frac{9,006}{2} = 4,503 \text{ units}$$

with a total annual order and holding costs of

$$\sqrt{2 \times 130 \times 280,800 \times 0.90} = \$8,106 / \text{year}$$

which is 67% lower than for the decentralized operation.

Essentially, centralization gains advantage by exploiting the economies of scale in placing orders. While the preceding discussion outlined a situation where the hospitals centralized purchasing *and* used a central warehouse, the latter is not essential. That is, the advantages of centralization can be achieved by simply centralizing the purchasing function. Under this scenario, each hospital will share its output flow rate information with the central coordinator. On consolidating the flow rates of each of the hospitals, the coordinator will place a single order with the supplier. The consolidated order can then be split and delivered to meet requirements of the respective hospitals. Obviously, such a practice will require capabilities in information technology and coordination.

▪▪▪ 6.6   Effect of Lead Times on Ordering Decisions

In many practical settings, process managers will have to make periodic ordering decisions. There are two fundamental questions that a process manager then needs to address:

1. How much to order?
2. When to reorder?

The first question depends on the trade-off between fixed costs of placing orders and the variable holding costs of carrying inventory resulting from ordering in quantities larger than one. An example of this essential trade-off was discussed in the previous section that led to the EOQ formula.

The second question depends on how long it takes to replenish inventory. *The time lag between the arrival of the replenishment and the time the order was placed is called the replenishment* **lead time**, which is denoted by L. Clearly, we should order L units of time before we expect the inventory level to drop to zero. (This was exactly what we did in Example 6.3.)

Instead of keeping track of time, we can keep track of inventory levels and reorder as soon as the inventory drops below a certain **reorder point**, *which is the available inventory at the time of placing an order.* We use ROP to denote the reorder point. Clearly, when we process continuously at a constant rate R, we should reorder when we have just enough inventory to cover requirements during the replenishment lead time L. Thus, the reorder point is found as

$$\text{Reorder point} = \text{Lead time} \times \text{Throughput}$$

$$ROP = L \times R \tag{6.7}$$

If the lead time L is less than the time between orders (which we calculated earlier as $t_z = Q/R$ in Section 6.4), then the reorder point is the inventory that we have on hand at the time of placing an order. The reorder point decision can be superimposed on the inventory buildup diagram as shown in Figure 6.6. Example 6.8 illustrates the reorder point concept.

Example 6.8
Recall that the replenishment lead time for ordering IV Starter Kits is $L = 1$ week. The reorder point is

$$ROP = L \times R = 1 \text{ week} \times 600 \text{ units/week} = 600 \text{ units}$$

Thus, whenever the input inventory level drops below 600 units, the process manager should place a new order with the supplier. Observe also that the 600 units is an in-transit inventory.

If, however, the lead time L is larger than the time between orders (i.e., $L > Q/R$), the reorder point will be larger than the order quantity Q. This means that at the time

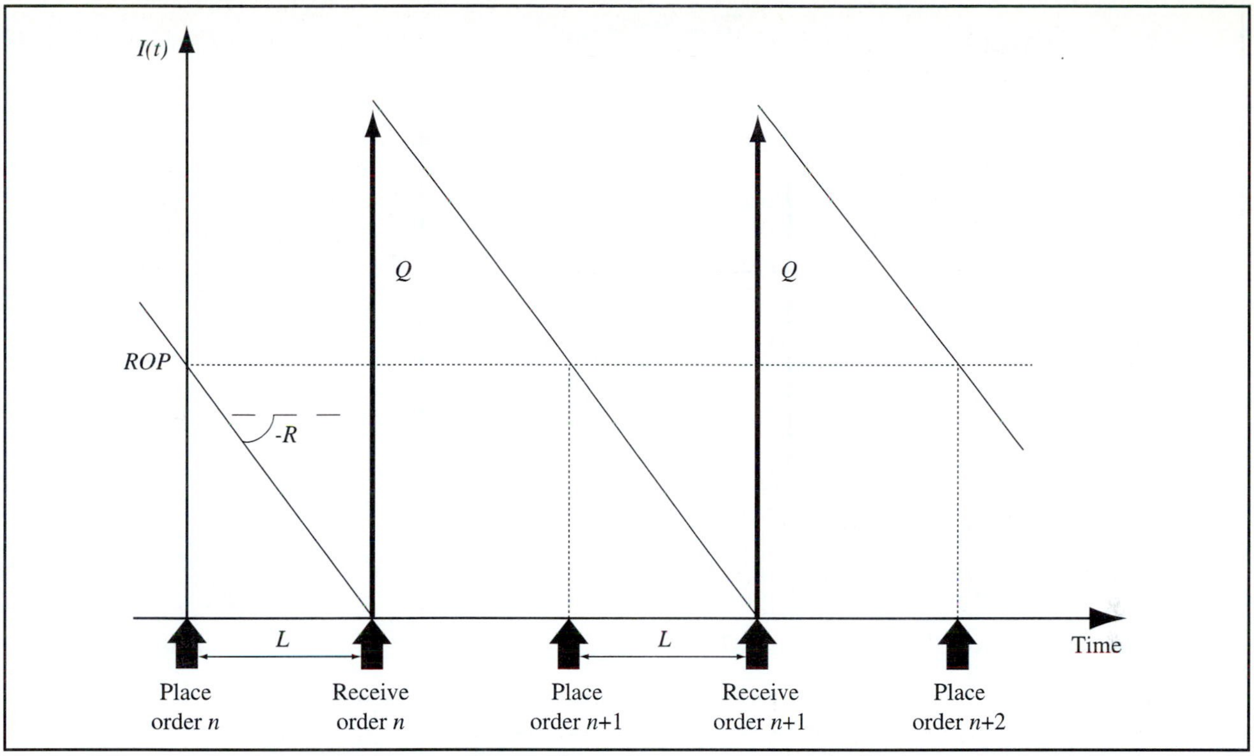

▪▪▪▪▪▪▪▪▪▪▪▪ **FIGURE 6.6** Ordering Decisions and the Reorder Point

we place our current order, there will be previous orders outstanding that will be received before the current order is received at a time L periods from now. In that case, *reorder point* measures *the sum of on-hand inventory and all outstanding orders* (called **on-order inventory**) at the time of placing an order, as illustrated by Example 6.9.

Example 6.9

Suppose the replenishment lead time for ordering IV Starter Kits is $L = 6$ weeks (instead of the 1 week assumed in Examples 6.1 and 6.8). With the demand rate $R = 600$ units per week, the reorder point becomes

$$ROP = L \times R = 6 \text{ weeks} \times 600 \text{ units/week} = 3{,}600 \text{ units}$$

In Example 6.5, we calculated that the optimal order size is $Q^* = 3{,}002$ so that the time between ordering is $Q/R = 5.003$ weeks, which is less than the new lead time L of 6 weeks. Thus, there will always be one previous order outstanding at the time of placing the current order. Indeed, in this case, the reorder point of 3,600 represents the sum of on-hand inventory (598) and one outstanding order ($Q^* = 3{,}002$) at the time of placing an order. The corresponding ordering decisions over time are shown in Figure 6.7.

So far, we have assumed that the output flow rate R and the lead time L are known with certainty. However, in reality this is rarely the case. For example, consumer demand is seldom known with certainty, and suppliers are not always reliable in their delivery schedules. We will see in the next chapter how to adjust the reorder point to incorporate a safety cushion, called safety inventory, to protect against this uncertainty.

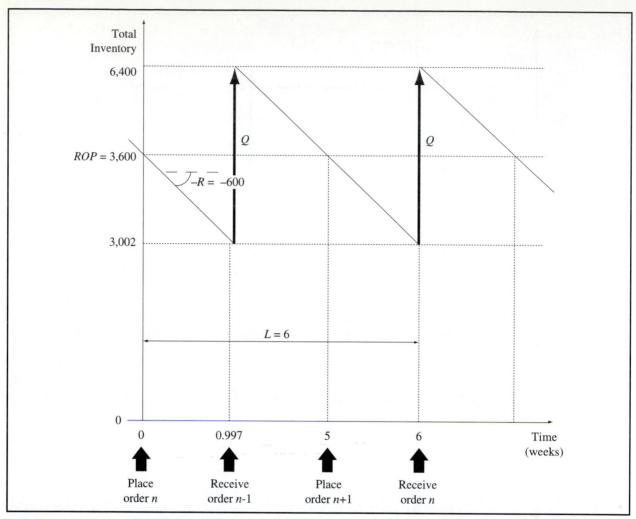

Total Inventory

6,400

$ROP = 3,600$

$-R = -600$

3,002

$L = 6$

0

0 0.997 5 6 Time (weeks)

Place order n | Receive order n-1 | Place order n+1 | Receive order n

▪▪▪▪▪▪▪▪▪▪▪ **FIGURE 6.7** Ordering Decisions and the Reorder Point for Example 6.9

▪▪▪ 6.7 Price Discounts: Forward Buying

In addition to fixed order costs, scale economies in procurement can be driven by price discounts that a supplier may offer to a buyer who purchases in large quantities. Consider the situation in Example 6.10.

Example 6.10

A buyer at the discount retailer, Kmart Inc., is considering ordering Colgate toothpaste for its stores. Demand for Colgate toothpaste is estimated to be 10,000 tubes per month. The fixed cost of an order—including administrative, transportation, and receiving—is estimated to be $100. The unit annual holding cost is 20%. The regular unit purchase price is $3. The manufacturer offers a one-time discount of 5% for units purchased over the next one month. What should the buyer do?

Price discounts take many forms. The type of discount policy described in Example 6.10 is *a short-term discount policy where discounts are offered for only a short period of time, known as a* **trade promotion**. The supplier offers incentives in the form of one-time opportunities to sell materials at reduced unit costs or perhaps notifies the buyer of an upcoming price increase and offers one last chance to order at the lower price. In both cases, of course, the buyer has an incentive to fill future needs by purchasing a single large quantity at the reduced price.

Forward Buying   Taking advantage of such an opportunity by *purchasing for future needs today is called* **forward buying**. We use Q^f to denote the quantity bought in response to a trade promotion. Once the trade promotion is over, the buyer will resume ordering at the regular (higher) price in the usual batches of size Q^* (or ordering a smaller batch size at the higher new cost). The resulting inventory buildup diagram is shown in bold in Figure 6.8—forward buying results in a big one-time increase in inventory. In dotted lines, the figure also shows the usual sawtooth profile without forward buying. How do we determine the impact of a trade promotion on forward buying by comparing Q^f with Q^*?

Consider process inflow at a normal price of $\$C$ per unit. At this price, the process manager normally orders Q^* units per order, but suppose a supplier offers a one-time discount of $\$d$ per unit. Let's say that for a certain period the price is

$$\$ (C - d)/\text{unit}$$

after which regular price $\$C$ will resume. The process manager must choose the quantity Q^f to order at the discounted price. To reduce the total material purchasing cost, the manager would like to increase order size. This change, however, will increase the amount of inventory held and thus increase holding cost. Note that there will be a savings on fixed ordering cost because the number of orders will be reduced. Our manager's goal is to strike an optimal trade-off that minimizes total cost. The optimal forward-buying quantity is computed in the Appendix at the end of this chapter as

$$Q^f = \frac{Rd}{(r + h)(C - d)} + \frac{C}{C - d} Q^* \tag{6.8}$$

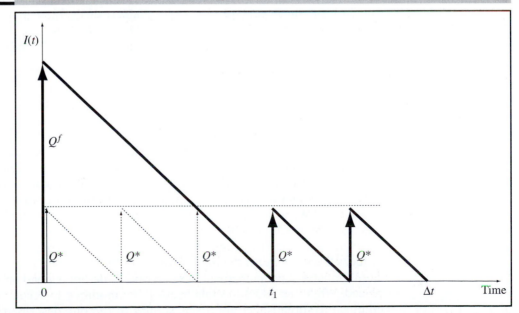

▪▪▪▪▪▪▪▪▪▪▪ **FIGURE 6.8** Forward Buy of Quantity Qᶠ with a One-Time Discount versus Regular Buy

Our process manager should then order either Q^f or the actual demand through the next anticipated trade promotion, whichever is smaller. The continued Example 6.10 quantifies the large inventory spikes that can result from forward buying.

Example 6.10 (Continued)

First, let us estimate the order quantity under the undiscounted purchase price. Observe that the unit annual holding cost is

$$H = 0.20 \times 3.00 = \$0.60$$

Then the regular order size is determined by the EOQ formula as

$$Q^* = \sqrt{\frac{2SR}{H}} = \sqrt{\frac{2 \times \$100 \times 120,000}{\$0.60}} = 6,325$$

With a one-time discount of 5% for units purchased over the next one month, the buyer has an incentive to forward buy. If we factor in the discount

$$d = (5\%)(\$3) = \$0.15$$

we arrive at the following purchase order (in lots):

$$Q^f = \frac{120,000 \times 0.15}{0.2 \times (3.00 - 0.15)} + \frac{3 \times 6,325}{3.00 - 0.15} = 38,236$$

The 5% discount would induce the Kmart buyer to increase its order size more than sixfold! The forward buy, therefore, will cover six normal order periods. The supplier, of course, will experience an enormous spike in demand followed by very low demand for a long period.

Thus, short-term trade promotions could motivate a retailer to forward buy large quantities of material, resulting in a substantial increase in inventory. According to a study of food distributors by Buzzell et al. (1990), forward-buy inventories normally amounted to 40% to 50% of total stocks. Of course, the total costs of trade promotions and resulting forward buy includes, in addition, added transportation and handling costs, higher administrative and selling costs that both suppliers and distributors incur, and costs of time buyers spend trying to evaluate deals. These added costs could be substantial. For example, Buzzell et al. (1990) report that the cost of forward buys in the nonperishable food-store products account for at least 1.15% to 2.0% of retail sales.

The Effect of Everyday Low Pricing   As we observed, order increases designed to take advantage of short-term discounts can generate significant increases in inventory—and thus material flow time—in the supply chain. This realization has led many firms to adopt a policy of **everyday low pricing (EDLP)**—a pricing policy whereby retailers charge constant, everyday low prices with no temporary discounts. With EDLP, customers will not exercise forward buying. The same argument can be used upstream in the supply chain. If wholesalers practice **everyday low purchase prices (EDLPP)**, *charging constant prices with no discounts,* retailers will not forward buy. Thus, flows in the entire chain will be smoother and total inventories lower than when forward buying is practiced. We will examine the implications of such policies for flows in supply chain management in Chapter 10.

Another class of discount policies is a quantity discount policy where a supplier reduces the unit price if the buyer buys more than a certain number of units. Such discount policies depend on quantities and usually do not depend on when the orders are placed. While the EOQ formula needs to be modified to accommodate quantity discounts, the spreadsheet approach, similar to the one described in Table 6.2 for an undiscounted case, can always be used to find the optimal order quantity. We skip the details of quantity discounts and refer the reader to inventory or supply-chain management texts such as Chopra and Meindl (2003) and Nahmias (2000).

111 6.8 Levers for Managing Inventories

We conclude by summarizing the most important ways of controlling the different types of inventories that we have discussed.

Theoretical Inventory   Theoretical in-process inventory, expressed as

$$I_{th} = R \times T_{th}$$

is determined by throughput R and theoretical flow time T_{th}. As discussed in Chapters 4 and 5, managing these two measures can control inventory. T_{th} can be reduced by any one of the following measures:

- Reducing critical activity times
- Eliminating non-value-adding activities
- Moving work from critical to noncritical activities (as defined in Chapter 4)
- Redesigning the process to replace sequential with parallel processing

Reducing process flow rate R can also reduce theoretical in-process inventory. This option, however, will reduce the economic value of output per unit of time. Regardless, theoretical in-process inventory is usually only a small fraction of total inventory and managers like to reduce it primarily in order to reduce flow time.

Cycle Inventory   Average cycle inventory is expressed as half the order size. Thus, cycle inventory can be reduced by reducing the order size. Recall that the optimal order size is given by the EOQ formula:

$$Optimal\ order\ size\ =\ \sqrt{\frac{2 \times Fixed\ cost\ per\ order \times Annual\ outflow\ rate}{Unit\ holding\ cost\ per\ year}}$$

Thus, the only sensible lever for reducing optimal cycle inventory (and hence the flow time) is to reduce the fixed order (or setup) cost. Simplifying the order process in conjunction with the use of information technology can reduce fixed order costs. Investing in setup or changeover time reduction or investing in flexible resources helps lower fixed setup costs. Negotiating everyday low prices with suppliers instead of seeking short-time trade promotions can reduce excessive cycle inventories resulting from forward buying.

Seasonal Inventory   Seasonal inventory results from temporary fluctuations in outflows, coupled with the high costs of adjusting capacity to meet them. Using pricing and incentive tactics to promote stable demand patterns can reduce it. Increasing resource flexibility so that resources can process at various flow rates to match demand fluctuations will also make it less expensive to adjust seasonal inventory levels. Similarly, using flexible resources to produce countercyclical products makes it possible to level the load without having to build up inventory. A classic example is a company that produces snowblowers in winter and lawn mowers in summer, both with a single flexible production process.

Safety Inventory   Safety inventory cushions the process against unexpected supply disruptions or surges in demand. The basic response to reducing its levels is reducing uncertainty in supply and demand. Ensuring reliable suppliers and stable demand patterns largely eliminates the need for safety inventories. We will discuss the role of safety inventory more fully in Chapter 7.

Speculative Inventory Speculative inventory permits a firm to do one of two things:

1. Reduce the total cost of purchasing materials
2. Increase profits by taking advantage of uncertain fluctuations in a product's price

Negotiating stable prices would eliminate speculative inventories and the associated portfolio risk.

SUMMARY ■■■■■■■

Inventory accumulates whenever there is a mismatch between supply and demand. Along with flow time and flow rate, inventory is the third basic measure of process performance. In this chapter, we provided inventory classification, reasons and costs for holding inventory, optimal decisions under economies of scale, and short-term price promotions.

Depending on its location in the process, inventory can be classified as either inputs, in-process, or outputs inventory. Firms carry inventory for several reasons. First, a minimal level of inventory, called theoretical inventory, is needed to maintain a desired level of throughput in equilibrium. Transportation of products from one location to another involves delays; inventory being moved is classified as in-transit or pipeline inventory. To exploit economies of scale in production, procurement, and transportation, firms produce, purchase, or transport larger quantities than what may be immediately required, leading to cycle inventory. Faced with a seasonal demand and a desire to maintain a constant processing rate, firms create seasonal inventory. Firms may carry safety inventory to protect against demand or supply uncertainty. Finally, depending on the nature of price changes (e.g., random or promotional), firms may carry speculative inventory or forward buy more than what is needed. While there are several reasons for carrying inventory, it also entails a cost. Specifically, inventory carrying cost consists of physical holding costs as well as opportunity costs of capital tied up.

Decisions about purchasing under economies of scale involve trading off the fixed costs of ordering with the cost of holding the cycle inventory. As the lot size per order increases, fewer orders are placed in a year, reducing the annual fixed order costs. Increasing the lot size, however, increases cycle inventory, resulting in higher holding costs. The optimal lot size is determined by the economic order quantity formula. To reduce the cycle inventory, the lot size must be decreased. A primary lever to achieve this is to reduce the fixed costs of ordering or setup. Setup time reduction and using technology to cut purchase orders are some direct ways to reduce fixed order costs. In addition, aggregating purchases across multiple locations can also reduce lot sizes and hence cycle inventory. In particular, cycle inventory decreases by a factor of the square root of the number of locations aggregated.

In addition to the lot size, which determines the order quantity, a process manager needs to determine when to reorder, a decision that involves monitoring the inventory level, and placing an order when the inventory level drops to a reorder point. If demand is known perfectly, the reorder point is given by the demand during the lead time of replenishment.

Finally, in response to short-term price reductions by a supplier, called a trade promotion, a buyer may order significantly more quantity than it normally does, leading to forward-buy inventory. Every day low pricing is an effective tool to counter the buildup of forward-buy inventories.

KEY EQUATIONS AND SYMBOLS ▪▪▪▪▪▪▪

(6.1) $I_{th} = R \times T_{th}$

(6.2) $H = (h + r)C$

(6.3) $I_{cycle} = Q/2$

(6.4) $TC = S\dfrac{R}{Q} + H\dfrac{Q}{2} + CR$

(6.5) $Q^* = \sqrt{\dfrac{2SR}{H}}$

(6.6) $TC^* = \sqrt{2SRH} + CR$

(6.7) $ROP = L \times R$

(6.8) $Q^f = \dfrac{Rd}{(r+h)(C-d)} + \dfrac{C}{C-d}Q^*$

where,

I_{th} = Theoretical inventory

R = Throughput or demand rate

T_{th} = Theoretical flow time

H = Total unit inventory holding cost

C = Unit variable cost

h = Unit physical holding cost as a fraction of unit variable cost

r = Unit opportunity cost of capital as a fraction of unit variable cost

I_{cycle} = Cycle inventory

Q = Order size

TC = Total annual cost

Q^* = Economic order quantity

TC^* = Total optimal annual cost

ROP = Reorder point

L = Replenishment lead time

Q^f = Optimal forward-buying quantity

KEY TERMS ▪▪▪▪▪▪▪

- Aggregate production planning
- Batch
- Batch size
- Chase demand strategy
- Cycle inventory
- Economic order quantity (EOQ)
- Economies of scale
- EOQ formula
- Everyday low pricing (EDLP)
- Everyday low purchase prices (EDLPP)
- Fixed order cost

- Fixed setup cost
- Forward buying
- In-process inventory
- Inputs inventory
- In-transit inventory
- Inventory holding cost
- Lead time
- Level-production strategy
- On-order inventory
- Opportunity cost
- Outputs inventory
- Physical holding cost

- Pipeline inventory
- Procurement batch
- Production batch
- Reorder point (ROP)
- Safety inventories
- Safety stock
- Seasonal inventories
- Speculative inventory
- Theoretical inventory
- Trade promotion
- Transfer batch
- Work-in-process inventory

DISCUSSION QUESTIONS ▪▪▪▪▪▪▪

6.1 Explain how better inventory management affects a firm's bottom line.

6.2 Why do firms carry inventory even though it is costly to do so?

6.3 What are the key trade-offs in determining the economic order quantity?

6.4 Explain why it is not absolutely critical to estimate the cost parameters accurately in implementing the economic order quantity model.

6.5 Explain why fixed costs must decrease by a factor of four when reducing cycle inventory only by one half.

6.6 How can the use of information technology result in lower inventory?

6.7 Discuss whether reduction in replenishment lead times will reduce cycle inventory.

6.8 What is the impact of short-term price promotions on the purchasing behavior of the buyer? What key trade-offs does the buyer make in determining the quantity to buy under promotion?

EXERCISES ▪▪▪▪▪▪▪

6.1 Suppose you purchase a $4-per-unit part from a supplier with which you assemble red widgets. On average, you use 50,000 units of this part each year. Every time you order this particular part, you incur a sizable ordering cost of $800 regardless of the number of parts you order. Your cost of capital is 20% per year.

a. How many parts should you purchase each time you place an order?

b. To satisfy annual demand, how many times per year will you place orders for this part?

6.2 BIM Computers Inc. sells its popular PC-PAL model to distributors at a price of $1,250 per unit. BIM's profit margin is 20%. Factory orders average 400 units per week. Currently, BIM works in a batch mode and produces a four-week supply in each batch. BIM's production process involves three stages:

- PC board assembly (the automatic insertion of parts and the manual loading, wave soldering, and laser bonding of electronic components purchased from outside sources)
- Final assembly
- Testing

When the firm wants to change production from one model to another, it must shut down its assembly line for half a day, which translates into four working hours. The company estimates that downtime costs half an hour of supervisory time and an additional $2,000 in lost production and wages paid to workers directly involved in changeover operations. Salaries for supervisory personnel involved amount to $1,500 per day.

Although BIM products are generally regarded as high quality, intense price competition in the industry has forced the firm to embark on a cost-cutting and productivity improvement campaign. In particular, BIM wants to operate with leaner inventories without sacrificing customer service. Releasing some of the funds tied up in outputs inventory would allow BIM to invest in a new product development project that is expected to yield a risk-adjusted return of 20% per annum. Assume 50 workweeks in a year and five working days in a week.

a. Determine BIM's total annual cost of production and inventory control.

b. Compute the economic batch size and the resulting cost savings.

6.3 Victor sells a line of upscale evening dresses in his boutique. He charges $300 per dress, and sales average 30 dresses per week. Currently, Victor orders a 10-week supply at a time from the manufacturer. He pays $150 per dress, and it takes two weeks to receive each delivery. Victor estimates his administrative cost of placing each order at $225. Because he estimates his cost of capital at 20%, each dollar's worth of idle inventory costs him $0.30 per year.

a. Compute Victor's total annual cost of ordering and carrying inventory.

b. If he wishes to minimize his annual cost, when and how much should Victor order in each batch? What will be his annual cost?

c. Compare the number of inventory turns under the current and proposed policies.

6.4 A retailer estimates her fixed cost for placing an order at $1,000. Presently, she orders in optimal quantities of 400 units. She has, however, heard of the benefits of *just-in-time purchasing*—a principle that advocates purchasing goods in smaller lots as a means of keeping inventory down. If she wishes to order in lots no larger than 50, what should her fixed ordering costs be?

6.5 Major Airlines would like to train new flight attendants in an economically rational way. The airline requires a staff of about 1,000 trained attendants to maintain in-flight service. Because of the nature of the job, attendants have a high propensity to quit, with average job tenure being about two years, hence the need to train new attendants. Major's training course takes six weeks, after which trainees take one week of vacation and travel time before entering the pool from which they are assigned to flight duty as needed to fill vacancies created by attrition. To reduce the dropout rate and ensure the continued availability of trained attendants, Major pays trainees $500 per month while they are training, vacationing, and waiting for assignment.

a. The cost of the training itself consists mainly of salaries for instructors ($220 per person per week) and support personnel ($80 per person per week). A training team consists of 10 instructors and 10 supporting personnel. The team is paid only for the time engaged in training, and pay is independent of both class size and the number of classes running simultaneously. Assume 50 workweeks in a year. Determine the most economical size of a trainee class, the annual total cost of this policy, and the time interval between starting consecutive classes. Draw the inventory-time diagram, showing when each batch will begin and end training, when each will take vacation time, and when each will be ready for duty.

b. Now modify the solution in part a so that only one class will be in training at one time. Note that this requirement means that a new class must start every six weeks. Determine the corresponding class size and the total annual cost of this operation. Compare your findings for this option with the optimum cost for the option described in part a and make a recommendation as to which option Major Airlines should choose.

6.6 National Bank operates a network of automated teller machines (ATMs). Cash withdrawals at an ATM average about $80. The bank estimates that the fixed cost of filling an ATM with cash is about $100 regardless of the amount of cash put in. Average numbers of cash withdrawals per week is about 150. How much cash should the bank keep at an ATM if its annual cost of money is 10%. How often should the bank replenish an ATM?

6.7 Gourmet Coffee (GC) is a specialty coffee shop that sells roasted coffee beans. It buys green beans, roasts them in its shop, and then sells them to the consumer. GC estimates that it sells about 150,000 pounds of coffee per year. Green beans cost about $1.50 per pound. In addition, there is a shipping charge that GC pays its supplier according to the following schedule:

Quantity Shipped	Shipping Cost per Pound
Less than 10,000 pounds	$0.17
Less than 15,000 pounds	$0.15
More than 15,000 pounds	$0.13

GC estimates its cost of capital at 15% per year. The administrative cost of placing an order (fax/phone/billing) and receiving the goods and so on is about $50 per order. In addition, to receive a shipment into its shop, GC rents a forklift truck for $350.

a. What is the optimal order quantity of beans for GC? What is the total annual cost?

b. GC is considering buying a forklift and building a ramp that will allow it to eliminate the rental cost of a forklift. GC will have to borrow money to finance this investment. If the life of the equipment is approximately five years, how much money should GC be willing to spend to buy a forklift and build a ramp? If the investment were made, what should be the optimal order policy for GC?

6.8 A supplier to Toyota stamps out parts using a press. Changing a part type requires the supplier to change the die on the press. This changeover currently takes four hours. The supplier estimates that each hour spent on the changeover costs $250. Demand for parts is 1,000 per month. Each part costs the supplier $100, and the supplier incurs an annual holding cost of 25%.

a. Determine the optimal production batch size for the supplier.

b. Toyota would like the supplier to reduce their batch size by a factor of four; that is, if the supplier currently produces Q parts per batch, Toyota would like them to produce $Q/4$ parts per batch. What should the supplier do in order to achieve this result?

6.9 Superfast Motors manufactures and sells a wide variety of motors to industrial customers. All motors cost about the same and are assembled on the same line. Switching over from assembling one motor to another requires about two hours. Superfast assembles motors to be stocked in a distribution center from where they are shipped as orders arrive. HP is the highest-selling motor (in terms of units sold) and LP the lowest selling.

a. Will the average cycle inventory of HP motors be:
   • Higher than the cycle inventory of LP motors
   • Lower than the cycle inventory of LP motors
   • Same as the cycle inventory of LP motors?

b. Will the average time spent by an HP motor in inventory be:
   • Higher than the time spent by an LP motor
   • Lower than the time spent by an LP motor
   • Same as the time spent by an LP motor?

6.10 Complete Computer (CC) is a retailer of computer equipment in Minneapolis with four retail outlets. Currently each outlet manages its ordering independently. Demand at each retail outlet averages 4,000 units per week. Each unit costs $200, and CC has a holding cost of 20% per annum. The fixed cost of each order (administrative plus transportation) is $900. Assume 50 weeks in a year.

a. Given that each outlet orders independently and gets its own delivery, determine the optimal order size at each outlet.

b. CC is thinking of centralizing purchasing (for all four outlets). In this setting, CC will place a single order (for all outlets) with the supplier. The supplier will deliver the order on a common truck to a transit point. Since individual requirements are identical across outlets, the total order is split equally and shipped to the retailers from this transit point. This entire operation has increased the fixed cost of placing an order to $1,800. If CC manages ordering optimally in the new setting, compute the average inventory in the CC system (across all four outlets).

MODELING EXERCISE ▌▌▌▌▌▌▌

www.prenhall.com/anupindi

For exercises and models using the evaluation software of iGrafx Process, insert the CD-ROM that is packaged with this book. An electronic copy of the User Guide is included on the CD. For more information on iGrafx, visit www.iGrafx.com. Detailed descriptions of the models may also be found at www.prenhall.com/anupindi.

Model

In Exercise 6.2, you were asked to determine the production and inventory costs of BIM Computer Inc.'s current policy as well as determine its optimal policy. In this modeling exercise, Exercise 6.2 has been prebuilt using iGrafx Process. You can use the model to evaluate the costs of the current policy as well as determine the optimal policy.

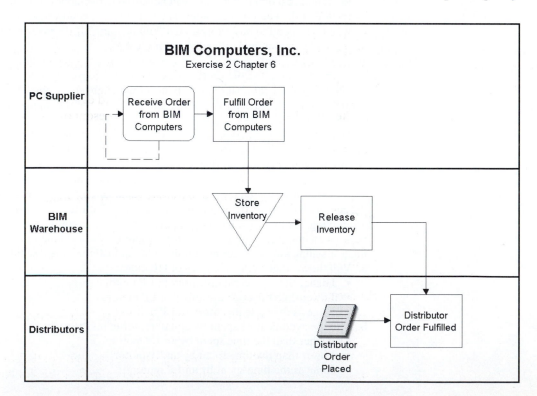

BIM Computers Inc. sells the PC-PAL model computer to distributors. Based on demand from its customers, BIM orders additional inventories from its supplier, assembles the computers, and ships them to distributors. Distributor orders for 400 units per week are placed evenly throughout the week. This translates to an order placed every 6 minutes (40 work hours × 60 minutes/400 units per week). When inventory is empty (i.e., $ROP = 0$), 1,600 (Q) units of inventory are ordered from the PC supplier and arrive instantaneously (i.e., $L = 0$) to fill the inventory. A simplified version of this process has been implemented with iGrafx 2003. For this process model, the BIM manufacturing steps are ignored.

Simulation

To simulate the production and inventory process at BIM Computers Inc., double-click on iGrafx document CH6EX2. This loads the simulation model within iGrafx Process. The main screen should have two panes. The left pane shows the Explorer bar with the following contents: Processes, Scenarios, and Reports. (If you do not see this, click on View and the Explorer bar from the menu item and ensure that the All Components view is chosen at the top of the Explorer bar.) You may view the model for this exercise by double-clicking on CH6EX2 under Processes. The Process Scenario tab gives details of the various parameters used in the simulation model. Finally, results of a simulation run may be viewed by double-clicking on Simulation Report under the Reports tab in the Explorer bar.

To simulate the model, from the Model menu, point to Run and choose Start. The default simulation length is set up for one year (equal to 250 days). A Simulation Progress window pops up at the right end of the screen. As soon as the simulation ends, the results of the simulation are displayed as a report. There are five tabs in a report. Select the Custom tab to see the customized report for this exercise.

Implementation

The process flow diagram is illustrated at the beginning of this section. The model is divided into three "swim lanes" representing distributors, the BIM warehouse, and the suppliers of PC inventory. Activities in the Distributors swim lane produce demand and receive BIM computers. iGrafx 2003 uses transactions to represent objects flowing through the process. The type of object represented can vary.

In the Distributors activities, transactions represent orders. In the BIM Warehouse activities, transactions represent PC inventory. These activities store PCs until released to distributors to fulfill orders. An inventory count is maintained, and when inventory reaches the reorder point (ROP), additional inventories of quantity Q are sent from the PC supplier.

In the PC Supplier activities, activities receive and fulfill requests for inventories from BIM computers. At the start of the simulation, a single transaction enters the process to seed the simulation with initial inventory.

Refer to the document in the CD for detailed explanations on the modeling approach for this exercise.

Performance Interpretation

The performance of the process is illustrated in the custom report. The report shows the following:

- *Number of orders* placed during the simulation. Observe that the number of orders includes even the last order placed just before the simulation ends. So if the simulation run length is set to 500 days, it will count the order placed at the end of 500th day even though the material delivered for this order will be used only to satisfy demand in the next order cycle.

- *Average inventory at BIM Computers,* which is the average (time-weighted) inventory in the BIM warehouse.
- *Annual holding costs* gives the annual cost of holding inventory.
- *Annual ordering costs* gives the annual cost of placing orders.
- *Annual purchasing costs* gives the annual variable cost of computers purchased.
- *Total annual costs* gives the sum of the previous three costs.
- *Total cumulative costs* lists the cumulative (over the duration of the simulation) costs at the warehouse, distributor, and supplier.
- *Total cumulative and average transaction statistics* gives a count of the number of units of demand processed, the total cumulative costs incurred, and the average cost incurred per unit of demand.
- *Elapsed time (in days)* is the number of days in the simulation run.

The data in the custom report are for the default simulation run of one year (250 days). Observe that based on the theoretical values in Exercise 6.2, we do not get complete (inventory) cycles in one year, and hence the average statistics do not match the theoretical values. To match with theoretical values, we will have to conduct a simulation run extending to two years (500 days).

SELECTED BIBLIOGRAPHY ▪▪▪▪▪▪▪

Buzzell, R. D., J. A. Quelch, and W. J. Salmon. 1990. "The Costly Bargain of Trade Promotions." *Harvard Business Review,* March–April, pages 1–9.

Chopra, S., and P. Meindl. 2003. *Supply Chain Management: Strategy Planning and Operations.* 2nd ed. Upper Saddle River, N.J.: Prentice Hall.

Hadley, G., and T. M. Whitin. 1963. *Analysis of Inventory Systems.* Upper Saddle River, N.J.: Prentice Hall.

Nahmias, S. 2000. *Production and Operations Analysis.* 4th edition. Homewood, Ill.: Irwin.

Peterson, R., and E. A. Silver. 1979. *Decision Systems for Inventory Management and Production Planning.* New York: John Wiley & Sons.

Sasser, W. 1976. "Match Supply and Demand in Service Industries." *Harvard Business Review,* November–December, pages 132–138.

▨▨▨▨▨▨▨ Appendix: Derivation of EOQ ▨▨▨▨▨▨▨ Formula and Forward-Buying Quantity

Derivation of EOQ Formula

Recall that the total annual costs is given by

$$TC = S \times \frac{R}{Q} + H \times \frac{Q}{2} + C \times R$$

Taking the first derivative of the total cost function TC with respect to Q yields

$$d(TC)/dQ = -SR/Q^2 + H/2$$

If we set the first derivative of the total cost function equal to zero (which is a condition to minimize TC), solving for Q yields the EOQ formula as

$$Q^* = \sqrt{\frac{2SR}{H}}$$

Calculation of Forward-Buying Quantity

The analysis involves comparing inventory pattern and costs with forward buying (indicated in bold in Figure 6.8) against the usual sawtooth pattern without forward buying (indicated in nonbold lines). Exact analysis is rather complex because the two cases can be effectively compared only for certain time intervals Δt—namely, those that leave us in the same ending inventory position in both cases. However, we can conduct an approximate analysis as follows (Peterson and Silver 1979):

1. Assume an interval Δt such that both cases can be effectively compared.
2. Now determine Q^f by maximizing the improvement of total costs over the forward-buying interval t_1.

First consider the case of forward buying. At a process throughput of R, a forward-buy order of size Q^f will be consumed by the time interval denoted as

$$t_1 = Q^f/R$$

The average inventory resulting from buying Q^f is then $Q^f/2$. The total relevant costs of buying a quantity Q^f then includes the one-time fixed order cost S, the total discounted material cost $Q^f(C - d)$, and the discounted holding cost for carrying $Q^f/2$ units in inventory for t_1 time units. We thus write the total ordering and inventory holding costs resulting from a forward buy of Q^f as follows:

$$TC^f = S + Q^f(C - d) + (r + h)(C - d)\frac{Q^f}{2}t_1$$

Now consider the case without forward buying. We will order EOQ amount

$$Q^* = \sqrt{\frac{2RS}{(r + h)C}}$$

perhaps multiple times during the period $[0, t_1]$. We can thus express total ordering and inventory costs during the period as (recall that earlier we assumed a time unit of one year)

$$TC^* = \left(\sqrt{2SR(r + h)C} + CR\right)t_1$$

Noting that $t_1 = Q^f/R$, we would like to select the value of Q^f that maximizes the following cost:

$$TC^* - TC^f = \sqrt{2SR(r + h)C}\left(\frac{Q^f}{R}\right)$$
$$+ CQ^f - S - Q^f(C - d)$$
$$- (r + h)(C - d)\frac{\left(Q^f\right)^2}{2R}$$

Using calculus, we find that at the optimal forward-buying quantity, the first derivative of this cost differential with respect to Q^f equals zero.

PART III

Process Flow Variability

7

Managing Flow Variability: Safety Inventory

▦ Introduction

In the 1990s, General Electric (GE) Lighting served its European customers through a distribution network that consisted of seven warehouses including three near Paris and one each in Austria, Belgium, Germany, and Switzerland. The network of multiple warehouses was built on the idea that it will allow GE Lighting to be "close to the customer." Contrary to expectations, establishing the distribution network led to an "inventory-service crisis." Inventory levels in the network were high, and customer service suffered. GE Lighting wanted to reevaluate its distribution strategy in Europe while also expanding to serve southern Europe. They faced several questions. What are the key drivers of inventory when customer demands are unpredictable? Should they invest in a better forecasting system? What should be the right inventory level? What service level is appropriate to offer? Should they continue to serve their customers using a decentralized network or build a central distribution facility to serve all customers?

GE Lighting ultimately consolidated the original seven warehouses into a single master distribution center in France to serve customers in Austria, Belgium, France, Germany, the Netherlands, Luxembourg, and Switzerland. In addition, to serve customers in other parts of Europe, it opened a facility in Sweden to serve the Scandinavian customers, one each in the United Kingdom and Italy to serve customers in those countries, and a distribution center in Spain that serves both Spain and Portugal (Harps, 2000).

Matching inflows (supply) and outflows (demand) is a critical aspect of managing any business process. In Chapter 6, we focused on economies of scale to explain why firms may plan supply in excess of demand and hold the resulting inventory. Actual supply may still fall short of demand because of unpredictable variability (uncertainty) in either supply or demand. This may result in process starvation, product shortages, lost sales, and customer dissatisfaction. Several companies find themselves in this perilous situation, often with severe financial consequences, as illustrated in Table 7.1. The process manager may respond by holding additional inventory—called safety inventory—as a cushion, or buffer, that absorbs fluctuations, thus maintaining stock availability despite variability in supply or demand.

In this chapter, we explore this protective function of inventories, its key determinants, and the managerial levers available to control these inventories. As in Chapter 6, our discussion applies equally to buffers at any one of three stages in a process: input (raw material), in process, and output (finished goods). For consistency, however, we refer to inflows into the buffer as supply and outflows from the buffer as demand.

To plan an adequate level of inventory, the process manager needs to forecast demand. The amount of safety inventory required will then depend on the accuracy of that forecast. In Section 7.1, we outline some general principles about forecasts that bear on the management of safety inventory. The rest of the chapter then examines these implications in greater detail. In Section 7.2, we begin by studying the amount of stockout protection provided by a given level of inventory and the amount of safety inventory required to provide a given level of protection. In Section 7.3, we consider the problem of determining the optimal level of protection that balances the expected costs of overstocking and understocking. Section 7.4 examines the factors affecting variability in supply and demand and thus the extent of safety inventory needed to provide certain levels of service. Sections 7.5 and 7.6 outline operational strategies for reducing variability by means of aggregation of demand and postponement of supply.

TABLE 7.1 Examples of Supply-Demand Mismatch

Toyota can't build ES 300s fast enough to meet customer cravings for them. Sales have been running 20% higher than Toyota expected. . . . Instead of waiting, some would-be buyers are defecting to the [Cadillac] Catera.

BusinessWeek, April 7, 1997

Sled Dogs Co., the Minneapolis-based maker and marketer of snow skates and accessories that has pioneered snow skating as a winter sport, posted a $4.4 million loss in 1996 because of write-offs on obsolete inventory and ultimately filed for bankruptcy.

Star Tribune, 1997

Cisco wrote off $2.5 billion of inventory in the first quarter of 2001.

The Street.com, April 2001

Taiwan's Macronix International Co., maker of flash memory and mask ROM incurred a net loss of (Taiwanese) $11.357 billion primarily due to inventory write-offs when demand from its main customer for mask ROM, Nintendo Co. Ltd. suffered in 2002.

Reuters

Finally, Section 7.7 summarizes the key levers for managing safety inventory and customer service in the face of demand variability.

▪▪▪ 7.1 Demand Forecasts and Forecast Errors

Until now, we have assumed that product demand is known and is constant over time. In reality, of course, demand usually varies over time. Although some variation is systematic and hence predictable (e.g., because of trends or seasonality), much of it results from unpredictable, unexplainable, random factors called noise. As *a process of predicting future demand,* **forecasting** is, among other things, an effort to deal with noise. Firms forecast a variety of factors, such as future customer demand, sales, resource requirements and availabilities, and interest rates.

Forecasting Methods A variety of forecast methods are available; they can be classified broadly as *subjective* or *objective.* Subjective methods are based on judgment and experience and include customer surveys and expert judgments. Objective methods are based on data analysis. The two primary objective methods are causal models and time-series analysis. **Causal models** *are forecasting methods that assume that in addition to the data, other factors influence demand.* For example, future sales could be a function of consumer prices. **Time-series analyses** *are forecasting methods that rely solely on past data.* Objective methods aim to filter out noise and estimate the effect of such systematic components as trends and patterns of seasonality or such causal factors as the effect of price on sales.

A detailed discussion of forecasting methods is beyond the scope of this book, but they are discussed in Chopra and Miendl (2003) and Nahmias (2000). Our focus in this section will be on some general characteristics of forecasts, as identified by Nahmias (2000), that process managers should understand—regardless of the forecasting method that they may use—to make rational decisions about process inventory. These general characteristics are the following:

1. **Forecasts are usually wrong**: Even if we could accurately estimate variations in the systematic components of a demand pattern, the presence of random noise that we can neither explain nor control leads to inaccuracy. Therefore, decisions made on the basis of a forecast (specified as a single number) could have unexpected consequences in terms of either higher costs or inadequate service.
2. **Forecasts should, therefore, be accompanied by a measure of forecast error**: A measure of forecast error quantifies the process manager's degree of confidence in the forecast. Our decisions (e.g., regarding inventory) should change with our confidence in the forecast—the greater the forecast error, the greater the chance of a stockout for a given level of safety inventory. We will study the exact relationship between the safety inventory, the service level, and the forecast error in Section 7.2.
3. **Aggregate forecasts are more accurate than individual forecasts**: For example, forecasting demand for sweaters by individual colors is less reliable than forecasting total demand for all sweaters. Intuitively, we know that aggregation reduces variability—or, more precisely, reduces the amount of variability relative to aggregate mean demand. Why? High- and low-demand patterns among individual products tend to cancel one another, thereby yielding a more stable pattern of total demand. As a result, less safety inventory is needed in the aggregate. This realization underlies the principle of reducing variability and safety inventory by pooling and centralizing stock—which we will discuss in Section 7.5.

4. **Long-range forecasts are less accurate than short-range forecasts**: Again, intuitively we know that events further in the future are less predictable than those that are more imminent. Every meteorologist knows that forecasting tomorrow's weather is easier than forecasting next week's weather. Likewise, matching supply and demand in the short run is easier than planning for the long term. The closer to the actual time of demand a manager can make supply decisions, the more information will be available to make those decisions. Short-range demand forecasts, therefore, will be more accurate than long-range demand forecasts, and less safety inventory will be needed. Section 7.6 focuses on the use of postponement strategies to exploit short-range forecasts.

In addition to incorporating hard quantitative data, forecasts should be modified to include qualitative factors such as managerial judgment, intuition, and market savvy. After all, forecasting is as much an art as a science, and no information should be ignored.

▪▪▪ 7.2   Safety Inventory and Service Level

If we grant that forecasts are usually wrong, we must also agree that planning supplies so that they merely match demand forecasts will invariably result in either excess inventories when supply exceeds demand or stockouts when demand exceeds supply, as illustrated in Example 7.1.

Example 7.1

Consider a GE Lighting warehouse near Paris and the procurement decisions faced by the warehouse manager for its industrial flood lamp. The throughput rate of lamps is, say, 2,000 units per day.[1] The warehouse manager orders a batch of 28,000 lamps every 14 days. He estimates that the cost of holding one lamp in inventory for one year is €20. Whenever the manager places an order, the replenishment is received in 10 days. The manager reorders whenever the inventory level drops to 20,000 units.

How was the throughput rate of 2,000 units per day established? It was perhaps based on some forecast of the number of lamps demanded, but the forecast inevitably will involve some error. Observe that the manager has set the reorder point (*ROP*) to 20,000 units and the replenishment lead time is 10 days. During that 10-day lead time, one of the following events will inevitably occur:

1. Actual requirements will fall below 20,000 units, resulting in excess inventory.
2. Actual requirements will exceed 20,000 units, resulting in a lamp stockout.

Only by extreme coincidence will actual demand be *exactly* 20,000 units. If demand is equally likely to be above or below 20,000, then there is a 50% probability that keeping an inventory of 20,000 units will result in a stockout.

Stockouts occur whenever demand exceeds supply; they have critical business implications. In the GE Lighting's Paris warehouse situation, lamp stockouts imply that customer demands will go unsatisfied. That may mean lost customers and lost revenue as well as loss of customer goodwill, which may lead to lost future sales. A comprehensive study on out-of-stock frequency in the retail sector (Gruen et al., 2002) has estimated that worldwide the out-of-stock frequency in these settings averages at 8.3%. The researchers estimate that a typical retailer loses about 4% of sales because of having items out of stock. A 4% loss of sales for the average firm in the grocery retail sector, for example, translates into earnings per share loss of 4.8%.

---

[1] All numbers in the examples are fictitious and used only to illustrate the concepts.

Sometimes, *customers may be willing to wait and have their needs satisfied later, in which case their demand is said to be* **backlogged**. Regardless, when a stockout occurs, customer needs are not immediately fulfilled, and this leads to some level of dissatisfaction. To avoid stockouts—and to provide better customer service—businesses often find it wise to keep extra inventory just in case actual demand exceeds the forecast. As mentioned earlier, *inventory in excess of the average or in excess of forecast demand* is called **safety inventory** or **safety stock**.

This definition of safety stock may seem to imply that it is always *positive*. Depending on costs and benefits of carrying inventory, however, it may be preferable to keep an inventory level that covers less-than-average demand, which yields a negative safety inventory. We will explore negative safety inventory in Section 7.3.

7.2.1 Service Level Measures

To determine the optimal level of safety inventory, the process manager should consider economic trade-offs between the cost of stockouts and the cost of carrying excess inventory. Although inventory-carrying costs are quantifiable (as identified in Chapter 6), unfortunately the intangible consequences of stockouts are difficult to evaluate in monetary terms. Consequently, the process manager often decides to provide a certain level of customer service and then determines the amount of safety inventory needed to meet that objective. The two commonly used measures of customer service are as follows:

- **Cycle service level** refers to either *the probability that there will be no stockout within an order cycle* or, equivalently, the proportion of order cycles without a stockout, where an order cycle is the time between two consecutive replenishment orders.
- **Fill rate** is *the fraction of total demand satisfied from inventory on hand.*

These measures are illustrated in Example 7.2.

Example 7.2

Suppose that a process manager observes that within 100 order cycles, stockouts occur in 20. Cycle service level is then

$$80/100 = 0.8, \text{ or } 80\%$$

Now suppose that in each order cycle in which a stockout occurred, we measure the extent of the stockout in terms of the number of units by which we were short. Specifically, suppose that total demand during the 100 cycles was 15,000 units and the total number of units short in the 20 cycles with stockouts was 1,500 units. The fill rate, therefore, is

$$13,500/15,000 = 0.9, \text{ or } 90\%$$

Depending on the business context, an 80% cycle service level or a 90% fill rate may not be acceptable.

Effective inventory policies can be devised to achieve a desired level of either measure of customer service. In most business-to-consumer transaction settings (e.g., retail sales), only information on sales is available, as true demand is rarely observed because of stockouts. This makes it difficult to measure fill rate, which requires knowledge of demand. Furthermore, analyzing inventory policies for cycle service level is often simpler than for the fill rate measure. In this book, we focus on cycle service level and refer to it simply as service level (*SL*). Discussions about inventory policies for the fill rate measure can be found in a supply chain management text (see, e.g., Chopra & Miendl, 2003).

In the rest of this section, we determine two items:

1. The service level provided by a given amount of safety inventory
2. The amount of safety inventory needed to provide a given level of service

Before we address these issues, we will describe a modification of the inventory policy (introduced in Chapter 6, Section 6.7) when demands are uncertain.

7.2.2   Continuous Review, Reorder Point System

In establishing an inventory system, a process manager must first decide how often the inventory level should be reviewed. The two choices are either reviewing it periodically (weekly, monthly) or continuously. Obviously, the decision will depend on the cost of the review. With the widespread use of information systems, this cost has been declining, and more businesses are opting for a continuous review system, which will also be our focus in this book.

Recall the two fundamental questions that a process manager must address once a review policy has been set:

- How much should I order?
- When should I reorder?

The answer to the first question depends on the trade-off between the fixed cost of placing orders and the variable holding cost of carrying the inventory that results from larger quantities. This trade-off is essentially what led to the development of the economic order quantity (EOQ) formula discussed in Chapter 6. *Having initially ordered a fixed quantity, the process manager monitors inventory level continuously and then reorders (a quantity perhaps equal to EOQ) once available inventory level falls to a pre-specified reorder point. This order policy, known as a* **continuous review**, **reorder point policy**, is essentially the one described in Chapter 6. Here we extend it to include uncertainty in *demand* and replenishment *lead time*.

In the sequel, we will use **boldface** notation to signify that the variable represented by the notation can take values that are uncertain or unknown. For example, $\mathbf{X}$ will be a variable that takes uncertain values; $\mathbf{X}$ is usually referred to as a random variable. The average value of $\mathbf{X}$ will be represented by an *italicized X,* and its standard deviation (a statistical measure of the variability of $\mathbf{X}$; see Appendix II for details) will be represented by the symbol sigma with a subscript X, that is, σ_X.

In this context, $\mathbf{R}$ will denote the (uncertain) *demand rate per unit of time* (day, week, month, or year). The average demand rate is R, which now represents the average rate at which inventory is depleted over time. Actual demand rate—and thus inventory level—will vary. Similarly, the (uncertain) replenishment lead time is denoted by $\mathbf{L}$ with an average value denoted by L. This delay can result from a combination of various delays in information, processing, or transportation. The variable is measured in the same time units (days, weeks, months, or years) as $\mathbf{R}$. If $\mathbf{R}$ is the number of flow units demanded per day, week, or month, then $\mathbf{L}$ is measured in the number of days, weeks, or months, respectively, that elapsed between the placing of an order and its receipt. Thus, when the available inventory level falls to the reorder point, a new order of size Q (a quantity perhaps equal to EOQ) is placed that arrives in $\mathbf{L}$ time periods. On receipt of this new order, of course, available inventory level increases by Q units.

Lead Time Demand   The reorder point inventory is used to meet flow-unit requirements until the new order is received $\mathbf{L}$ periods later. The risk of stockout occurs during this period of replenishment lead time. The *total flow-unit requirement during replenishment lead time* is called **lead time demand** and is designated by **LTD**. In general, if either flow rate $\mathbf{R}$ or lead time $\mathbf{L}$ is uncertain, total lead time demand **LTD** will also be uncertain. Uncertainty in flow rate results from less-than-perfect forecasting (which is inevitable). Uncertainty in lead time may be due to a supplier's unreliability in delivering on-time orders. When the leadtime demand exceeds the reorder point, a stockout occurs, as illustrated in the following example.

Example 7.1 (Revisited)

Recall that the average leadtime demand is determined to be 20,000 units (see Example 7.1) and the reorder point was set at 20,000 units. Suppose, however, that the manager observes that actual leadtime demand fluctuates between 15,000 and 25,000 units. Because leadtime demand is uncertain, actual leadtime demand is less than 20,000 in some replenishment cycles and larger in others. When the latter situation occurs, we have a stockout.

Let the average leadtime demand be denoted by LTD and its standard deviation by σ_{LTD}. Suppose that the reorder point is set at the average lead time demand, or $ROP = LTD$. Assume further that the distribution (see Appendix II) of leadtime demand is symmetric around its mean. This means that if we carry just enough inventory to satisfy forecast demand during lead time (with a mean LTD), then actual leadtime demand will exceed forecast demand in 50% of our order cycles. We will suffer stockouts, and our service level SL will be 50%. To reduce our stockout risk, we may decide to order earlier by setting the reorder point larger than the average leadtime demand. The additional amount that we carry in excess of the average requirements is the safety inventory, denoted by I_{safety}. That is,

$$I_{safety} = ROP - LTD$$

Thus, we have reorder point inventory expressed as follows:

$$ROP = \text{Average lead time demand} + \text{safety stock} = LTD + I_{safety} \qquad \textbf{(7.1)}$$

Figure 7.1 illustrates a continuous review reorder point system when the lead time demand is uncertain. As shown, inventory level fluctuates over time and is not depleted

FIGURE 7.1 Continuous Review Reorder Point System

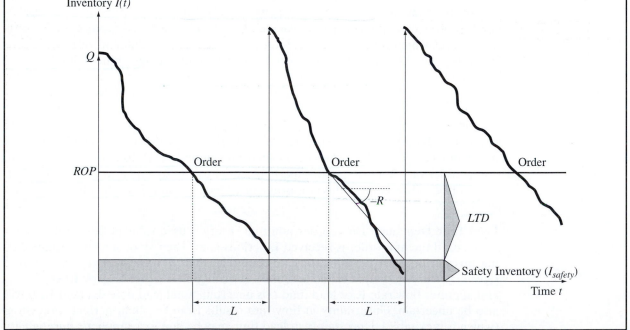

uniformly. Specifically, the on-hand inventory when an order arrives varies between cycles. When actual lead time demand is *smaller* than its average value of *LTD* (as in the first cycle in Figure 7.1), the on-hand inventory just before the next order arrives is greater than the safety inventory (I_{safety}). If, however, the actual lead time demand is larger than its average value of *LTD* (as in the second cycle in Figure 7.1), the on-hand inventory just before the next order arrives is smaller than the safety inventory. Because the average lead time demand is *LTD,* the average on-hand inventory just before the next order arrives will be equal to the safety inventory (I_{safety}).

Recall from Chapter 6 that average inventory with an order of size *Q* equals *Q*/2 and is called cycle inventory, I_{cycle}. When lead time demand is uncertain, we carry safety inventory I_{safety} as well, so that the total average inventory is now

$$I = I_{cycle} + I_{safety} = Q/2 + I_{safety} \qquad (7.2)$$

Because the average flow rate is *R,* the average flow time is expressed by Little's law as follows:

$$T = I/R = (Q/2 + I_{safety})/R$$

It represents the average amount of time a typical flow unit waits in inventory before being used.

7.2.3 Service Level Given Safety Inventory

Service level is measured by the probability (or the proportion of time) that the actual leadtime demand will not exceed the reorder point. Figure 7.2 illustrates the relationship between the distribution of lead time demand **LTD**, the reorder point *ROP*, and the corresponding service level *SL*. In Figure 7.2, the area under the density curve to the left of the reorder point is the probability *SL* that leadtime demand will be less than the reorder point.

Formally, this area can be written as

$$SL = \text{Prob}(\textbf{LTD} \le ROP) \qquad (7.3)$$

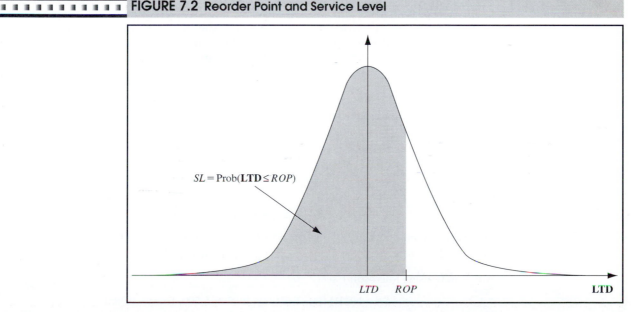

FIGURE 7.2 Reorder Point and Service Level

To compute this probability, we need to know the probability distribution of the random variable **LTD**. It is common to assume that **LTD** is normally distributed with mean *LTD* and standard deviation σ_{LTD}. Thus, the probability density function of **LTD** (representing the probability of different values of **LTD**; see Appendix II for details) is bell shaped—symmetric around *LTD* with a spread representing the magnitude of σ_{LTD}—where larger values of σ_{LTD} correspond to a more dispersed distribution. It can then be shown (see the Appendix at the end of this chapter) that the area covered to the left of the reorder point in the density function for leadtime demand is the same as the area covered to the left of a corresponding constant, represented by *z*, to the left of a normal density with mean of 0 and standard deviation of 1. Formally,

$$SL = \text{Prob}(\textbf{LTD} \leq ROP) = \text{Prob}(\textbf{Z} \leq z)$$

where **Z** is a *standard normal random variable* with mean 0 and standard deviation 1 and *z* measures the safety inventory I_{safety} relative to the standard deviation of lead time demand σ_{LTD}. That is,

$$I_{safety} = z \times \sigma_{LTD} \tag{7.4}$$

or

$$z = \frac{I_{safety}}{\sigma_{LTD}}$$

Thus, for any given value of *z,* the service level *SL* can now be read from the standard normal table given in Appendix II. The service level can also be computed directly in Microsoft Excel as follows:

$$SL = \text{NORMDIST}\ (ROP,\ LTD,\ \sigma_{LTD},\ \text{True})$$

Example 7.3 illustrates the computation of service level for a given safety inventory.

Example 7.3

In Example 7.1, the average lead time demand for lamps at GE Lighting's Paris warehouse was determined to be 20,000 units. Actual demand, however, varies daily. Suppose, then, that the standard deviation of lead time demand is estimated to be 5,000 units. The warehouse currently orders a 14-day supply of lamps each time the inventory level drops to 24,000 units. How do we determine service level in terms of the proportion of order cycles over which the warehouse will have stock to meet customer demand? What are the average total inventory and the average flow time?

We know the following: The lead time demand **LTD** has mean *LTD* = 20,000 units and standard deviation σ_{LTD} = 5,000. Safety inventory can be expressed as follows:

$$I_{safety} = ROP - LTD$$
$$= 24,000 - 20,000 = 4,000$$

which, when measured as the number of standard deviations, corresponds to

$$z = \frac{I_{safety}}{\sigma_{LTD}}$$

or

$$z = 4{,}000/5{,}000 = 0.8$$

Using the standard normal tables (Appendix II), we now find the service level to be

$$SL = \text{Prob}(\textbf{Z} \leq 0.8) = 0.7881$$

Alternately, using Microsoft Excel,

$$SL = \text{NORMDIST}\ (24{,}000, 20{,}000, 5{,}000, \text{True}) = 0.7881$$

To summarize, in 78.81% of the order cycles, the warehouse will not have a stockout.

Recall from Example 7.1 that the warehouse manager orders $Q = 28,000$ units. Thus, the corresponding cycle inventory

$$I_{cycle} = 28,000/2 = 14,000$$

With safety inventory

$$I_{safety} = 4,000$$

the average total inventory is

$$I = I_{cycle} + I_{safety} = 18,000 \text{ units}$$

for an average annual holding cost of

$$€20 \times 18,000 = €360,000/\text{year}$$

Average flow time, therefore, is

$$T = I/R = 18,000/2,000 = 9 \text{ days}$$

7.2.4   Safety Inventory Given Service Level

Managers often want to determine the safety inventory and reorder point required to provide a desired level of service. In this case, in Figure 7.2 we know the service level *SL* and want to compute the reorder point *ROP*. To proceed, we must reverse the computational procedure in Section 7.2.3. Knowing *SL*, we first determine the z value from the standard normal tables (Appendix II) such that

$$SL = \text{Prob}(\mathbf{Z} \leq z)$$

Given *SL*, the z value can also be computed directly in Microsoft Excel as follows:

$$z = \text{NORMSINV}(SL)$$

We can then compute the safety inventory

$$I_{safety} = z \times \sigma_{LTD}$$

and then the reorder point

$$ROP = LTD + I_{safety}$$

Alternately, the reorder point can be directly computed using Microsoft Excel as

$$ROP = \text{NORMINV}(SL, LTD, \sigma_{LTD})$$

Thus, to determine the reorder point for a desired service level, we need information regarding average lead time demand *LTD* and its standard deviation σ_{LTD}. These figures in turn will depend on flow rate **R** (its average and standard deviation) and lead time of supply **L** (its average and standard deviation). To keep our focus on the interaction between service levels and safety inventory, we assume in this section that the average and standard deviation of leadtime demand are known. We discuss methods for estimating information about lead time demands in Section 7.5. Example 7.4 illustrates the computation of the safety inventory and reorder point to achieve a given service level.

Example 7.4

Reconsider Example 7.3. We determined that with a safety inventory of 4,000 units, the provided service level was 78.81%. Recently, customers of the Paris warehouse have started complaining about the frequent stockout of lamps when they placed their orders with the warehouse. In response, the warehouse manager is considering increasing the service level but does not know how much the increase may cost in extra inventory. He wants to evaluate the cost of providing service

TABLE 7.2 Safety Inventory versus Service Level

Service Level (SL)	z Value	Safety Inventory (I_{safety})	Reorder Point (ROP)
85%	1.04	5,200	25,200
90%	1.28	6,406	26,406
95%	1.65	8,246	28,246
99%	2.33	11,686	31,686

levels of 85%, 90%, 95%, and 99%. How will he determine how much safety inventory should be carried to provide these levels?

Recall first that the average (LTD) and standard deviation (σ_{LTD}) of the leadtime demand were 20,000 and 5,000 units, respectively. Now consider a service level of 85%. To determine the corresponding value of z, we must find that value of z such that

$$\text{Prob}(\mathbf{Z} \leq z) = 0.85$$

Using the standard normal tables, one can read the z value for 85% service level as 1.04. Alternately, in Microsoft Excel, we will write

$$z = \text{NORMSINV}(0.85) = 1.04$$

Safety inventory is therefore $I_{safety} = z \times \sigma_{LTD} = 1.04 \times 5,000 = 5,200$ units, and the reorder point is $ROP = LTD + I_{safety} = 20,000 + 5,200 = 25,200$ units. We repeat this process for each desired service level—reading the z value, computing the safety inventory, and calculating the reorder point. The results are summarized in Table 7.2, where we observe that required safety inventory increases with service level. Whereas an increase of 5% in service, from 85% to 90%, requires an additional safety inventory of 1,206 units, the next 5% increase in service level, from 90% to 95%, requires an additional safety inventory of 1,840 units. Thus we observe a nonlinear relationship between safety inventory and service level.

Increasing service level increases the required safety inventory *more than proportionately*—as seen in Figure 7.3. Because providing higher levels of service gets

FIGURE 7.3 Safety Inventory versus Service Level

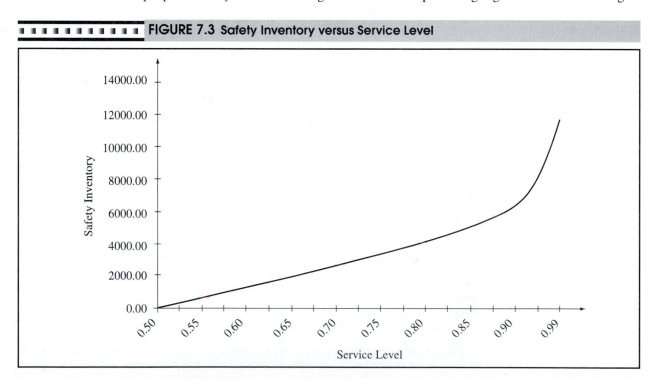

increasingly more expensive in terms of inventory holding cost, the process of selecting service and safety inventory levels is an important strategic decision. A firm may choose, for instance, to provide high-quality service in terms of product availability, or it may choose to be a low-cost supplier by holding down inventory costs. In either case, it is positioning itself along the service versus cost trade-off curve displayed in Figure 7.3. Our aim in providing Example 7.4 and Table 7.2 is to show how that position could be operationalized. For example, if the warehouse decides to position itself as a company providing high service at a 99% level, then it must carry a safety inventory of approximately 11,686 units along with the entailing cost.

▪▪▪ 7.3 Optimal Service Level: The Newsvendor Problem

Thus far, we have derived safety inventory for a desired level of customer service. However, what level of service should a firm offer? An optimal service level should balance the benefits of improved service in terms of supply continuity and customer satisfaction with the additional costs of holding required safety inventory. In this section, we analyze this problem in a simpler context with a problem involving only one order cycle. The *qualitative* principles that emerge in the upcoming discussion carry over to this discussion of the reorder point model.

A large proportion of retail sales involves "fashion goods" with short product life cycles of a few months. Usually, the retailer has only one or two buying opportunities, and at the end of the product life cycle, remaining items must be marked down for sale or even disposed of at a loss. Newspapers and magazines, for example, have limited lives (a day, a week, a month) at the end of which they lose most of their value. Perishable grocery items—fish, produce, bread, and milk—also have limited shelf lives and must be discarded after expiration dates. Seasonal items like Christmas trees, snowblowers and lawn mowers, and summer and winter apparel are bought and sold only at certain times of the year. In these cases, purchasing too few or too many items in relation to uncertain customer demand entails tangible costs. Because margins are usually high before the end of the season, retailers with insufficient inventory lose potential profits. Conversely, because postseason markdowns can be significant, those with excess inventory lose money through lower margins.

Thus, it is important to perform economic analysis in order to determine the optimal order quantity. Such an analysis should balance the expected costs of ordering too little (such as customer dissatisfaction and the opportunity cost of lost revenue) with the expected costs of ordering too much (such as markdowns and disposal costs). In the operations literature, *this basic model of decision making under uncertainty whereby the decision maker balances the expected costs of ordering too much with the expected costs of ordering too little to determine the optimal order quantity* is discussed as the **newsvendor problem**. It differs from the EOQ inventory model (illustrated in Chapter 6), which focuses on scale economies and, more importantly, assumes no uncertainty. The newsvendor model, which is a basic model for decision making under uncertainty, highlights the role of uncertainty, assumes no scale economies, and boasts a wide variety of applications, as illustrated at the end of this section. Let us consider Example 7.5.

Example 7.5

Big George Appliances[2] is an electronics superstore in Ann Arbor, Michigan. It sells consumer electronics items as well as appliances. Big George is considering carrying a newly introduced plasma HDTV for Christmas holiday sales. Each HDTV can be sold at $2,500. Big George can

---

[2]All numbers in the example are fictitious and used only to illustrate the concepts.

TABLE 7.3 Demand for HDTV at Big George

Demand r	Probability Prob(R = r)	Cumulative Probability Prob(R ≤ r)	Complementary Cumulative Probability Prob(R > r)
100	0.02	0.02	0.98
110	0.05	0.07	0.93
120	0.08	0.15	0.85
130	0.09	0.24	0.76
140	0.11	0.35	0.65
150	0.16	0.51	0.49
160	0.20	0.71	0.29
170	0.15	0.86	0.14
180	0.08	0.94	0.06
190	0.05	0.99	0.01
200	0.01	1	0

purchase each unit for $1,800. Any unsold TVs can be salvaged for $1,700. The retailer estimates that the demand for this new HDTV will be between 100 and 200 units with probability weights as given in Table 7.3. Big George needs to determine the number of HDTVs to be purchased for this season's sales.

We use the following notation in Table 7.3. The uncertain demand for HDTV is represented by **R**. The variable **R** can take various values, denoted by r, ranging from 100 to 200; this is column 1. The probability of a particular demand value r is given by $\text{Prob}(\mathbf{R} = r)$ and is listed in column 2. The cumulative probability, written as $\text{Prob}(\mathbf{R} \leq r)$, representing the chance that demand **R** will be less than or equal to a particular value r, is given in column 3. Finally, the last column gives the complementary cumulative probability, written as $\text{Prob}(\mathbf{R} > r)$, which is the probability that the demand **R** will exceed a particular value r. Using data from Table 7.3, we can compute the average demand as the weighted average of all possible demand values between 100 and 200 and their respective probabilities. Let $\bar{R}$ represent this average. Notationally, if x takes values from 1 to k, we write $\sum_{x=1}^{k} x$ to represent the sum of all values of x ranging from 1 to k. Using this notation, we write

$$\bar{R} = \sum_{demand=100}^{200} demand \times probability$$
$$\bar{R} = \sum_{r=100}^{200} r \times \text{Prob}(\mathbf{R} = r) = 151.60 \text{ units}$$

This estimate of the average demand, $\bar{R}$, represents the forecast of sales. If there were no uncertainty in demand for the HDTVs, then Big George should purchase 152 units. With uncertain demand, however, there is a 49% probability that actual demand will exceed 150, resulting in a stockout and lost revenue. There is also a 51% chance that at least one HDTV will be left over to be salvaged at a loss. Thus, ordering the mean demand may not maximize profitability.

To facilitate the determination of the optimal order quantity, we first outline a procedure to estimate the expected profits for a particular order quantity, say, $Q = 160$ units. First, we recall the following facts:

- If actual demand is 160 or higher, all 160 units will be sold at a profit of $700 each.
- If the demand is fewer than 160 units, some of the 160 units will have to be disposed of at a loss of $100 each (the difference between the purchase price and the salvage value).

Thus, every unit sold fetches a unit profit of $700, and every unsold unit costs $100. Given an order quantity, we can compute the gross profit for every possible demand scenario (ranging from demand values of 100 to 200). Each demand scenario, however, occurs with a known probability, as given in Table 7.3. For example, if the order quantity is 160 and the demand realized is

TABLE 7.4 Order Quantity versus Expected Profits

Order Quantity (Q)	Expected Profit
100	$70,000
110	$76,840
120	$83,280
130	$89,080
140	$94,160
150	$98,360
160	$101,280
170	$102,600
180	$102,720
190	$102,200
200	$101,280

100, Big George will then sell 100 units at a profit of $700 each. However, 60 units will be left unsold, incurring a loss of $100 each. The gross profit for demand value of 100 is then $(100 \times \$700 - 60 \times \$100) = \$64,000$. The chance of a demand realization of 100 is $\text{Prob}(\mathbf{R} = 100) = 0.02$. Observe that under each of the scenarios, when demand realized is greater than or equal to 160 units, sales will be 160 units, and there will be no excess units left over, giving gross profits of $160 \times \$700 = \$112,000$. These scenarios, cumulatively, will occur with probability $\text{Prob}(\mathbf{R} \geq 160)$. By multiplying the gross profit under a given scenario with its probability and then summing across all possible scenarios, we can compute the expected profit of a given order quantity. For an order quantity of 160 units, the expected profit is computed as follows:

$$(100 \times 700 - 60 \times 100)\, \text{Prob}(\mathbf{R} = 100) + (110 \times 700 - 50 \times 100)\, \text{Prob}(\mathbf{R} = 110)$$
$$+ (120 \times 700 - 40 \times 100)\, \text{Prob}(\mathbf{R} = 120) + \ldots + (160 \times 700)\, \text{Prob}(\mathbf{R} \geq 160)$$
$$= \$101,280$$

A similar approach can be used to determine the expected profit resulting from an order quantity of $Q = 110, \ldots, 200$. The expected profits for these order quantities are displayed in Table 7.4.

The order quantity that yields maximum profit equals 180 units—which is our desired order quantity. The optimal order size is larger than expected demand because with uncertain demand, we do not simply order the expected value of demand. Rather, our decision depends on a broader range of economic considerations, including price, purchasing cost, and salvage value of the unit.

The generic problem can be stated as follows: Consider a retailer who sells ski parkas. Let $\mathbf{R}$ denote the uncertain demand for this product. Every ski parka sold during the season fetches retail price of p per unit. Any parka not sold during the season can be disposed of at a markdown price of v per unit. The unit purchase cost (wholesale price paid by the retailer) of one parka is c. The retailer must decide how many parkas to order. Suppose the retailer decides to order Q parkas. As a consequence, the various cash flows can be described as follows:

- **In-season sales**: The number of parkas sold during the season will depend on the realized demand and will be given by the lesser of the demand and the quantity stocked and is equal to $min\,(Q, \mathbf{R})$; Each of these parkas generate a revenue of p, giving a total revenue $p \times min\,(Q, \mathbf{R})$.
- **Markdown sales**: Parkas not sold during the regular season will be salvaged at the end of the season. The number of parkas left over at the end of the season is given by $max\,(Q - \mathbf{R}, 0)$, each earning a revenue of v. The total revenues earned from markdown sales is then $v \times max\,(Q - \mathbf{R}, 0)$.

- **Purchase cost**: Finally, the retailer purchases Q parkas at a unit cost of c per unit, resulting in a total purchase cost of cQ.

The realized value of in-season sales and markdown sales will differ depending on the demand that materializes. The retailer, however, has to make her decision before observing the demand. She chooses an order quantity Q that optimizes the expected value of the profits given as

$$\text{Expected profit} = \text{Expected in-season sales} + \text{Expected markdown sales}$$
$$- \text{Purchase cost}$$

Marginal Analysis   A more insightful approach to understanding the trade-offs involved in deciding optimal order quantity entails **marginal analysis**: *comparing expected costs and benefits of purchasing each incremental unit.* First we must define the following:

- **Net marginal benefit** *is the difference between the unit price of the product and unit marginal cost of procurement.* The net marginal benefit from each additional unit, denoted by *MB*, is its contribution margin. If the unit retail price is p and the unit purchase cost is c, then

$$MB = p - c$$

  In practice, it may also include the opportunity cost of lost goodwill had the unit not been stocked but were demanded.
- **Net marginal cost** *is the difference between unit marginal cost of procurements and its salvage unit.* The net marginal cost of stocking an additional unit, denoted by *MC*, is the effective cost if the unit remains unsold under conditions of low demand. If the unit salvage value is v and the purchase cost is c, then

$$MC = c - v$$

We receive the net marginal benefit only when the additional unit sells, which will occur whenever demand exceeds Q. At any order quantity, Q, the expected marginal benefit from ordering an additional unit is

$$MB \times \text{Prob}(\mathbf{R} > Q)$$

At the same time, we suffer the net marginal cost only when the additional unit does not sell, which will occur whenever demand is no more than Q. The expected marginal cost of having a unit left over is

$$MC \times \text{Prob}(\mathbf{R} \leq Q)$$

Note that *while the expected marginal benefit from purchasing an additional unit is decreasing, expected marginal cost is increasing in the order quantity* Q. As long as expected benefit is greater than expected cost, Q should be increased until the reverse is true. Thus, the optimal Q is the first value Q^* for which the expected cost of ordering an additional unit exceeds the expected benefit; that is,

$$MC \times \text{Prob}(\mathbf{R} \leq Q^*) \geq MB \times \text{Prob}(\mathbf{R} > Q^*)$$

Since

$$\text{Prob}(\mathbf{R} > Q) = 1 - \text{Prob}(\mathbf{R} \leq Q)$$

the condition for optimality of Q^* can be rewritten as follows:

$$MC \times \text{Prob}(\mathbf{R} \leq Q^*) \geq MB \times [1 - \text{Prob}(\mathbf{R} \leq Q^*)]$$

Rearranging terms, we arrive at an optimal order quantity as *the smallest value Q^* such that*

$$\text{Prob}(\mathbf{R} \le Q^*) \ge \frac{MB}{MB + MC}$$

Thus, computing optimal order quantity is a two-step procedure:

1. Compute the ratio $\dfrac{MB}{MB + MC}$.
2. Determine optimal order quantity, Q^*, from the cumulative distribution of demand **R**.

We illustrate this procedure in Example 7.6.

Example 7.6
We now apply these principles to the problem of ordering HDTVs for Big George Appliances. Recall that

$$MB = p - c = 2{,}500 - 1{,}800 = \$700$$

and

$$MC = c - v = 1{,}800 - 1{,}700 = \$100$$

Thus,

$$\frac{MB}{MB + MC} = \frac{700}{700 + 100} = 0.875$$

From the cumulative distribution of demand in Table 7.3 (column 3), we find that

$$\text{Prob}(\mathbf{R} \le 180) = 0.94$$

and

$$\text{Prob}(\mathbf{R} \le 170) = 0.86$$

Therefore, the smallest Q^* such that $\text{Prob}(\mathbf{R} \le Q^*) \ge 0.876$ is $Q^* = 180$.

We can simplify this procedure even further. It is often more convenient, for instance, to assume that demand is a continuous random variable, whereby all (noninteger) values of **R** and Q become possible. If we make this assumption, then at optimal Q we can exactly balance out the marginal benefit of increasing Q (by a fractional amount) with the loss of keeping Q at its current level. Thus,

$$MC \times \text{Prob}(\mathbf{R} \le Q^*) = MB \times [1 - \text{Prob}(\mathbf{R} \le Q^*)]$$

which gives us an optimal order quantity, Q^*, that satisfies the following relationship:

$$\text{Prob}(\mathbf{R} \le Q^*) = \frac{MB}{MB + MC}$$

Recall from Section 7.2 that cycle service level was defined as the probability of not stocking out in a cycle. If demand is represented by **R** and order quantity by Q, then cycle service level is $\text{Prob}(\mathbf{R} \le Q)$. Because Q^* is optimal order quantity determined by the economic trade-off between costs of under- and overstocking, $\text{Prob}(\mathbf{R} \le Q^*)$ is the optimal probability of not stocking out. Therefore, using the earlier relationship for Q^*, the optimal service level SL^* is given by the following formula:

$$\text{Newsvendor formula:} \quad \boxed{SL^* = \text{Prob}(\mathbf{R} \le Q^*) = \frac{MB}{MB + MC}} \qquad \text{(7.5)}$$

Note that optimal service level depends only on the net marginal benefit and cost of stocking a unit and not on the probability distribution function. Furthermore, it increases with the net marginal benefit, *MB,* and decreases with the net marginal cost, *MC.* Thus, *the more expensive stockouts and/or the lower the cost of disposing of excessive inventory, the higher the optimal service level.* For Examples 7.5 and 7.6, optimal service level is computed as equal to

$$\frac{MB}{MB + MC} = 0.875$$

Knowing our optimal service level, we can now determine optimal order quantity from the probability distribution of demand. Let us assume, for example, that demand is normally distributed with mean R and standard deviation σ_R. In that case, the optimal order quantity Q^* can be determined in one of two ways:

1. From the standard normal tables given in the Appendix II, we first determine z corresponding to the optimal service level SL^* and then compute

$$Q^* = R + z \times \sigma_R$$

2. Or, from the Excel function,

$$Q^* = \text{NORMINV}\,(SL^*, R, \sigma_R)$$

We illustrate this computation in Example 7.7.

Example 7.7

Recall that in Example 7.5, $R = 151.60$. The variance of R can be computed as *the average squared deviation from its mean,* or

$$\sigma_R^2 = \sum_{r=100}^{200} [(r - R)^2 \times \text{Prob}(\mathbf{R} = \text{r})] = 503.44$$

Taking its square root gives the standard deviation $\sigma_R = 22.44$ units—a figure that measures the variation in actual demand around its mean. We need Q^* such that

$$\text{Prob}(\mathbf{R} \le Q^*) = 0.875$$

Looking up the normal tables, we find that $z = 1.15$ and

$$Q^* = R + z \times \sigma_R = 151.60 + 1.15 \times 22.44 = 177.41$$

Alternately, using the Microsoft Excel formula, we get

$$Q^* = \text{NORMINV}\,(0.875, 151.60, 22.44) = 177.41$$

which is close to our earlier answer of 180 units. The discrepancy arises because we approximated discrete demand probability density in Example 7.5 with a continuous probability density.

In the newsvendor model, the difference between the optimal order quantity Q^* and the mean demand R is the single-order equivalent of safety inventory I_{safety} that we considered in the preceding section. Thus, the qualitative conclusions of this section apply to the preceding discussion. Of course, the economics of the situation could be such that the optimal order quantity is below the mean demand, in which case we say that the firm carries a negative safety stock. This will occur, for example, when optimal service level is below 50%. With uncertain demand, therefore, we determine optimal service level—and corresponding safety inventory—by balancing the expected marginal benefit of an additional unit with those of expected marginal cost. Intuitively, we rationalize that if the net marginal benefit is twice the net marginal cost, we need an order quantity that gives us a probability of overstocking that is twice the probability of understocking. To summarize, the optimal service level increases with the net marginal benefit and decreases with the net marginal cost. The order quantity increases with the optimal service level and the mean and the standard deviation of demand.

The newsvendor model is a fundamental model for decision making under uncertainty and has applications in a wide variety of areas. Consider the following:

1. *Matrix Reloaded* has just been released on VHS for the rental market. Blockbuster needs to place orders for the tape. The studio charges a unit price for each tape Blockbuster purchases. The rental lifetime of a typical tape is about six weeks. Blockbuster can rent the tape several times during this period and then sell it off at a steep discount as a previewed tape. How many tapes of *Matrix Reloaded* should Blockbuster stock?

2. The IRS code allows employees to set aside a certain part of their salary into a health care Flexible Savings Account (FSA) earmarked for health care expenses. The amount set aside for a given year must be committed to by the end of the previous year. During the year, an employee can use these moneys, tax free, to cover qualified health care expenses. However, any amount not claimed during the year is forfeited. The health care needs of a family cannot be accurately forecasted. How much money should an employee set aside in their FSA?

3. Northwest Airlines needs to determine the number of reservations to accept for the 7:00 a.m. flight from Detroit to San Francisco. The plane has a capacity of 350 seats. Passengers always make last-minute changes to their travel plans, resulting in cancellation of their reservations. Therefore, accepting exactly 350 reservations may result in some unused seats because of cancellations. If more than 350 reservations are taken and everyone shows up, then some passengers need to be bumped at a cost. How many reservations should Northwest take for this flight?

4. Amgen is gearing up for the introduction of Enbrel, a breakthrough drug for arthritis. There is a wide range of estimates for the potential market for Enbrel. However, because of the long lead time for building a plant, Amgen must decide on capacity long before the product is launched. If demand ultimately outstrips capacity, there is the potential of lost revenue or of excessive costs of subcontracting. On the other hand, too little demand will result in capital tied up in unused capacity. How much capacity should Amgen build?

▪▪▪ 7.4   Lead Time Demand Variability

The rest of this chapter considers sources of demand variability and operational strategies for reducing this variability.

Recall that lead time demand **LTD** refers to the flow unit requirement from the time an order is placed until it is received. We carry safety inventory to satisfy this requirement a proportion of time corresponding to the service level. As discussed, both the safety inventory and the service level depend critically on the variability in the leadtime demand—if the leadtime demand were constant and known, we could guarantee 100% service level with no safety inventory. In this section, we consider factors that affect the service level and the safety inventory by contributing to variability in the leadtime demand.

7.4.1 Fixed Replenishment Lead Time

For the sake of simplicity, we first consider the case of known (fixed) replenishment lead time L measured in periods (days, weeks, months). We assume that our supplier is perfectly reliable, and we postpone the discussion of variability in lead times to Section 7.4.2.

First, let $\mathbf{R}_t$ denote (uncertain) demand in period t. For a supply lead time of L number of periods, total lead time demand will be

$$\mathbf{LTD} = \mathbf{R}_1 + \mathbf{R}_2 + \ldots + \mathbf{R}_L$$

We will assume that demand levels between periods are independent and follow the same distribution—that is, they are *independent and identically distributed random variables*. Average leadtime demand, therefore, will be given by

$$LTD = L \times R \qquad\qquad (7.6)$$

where L is lead time in number of periods and R is average demand per period. Since L is constant, variability in the leadtime demand arises from variability in the periodic demand. As noted, the statistical measure of variability is its standard deviation. Let σ_R be the standard deviation of demand (flow rate) per period (day, week, or month). Statistically, to compute the standard deviation σ_{LTD} of the leadtime demand, it is convenient to first estimate the variance of the leadtime demand given by σ_{LTD}^2 as

$$\sigma_{LTD}^2 = \sigma_R^2 + \sigma_R^2 + \cdots + \sigma_R^2 = L \times \sigma_R^2$$

This follows from the fact that *the variance of the sum of L independent random variables equals the sum of their variances*. Thus, standard deviation of lead time demand is

$$\sigma_{LTD} = \sqrt{L} \times \sigma_R \qquad\qquad (7.7)$$

If we know the lead time of supply and the variability in demand per period, we can compute safety inventory to achieve a desired level of service using ideas discussed in Section 7.2.4.

In addition to its dependence on service level (discussed in Section 7.2), safety inventory also depends on the standard deviation of lead time demand, which depends in turn on both length of supply lead time and variability in demand. Specifically, greater variability in lead time demand results from longer lead time, more variable demand per period, or both. More safety inventory is also needed to provide a desired level of service.

Example 7.8

GE Lighting's Paris warehouse manager wants to know if he can reduce procurement costs. The transportation department has proposed that material be shipped by ocean freight, which will reduce the per unit cost but increase the replenishment lead time to 20 days from the present 10 days. The manager needs to know the ramifications of this proposal. What impact, if any, would the new proposal have on the inventory carried in the warehouse?

We proceed in the following manner. Recall from Example 7.1 that the average daily demand R is 2,000 units. Recall also from Example 7.3 that the standard deviation of leadtime demand was specified as 5000. This was estimated based on a standard deviation of daily demand, σ_R, of 1,581 and a replenishment leadtime of 10 days. For the new lead time of $L = 20$ days, we can compute the standard deviation of the leadtime demand as follows:

$$\sigma_{LTD} = \sqrt{L} \times \sigma_R = \sqrt{20} \times 1,581 = 7,070 \text{ units}$$

For 95% service level, required safety inventory is expressed as

$$I_{safety} = z \times \sigma_{LTD} = 1.65 \times 7,070 = 11,666 \text{ units}$$

For a similar service level, when replenishment lead time was 10 days, the safety inventory was estimated in Example 7.4 to be 8,246 units. Thus, under the new proposal, the safety inventory increases by 3,420 units (or 41.4%) from 8,246 to 11,666 because of an increase in replenishment lead time. The additional cost of this inventory has to be traded off with any reduction in transportation cost to determine whether to accept the new proposal.

Example 7.8 illustrates the connection between replenishment lead time and safety inventory. This has managerial implications covering several issues, such as transportation mode choice and supplier selection and sourcing. A decision on transportation mode choice, such as air freight versus ocean freight, impacts the replenishment lead time. This in turn affects the safety inventory necessary to provide a specific service level, as shown in Example 7.8.

Similarly, from a sourcing perspective, suppose we can choose between two suppliers, one that offers a lower price but a longer lead time and the other that offers a shorter time but a higher price. In such situations, selecting a supplier on the basis of the price alone could result in the need to carry larger safety inventory—a decision that may increase total cost. Both contexts, then, call for a decision-making framework based on total costs, including material, transportation, and inventory costs.

7.4.2   Variability in Replenishment Lead Time

In addition to its duration, variability in lead time is also an important contributor to variability in the leadtime demand. To develop some intuition for the effect of variability in lead time, suppose that while demand rate R is fixed and known, lead time is a random variable, $\mathbf{L}$, with mean L and standard deviation σ_L. In this case, uncertain lead time demand is expressed as

$$\mathbf{LTD} = R \times \mathbf{L}$$

It has mean

$$LTD = R \times L$$

and variance

$$\sigma_{LTD}^2 = R^2 \times \sigma_L^2$$

The last expression follows from the fact that *the variance of a constant times a random variable is equal to the square of that constant times the variance of the random variable.*

More generally, suppose that both demand rate $\mathbf{R}$ and lead time $\mathbf{L}$ are random variables. If so, the leadtime demand is *the sum of a random number of random variables.* To compute the required safety inventory, therefore, we must compute the mean and the variance of the leadtime demand. Since the average lead time is L and average flow rate is R, it is clear that the average leadtime demand is

$$LTD = L \times R$$

Assuming that the demand and replenishment lead times are independent random variables, the variance of the leadtime demand can be computed by combining two special cases:

1. Variance of the leadtime demand when flow rate is random but the lead time is fixed (a situation discussed in the previous section)
2. Variance of the leadtime demand when the flow rate is constant but lead time is random (a situation discussed at the beginning of this section)

Total variability in the leadtime demand is then the sum of the two individual effects:

$$\sigma^2_{LTD} = L\sigma^2_R + R^2\sigma^2_L$$

The standard deviation of the leadtime demand is then computed by taking the square root of the variance of the leadtime demand and is given by the following formula:

$$\sigma_{LTD} = \sqrt{L\sigma^2_R + R^2\sigma^2_L} \tag{7.8}$$

The exact derivation of this intuitive explanation can be found in Ross (1972). The impact of variability in lead time on safety inventory is illustrated in Example 7.9.

Example 7.9

Return for a moment to Example 7.1 and suppose that the replenishment lead time has recently become more variable. Specifically, suppose that the replenishment lead time has a mean of 10 days and a standard deviation of 2 days (with all remaining data as specified in Example 7.1). How much safety inventory does the Paris warehouse need in order to provide a 95% service level?

Again, we start with the following data:

$$L = 10, \sigma_L = 2, R = 2,000, \sigma_R = 1,581$$

Thus, we see that

$$\sigma^2{}_{LTD} = (10)(1,581)^2 + (2,000)^2(2)^2 = 40,995,610$$

or

$$\sigma_{LTD} = 6,402.78$$

Therefore, safety inventory must be

$$I_{safety} = 1.65 \times \sigma_{LTD} = 10,565 \text{ units}$$

compared with only 8,246 units needed if lead time were *exactly* 10 days.

We can arrive at an intuitive understanding of this increase. With variability in lead time, it is likely that actual lead time of supply will often be larger than 10 days. The process manager must now account for this increase by carrying more safety inventory.

Thus, variability in lead time of supply increases the safety inventory. Lead time variability, therefore, has a significant impact on safety inventory requirements (and on material cycle time). Reliable suppliers who make on-time deliveries contribute directly to a firm's bottom line and level of customer service.

In summary, we have shown how uncertainty in demand and supply affects raw material and product availability. To provide better service in the face of uncertainty, firms carry safety inventory. Three key factors affect the amount of safety inventory that a company carries under given circumstances:

1. Level of customer service desired
2. The average and the uncertainty in demand
3. The average and the uncertainty in replenishment lead time

In turn, there are two primary levers for reducing the level of safety inventory:

1. Reducing both the average and standard deviation replenishment lead time
2. Reducing demand variability

Although improved forecasting can reduce variability in demand, too many firms tend to think it is their only option. Better forecasting can help, but it is not a panacea. As discussed, reducing the lead time and reducing its variability are also important levers. In Sections 7.5 and 7.6, we explore two further ways of reducing variability: aggregating demand and using shorter-range forecasts.

▪▪▪ 7.5　Pooling Efficiency through Aggregation

Recall from Section 7.1 the third characteristic of forecasts: aggregate forecasts are more accurate than individual forecasts. The basic concept of **aggregation**—*pooling demand for several similar products*—can be applied broadly. Indeed, firms often aggregate sales according to various geographical regions and/or types of products. Improved forecast accuracy due to aggregation is simply a statistical property, and we can devise important operational strategies to exploit this property in effective inventory management.

7.5.1　Physical Centralization

Suppose a firm stocks its product in multiple warehouses to serve geographically dispersed customers. Because all the locations face uncertain demand, each should carry some safety inventory. Assume that the company's warehousing operations are *decentralized*—that each warehouse operates independently of the others. It is possible, then, that one warehouse will be out of stock while another has the product in stock. Although the total distribution system has sufficient inventory, it may be held at the wrong location. As a result of this imbalance of inventory, some customer demand may not be satisfied.

Suppose, however, *that the firm can consolidate all its stock in one location from which it can serve all its customers.* We will call this alternative system the **physical centralization** of inventory. Because centralization eliminates the possibility of stock imbalance, all customer demand will be met as long as there is inventory in the system. The centralized system, therefore, will provide *better* customer service than the decentralized network and will do so with the *same* total inventory. Equivalently, to provide the same level of service as in the decentralized system, the centralized system would need *less* inventory.

Let us make these claims more precise. Suppose that a firm serves locations 1 and 2, and assume that the respective lead time demands—**LTD**$_1$ and **LTD**$_2$—are statistically identically distributed, each with mean of *LTD* and standard deviation of σ_{LTD}. To provide a desired level of service *SL,* each location must carry safety inventory

$$I_{safety} = z \times \sigma_{LTD}$$

where z is determined by the desired service level (as discussed in Section 7.2). If each facility faces identical demand and provides identical service levels, the total safety inventory in the decentralized system is equal to

$$I^d_{safety} = 2 \times z \times \sigma_{LTD}$$

Independent Demands　Consider centralizing the two inventories in one location when lead time demands at the two locations are independent. This centralized pool will now serve the total lead time demand

$$\mathbf{LTD} = \mathbf{LTD}_1 + \mathbf{LTD}_2$$

Recall that the mean and the variance of a sum of independent random variables are, respectively, equal to the sum of their means and variances. The mean of total lead time demand faced by the central warehouse is thus

$$LTD + LTD = 2\,LTD$$

Its variance is

$$\sigma^2{}_{LTD} + \sigma^2{}_{LTD} = 2\sigma^2{}_{LTD}$$

The standard deviation of the leadtime demand at the centralized location, therefore, is $\sqrt{2}\sigma_{LTD}$. Note that although consolidation of demands doubles the mean, the standard deviation increases only by a factor of $\sqrt{2}$ or 1.414.

Intuitively, we understand that high and low demands in the two locations will tend to counterbalance each other, thereby yielding a more stable total demand. Safety inventory carried in the centralized system is then equal to

$$I^c_{safety} = z \times \sqrt{2}\,\sigma_{LTD}$$

Comparing the safety inventories carried by decentralized (I^d_{safety}) and centralized (I^c_{safety}) systems, we observe that when both systems offer the same level of service, the total safety inventory required by the centralized operation is $\dfrac{1}{\sqrt{2}}$ times the required total safety inventory in the decentralized operation. That is, the safety inventory in a centralized system is less than in a two-location decentralized system by a factor of $\dfrac{1}{\sqrt{2}}$.

We can generalize our analysis of the benefits of centralizing two locations to consider the centralization of N locations. The safety inventory needed when N locations are centralized is given by

$$I^c_{safety} = z \times \sqrt{N}\,\sigma_{LTD} \tag{7.9}$$

A similar N location decentralized network will require a safety inventory investment of N times the safety inventory in each warehouse, which will total $N \times z \times \sigma_{LTD}$. Thus, centralization will reduce safety inventory investment by a factor of $\sqrt{N}$. The concept of centralization is illustrated in Example 7.10.

Example 7.10

Recall that GE Lighting operated seven warehouses. An internal task force had recommended that it consolidate all the seven warehouses into one central warehouse to serve customers in Austria, Belgium, France, Germany, the Netherlands, Luxembourg, and Switzerland. Assume that the replenishment lead time to this central warehouse will remain at 10 days. What will be the impact of accepting the task force recommendations?

In the current decentralized system, each warehouse orders independently of the other warehouses. In Example 7.4, we estimated that a warehouse facing average lead time demand of 20,000 units with a standard deviation of 5,000 units needs to carry a safety inventory of $I_{safety} = 8,246$ to provide a 95% service level. Assuming that each of the other warehouses faces similar demand patterns and wants to offer the same service level, the total safety inventory carried across the seven warehouses will be

$$I^d_{safety} = 7 \times 8,246 = 57,722$$

If the task force recommendation is accepted, the single central warehouse will face a total lead time demand with mean and standard deviation of

$$LTD = 7 \times 20,000 = 140,000$$
$$\sigma_{LTD} = \sqrt{7} \times 5,000 = 13,228.8$$

To provide a 95% service level, the central warehouse must carry a safety inventory:

$$I^c_{safety} = 1.65 \times \sigma_{LTD} = 1.65 \times 13,228.8 = 21,828$$

Thus, we see that the required safety inventory with the single central warehouse is 35,894 less than that required under the current decentralized network of seven warehouses. This reduction represents a decrease in safety inventory of 62%, or reduction by a factor of $\sqrt{7} = 2.65$.

Square Root Law   The savings illustrated in Example 7.10 results from the **square root law**, which states that *total safety inventory required to provide a specified level of service increases by the square root of the number of locations in which it is held.* This principle is displayed graphically in Figure 7.4.

In addition to the benefits of reducing the safety inventory, centralization also reduces the cycle inventory, as we saw in Chapter 6. The reduction in cycle inventory results from the fact that centralization allows better use of economies of scale in procurement and production. Physical centralization is a common practice for retailers with catalog and mail-, telephone-, or Internet-order operations.

Correlated Demands   In the previous discussion, we have shown the benefits of centralization when demands in the various locations were *independent*. Does centralization offer similar benefits when demands in the multiple locations are correlated? Suppose that a firm serves locations 1 and 2 with lead time demands—**LTD**$_1$ and **LTD**$_2$—that are statistically identically distributed but correlated. We represent the correlation of demand between the two locations with a correlation coefficient ρ (pronounced as *rho*). The mean of the total lead time demand is thus

$$LTD + LTD = 2\,LTD$$

▌ ▌ ▌ ▌ ▌ ▌ ▌ ▌ ▌ ▌ ▌ **FIGURE 7.4 Square Root Law of Pooling**

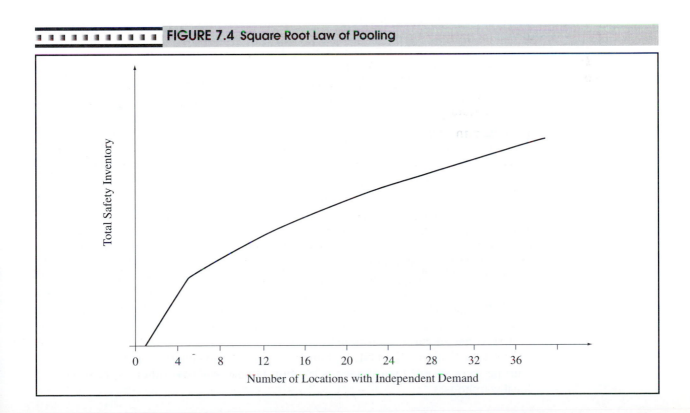

Its variance is

$$\sigma^2_{LTD} + \sigma^2_{LTD} + 2\rho\, \sigma^2_{LTD} = 2(1 + \rho)\sigma^2_{LTD}$$

Therefore, the total safety inventory in the centralized system is

$$I^c_{safety} = z \times \sqrt{2(1 + \rho)}\, \sigma_{LTD} \tag{7.10}$$

The total safety inventory required in the decentralized system is

$$I^d_{safety} = 2 \times z \times \sigma_{LTD}$$

Therefore, the safety inventory in the two-location decentralized system is larger than in the centralized system by a factor of

$$\sqrt{\frac{2}{(1 + \rho)}}$$

When the demands of the two locations are independent, the correlation coefficient $\rho = 0$ and the safety inventory in the decentralized system is larger by a factor of $\sqrt{2}$, as discussed earlier. The advantage of a centralized system increases as the demands on the two locations become negatively correlated. The advantage of a centralized system, however, diminishes as the demands in the two locations become positively correlated. In fact, if demand is perfectly positively correlated (i.e., $\rho = 1$), centralization offers no benefits in the reduction of safety inventory. The benefits of economies of scale discussed in Chapter 6, however, remain.

Disadvantages of Centralization If centralization of stocks reduces inventory, why doesn't everybody do it? In addition to inventory costs, at least two other factors need to be considered in making the decision. First is the *response time* to the customer, which measures the time taken to satisfy the customer demand. Second is the *shipment cost* of sending the goods to the customer from the warehouse. In the previous analysis, we assumed that both centralized and decentralized operations have *identical response times* and *identical shipment costs*. Hence, inventory costs remained the only determining factor. In practice, a centralized location is typically farther away from some customer locations than are some decentralized locations; centralization may entail longer response times when units must be shipped to more distant customers. It may also be more expensive to transport products to customers located at vastly different distances from the central location. If, in addition, response time and/or shipping costs increase such that overall demand decreases, then serving every customer from a single facility may not be optimal. In such situations, decentralized locations may improve response times and service levels. With decentralized locations, proximity to customers may also lead to better understanding their needs and developing closer relationships.

In addition, as described in Harps (2000), companies need to be aware of the cultural, linguistic, and regulatory barriers in some parts of the world (e.g., Europe and Asia) that may inhibit them in centralizing their operations. In fact, GE Lighting's decision, as illustrated at the beginning of this chapter, demonstrates that companies indeed consider these factors important. The trade-offs involved in centralization versus decentralization led GE Lighting to build a hybrid network where some parts of Europe were served by a single distribution facility, whereas others were served by local warehouses.

7.5.2 Principle of Aggregation and Pooling Inventory

It is important to stress that the inventory benefits outlined in the previous subsection result from the statistical principle called the **principle of aggregation**, which states that *the standard deviation of the sum of random variables is less than the sum of the individual standard deviations.* In all the examples discussed in Section 7.5.1, total inventory is physically located at a central location to enable the seller to aggregate demand across various regions. Physical consolidation, however, is not essential. As long as *available inventory is shared among various sources of demand—a practice known as* **pooling inventory**—we achieve the benefits of aggregation. As the following examples indicate, the concept of pooling inventory can be applied in various ways other than physical centralization.

Virtual Centralization Consider a distribution system with warehouses in two locations, A and B. Each location carries some safety stock to provide a given level of service. Suppose now that at a given time, demand for a product in location A exceeds the available local stock. The product, however, is available at location B. Customer demand at location A can then be satisfied with stock at location B. Likewise, if at any time location B is out of stock on an item that is available at location A, the product can be shipped to location B to satisfy customer demand. To accommodate this option, however, a system must satisfy two criteria:

1. Information about product demand and availability must be available at both locations.
2. Shipping the product from one location, B, to a customer at another location, A, must be fast and cost effective.

If these two requirements are met and correlation of demand is less than one, pooling is effective—inventory at any location can be shared by demands at all other locations. Because pooling is achieved by keeping the inventories at decentralized locations instead of physically consolidating them at one location, we call it virtual centralization. Formally, **virtual centralization** *is a system in which inventory pooling in a network of locations is facilitated using information regarding availability of goods and subsequent transshipment of goods between locations to satisfy demand.*

Machine-tool builder Okuma America Corporation, a subsidiary of Japan's Okuma Corporation, is an example of a company that is moving its distribution network toward virtual centralization. Each of its 46 distributors in North and South America has access to Okumalink, a shared information technology system that provides information about the location and availability of machine tools stored in Okuma warehouses in Charlotte, North Carolina, and in Japan. Okumalink is currently being upgraded to allow channel members to connect with one other directly, thereby facilitating intrachannel exchanges of products and parts (Narus & Anderson, 1996). Similarly, in the event of a stockout, orders placed to a distribution center in W.W. Grainger, a large industrial distributor, may be fulfilled from another distribution center in the network that has available stock.

Specialization A firm may have several warehouses, each of which stocks several products. Safety inventory for each product, however, may be allocated to a particular warehouse that specializes in that product. Even though there are several warehouses, there is for each product only one specialized warehouse that carries the entire safety inventory. Each warehouse effectively pools with all the others the inventory for the product in which it specializes.

This system is particularly useful when the local demand that each warehouse serves is more or less unique to the product. For example, suppose there are two warehouses, one each at locations A and B. Suppose inventory consists of two products, P1 and P2. In addition, suppose a large fraction of demand at location A is for product P1 and a large fraction of that at location B is for product P2. Then location A's warehouse may be specialized to carry all the safety stock for product P1, and location B may be specialized for product P2. If location B (or A) requires any units of P1 (or P2), it could be shipped from location A (or B). Under this arrangement, safety inventory for each product is reduced because each inventory is now centralized at one location. Furthermore, because centralization is based on the local demand patterns, response times and shipping costs are also less than they would be if all products were physically centralized at one warehouse.

Component Commonality   Our examples thus far have focused on pooling efficiency by means of aggregating demand across multiple geographic locations. The concept of pooling can also be exploited when aggregating demand across various products. Consider a computer manufacturer (such as Dell, Hewlett Packard, or Apple) that typically offers a wide range of models. Although models vary considerably, a few common components are used across product lines, such as similar central processing units or DVD or CD-RW drives.

To offer variety, firms have a few options. They can, for instance, *produce in anticipation of product demand*—a **make-to-stock** strategy. To provide a desired service level, the firm would then need sufficient safety inventory of each final product. Conversely, the firm may decide to *produce in response to customers orders*—a **make-to-order** strategy. Under this strategy, a firm keeps its entire inventory in components and builds the final product as and when customers place orders. To determine the safety inventory of those components common to various product lines, the firm aggregates demand for the products that share specific components. Component commonality thus allows the firm to reduce inventory investment while maintaining the same level of service and offering product variety.

Risk pooling of common-component demand across various products is akin to the practice of physical centralization that we described earlier. Safety inventory of common components will be much lower than the safety inventory of unique components stored separately for different finished products. In addition, in a make-to-order situation, holding costs will be less because inventory of components has accumulated no added value. There is, however, at least one key drawback. In a make-to-order situation, the customer must wait for the firm to produce the product, whereas the make-to-stock product is available for immediate consumption. Therefore, if flow times in production can be shortened until they are *shorter in duration than the wait that the consumer is willing to endure*, then a make-to-order strategy has significant benefits.

Product Substitution   Often, one product can substitute to fill excess demand for another. The ability to provide substitute products improves the effective level of service by pooling safety inventory across multiple products. Substitution, therefore, reduces the level of safety stock needed for a given level of customer service. To exploit this, however, a firm needs to gather information on substitution patterns.

▪▪▪ 7.6   Shortening the Forecast Horizon through Postponement

As noted in Section 7.1, forecasts further into the future tend to be less accurate than those of more imminent events. Quite simply, as time passes, we get better information and so can make better predictions. Because shorter-range forecasts are more accurate, inventory-planning decisions will be more effective if supply is postponed closer to the point of actual demand.

Postponement (or Delayed Differentiation)   Consider a garment manufacturer who makes blue, green, and red T-shirts. The firm is considering two alternate manufacturing processes:

1. Process A calls first for coloring the fabric, which takes a week, and then assembling the T-shirt, which takes another week.
2. Process B calls first for assembling T-shirts from white fabric, which also takes one week, and then coloring the assembled shirts—a process that, as in process A, takes one week.

Both processes, therefore, take a total of two weeks. Does one have any advantage over the other? With process A, the manufacturer must forecast demand for T-shirts in every color that will sell in two weeks. Although total flow time per T-shirt is the same under both processes A and B, by reversing the assembly and dyeing stages, process B has essentially postponed the color differentiation until one week closer to the time of sale. *This practice of delaying part of a process in order to reduce the need for safety inventory is well known as* **postponement** *or* **delayed differentiation**. Because it is easier to more accurately forecast demand for different colored T-shirts for next week than demand for the week after next, process B will entail less safety inventory of colored T-shirts than process A.

Process B also has another advantage. In deciding the number of white T-shirts to assemble in the first phase, the manufacturer can make an aggregate forecast across all colors (as discussed, aggregation reduces variability). Process B, then, boasts reduced variability for two reasons:

1. It aggregates demands by color in the first (assembly) phase.
2. It requires shorter-range forecasts of individual T-shirts needed by color in the second (dyeing) phase.

Both result in less demand variability and hence require less total safety inventory.

Clothing maker Benetton (Signorelli & Heskett, 1989) was an early pioneer in postponement strategies. Another company that has found this particular process innovation beneficial is Hewlett Packard (HP), which builds Deskjet printers for worldwide sales (Kopczak & Lee, 2001). For example, one major difference between printers destined for North America and those bound for Europe is their power-supply rating. Initially, the HP Deskjet printer was designed to include a specific power supply (110 or 220 volts) in the assembly process—the plant would make printers specific to each geographical location. But in rethinking its distribution system, HP redesigned the printer so that the power-supply module could be installed at the very end of the production process (in fact, it is installed by the distributor). Thus, the plant was producing a generic printer and postponing differentiation until the distribution stage. The more recent HP Deskjet printers carry the postponement concept even further. These printers can be used as either color or black-and-white printers simply by inserting the appropriate cartridge. Because this customization process is actually performed by the consumer, HP has no need to forecast separate demand for color and black-and-white printers.

▪▪▪ 7.7   Levers for Reducing Safety Inventory

In this chapter, we first recognized the role of uncertainty and variability in process inflows and outflows and introduced the notion of *safety inventory* as a buffer against uncertainty in supply and/or demand.

We can identify the following levers for reducing flow variability and the required safety inventory (and thus flow time):

1. Reduce demand variability through improved forecasting
2. Reduce replenishment lead time
3. Reduce variability in replenishment lead time
4. Pool safety inventory for multiple locations or products, whether through physical or virtual centralization or specialization or some combination thereof
5. Exploit product substitution
6. Use common components
7. Postpone product-differentiation processing until closer to the point of actual demand

SUMMARY ■ ■ ■ ■ ■ ■ ■

Firms carry *safety inventory* of inputs and outputs as protection against possible stockouts resulting from unexpected supply shortages and demand surges. The goal is to ensure that flow units are available to meet the company's production needs and customer requirements despite supply and demand uncertainty. The probability that flow units will be available to satisfy requirements is called service level, which measures the degree of stockout protection provided by a given amount of safety inventory—the higher the level of safety inventory, the higher the level of service provided. The optimal service level balances the net marginal benefit of each additional unit with its net marginal cost as given by the newsvendor formula.

Both the service level provided and the safety inventory required depend on *variability* in flow rates—reducing variability increases the service level that is provided by a given amount of safety inventory and decreases the amount of safety inventory that is necessary to provide a given level of service. Variability of flow rates in turn depend on the forecast errors and the mean and variability of replenishment lead times. Therefore, better forecasting and fast and reliable suppliers are key to reducing investment in safety inventory. Pooling inventories to satisfy aggregate demand across multiple regions can also effectively decrease variability of flow rates and hence safety inventory. The square root law suggests that when demands are independent across regions, pooling reduces safety inventory by a factor of the square root of the number of locations aggregated. The aggregation principle can be operationalized in several other ways including virtual centralization, specialization, and component commonality. Finally, since forecast errors decrease closer to the point of sale, strategies to postpone critical decisions on differentiation will allow a firm to reduce safety inventory without sacrificing service level.

KEY EQUATIONS AND SYMBOLS ■ ■ ■ ■ ■ ■ ■

(7.1) $ROP = LTD + I_{safety}$

(7.2) $I = I_{cycle} + I_{safety} = Q/2 + I_{safety}$

(7.3) $SL = \text{Prob}(\mathbf{LTD} \leq ROP)$

(7.4) $I_{safety} = z \times \sigma_{LTD}$

(7.5)   Newsvendor formula: $SL^* = \text{Prob}(\mathbf{R} \leq Q^*)$
$$= \frac{MB}{MB + MC}$$

(7.6) $LTD = L \times R$

(7.7) $\sigma_{LTD} = \sqrt{L}\,\sigma_R$ (fixed lead time case)

(7.8) $\sigma_{LTD} = \sqrt{L\sigma_R^2 + R^2\sigma_L^2}$ (variable lead time case)

(7.9) $I_{safety}^c = z \times \sqrt{N}\,\sigma_{LTD}$ (N locations and no correlation

(7.10) $I_{safety}^c = z \times \sqrt{2(1 + \rho)}\,\sigma_{LTD}$
(two locations with correlation demand)

where
ROP = Reorder point
LTD = Average lead time demand
I_{safety} = Safety inventory
Q = Order size
I = Average inventory
SL = Service level
z = Service level factor
σ_{LTD} = Standard deviation of lead time demand
SL^* = Optimal service level

MB = Net marginal benefit from each additional unit
MC = Net marginal cost of each additional unit
R = Average demand rate
σ_R = Standard deviation of period demand
L = Average replenishment lead time
σ_L = Standard deviation of replenishment lead time
I_{safety}^c = Safety inventory upon centralization
ρ = Demand correlation

KEY TERMS

- Aggregation
- Backlogged
- Causal models
- Continuous review, reorder point policy
- Cycle service level
- Delayed differentiation
- Fill rate
- Forecasting

- Lead time demand
- Make-to-order
- Make-to-stock
- Marginal analysis
- Net marginal benefit
- Net marginal cost
- Newsvendor problem
- Physical centralization
- Pooling inventory

- Postponement
- Principle of aggregation
- Safety inventory
- Safety stock
- Square root law
- Time-series analyses
- Virtual centralization

DISCUSSION QUESTIONS

7.1 What is the role of safety inventory?

7.2 Discuss the pros and cons of different ways to measure service level.

7.3 How does service level impact the level of safety inventory?

7.4 Consider two products with the same margins but with different costs. Which product should have a higher service level, and why?

7.5 If the quality of goods provided by suppliers is identical, purchasing goods based on lowest price is the best strategy. Discuss.

7.6 It takes the same amount of inventory to operate a single warehouse system as a four warehouse distribution network. True or false? Explain.

7.7 Going online allows a firm to supply online orders from a centralized location rather than using many retail outlets because customers are willing to wait a little for the online order to be delivered. Do you think that the inventory benefits of this centralization will be higher for staple grocery products like cereal and pasta or for products like music CDs and DVDs? Explain.

7.8 Several decades back, manufacturers of paint used to produce paint of appropriate colors and sizes to be sold in retail stores. Today, consumers go to retail stores and select the color they wish, and the retailer mixes the pigment into a base paint to make the chosen color. Discuss what impact, if any, this strategy has on safety inventories.

EXERCISES

7.1 MassPC Inc. produces a 4-week supply of its PC Pal model when stock on hand drops to 500 units. (It takes 1 week to produce a batch.) Factory orders average 400 units per week, and standard deviation of forecast errors is estimated at 125 units.

a. What level of customer service is MassPC providing to its distributors in terms of stock availability?

b. MassPC wants to improve customer service to 80%, 90%, 95%, and 99%. How will such improvements affect the company's reorder policy and its annual costs?

7.2 Weekly demand for diskettes at a retailer is normally distributed with a mean of 1,000 boxes and a standard deviation of 150. Currently, the store places orders via paper that is faxed to the supplier. Assume 50 working weeks in a year and the following data:
   - Lead time for replenishment of an order is 4 weeks.
   - Fixed cost (ordering and transportation) per order is $100.
   - Each box of diskettes costs $1.
   - Annual holding cost is 25% of average inventory value.
   - The retailer currently orders 20,000 diskettes when stock on hand reaches 4,200.
   a. Currently, how long, on average, does a diskette spend in the store? What is the annual ordering and holding cost under such a policy?
   b. Assuming that the retailer wants the probability of stocking out in a cycle to be no more than 5%, recommend an optimal inventory policy (a policy regarding order quantity and safety stock). Under your recommended policy, how long, on average, would a box of diskettes spend in the store?
   c. Claiming that it will lower lead time to 1 week, the supplier is trying to persuade the retailer to adopt an electronic procurement system. In terms of costs and flow times, what benefits can the retailer expect to realize by adopting the electronic procurement system?

7.3 The Home and Garden (HG) chain of superstores imports decorative planters from Italy. Weekly demand for planters averages 1,500 with a standard deviation of 800. Each planter costs $10. HG incurs a holding cost of 25% per year to carry inventory. HG has an opportunity to set up a superstore in the Phoenix region. Each order shipped from Italy incurs a fixed transportation and delivery cost of $10,000. Consider 52 weeks in the year.
   a. Determine the optimal order quantity of planters for HG.
   b. If the delivery lead time from Italy is 4 weeks and HG wants to provide its customers a cycle service level of 90%, how much safety stock should it carry?
   c. Fastship is a new shipping company that promises to reduce the delivery lead time for planters from 4 weeks to 1 week using a faster ship and expedited customs clearance. Using Fastship will add $0.2 to the cost of each planter. Should HG go with Fastship? Why or why not? Quantify the impact of the change.

7.4 Johnson Electronics sells electrical and electronic components through catalogs. Catalogs are printed once every two years. Each printing run incurs a fixed cost of $25,000, with a variable production cost of $5 per catalog. Annual demand for catalogs is estimated to be normally distributed with a mean of 16,000 and standard deviation of 4,000. Data indicates that, on average, each customer ordering a catalog generates a profit of $35 from sales. Assuming that Johnson wants only one printing run in each two-year cycle, how many catalogs should be printed in each run?

7.5 As owner of Catch-of-the-Day Fish Shop, you can purchase fresh fish at $18 per crate each morning from the Walton Fish Market. During the day, you sell crates of fish to local restaurants for $120 each. Coupled with the perishable nature of your product, your integrity as a quality supplier requires you to dispose of each unsold crate at the end of the day. Your cost of disposal is $2 per crate. You have a problem, however, because you do not know how many crates your customers will order each day. To address this problem, you have collected the several days' worth of demand data shown in Table 7.5. You now want to determine the optimal number of crates you should purchase each morning.

7.6 The residents of Bucktown, Illinois, place their trash at the curb each Wednesday morning to be picked up by municipal crews. Experience shows that the total amount of trash put out has a normal distribution with a mean of 35 tons and a standard deviation of 9 tons. Crews of full-time city employees assigned to trash collection collect trash. Each crew can collect 5 tons of trash per working day. The city has plenty of trucks of the kind used for trash

TABLE 7.5 Demand at Catch of the Day Fish Shop

Demand	0	1	2	3	4	5	6	7	8	9	10	11	12	13	14	15
Frequency	0	0	0	1	3	2	5	1	6	7	6	8	5	4	1	3

collection. The marginal cost of operating one trash collection crew for one working day, including both personnel-related costs and truck-related costs, is reckoned at $625. Whatever trash remains at the end of the work day *must* be collected that evening by an outside contractor who charges $650 per ton.

How many crews should the city assign to trash collection? For simplicity, treat the number of crews as a continuous variable.

7.7 Northwest Airlines runs daily flights from Detroit to Amsterdam. They face a fixed cost of $70,000 for each flight independent of the actual number of passengers on the plane. There are 310 seats available on a plane. One-way tickets generate revenues of $600 apiece when used but are fully refundable if not used. On a typical weekday, the airline estimates that the number of no-shows will range between 0 and 20; all intermediate values are equally likely.

By law, an airline is allowed to overbook flights, but must give compensation of $250 to all ticketed passengers not allowed to board. In addition, it must provide those passengers with alternative transportation on another carrier (the cost of providing the alternative transportation just wipes out the $600 revenue). How many tickets should Northwest book on its flight from Detroit to Amsterdam?

7.8 A mail-order firm has four regional warehouses. Demand at each warehouse is normally distributed with a mean of 10,000 per week and a standard deviation of 2,000. Annual holding cost is 25%, and each unit of product costs the company $10. Each order incurs an ordering cost of $1,000 (primarily from fixed transportation costs), and lead time is 1 week. The company wants the probability of stocking out in a flow to be no more than 5%. Assume 50 working weeks in a year.

   a. Assuming that each warehouse operates independently, what should be the ordering policy at each warehouse? How much safety stock does each warehouse hold? How much average inventory is held (at all four warehouses combined) and at what annual cost? On average, how long does a unit of product spend in the warehouse before being sold?

   b. Assume that the firm has centralized all inventories in a single warehouse and that the probability of stocking out in a cycle can still be no more than 5%. Ideally, how much average inventory can the company now expect to hold and at what cost? In this case, how long will a unit spend in the warehouse before being sold?

7.9 Hi-Tek is a retailer of computer equipment in the greater Chicago region with four retail outlets. Currently, each outlet manages its ordering independently. Demand at each retail outlet averages 4,000 units per week. Each unit costs $200, and Hi-Tek has an annual holding cost of 20%. The fixed cost of each order (administrative + transportation) is $900. Assume 50 weeks in a year.

   a. Given that each outlet orders independently and gets its own delivery, determine the optimal order size at each outlet.

   b. On average, how long (in weeks) does each unit spend in the Hi-Tek system before being sold?

   c. Hi-Tek is thinking of centralizing purchasing (for all four outlets). In this setting, Hi-Tek will place a single order (for all outlets) with the supplier. The supplier will deliver the order on a common truck to a transit point. Since individual requirements are identical across outlets, the total order is split equally and shipped to the retailers from this transit point. This entire operation will increase the fixed cost of placing an order to $1,800. If Hi-Tek manages ordering optimally, determine the average inventory across all four outlets in the new Hi-Tek system.

MODELING EXERCISE

www.prenhall.com/anupindi

For exercises and models using the evaluation software of iGrafx Process, insert the CD-ROM that is packaged with this book. An electronic copy of the User Guide is included on the CD. For more information on iGrafx, visit www.iGrafx.com. Detailed descriptions of the models may also be found at www.prenhall.com/anupindi.

Model

In Exercise 7.1, you were asked to determine the production and inventory costs of MassPC Inc.'s current policy as well as determine its optimal policy. In this modeling

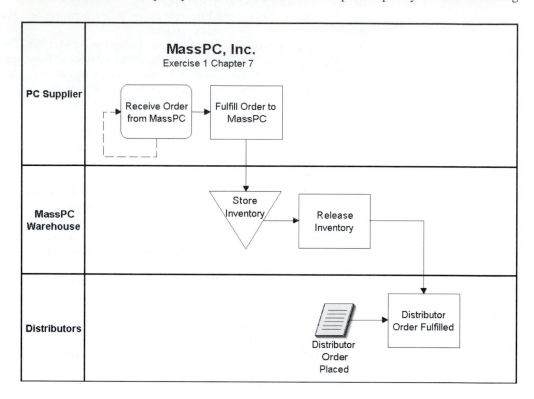

exercise, Exercise 7.1 has been prebuilt using iGrafx Process. You can use the model to evaluate the costs of the current policy as well as determine the optimal policy.

MassPC Inc. sells the PC-PAL model computer to distributors. The demand faced by MassPC is 400 units per week with a standard deviation of 125 units per week. The company has a reorder point $ROP = 500$ units. The lead time is 1 week, or 2,400 minutes (at 40 work hours per week). The current order size is 1,600 units. A simplified version of this process has been implemented with iGrafx 2003. For this process model, the BIM manufacturing steps are ignored.

Simulation

To simulate the production and inventory process at MassPC Inc., double-click on iGrafx document CH7EX1. This loads the simulation model within iGrafx Process. The main screen should have two panes. The left pane shows the Explorer bar with the following contents: Processes, Scenarios, and Reports. (If you do not see this, click on View and the Explorer bar from the menu item and ensure that the All Components view is chosen at the top of the Explorer bar.) You may view the model for this exercise by double-clicking on CH7EX1 under Processes. The Process Scenario tab gives details of the various parameters used in the simulation model. Finally, results of a simulation run may be viewed by double-clicking on Simulation Report under the Reports tab in the Explorer bar.

To simulate the model, from the Model menu, point to Run and choose Start. The default simulation length is set up for two years (equal to 500 days). A Simulation

Progress window pops up at the right end of the screen. As soon as the simulation ends, the results of the simulation are displayed as a report. There are five tabs in a report. Select the Custom tab to see the customized report for this exercise.

Implementation

The process flow diagram is illustrated at the beginning of this section. The model is divided into three "swim lanes" representing distributors, the MassPC warehouse, and the suppliers of PC inventory. Activities in the Distributors swim lane produce demand and receive MassPC computers. iGrafx 2003 uses transactions to represent objects flowing through the process. The type of object represented can vary.

In the Distributors activities, transactions represent orders. In the MassPC Warehouse activities, transactions represent PC inventory. These activities store PCs until released to distributors to fulfill orders. An inventory count is maintained and when inventory reaches the reorder point (ROP), additional inventories of quantity Q are sent from the PC supplier. To calculate the service level, each time a unit is requested from the inventory, the model checks if inventory stock is empty.

In the PC Supplier activities, activities receive and fulfill requests for inventories from MassPC. At the start of the simulation, a single transaction enters the process to seed the simulation with initial inventory.

Refer to the document in the CD for detailed explanations on the modeling approach for this exercise.

Performance Interpretation

The performance of the process is illustrated in the custom report. The report shows the following:

- *Number of orders* placed during the simulation. Observe (as in Chapter 6) that the number of orders includes even the last order placed just before the simulation ends. So if the simulation run length is set to 500 days, it will count the order placed at the end of the 500th day, which is used only for the next order cycle.
- *Number of stockouts* measures the cumulative number of stockouts during the simulation.
- *Service level* estimates the cycle service level.
- *Average inventory at MassPC computers,* which is the average (time-weighted) inventory in the MassPC warehouse.
- *Annual holding costs* gives the annual cost of holding inventory.
- *Annual ordering costs* gives the annual cost of placing orders.
- *Annual purchasing costs* gives the annual variable cost of computers purchased.
- *Total annual costs* gives the sum of the previous three costs.
- *Total cumulative costs* lists the cumulative (over the duration of the simulation) costs at the warehouse, distributor, and supplier.
- *Total cumulative and average transaction statistics* gives a count of the number of units of demand processed, the total cumulative costs incurred, and the average cost incurred per unit of demand.
- *Elapsed time (in days)* is the number of days in the simulation run.

The data in the custom report are for the default simulation run of two years (500 days). To get good estimates of service level, given the randomness in demand, you need to run the simulation for longer durations.

SELECTED BIBLIOGRAPHY ⊓⊓⊓⊓⊓⊓

Chase, R., F. R. Jacobs, and N. Aquilano. 2004. *Production and Operations Management.* 10th ed. New York: McGraw-Hill/Irwin.

Chopra, S., and P. Miendl. 2003. *Supply Chain Management: Strategy Planning and Operations.* 2nd ed. Upper Saddle River, N.J.: Prentice Hall.

Gruen, T. W., D. S. Corsten, and S. Bharadwaj. 2002. *Retail Out-of-Stocks: A Worldwide Examination of Extent, Causes, and Consumer Responses.* Washington, D.C.: Grocery Manufacturers of America, Industry Affairs Group.

Harps, Leslie H. 2000. "Pan-European Distribution." *Logistics Management,* February, 2, 39.

Kopczak, L., and H. L. Lee. 2001. "Hewlett Packard: Deskjet Printer Supply Chain." *Graduate School of Business, Stanford University, case study #GS-3A.*

Nahmias, S. 2000. *Production and Operations Analysis.* 4th ed. New York: McGraw-Hill/Irwin.

Narus, J., and J. S. Anderson. 1996. "Rethinking Distribution: Adaptive Channels." *Harvard Business Review,* 112–20, July-August.

Ross, S. 1972. Introduction to Probability Models. Academic Press, New York.

Signorelli, S., and J. L. Heskett. 1989. "Benetton (A)." *Harvard Business School Case Study,* 1–20. HBS case #9-685-014.

Appendix: Calculating Service Level for a Given Safety Inventory

The service level for a given ROP is given by

$$SL = \text{Prob}(\mathbf{LTD} \leq ROP)$$

To calculate SL, recall first that if $\mathbf{LTD}$ is normally distributed with mean LTD and standard deviation σ_{LTD}, then

$$\mathbf{Z} = (\mathbf{LTD} - LTD)/\sigma_{LTD}$$

is also normally distributed with mean 0 and standard deviation 1 and is known as the *standard normal random variable.*

Furthermore, a given level of safety inventory, I_{safety}, can be measured as a multiple, z, of the standard deviation σ_{LTD} of $\mathbf{LTD}$. Thus, we can say the following:

$$I_{safety} = z \times \sigma_{LTD}$$

Using the fact that $ROP = I_{safety} + LTD$, we write

$$z = \frac{ROP - LTD}{\sigma_{LTD}}$$

Therefore, we can say the following:

$$SL = \text{Prob}(\mathbf{LTD} \leq ROP)$$
$$= \text{Prob}\left(\frac{\mathbf{LTD} - LTD}{\sigma_{LTD}} \leq \frac{ROP - LTD}{\sigma_{LTD}}\right)$$
$$= \text{Prob}(\mathbf{Z} \leq z)$$

CHAPTER 8

Managing Flow Variability: Safety Capacity

Introduction
8.1 Service Process and Its Performance
8.2 Effect of Variability on Process Performance
8.3 Drivers of Process Performance
8.4 Performance Improvement Levers
8.5 Effect of Pooling Capacity
8.6 Effect of Blocking and Abandonment
8.7 Capacity Investment Decisions
8.8 Variability in Process Performance
8.9 Managing Customer Perceptions and Expectations
Summary
Key Equations and Symbols
Key Terms
Discussion Questions
Exercises
Modeling Exercise
Selected Bibliography
Appendix: The Exponential Model with Finite Buffer Capacity

▪▪▪ Introduction

B. B. Lean, a U.S. mail-order retailer of casual apparel, outsources its call center operations to DesiCom in Banglore, India. Customers call a toll-free number to place their orders with customer service representatives (CSRs) who provide product information, take down their orders, and set up shipping and billing schedules. Each caller gets connected to a CSR, is put on hold to wait for one, or gets a busy signal. Customers who are put on hold for excessive lengths of time may decide to abandon the queue and hang up, while those who are blocked by busy signals do not enter the system at all. In either case, they may call back later, or they may contact and buy from a competitor, costing B. B. Lean profit from lost sales. Figure 8.1 shows the call center process that customers go through.

Lately, customers have been complaining about the difficulty in accessing the call center and the excessive time spent on hold waiting for a CSR. Since the call center is the retailer's main source of sales, management is concerned about its performance

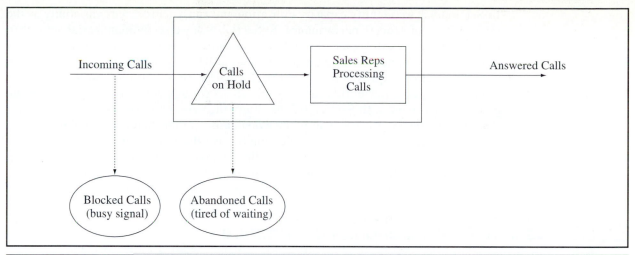

▪▪▪▪▪▪▪▪▪▪▪▪ **FIGURE 8.1** The Service Call Center at DesiCom

and its effect on the retailer's bottom line. They have asked DesiCom to identify the causes of customer delays and make appropriate changes in the call center design and operation to improve its performance, with the goal of providing greater customer satisfaction, leading to higher sales.

In this chapter, we study how to model and analyze such processes in order to gain managerial insights into their performance measurement and improvement. As we will see, the fundamental problem in managing these processes is that of matching the processing capacity with variable demand. In Chapters 6 and 7, we studied the role of inventory in matching supply with demand in *make-to-stock* operations, wherein products are manufactured and then stocked in advance of demand. As we saw, raw materials flow into input buffers to be processed into finished products that are stored in output buffers until needed to fill the customer demand. Excess flow into a buffer accumulates as inventory that entails holding costs but also serves two important functions: permitting economies of scale and providing a protection against stockouts due to variability in inflows and outflows. The most economical level of inventory then balances these costs and benefits so as to provide an optimum degree of product availability.

In this chapter, we study *make-to-order* processes such as job shops and service operations (such as the DesiCom call center) wherein we cannot produce and store inventory of finished orders in advance of demand. The process manager must therefore maintain sufficient capacity to process customer orders as they come in. These orders now become inflow units that may have to wait in input buffers before being processed by the available resources, while completed orders leave the process as outflow units. The queue of customer orders waiting to be processed is then the inventory of inflow units that entails cost due to customer dissatisfaction with long delays (flow times) in getting their orders processed. In this chapter, we will identify the causes of these queues and delays and suggest appropriate managerial actions to reduce them to improve the process performance. For concreteness, we will focus on managing service processes, although the concepts, methods, and conclusions of this chapter are equally applicable to manufacturing in job shops and other make-to-order processes.

In Section 8.1, we describe a typical service process and outline key measures of its performance in terms of queues (inventories) and delays (flow times). In Section 8.2, we discuss the effect of variability in inflow and processing times on these measures.

In Section 8.3, we identify capacity utilization and (unsynchronized) variability as the main drivers of process performance. In Section 8.4, we study managerial actions to improve process performance by reducing variability, increasing safety capacity, and synchronizing capacity with demand. In Section 8.5, we show how pooling capacity across processes improves its overall performance. In Section 8.6, we consider the effect of limited input buffer capacity and the resultant blocking of arrivals on the process performance. In Section 8.7, we study the economics of capacity investment decisions. In Section 8.8, we analyze the worst-case—rather than the average—analysis of process performance. Finally, in Section 8.9, we discuss how to manage customer perceptions and expectations to mitigate the adverse effect of delays and congestion on customer satisfaction. We summarize the chapter by outlining the key levers for improving process performance in terms of flow times and inventories.

▮▮▮8.1 Service Process and Its Performance

Recall that any business process is defined by its inputs, outputs, network of activities and buffers, resources, and information flows. In the previous chapters, we emphasized flow rate, flow time, and inventory as the key operational measures of process performance. We also discussed various levers that drive these measures. In the preceding chapter, we studied the role of inventories in matching available supply with variable demand in make-to-stock operations. In this chapter, we consider make-to-order processes, such as job shops and service processes, where there can be no inventory of finished orders. Make-to-order processes are characterized by (1) variability in inflows as well as in order processing time and (2) the role of capacity—rather than inventory—in dealing with it. In general, most processes involve a combination of make-to-stock and make-to-order operations. For example, a computer manufacturer like Dell may produce and stock partially assembled computers in advance of demand but finish the final assembly to customer specifications only after an actual order is received. Similarly, a fast-food restaurant such as McDonald's may prepare partially cooked and assembled sandwiches before the rush hour and then complete the orders to individual requirements as customers come in. In such hybrid operations, the process manager can manipulate both inventory (of partially finished products) and capacity (to finish the processing) in trying to match supply with demand. However, to understand these two levers more clearly, we have isolated them by focusing first on inventory alone in a purely make-to-stock process in the preceding chapter and on capacity alone in purely make-to-order processes in this chapter. Moreover, for concreteness, we will address service processes, although our analysis is also applicable to other make-to-order processes. Accordingly, we specialize the general business process terminology to discuss service processes in a more natural language, although, for consistency and simplicity, we will continue to use the same general notation as in the previous chapters.

8.1.1 Service Processes

In a service process, it is natural to refer to a flow unit as a *customer* (or a *job order*). Thus, customers at bank teller windows, drive-through restaurants, and supermarket checkouts, as well as passengers checking in at airline counters and patients taken to hospital emergency rooms, are all customers arriving ("flowing in") for service ("processing"). Similarly, telephone calls ringing at call centers, information packets transmitted to data processing centers, planes landing at airports, and ships or trucks arriving at loading docks are also examples of "customers" arriving to be "served" by the available resources. Finally, work orders submitted to job shops, projects undertaken by consulting firms, and cars driven to auto repair garages can also be viewed as customer arrivals to service facilities.

A resource unit that processes a customer may therefore be called a *server*. Thus, a passenger at an airline counter, a telephone call at a call center, a truck at a loading dock, and a loan application at a bank are processed by "servers" like airline agents, CSRs, docking crews, and loan officers, respectively. If a server is not immediately available, the arriving customer must join and wait in *queue,* which now corresponds to flow units waiting to be processed in the input buffer.

In each case, arrival of a customer (order) represents demand for processing. However, unlike in the make-to-stock environment, the process manager cannot meet this demand by processing and storing finished orders (completed bank transactions, baggage check-ins, medical treatments, or car repairs) ahead of time; in fact, often order processing may not even begin until *after* the order is received. Without the benefit of inventory of completed orders, customers may have to wait if the resources required to process them are not immediately available. This is equivalent to customers having to wait for physical products because of insufficient inventory of finished goods in make-to-stock situations. Customer orders waiting in queue to be processed then constitute "inventory" of inflow units that accumulates in the input buffer because of insufficient capacity to process them. The cost of holding this inventory arises from the customer dissatisfaction with delay in completing their orders. The process manager must balance this cost of customer delay against the cost of investment in additional capacity required to reduce it.

In addition to insufficient processing capacity, customer waiting occurs because of variability in their arrival and processing times, as we saw in the Vancouver Airport example in Chapter 3. Variability in customer arrival times arises from the fact that the process manager has only limited control over the customer inflow. Even with reservations, appointments, and careful scheduling, the actual times of customer arrivals display significant variability. Moreover, given the customized nature of make-to-order operations, their individual order processing times are also significantly more variable than those in make-to-stock operations. For example, job shops typically handle a wide variety of orders, each with different processing requirements, so their processing times are also more variable than in flow shops, which tend to focus on producing only a limited variety of products. Similarly, patients coming to a hospital emergency room have widely differing ailments, so the time required to treat each is very different as well. As we will see, this variability in customer arrival and processing times degrades the process performance in terms of customer delays (flow times) and queues (inventories). Again, the process manager must balance the cost of reducing this variability against the benefit of improved performance.

In a **single-phase service process**, *each customer is processed by one server, and all tasks performed by that server are combined into a single activity.* An example is the DesiCom call center where each CSR handles all requirements of each caller. In a more complex *processing network,* multiple servers may process each customer, and processing may involve different activities performed in the order specified by a process flowchart. For example, processing an insurance claim involves several steps, such as policy verification, loss determination, and claim settlement, each involving different agents and information resources. Although in Chapters 4 and 5 we analyzed flow times and flow rates in such processing networks, we did not consider variability in inflow and processing times. In this chapter, our focus will be on this variability and how to deal with it by managing the process capacity. However, to keep the analysis simple, we will suppress other process details and treat the entire process as a single activity that is performed by one resource unit. The resulting single-phase process model is easier to analyze and still brings out most of the key managerial insights that we wish to gain.

A single-phase service process may have multiple servers in one resource pool, with each server performing the same set of activities on one customer at a time. With multiple servers, customer arrivals may form either a single queue that feeds into all servers or multiple queues, one for each server. **Service order discipline** *is a specification of the sequence in which waiting customers are served.* We will always assume that customers are served in the order of their arrival; that is, the service order discipline is *first-come/first-served* or *first-in/first-out (FIFO).* In a single-phase service process, there is no output buffer since customers exit the process as soon as they are served. For example, in the DesiCom call center, customers hang up as soon as they finish speaking with CSRs. Finally, to simplify the exposition, in this section we will assume that all customer arrivals are accommodated and eventually served; refinements in which some arrivals may be blocked from joining the queue or some may leave due to long waits will be discussed later in Section 8.6.

8.1.2 Service Process Attributes

In a typical single-phase service process, customers arrive, wait for service, and are processed by one of the available servers in the FIFO order. Customer flow through the service process is then characterized by its attributes that determine the demand for and supply of service.

- The **inflow rate** R_i *is the average rate of customer arrivals per unit time,* which represents the demand for service. The **interarrival time**, which is *the average time between customer arrivals*, is then $1/R_i$ time units.
- The **processing time** T_p *is the average time required by a server to process a customer.* Observe that for a single-phase service process, the processing time is the same as the activity time (Chapter 4) and the unit load (Chapter 5). The average **processing (or service) rate** of a server is then $1/T_p$ customers per unit time. It is the *unit server capacity* and represents the processing *speed* of each server.
- All servers together form a single **resource pool**, and the number of servers in the pool is denoted by c. In a single-phase queuing process, each server processes one customer at a time, so that c is also the maximum number of customers that can be processed simultaneously and represents the *scale* of the processing operation.
- The **process capacity** (also called **service rate**) R_p is then *the total processing rate at which customers are processed by servers in the resource pool*, so that

$$R_p = \frac{c}{T_p} \qquad (8.1)$$

computed as *scale × speed.* Process capacity measures the supply of service in terms of the maximum number of customers that can be processed by the resource pool per unit time.
- As customers arrive into the process for service, they may have to wait to get served. *The maximum number of customers that can wait in queue is called the* **buffer capacity** to be denoted by K. We will assume for now that buffer capacity is infinite and postpone the discussion of the effect of finite buffers on blocking arrivals until Section 8.6.

8.1.3 Service Process Performance

Key performance measures of a service process can be expressed in terms of the usual flow rate, flow time, and inventory measures discussed earlier for general business processes:

1. **Flow rate-related measures of process capacity**

   - **Throughput rate** R is *the average rate at which customers flow through the process.* In a simple service process without blocking or abandonment, it is simply the smaller one of the customer arrival rate (demand) and the maximum processing rate (supply), so that

$$R = \min(R_i, R_p) \tag{8.2}$$

   - **Capacity utilization** ρ is *the average fraction of the resource pool capacity that is occupied in processing customers* and, as in Chapter 5, is given by

$$\rho = \frac{R}{R_p} \quad \text{— throughput} \atop \text{— process capacity} \tag{8.3}$$

Note that, if $R_i < R_p$ (i.e., the available supply of service is more than sufficient to meet the demand for service), then the throughput is $R = R_i$ and $\rho = R_i / R_p < 1$, so that some of the available capacity is unutilized. If, on the other hand, $R_i \geq R_p$, then $R = R_p$ and $\rho = 1$, and the resource pool is constantly busy processing customers. As we will see, $\rho < 1$ is essential for stability of a service process if there is any variability in inflow and processing times at all.

   - **Safety capacity** R_s is *the excess processing capacity (supply) available to handle the customer inflows (demand)* and is given by

$$R_s = R_p - R_i \tag{8.4}$$

Note that, if $R_i < R_p$, then $R_s = R_p - R_i > 0$. However, if $R_i \geq R_p$, then $R_s = 0$, and all the available capacity is busy processing arrivals. As we will see, some safety capacity is necessary to deal with any variability in arrival and processing times. The concept of safety capacity is the make-to-order process equivalent of safety inventory in make-to-stock processes that was necessary to limit stockouts. Both safety inventory and safety capacity represent cushions that the process must carry to ensure availability of products and resources in the event of excess demand or shortfall in supply. Note that the two conditions

$$\text{capacity utilization } \rho < 1$$

and

$$\text{safety capacity } R_s > 0$$

are equivalent. Both mean that $R_i < R_p$ or that, on average, the supply of service is more than sufficient to handle the demand for service.

2. **Flow time-related measures of customer delay**

   - The average **waiting time** T_i is the time that a customer spends in queue (input buffer).
   - Since we are considering a single-phase service process, the *average theoretical flow time* is the average **processing time** of a customer denoted by T_p.

- The average **flow time in the process** T is, as defined in Chapter 4, *the average time that a customer spends waiting in queue and being served*, so that

$$T = T_i + T_p \tag{8.5}$$

- **Flow time efficiency**, as defined in Chapter 4, is *the proportion of time that a customer spends being served rather than waiting in queue*, computed as T_p / T. Since waiting is generally considered to be a non-value-adding activity, flow-time efficiency measures the productive fraction of time that a flow unit spends in the process.

3. **Inventory-related measures of customer queues**
   - The average **queue length** is the *average number of customers waiting for service*, which is the average inventory in the input buffer, denoted by I_i.
   - The average **number of customers in service** is the *average in-process inventory*, denoted by I_p. Since each customer is served by one server, I_p is also the average number of servers that are busy processing customers.
   - The average **total number of customers in the process** is then the *average total inventory I within the process boundaries*, which includes customers in queue and those in process, so that $I = I_i + I_p$.

Although we have described a service process and its performance in more natural terms, we have already seen these concepts in the previous chapters, so we have kept the same general notation. In fact, most of the process flow concepts introduced in Chapters 3 to 5 were inspired by the analysis of queuing systems, where Little's law was originally derived. For simplicity and consistency, we have employed a uniform notation to discuss a service process (or, more generally, a make-to-order process) as a special case of general business processes. This terminology and notation for make-to-order processes are summarized in Figure 8.2, which is very similar to Figure 6.1 in Chapter 6 for make-to-stock processes, the only difference being the absence of an output buffer since there is no inventory of completed orders.

These concepts can be illustrated by Example 8.1, which is simply a continuation of Example 3.1 of Chapter 3.

Example 8.1

Consider passenger arrivals at the Vancouver International Airport security checkpoint. Each passenger places his or her carry-on luggage on a moving belt to be scanned by an X-ray machine. Each passenger is a customer, and the X-ray scanner is the server, which processes

▪▪▪▪▪▪▪▪▪▪▪▪ **FIGURE 8.2 Service Process Flows, Delays, and Queues**

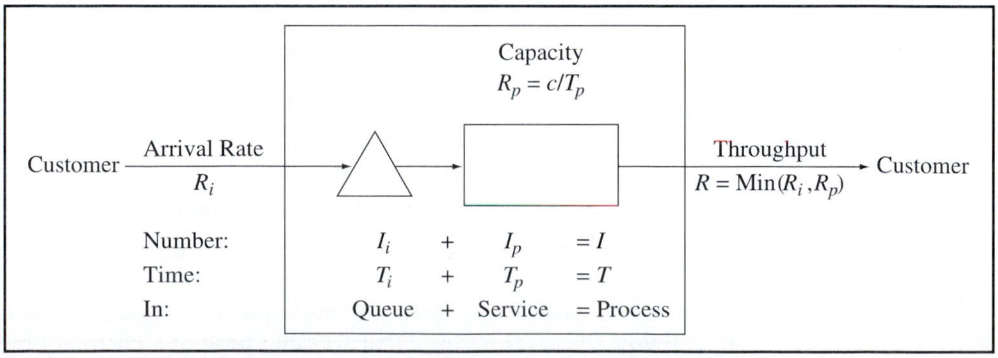

Capacity
$R_p = c/T_p$

Customer — Arrival Rate $\dfrac{}{R_i}$ → △ →

Throughput
$R = \mathrm{Min}(R_i, R_p)$ → Customer

Number:	I_i	+	I_p	$= I$
Time:	T_i	+	T_p	$= T$
In:	Queue	+	Service	$=$ Process

customers in the FIFO order. The queue capacity is practically unlimited, so no one gets blocked from joining the queue. Moreover, all passengers must go through security check, so no one abandons the queue, even with long waits. Recall that, on average, a customer carries 1.5 bags and that the X-ray machine can scan 18 bags per minute. Alternately, we say that the X-ray machine can scan bags of up to 12 passengers per minute, so the scanner's processing rate is 12 per minute, and the average time to process a passenger is $T_p = 1/12$ minute, or 5 seconds. With one scanner, $c = 1$, the total processing rate is also $R_p = 12$ per minute. Prior to rescheduling flights, the peak arrival rate (from 9:10 a.m. to 9:30 a.m.) is estimated to be $R_i = 15$ per minute, so the average interarrival time is $1/15$ minute, or 4 seconds. The passenger throughput rate is therefore $R = \min(15, 12) = 12$ per minute.

Since one customer arrives every 4 seconds and each customer requires 5 seconds to be processed, the queue (inventory) will build up at the net rate of $R_i - R_p = 3$ per minute. Since $R_i > R_p$, the scanner capacity is insufficient to handle the passenger inflow. There is no safety capacity, so $R_s = 0$, and capacity utilization is $\rho = 1$, so the X-ray machine is busy 100% of the time. Figure 8.3 shows passenger arrival and departure times and the time that each spends in the process, assuming that they arrive *exactly* 4 seconds apart and are processed in *exactly* 5 seconds. It is clear that each successive arrival will spend more and more time waiting and that the queue will keep building up. If this were to continue indefinitely, delays and queues would grow without limit, so in the long run, both T and I are infinite.

Recall that, after rescheduling flights, the customer arrival rate drops to $R_i = 10$ per minute (see Table 3.3), or one every 6 seconds. The new arrival rate is below the processing rate $R_p = 12$ per minute (or one every 5 seconds), and the scanner will be able to handle all arrivals. Now the throughput rate becomes $R = \min(10, 12) = 10$ per minute, the scanner has safety capacity of $R_s = R_p - R_i = 12 - 10 = 2$ per minute, and the capacity utilization is $\rho = R_i / R_p = 10/12$, or 0.8333. Thus, the scanner is busy 83.33% of the time and idles the remaining 16.67% of the time. Equivalently, since the interarrival time is 6 seconds and the processing time is 5 seconds, the scanner is busy 5 seconds out of every 6 seconds between arrivals, so it is busy 5/6, or 83.33%, of the time. Also note that 83.33% of the time there is one customer being scanned and that 16.67% of the time there is none, so the average number of customers being scanned at any instant is $I_p = (1)(0.833) + (0)(0.167) = 0.833$. Since each customer is being scanned by one server, $I_p = 0.833$ is also the average number of servers (out of one) busy processing at any instant. Finally, note that if the interarrival and processing times are *exactly* 6 and 5 seconds, respectively, no one has to wait in queue, so $I_i = 0$ and $T_i = 0$ as well (see Figure 8.4).

▪▪▪▪▪▪▪▪▪▪▪ **FIGURE 8.3 Flow Times with an Arrival Every Four Seconds**

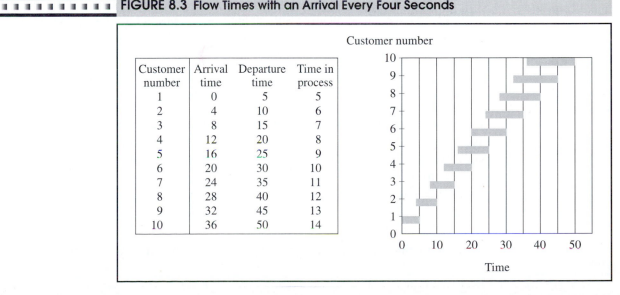

Customer number

Customer number	Arrival time	Departure time	Time in process
1	0	5	5
2	6	11	5
3	12	17	5
4	18	23	5
5	24	29	5
6	30	35	5
7	36	41	5
8	42	47	5
9	48	53	5
10	54	59	5

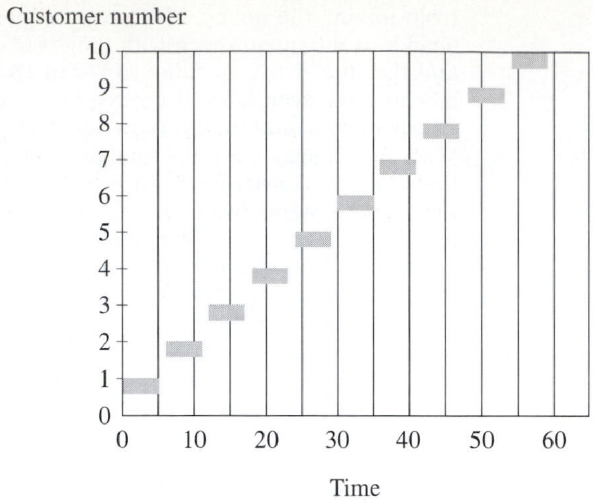

Time

FIGURE 8.4 Flow Times with an Arrival Every Six Seconds

This example brings out one obvious but important reason why delays and queues occur: *If the interarrival and processing times are constant, queues will develop if and only if the arrival rate is greater than the processing rate*.

Although the arrival rate may exceed the processing rate over some time intervals, the long-run stability of a service process requires that, on average, the processing rate (supply of service) be sufficiently high to process all arrivals (demand for service). This requirement that $R_i < R_p$ (so that throughput $R = R_i$, capacity utilization $\rho < 1$, and safety capacity $R_s > 0$) will be called the **stability condition**, *which is the requirement that the average inflow rate should be strictly less than the average processing rate to ensure a stable process*. Note that this terminology is consistent with discussion in Section 3.4 in Chapter 3, where we called a process stable if its outflow rate equals the inflow rate, which was then called the throughput rate.

The stability condition is necessary for limiting delays and queues; if it is not satisfied, delays and queues will grow without limit. As we saw in Example 8.1, prior to flight rescheduling, the arrival rate $R_i = 15$ per minute exceeded the processing rate of $R_p = 12$ per minute, so the process was not stable. After staggering flights, the arrival rate dropped to $R_i = 10$ per minute, which is less than the processing rate, and the process becomes stable. We will assume throughout this chapter that the stability condition holds.

8.1.4 Relationships between Performance Measures

With the throughput rate $R = \min(R_i, R_p)$, we can apply Little's law to derive relationships between the number of customers and their flow times in various stages of the process to relate the average waiting time in queue (T_i) and the average number of customers in queue (I_i) as

$$I_i = R \times T_i \tag{8.6}$$

the average time in service (T_p) and the average number of customers in service (I_p) as

$$I_p = R \times T_p \tag{8.7}$$

and the average total time in process (T) and the average number of customers in process (I) as

$$I = R \times T \tag{8.8}$$

Recall that the capacity utilization is defined as $\rho = R / R_p$, where $R_p = c / T_p$, so that $\rho = RT_p / c$. Since, by Little's law, $I_p = R \times T_p$, we have

$$\rho = \frac{I_p}{c}$$

as an alternate and more intuitive definition of capacity utilization: it is *the average fraction of the total number of servers that is busy processing customers*. Equivalently, it is *the average fraction of time that each server is busy processing a customer*.

As we saw in Example 8.1, after staggering flights, the capacity utilization drops from $\rho = 1$ to 0.8333, and the queue disappears. Thus, making the process stable by reducing its capacity utilization (or, equivalently, by increasing the safety capacity) has a positive effect on the process performance in terms of reduced delays and queues. Note that the capacity utilization $\rho = R_i T_p / c$ can be decreased (or the safety capacity $R_s = c / T_p - R_i$ can be increased) by the following means:

- Decreasing the average inflow rate R_i
- Decreasing the average processing time T_p
- Increasing the number of servers c

We have already seen in the X-ray scanner example how staggering flights reduced the passenger arrival rate at the security check. The processing time could be reduced by purchasing a faster scanner, hiring better-trained security officers, restricting the number of carry-on bags per customer, and so forth. Finally, installing a second belt and scanner would double the processing capacity and reduce the capacity utilization by half.

Naturally, process managers prefer high capacity utilization and low idle time because it means fuller use of resources. In fact, ideally, they would prefer 100% utilization, so that $R_i = R_p$, and there is no idle capacity. If the interarrival and processing times are constant, there still will be no queues, since the process has just enough capacity to handle all arrivals. Thus, in Example 8.1, if the interarrival and processing times are *exactly* 4 seconds, the X-ray scanner will be able to handle up to $R_i = R_p = 15$ passenger arrivals per minute (one every 4 seconds). However, as we will see in the next section, if there is *any* variability in arrival and processing times at all, then we must have some safety capacity $R_s = R_i - R_p > 0$ and $\rho < 1$; otherwise, queues will again grow indefinitely. In fact, as we will see in the next section, if there is any variability in the interarrival and/or processing times, queues will develop, even when there is excess capacity ($R_s > 0$) or underutilized capacity ($\rho < 1$).

▪ ▪ ▪ 8.2   Effect of Variability on Process Performance

Our analysis of Example 8.1 was based on the assumption that interarrival times and processing times are known and constant. We saw that in the absence of variability, we can guarantee that customers will not have to wait by ensuring that the processing capacity exceeds the arrival rate—that is, by keeping some safety capacity. As we mentioned in the previous section, however, service processes are characterized by a high degree of variability in customer arrival and processing times. At a call center (such as DesiCom), for example, customers do not call at regular intervals, nor does a CSR spend exactly the same amount of time with each caller. Similarly, at the airport security check, passengers do not arrive at evenly paced times, nor do they all need exactly the same amount of time to be checked out. Such *unpredictable or random variability that a service process experiences is called* **stochastic variability**, which we must distinguish from more predictable changes over longer periods of time that we have called seasonal variability. Example 8.2 illustrates how stochastic variability may lead to a queue buildup even in a stable process.

Example 8.2

Recall that at the security checkpoint of Vancouver International Airport, after staggering flights, the average passenger arrival rate is 10 per minute, or one every 6 seconds, whereas the average X-ray scanning rate is 12 per minute, or one every 5 seconds. However, now suppose the actual arrival and processing times are not constant but variable. In particular, suppose we observe the interarrival times of 10 passengers to be 10, 10, 2, 10, 1, 3, 7, 9, and 2 seconds, which average to 6 seconds, as before. Similarly, suppose we clock their processing times to be 7, 1, 7, 2, 8, 7, 4, 8, 5, and 1 second, which average to 5 seconds, again as before. With these observations, let us track times of passenger arrivals and departures and the number of customers in the process (in queue as well as in service) and plot them as in Figure 8.5.

▪▪▪▪▪▪▪▪▪▪▪▪ **FIGURE 8.5** Effect of Variability in Arrivals and in Processing

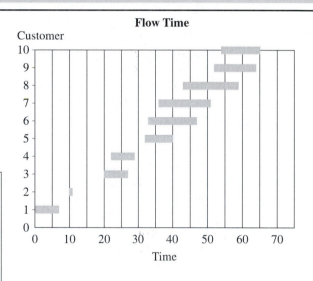

Customer number	Arrival time	Processing time	Time in process
1	0	7	7
2	10	1	1
3	20	7	7
4	22	2	7
5	32	8	8
6	33	7	14
7	36	4	15
8	43	8	16
9	52	5	12
10	54	1	11

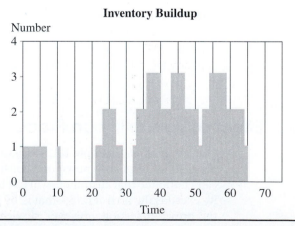

Now note that while customers 1, 2, 3, and 5 do not have to wait, all others do. Comparing with Example 8.1, where the interarrival and service times were *exactly* 6 and 5 seconds, respectively, and there was no waiting, we conclude that variability in these times leads to waiting and queues.

This example illustrates the second reason for delays and queues in service processes: *Even when the stability condition holds, variability in arrival and processing times may lead to customer delays and queues.*

To understand the reason, note that customer 2 needs only 1 second to be processed, and the next one does not come in for another 10 seconds, so the scanner is idle for 9 seconds after processing customer 2. Unfortunately, we cannot produce and store its scanning service or utilize its idle capacity for later use to process customer 4 when he arrives, who must therefore wait while customer 3 is being processed. The basic problem is that a completed service is nonstorable and processing capacity is perishable; if we do not use it, we have to lose it. In Example 8.2, the server is busy an average of 83.33% of the time, just as in Example 8.1. However, because of variability in arrival and processing times in Example 8.2, the server alternates between cycles of busy and idle periods, and its processing capacity during idle periods cannot be utilized to serve customers arriving during busy periods later who must therefore wait.

In general, with variability, some customers have short interarrival times, while others have long interarrival times. Similarly, some customers have short processing times, while others have long processing times. When short interarrival times coincide with long processing times, queues build up. In essence, this is due to an imbalance between inflows and outflows and the inability to shift processing times between customers and across time. The situation could be mitigated if we could match the arrival times (demand) and processing times (supply) for more uniform capacity utilization, as we see next.

Effect of Synchronization between Arrival and Processing Times   Variability alone does not cause queues to build up. Queues build up because the variability in processing times is *independent* of the variability in interarrival times. In Example 8.2, customer 4 has a short interarrival time and arrives 2 seconds after customer 3. Customer 3, however, has a long processing time of 7 seconds, causing customer 4 to wait for 5 seconds. If interarrival and processing times could be synchronized (or positively correlated), waiting times would be reduced significantly. Indeed, if short interarrival times of customers are coupled with short processing times of their predecessors and long interarrival times are coupled with long processing times, queues will not build up, as Example 8.3 shows.

Example 8.3
Suppose in Example 8.2 that the processing times of the 10 arrivals can be rearranged to be 8, 8, 2, 7, 1, 1, 7, 7, 4, and 5 (while keeping their arrival times at 0, 10, 20, 22, 32, 33, 36, 43, 52, and 54, as before). Now only passenger 10 will have to wait for 3 seconds despite variability in interarrival and processing times. The first passenger leaves at time 8, while the second arrives at time 10. The second passenger leaves at time 18, while the third arrives at time 20, and so forth. Note that, as before, the capacity utilization factor is still 0.833. In fact, since the previously mentioned processing times were merely reshuffled from those in Example 8.3, they have the same mean and variability as before. However, better synchronization between supply and demand has led to significantly less waiting.

Unfortunately, because of the idiosyncratic nature of individual processing requirements in service and other make-to-order operations, we cannot interchange processing times across customer arrivals over time and achieve synchronization to reduce their waiting times. In Section 8.4.3, we will study strategies for achieving some degree of synchronization between interarrival and processing times.

For now, we may state the following observation about the corrupting influence of stochastic variability: *Queues form when the customer arrival rate is—at least temporarily—greater than the rate at which customers are being processed. If the interarrival and/or processing times display variability that is not synchronized, queues may form **even if** the average interarrival time is longer than the average processing time—that is, even when there is some safety capacity and the capacity utilization is less than 100%.*

To summarize the key insights of this and the preceding sections, the main causes of delays and queues are the following:

1. High, unsynchronized variability in
   - Interarrival times
   - Processing times

2. High capacity utilization $\rho = R_i / R_p$ or low safety capacity $R_s = R_i - R_p$ due to
   - High inflow rate R_i
   - Low processing rate $R_p = c / T_p$, which may be due to small-scale c and/or slow speed $1 / T_p$

In Chapters 3 through 5, we learned how the process performance depends on the *average* flow times and *average* flow rates. The key lesson of this section is that *variability* in these factors also matters. Even if the process has sufficient capacity to handle inflows, *on average,* variability in these factors still degrades the process performance. Both of these factors are studied in greater detail in the next section.

▮▮▮ 8.3   Drivers of Process Performance

The two key drivers of process performance—stochastic variability and capacity utilization—are determined by two factors:

1. The mean and variability of interarrival times
2. The mean and variability of processing times

In practice, interarrival times can be measured by tracking either arrival times or the total number of arrivals during a fixed time period. Likewise, processing times can be measured for different customers. The mean interarrival and processing times can then be estimated by computing the averages. Variability in the interarrival and processing times can be measured by variance (or standard deviation), which indicates its dispersion around the mean. Higher standard deviation means greater variability. However, standard deviation alone may not provide a complete picture of variability. For example, if the mean processing time is 2 minutes, standard deviation of 1 minute represents significantly more variability than if the mean processing time was 10 minutes. Thus, we should measure variability in time relative to its mean. One such measure is obtained by computing *the ratio of the standard deviation to the mean,* which is called the **coefficient of variation**. We denote the coefficients of variation of interarrival and processing times by C_i and C_p, respectively. The greater the coefficient of variation, the more variable the time is in relation to its mean. We next quantify how variability and capacity utilization jointly affect process performance.

8.3.1 The Queue Length Formula

The following *approximate* expression shows how the average queue length (input inventory) I_i depends on the coefficients of variation C_i and C_p of interarrival and processing times as well as the capacity utilization $\rho = R_i / R_p$ and the number of servers c (details may be found in Chapter 8 of Hopp and Spearman [1996]):

$$I_i = \frac{\rho^{\sqrt{2(c+1)}}}{1-\rho} \times \frac{C_i^2 + C_p^2}{2} \tag{8.9}$$

This equation will be referred to as the **queue length formula**—*a formula which shows how the average queue length depends on the capacity utilization, number of servers and variability in arrival and processing times.* Note that the average queue length I_i is a product of two factors. The first factor

$$\frac{\rho^{\sqrt{2(c+1)}}}{1-\rho}$$

captures the *capacity utilization effect,* which shows that the queue length increases rapidly as the capacity utilization ρ increases to 1. As the processing capacity approaches the inflow rate (or, equivalently, as the safety capacity approaches zero), the average queue length (and hence waiting time) approaches infinity.

The second factor,

$$\frac{C_i^2 + C_p^2}{2}$$

captures the *variability effect,* which shows that the queue length increases as the variability in interarrival and processing times increases. Note that the effects of variability in interarrival and processing times on the queue length are similar and additive (because the formula assumes that the interarrival and processing times are independent). The variability effect in the queue length formula shows that, whenever there is variability in arrivals or in processing—as is the case in practice—queues will build up and customers will have to wait, *even if the processing capacity is not fully utilized.*

The queue length formula can be illustrated graphically in Figure 8.6 by the **throughput delay curve**, *which is a graph which displays the average flow time of a process as a function of capacity utilization.* It shows how the average flow time (waiting in queue and in process) increases with the capacity utilization for different levels of variability. In particular, it shows that the average flow time increases rapidly with capacity utilization and variability.

The queue length formula can be used to approximately compute the process performance measures, as illustrated in Example 8.4, which also illustrates the effect of increasing capacity on the process performance.

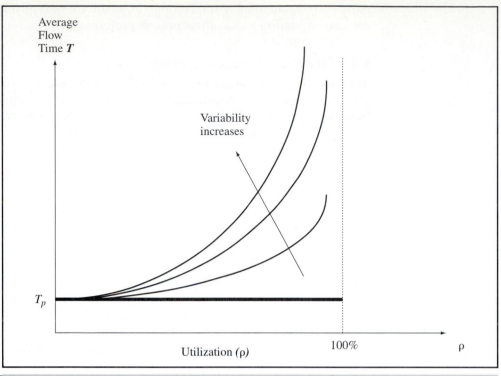

▪▪▪▪▪▪▪▪▪▪▪▪ **FIGURE 8.6 Throughput Delay Curve**

Example 8.4

Suppose, as in Examples 8.2 and 8.3, that we observe the interarrival times of 10 passengers to be 10, 10, 2, 10, 1, 3, 7, 9, and 2 seconds. The average interarrival time is then 6 seconds (so the average arrival rate is $R_i = 1/6$ per second) with a standard deviation of 3.937 seconds, so the coefficient of variation is $C_i = 3.937/6 = 0.6562$. Similarly, if their processing times were observed to be 7, 1, 7, 2, 8, 7, 4, 8, 5, and 1 seconds, the average processing time can be computed to be 5 seconds (so the average processing rate is $R_p = 1/5$ per second) with a standard deviation of 2.8284 seconds, so the coefficient of variation is $C_p = 2.8284/5 = 0.5657$. Furthermore, since $R_i < R_p$, throughput $R = R_i$. With $c = 1$, and $\rho = R/R_p = 0.8333$, we can estimate the average number of passengers in queue by the queue length formula

$$I_i = \frac{0.8333^2}{1 - 0.8333} \times \frac{0.6562^2 + 0.5657^2}{2} = 1.5633$$

Thus, *on average,* there will be 1.5633 passengers waiting in line, *even though, on average, we have sufficient processing capacity* $R_p = 1/5$ per second to handle the inflow rate $R_i = 1/6$ per second, or we have safety capacity of $R_s = R_p - R_i = 1/5 - 1/6 = 0.0333$ per second.

To compute other performance measures, we can use Little's law and basic definitions. Thus, the average time that a passenger will spend in queue is $T_i = I_i/R = (1.5633)(6) = 9.38$ seconds. With $T_p = 5$ seconds in processing, on average, the total time each passenger spends in the process is $T = 14.38$ seconds. Again, by Little's law, on average, the total number of passengers in the process is $I = R \times T = 14.38/6 = 2.3967$. Equivalently, the average number of customers in process is $I_p = RT_p = 5/6 = 0.8333$, and $I = I_i + I_p = 1.5633 + 0.8333 = 2.3966$.

Suppose, in order to improve the process performance, we decide to increase the processing capacity by adding a second scanning machine. Now $c = 2$, the total processing rate doubles to $R_p = c/T_p = 2/5 = 0.4$ passengers per second, and capacity utilization is reduced to

$\rho = R/R_p = \frac{1}{6}/0.4 = 0.4167$ (so the safety capacity is increased to $R_s = R_p - R_i = 2/5 - 1/6 = 0.2333$ per second). Substituting these values in the queue length formula, the average number of passengers in queue becomes

$$I_i = \frac{0.4167^{\sqrt{2(2+1)}}}{1 - 0.4167} \times \frac{0.6562^2 + 0.5657^2}{2} = 0.075361$$

Other performance characteristics can be computed as done here. We summarize the results in the following table:

c	ρ	R_s	I_i	T_i	T	I
1	0.8333	0.0333	1.5633	9.38	14.38	2.3966
2	0.4167	0.2333	0.07536	0.45216	5.45216	0.9087

Thus, reducing the capacity utilization (or increasing the safety capacity) improves process performance in terms of reduced queues and delays.

The queue length formula identifies two key drivers of process performance: capacity utilization and variability in interarrival and processing times. It, in conjunction with Little's law, also permits us to compute various measures of process performance. However, the queue length formula is only an approximation and not an exact relationship. To obtain an exact expression, one must make specific assumptions about the probability distributions of interarrival and processing times. The best-known and most tractable model for representing variability in these is the exponential model that we outline next. It turns out that in this case, and with one server, the queue length formula gives exact results.

8.3.2 The Exponential Model

In this model, the interarrival and processing times are assumed to be independently and exponentially distributed with means $1/R_i$ and T_p, respectively. Independence of interarrival and processing times means that the two types of variability are completely unsynchronized. As for the exponential distribution, it is mathematically described in Appendix 2, but we indicate here key implications underlying this assumption. In essence, it represents complete randomness in interarrival and processing times. For example, if we assume that times between passenger arrivals are independent and exponentially distributed with a mean of 6 seconds, then at *any* instant, the time until the next arrival is completely independent of the time of the last arrival. This *memorylessness* property of arrival times means that, regardless of how long it has been since the last arrival, we should expect to wait for another 6 seconds for the next arrival. Similarly, if processing times are exponentially distributed with a mean of 5 seconds, then regardless of how long a person has already been processed, he should expect to spend yet another 5 seconds before being released. Again, it implies that the actual time required for processing is totally unpredictable on the basis of the past.

If the interarrival time is exponentially distributed with mean $1/R_i$, then the probability that the time between two arrivals will exceed any specific value t is given by

$e^{-R_i t}$, where the mathematical constant $e = 2.718282$ is the base of the natural logarithm. This probability can be calculated by using the EXP function in Excel, as shown in Example 8.5.

Example 8.5

Suppose the time between consecutive passenger arrivals at the airport security X-ray scanner is exponentially distributed with a mean of 6 seconds. The average arrival rate R_i is thus 1/6 per second. Then the probability that the time between two consecutive arrivals will exceed 10 seconds is given by $e^{-10/6} = \text{EXP}(-1.667) = 0.1888$. Similarly, if the time required to scan one customer's bags is exponentially distributed with a mean of 5 seconds, then the chance that it will take no more than 3 seconds is given by $1 - e^{-3/5} = 1 - \text{EXP}(-0.6) = 0.451188$.

It turns out that the exponential distribution assumption greatly facilitates mathematical analyses leading to computation of process performance measures. For example, the standard deviation of the exponential distribution is the same as its mean, so its coefficient of variation is 1. If there is a single server, as in the X-ray scanner illustration, substituting $c = 1$ and $C_i = C_p = 1$ into the queue length formula yields

$$I_i = \frac{\rho^2}{1-\rho}$$

from which all other performance measures can be calculated by using Little's law and the basic definitions summarized in Figure 8.2. In particular, the average total time that a customer spends in the process turns out to be

$$T = \frac{1}{R_p - R_i} = \frac{1}{R_s}$$

With multiple servers ($c \geq 2$), the exact formulas for computing the queue length and wait are available but complicated, even with the exponential distribution assumption. The Appendix to this chapter provides these formulas in the case with finite input buffer capacity K (so that once there are K customers in queue, any new arrivals are blocked from joining the queue). These formulas are also programmed in an Excel spreadsheet called Performance.xls, which can be downloaded from Prentice Hall's Web site at www.prenhall.com/anupindi. The spreadsheet Performance.xls requires specification of four inputs: average inflow rate (R_i), average processing time (T_p), number of servers (c), and the buffer capacity (K). We will study implications of limited buffer capacity K later in Section 8.7. For now, we can use the spreadsheet to perform the computations by setting K equal to some large number such that the buffer rarely gets full. Depending on the problem setting, usually a value of 50 to 200 should suffice. This spreadsheet then calculates key performance characteristics for any exponential model with the number of servers $c \geq 1$. We illustrate these calculations in the airport security example, this time assuming that the interarrival and processing times are exponentially distributed.

Example 8.6

To use the Performance.xls spreadsheet, we enter the following inputs: arrival rate $R_i = 10$ (per minute), processing time $T_p = 0.0833$ minutes (5 seconds), number of servers $c = 1$, and buffer capacity $K = 50$. The spreadsheet yields $I_i = 4.162$, $T_i = 0.416$ minutes, $T = 0.499$ minutes, $I = 4.995$, and $\rho = 0.8333$.

If we add another X-ray machine to improve the performance, we simply need to change $c = 2$, and the spreadsheet calculates $I_i = 0.175$, $T_i = 0.018$ minutes, $T = 0.101$ minutes, $I = 1.008$, and $\rho = 0.4167$. The following table summarizes these results:

c	ρ	R_s	I_i	T_i	T	I
1	0.8333	0.0333	4.162	0.416	0.499	4.995
2	0.4167	0.2333	0.175	0.018	0.101	1.008

Note that, although qualitatively similar, results in Examples 8.4 and 8.6 are different. That is because in Example 8.4 we permitted general probability distributions of interarrival and processing times and used the queue length formula to obtain *approximate* results, whereas in Example 8.6 we obtained *exact* results but had to assume exponential distributions for interarrival and processing times. Furthermore, the variability in interarrival and processing times has increased from Example 8.4 to Example 8.6. Consequently, we observe that delays and average number of customers waiting also increase.

We conclude that even though the process is stable ($\rho < 1$) and we have safety capacity $R_s > 0$, customers will encounter delays and queues due to variability in the arrival and processing times. In the next section, we consider managerial actions to improve these measures of process performance.

▮▮▮ 8.4   Performance Improvement Levers

In the preceding two sections, we saw that degradation in process performance (in terms of delays and queues) occurs because of high, unsynchronized variability in arrival and processing rates and high capacity utilization (or low safety capacity). Therefore, the key levers to improve process performance (decrease delays and queues) are the following:

1. Decrease variability in customer interarrival and processing times
2. Decrease capacity utilization (or increase safety capacity) either by
   a. decreasing the arrival rate or increasing the unit processing rate, or by
   b. increasing the number of servers
3. Synchronize the available capacity with demand

We discuss concrete managerial actions for controlling these three levers.

8.4.1   Variability Reduction Levers

As discussed before, variability in interarrival and processing times can be expressed in terms of the coefficients of variation (standard deviation as a fraction of the mean) of their probability distributions. From the queue length formula in Section 8.3, note that the average queue length (and hence waiting time in queue) is directly proportional to the sum of the squares of the two coefficients of variation of interarrival and processing times.

Hence, one lever to decrease the average queue length and waiting time is to reduce variability in arrival and processing times. By planning for more regular arrival patterns, one can reduce the variability in arrival times. In manufacturing, for example, it means choosing more reliable suppliers who will deliver more consistently within narrower time windows. (Recall from Chapter 7 that less variability in the delivery lead time also results in reduced safety inventory.)

Even in service operations where there is only limited control over customer arrivals, it is possible to make arrivals more predictable through scheduling, reservations, and appointments. For example, airlines, hotels, medical offices, and restaurants try to match available capacity with uncertain demand through reservations and appointments. However, because of late arrivals and no-shows, variability in arrival times cannot be eliminated completely.

To reduce variability in processing times, we must first understand its source. In some instances, a common resource is used for producing a variety of products, each requiring very different processing times. In such situations, we can reduce the processing time variability by limiting product variety or specializing resources to perform a narrow range of processing. Examples include standard express-meal packs in fast food restaurants, specialized teller windows at banks, and separate extensions for different types of telephone calls. In some cases, processing times are variable because of a lack of process standardization or insufficient workforce training in standard operating procedures. The solution then is to standardize the process to reduce worker discretion and to set up worker training programs in these standardized procedures. Toyota, for example, defines an exact sequence of activities for each workstation, resulting in a reduction in the variability in processing times as well as in the average processing time. Similarly, because of learning by doing, more experienced workers tend not only to process faster but also to do so with higher consistency in terms of the processing time (as well as output quality). Therefore, any managerial actions and incentives aimed at maintaining a stable workforce and low turnover rate will lead to shorter and more consistent processing times and better process performance in terms of shorter queues and delays.

In spite of these strategies, it is impossible to eliminate all sources of variability. Banks, for example, cannot force customers to come in at regular intervals; after all, each customer decides when to go to the bank independently of others. Likewise, banks cannot eliminate processing time variability completely because different customers have different transaction needs, and all these cannot be standardized. In fact, the primary virtue of make-to-order processes is their ability to provide customization. Thus, given the presence of unavoidable variability in inflow and processing times, managers must deal with it by investing in some safety capacity, as we discuss next.

8.4.2 Capacity Utilization Levers

The queue length formula shows that decreasing capacity utilization will decrease delays and queues. To decrease capacity utilization $\rho = R_i/R_p$ (or increase safety capacity $R_s = R_i - R_p$), we can either decrease the inflow rate R_i or increase the processing rate R_p. We discuss managerial actions for each.

Managing Arrivals　In manufacturing, reducing the arrival rate R_i requires scheduling procurements of raw materials only as needed and hence in small quantities; this minimizes the input inventory. In Chapter 6, we have already seen the benefits of batch size reduction on average inventories and flow times. In Chapter 10, we will see other implications of this *just-in-time* procurement strategy.

In service operations, we have only limited control over customer arrival rate. Moreover, if the mission of a service process is to attract and serve customers or if customers pay for service, it does not make sense to reduce their arrival rate. However, it may be possible to shift customer arrivals across time to make them less variable with lower peak rates through better scheduling, differential pricing, offering alternative types of service, or even imploring them to shift demand over time. We have already seen in the airport security example that staggering the flight schedule led to reduced arrival rate at the X-ray scanner. Differential pricing also provides incentives to customers to shift their demand away from peak periods. Reduced prices for matinee shows, early-bird dinner specials in restaurants, off-season rates for hotels, and lower telephone and electric utility rates during off-business hours are some examples. Similarly, by encouraging customers to use online services, ATMs, fax machines, and e-mail, banks aim to reduce the need for customers to come to the bank, thereby reducing the arrival rate and congestion. Finally, organizations may also try appealing to customers to call during off-peak periods, do their holiday shopping early, file income tax returns early and online, and so forth. Since these actions try to influence the demand pattern, they are called **demand management strategies**. The overall objective is to try to reduce the arrival rate during peak periods of congestion as well as to reduce variability in inflows, resulting in reduced delays and queues.

Managing Capacity   Capacity utilization $\rho = R_i/R_p$ can also be reduced (and safety capacity increased) by increasing the average processing rate R_p. As we saw in Chapter 5, the processing capacity $R_p = c/T_p$ can be increased by either increasing the number of servers c or decreasing the average processing time T_p, and both alternatives involve costs. Generally, the cost of providing sufficient capacity to eliminate delays completely cannot be justified on economic grounds. The role of the operations analyst, therefore, is to design a service process that achieves an acceptable balance between the operating costs and the delays suffered by customers. We will study the economics of optimal capacity investment decisions in greater detail in Section 8.7.

8.4.3   Synchronization of Capacity with Demand

As we saw in Section 8.2, queues build up not just because of variability in inflow and processing times but also because these two sources of variability are unsynchronized. In Section 8.3, the queue length formula as well as the exponential model assumed that inflow times and processing times are independent random variables. Therefore, as we saw in the preceding two subsections, reducing delays and queues requires reducing these two types of variability or reducing the capacity utilization by adding safety capacity. In this section, we consider strategies for synchronizing capacity with variable demand so as to reduce delays and queues.

In general, synchronization of supply and demand requires managing either the supply (capacity) or the demand (arrival rates). Now, continually adjusting capacity in response to demand may not be economical or even feasible. For example, we cannot change the number of rooms in a hotel or tables in a restaurant as guests come in. In such cases, we must manage demand. As we have seen previously, off-season hotel rates and differential pricing are economic incentives designed to even out demand to align with the available supply.

In the short term, personnel adjustments are easier to implement than changing capital resources. Strategies to synchronize capacity with demand are observed at checkout counters in supermarkets, fast-food restaurants, and drugstores. There, servers often tend to work faster as the queues get longer, which is an attempt to synchronize the processing rate with the arrival rate. In addition, the store manager may open extra checkout counters as the number of customers waiting exceeds a specified limit. Personnel involved in less time-critical tasks (such as replenishing shelves or cleaning up aisles) are used to staff the newly opened counters, thereby temporarily increasing the processing capacity. Once the queue diminishes, these temporary servers return to their original duties. This capacity adjustment strategy is also common in call center operations, where backroom employees or management personnel staff telephone lines when queues get too large. As we will study in Chapter 9, "control limit policy" specifies triggers as to when to adjust the capacity (up or down) dynamically over time depending on the queue length. This capacity adjustment strategy also illustrates the advantages of pooling the available total capacity across different tasks, but it requires that all personnel are trained to perform different tasks. It illustrates the importance of resource flexibility in reducing the permanent capacity requirements, as we will see in Chapter 10. In any case, this short term capacity adjustment enables synchronization of capacity with demand and improves the process performance in terms of reduced waiting times.

In a somewhat longer time frame, synchronization of capacity with demand is easier to implement. In several businesses—for example, call centers, banks, and fast-food restaurants—demand for service varies by the time of the day and the day of the week. Much of this seasonal variability can be anticipated with a high degree of accuracy. The process managers can then plan the required capacity (personnel) to match the expected demand. McDonald's, for instance, plans the required number of personnel in 15-minute intervals by scheduling their breaks and work start times and using part-time workers.

Finally, in manufacturing operations, if the output of one workstation is an input into the next, managers can synchronize the arrival and processing rates by limiting the size of the buffer that is allowed to build up between the two workstations. The feeder workstation is then forced to stop once its output buffer is full. This method of synchronization decreases the in-process inventory and waiting time but also results in some loss of throughput, as we will see later.

▮▮▮ 8.5   Effect of Pooling Capacity

Thus, given the variability in arrival and processing times, performance improvement requires investment in safety capacity to reduce capacity utilization. We saw that one lever to increase capacity is to increase the number of servers. As we shall now see, not only the number of servers but also *how* they are organized has a significant impact on process performance. To illustrate, suppose in the airport security example that the airport authority decides to invest in an additional X-ray scanner in an effort to reduce passenger waiting times. Now the operations manager must decide how best to utilize the two scanners. Specifically, she has two choices of process design, shown in Figure 8.7:

- In design A, customer arrivals are evenly and randomly split into two streams, one for each X-ray scanner, and each scanner has its own queue. (This could be done, for example, by assigning one scanner for checking passengers on half the flights and the other for the remaining half. Alternately, the two scanners could be physically separated, so that on average half the passengers choose one and the other half chooses the other.)
- In design B, all passengers join a single queue, and each passenger is scanned by the next available scanner.

Assuming that both designs require the same resource investment, which one would yield better process performance in terms of flow time and resource utilization? Let us analyze the specifics in the airport security example.

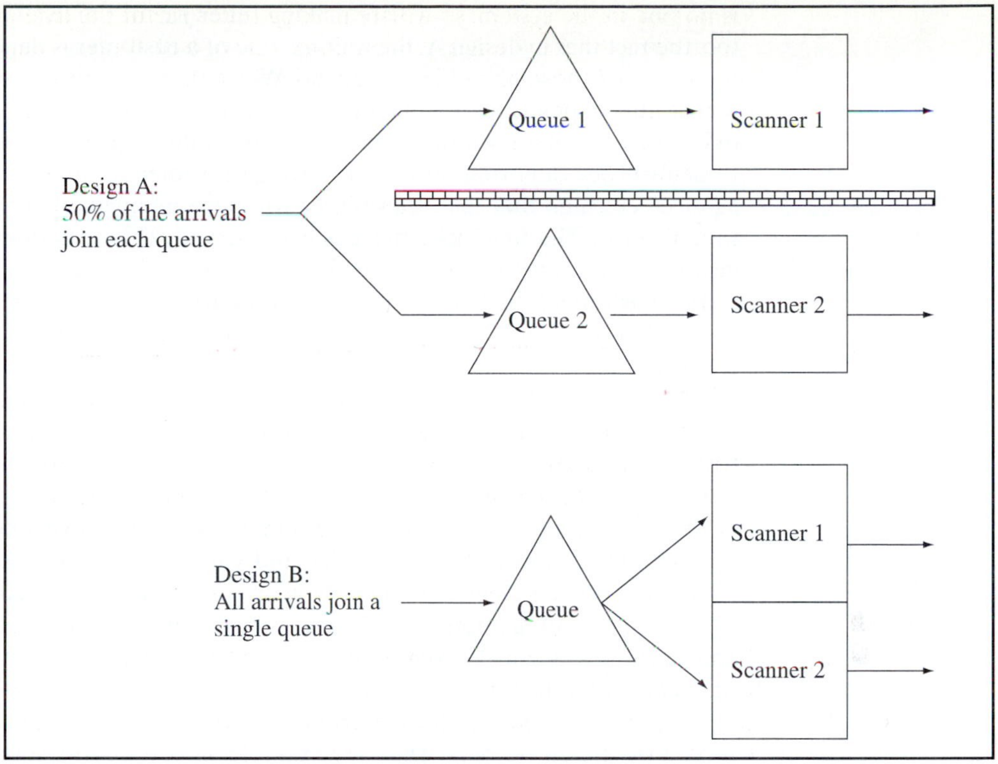

FIGURE 8.7 Pooling Capacity

Example 8.7

With process design A, we have two independent and identical service processes, each with one-half the arrival rate as before. Thus, each process has the arrival rate $R_i = 10/2 = 5$ per minute (so the mean interarrival time is 1/5 minute, or 12 seconds), while the average processing time of each is $T_p = 5$ seconds (or the processing rate is $R_p = 1/5$ per second, or 12 per minute), as before. We may use the Performance.xls spreadsheet with $R_i = 5$ per minute, $T_p = 0.0833$ minutes, $c = 1$, and $K = 50$ as inputs. The spreadsheet calculates various performance characteristics, including total flow time $T = 0.143$ minutes, or 8.58 seconds. This is a significant improvement over $T = 30$ seconds that we saw in Example 8.4 with one scanner handling all arrivals. Note that capacity utilization of each process now reduces by 50% to 0.4165, so each scanner is busy only 41.65% of the time.

Now consider process design B, where all customers join a single queue at the arrival rate $R_i = 10$ per minute and are served by the next available one of the two scanners (so $c = 2$) in $T_p = 5$ seconds = 0.0833 minutes. The total processing rate is now $R_p = c/T_p = 24$ per minute. In the Performance.xls spreadsheet, we enter $R_i = 10$ per minute, $T_p = 0.0833$ minutes, $c = 2$, and $K = 50$ and get $T_i = 0.017$ minutes, or 1.02 seconds, and $T = 6.02$ seconds, which represents a 33% improvement over design A. Other measures are also significantly better than with design A. Note that the capacity utilization is $\rho = R_i/R_p = 10/24 = 0.4165$, which is the same as for design A, so each scanner is again busy for 41.65% of the time (which is also the average fraction of scanners that are busy).

This example illustrates advantages of **pooling capacity**—*the sharing of available capacity among various sources of demand (or arrivals)*—in terms of reduced waiting times and queues. With two separate queues, it is possible that one server has customers waiting, while the other is idle. With pooling the queues, a server will be idle only if there is no one in the system, so we are making fuller use of the available capacity. Consider, too, the fact that in design A, the waiting time of a customer is dependent on the processing times of those ahead in the queue. When there are independent queues for each server, this dependence is very strong. If, on the other hand, two servers serve a single queue, a customer's waiting time is only partially dependent on each preceding customer's processing time. If the preceding customer requires a long processing time, chances are high that the other server will become available to serve the waiting customer before the first customer has been served. This situation not only reduces our customer's waiting time but also makes it less dependent on the processing times of preceding customers. This insight leads us to the following important observation: *Pooling available safety capacity to serve all customers improves the performance of a service process.*

It is worth noting the similarity of this statement to the one about safety inventory that we made in Chapter 7. There, we observed that centralization (pooling) of inventories improves customer-service level for the same total inventory investment. Likewise, we have just seen here that pooling safety capacity improves service in terms of reduced queue length and waiting time for the same investment in capacity. Just as pooling inventories reduces total demand variability and improves customer service, combining queues reduces variability in arrivals and leads to reduced waiting times.

Pooling is often implemented in banks, post offices, departments of motor vehicles, and even in call centers where all customers call one number and are then routed to the next available agent. Note that if arrivals can see and switch between queues, then having separate queues for different servers is equivalent to a single queue that is served by the entire pool. Thus, for example, in restaurants such as McDonald's, each cash register has a separate queue of customers waiting to place orders. However, if a server becomes idle, he takes orders from customers in adjacent lines (although perhaps not necessarily in the FIFO fashion).

▪▪▪▪ 8.6 Effect of Blocking and Abandonment

Until now, we have assumed that the throughput rate of a process is limited only by its inflow rate and the maximum processing rate of its resources. In this section, we consider the possibility that some of the arrivals may not be able to enter the process at all and that some who do enter may choose to leave before being served because of long delays. We then evaluate the process performance in terms of flow time, inventory, and flow rates.

In most real-world operations, **blocking** means *arrivals cannot get into the process because input buffers have only limited capacity to accommodate them before being processed.* For example, waiting rooms in a restaurant, storage bins for purchased parts, or telephone lines at a call center all have limited buffer capacity to hold arrivals. Recall that the maximum number of customers that can wait in queue is called the buffer (queue or waiting room) capacity and is denoted by K; when the buffer is full, new arrivals are turned away. In the DesiCom call center suppose, for example, there are two servers and six telephone lines. Then at most four callers can be put on hold, so the buffer capacity $K = 4$. Once that capacity is reached, any new caller will get a busy signal and cannot enter the system. Blocked arrivals represent loss of business if they do not call back.

In addition to blocking, even if they are able to join the queue, some of the *customers who have to wait long for service may get impatient and leave the process before being served,* which is called **abandonment**. Again, if they do not return, it means lost business.

To analyze these situations, we need to introduce some additional notation. *The average fraction of arrivals blocked from entering the process because the input buffer is full* is referred to as the **proportion blocked** and is denoted by P_b. Thus, even though the potential customer arrival rate is R_i, only fraction $1 - P_b$ gets in, so the net rate at which customers join the queue is $R_i(1 - P_b)$. Moreover, out of those customers who do get in, *a certain fraction of customers P_a may abandon the process, which is referred to as the* **proportion abandoning**, denoted as P_a. Thus, the net rate at which customers actually enter, get served, and exit the process is $R_i(1 - P_b)(1 - P_a)$. The resulting throughput rate can then be calculated as

$$R = \min[R_i(1 - P_b)(1 - P_a), R_p] \tag{8.10}$$

The average waiting time T_i now refers to the waiting time of only those customers who get into the system and are served. Moreover, fractions of customers blocked P_b and abandoned P_a are also important measures of process performance since they affect the process throughput rate R.

Unfortunately, with finite buffer capacity, blocking, and abandoning, we can no longer use the queue length formula to compute the key performance measures. We must now resort to more complicated formulas or simulation. These formulas are provided in the Appendix at the end of this chapter in the special case without abandoning (so that $P_a = 0$), with number of servers $c \geq 1$, finite buffer capacity K, and exponentially distributed interarrival and processing times. They are also programmed on the Performance.xls spreadsheet that was mentioned earlier. Again, we enter the inputs: average arrival rate R_i, average processing time T_p, number of servers c, and buffer capacity K. The spreadsheet calculates the probability of blocking P_b, the average number in queue I_i and in the system I, the average waiting time in queue T_i and in the system T, the capacity utilization ρ, and so forth. We illustrate these computations in Example 8.8 for the call center application mentioned in the introduction to this chapter.

Example 8.8

Suppose that the DesiCom call center is currently staffed by one CSR who takes an average of 2.5 minutes to process a call and that calls come in at an average rate of 20 per hour. Suppose there are six telephone lines, so that, at most, five customers can be put on hold. DesiCom would like to estimate the proportion of callers who get a busy signal and are thus lost to competition. They would also like to know the average time that a customer has to wait for a CSR to become available. Finally, they would like to know the effect of adding more telephone lines on various performance measures.

In this case, we have a service process with finite buffer capacity, and we are given the following information:

Arrival rate: R_i = 20 per hour = 0.333 per minute
Processing time: T_p = 2.5 minutes (or the processing rate R_i = 24 per hour)
Number of servers: c = 1
Buffer capacity: K = 5

With this data input into the Performance.xls spreadsheet, we get

Probability of blocking: P_b = 0.0771
Average number of calls on hold: I_i = 1.52
Average waiting time in queue: T_i = 4.94 minutes
Average total time in the system: T = 7.44 minutes
Average total number of customers in the system: I = 2.29

Thus, 7.71% of all callers get a busy signal and are thus turned away, or 92.29% of the 20 calling each hour get through. Assuming that no one abandons the queue ($P_a = 0$), the throughput rate, therefore, is

$$R = \min[R_i(1 - P_b), R_p] = \min[20 \times (1 - 0.0771), 24] = 18.46 \text{ calls/hour}$$

TABLE 8.1 Effect of Buffer Capacity on Process Performance

Number of lines	5	6	7	8	9	10
Number of servers c	1	1	1	1	1	1
Buffer capacity K	4	5	6	7	8	9
Average number of calls in queue I_i	1.23	1.52	1.79	2.04	2.27	2.47
Average wait in queue T_i (minutes)	4.10	4.94	5.72	6.43	7.08	7.67
Blocking probability P_b [%]	10.04	7.71	6.03	4.78	3.83	3.09
Throughput R (units/hour)	17.99	18.46	18.79	19.04	19.23	19.38
Resource utilization ρ	0.749	0.769	0.782	0.793	0.801	0.807

The server utilization is

$$\rho = \frac{R}{R_p} = \frac{18.46}{24} = 0.769$$

In other words, the CSR is busy only 76.9% of the time and idle for 23.1% of the time. Because of variability, however, there are enough periods during which 1.52 callers are on hold and 7.71% of all callers (or 1.51 callers per hour) get a busy signal and never get into the process, resulting in lost sales.

To study the effect of adding more telephone lines, we simply change the value of K and see how it affects key performance measures. Table 8.1 summarizes the results (rounded up to two decimal places).

Note that, as the buffer capacity (number of telephone lines) is increased, the blocking probability declines, and more callers get into the system. Interestingly, the waiting time of the callers who do get in *increases*. As a result (although not explicitly included in the model), the chance of some customers abandoning the queue because of longer waits may go up. Thus, increasing the buffer capacity has two opposing effects: decreasing the blocking rate P_b by letting more arrivals get in and perhaps increasing the abandonment rate P_a because of longer delays. The optimal buffer size should take into account the net loss in sales due to blocking and abandonment.

■■■ 8.7 Capacity Investment Decisions

As we saw in Sections 8.4 and 8.6, process performance can be improved by investing in the processing capacity or the buffer capacity. In this section, we will use the DesiCom call center example to show how managers can apply the analytical tools introduced so far to make optimal capacity investment decisions. As always, these decisions should be based on financial measures of process performance, which in turn are linked to the operational measures that we have studied. For example, customers blocked from entering the call center cost the retailer potential revenue if they do not call back. If they do enter and queues are long, they have to wait on hold for long periods of time, during which the call center may have to pay telephone charges. Long waits also mean customer dissatisfaction and some customers abandoning the queue, again resulting in lost potential revenue. Such inconvenience of waiting may also show up as lost future revenue if disgruntled customers decide to take their future business elsewhere. Capacity utilization represents the fraction of time that each sales representative is productively used, as idleness represents a waste of resources. Thus, each of the operational performance measures—blocking, abandonment, queues, and delays—has a direct bearing on economic measures—revenues and costs. Capacity investment decisions should balance benefits of improved performance against the cost of investment required.

8.7.1 The Economics of Buffer Capacity

Consider first the financial impact of increasing the input buffer capacity. Although adding buffer capacity is costly, it will decrease the blocking rate and increase the process throughput. However, as we saw in Example 8.8, adding to the buffer capacity also increases the waiting time. The goal, then, is to find an optimal trade-off, as illustrated in Example 8.9.

Example 8.9

Continuing Example 8.8, assume that any caller who receives a busy signal simply hangs up and orders from a competitor. Also assume that the average loss to the retailer in contribution margin is $100 per customer lost to competition. With a single server and the current total of six telephone lines, what is the hourly loss due to the inability of some callers to get through?

Furthermore, suppose that after a customer call gets in, each minute spent waiting on hold costs the retailer $2 in terms of lost goodwill (which may affect future sales). If each telephone line costs $5 per hour, what is the optimal number of telephone lines the call center should lease?

Note that the call center incurs four types of costs:

1. Cost of servers' wages, say, $20 per hour
2. Cost of leasing a telephone line, assumed to be $5 per line per hour
3. Cost of lost contribution margin for callers getting busy signals, assumed to be $100 per blocked call
4. Cost of waiting by callers on hold, assumed to be $2 per minute per customer

Now, with $c = 1$ and $K = 5$, the cost of servers is $20 c = \$20$ per hour, and the cost of leasing telephone lines is $\$5(K + c) = (5)(5 + 1) = \$30$ per hour.

We determined in Example 8.8 that the average number of customers blocked because of busy signals is

$$R_i P_b = (20)(0.0771) = 1.542/\text{hour}$$

The contribution margin lost because of blocking is therefore

$$\$100 \, R_i P_b = (100)(1.542) = \$154.2/\text{hour}$$

Performance.xls gave the average number of customers on hold as $I_i = 1.52$. If each waiting customer costs $2 per minute, or $120 per hour, the hourly waiting cost will be

$$\$120 \, I_i = (120)(1.52) = \$182.4/\text{hour}$$

The total operating cost, therefore, is

$$\$(20 + 30 + 154.2 + 182.4) = \$386.6/\text{hour}$$

Changing the number of telephone lines changes the buffer capacity K, and, as above, we can compute the total cost per hour, as summarized in Table 8.2, where figures are rounded to one decimal place. It can be seen that the total cost is minimized by leasing six lines, so the current situation is indeed optimal for the call center.

From this example, note that the total operating cost goes up by leasing additional telephone lines. In fact, leasing more lines not only costs more but also increases the cost of waiting time experienced by callers who do get in. In this instance, the waiting time of a caller is so expensive that the firm is better off not serving some customers at all than first admitting them and then subjecting them to long waits. Conversely, leasing

TABLE 8.2 Effect of Buffer Capacity on Total Cost

Number of telephone lines n	5	6	7	8	9	10
Number of CSRs c	1	1	1	1	1	1
Buffer capacity $K = n - c$	4	5	6	7	8	9
Cost of servers (\$/hour) = 20 c	20	20	20	20	20	20
Cost of telephone lines (\$/hour) = 5 n	25	30	35	40	45	50
Blocking probability P_b (%)	10.04	7.71	6.03	4.78	3.83	3.09
Lost margin due to blocking (\$/hour) = \$100 $R_i P_b$	200.8	154.2	120.6	95.6	76.6	61.8
Average number of calls in queue I_i	1.23	1.52	1.79	2.04	2.27	2.47
Hourly cost of waiting (\$/hour) = \$120 I_i	147.6	182.4	214.8	244.8	272.4	296.4
Total cost of service, blocking, and waiting (\$/hour)	393.4	386.6	390.4	400.4	414	428.2

fewer than six lines is also nonoptimal because it leads to increased blocking and a greater loss of contribution margin on the customers that are turned away than the savings in the cost of leasing the telephone line. The optimal buffer size thus correctly balances these two types of costs.

8.7.2 The Economics of Processing Capacity

Next we consider the problem of determining the optimal processing capacity (in terms of the number of servers) for a given buffer capacity so as to minimize the total cost. Again, the total cost includes the cost of providing service as well as losses due to blocking and waiting. We illustrate by determining the optimal number of servers in the call center example.

Example 8.10

Suppose the DesiCom call center has decided to lease six telephone lines, with an hourly average of 20 incoming calls. As before, each caller who gets a busy signal generates a contribution margin loss of \$100, and each minute spent by a customer on hold costs \$2 in terms of goodwill. Recall that each CSR takes 2.5 minutes to process one call and is paid \$20 per hour. How many CSRs should the call center hire?

Since the total number of telephone lines is fixed at $n = 6$, the buffer capacity depends on the number of servers as

$$K = 6 - c$$

For example, if there are two servers, no more than four callers can be on hold while two are being served. The total hourly cost, then, consists of the following:

- Fixed cost of the six line charges: \$30
- Cost of servers' wages: \$20 c
- Cost of blocking: \$100 $R_i P_b$
- Cost of waiting: \$120 I_i

Our computations of the total cost for different numbers of servers (rounded to the nearest dollar) using the Performance.xls spreadsheet are summarized in Table 8.3. It follows that DesiCom should staff its call center with three CSRs.

Note that the effect of adding a second server is to reduce the total cost by \$386.60 − \$97.80 = \$288.80, while adding a third server saves an additional \$97.80 − \$94.20 = \$3.60. Thus, the result of increasing capacity displays *diminishing marginal returns*. In fact, adding a fourth server *increases* the total cost, because the additional benefits (in terms of reduced blocking and waiting) are exceeded by the additional cost of providing service.

TABLE 8.3 Effect of Process Capacity on Total Cost

c	K	Blocking P_b (%)	Lost calls $R_i P_b$ (number/hour)	Queue Length I_i	Total Cost ($/hour)
1	5	7.71%	1.542	1.52	$30 + 20 + (1.542 \times 100) + (1.52 \times 120) = 386.6$
2	4	0.43%	0.086	0.16	$30 + 40 + (0.086 \times 100) + (0.16 \times 120) = 97.8$
3	3	0.09%	0.018	0.02	$30 + 60 + (0.018 \times 100) + (0.02 \times 120) = 94.2$
4	2	0.04%	0.008	0.00	$30 + 80 + (0.008 \times 100) + (0.00 \times 120) = 110.8$

In Examples 8.9 and 8.10, we held the buffer capacity or the processing capacity fixed and determined the optimal investment in the other. A more general problem is to determine both optimal buffer capacity and processing capacity simultaneously. Also in both examples we assumed specific values for the cost of lost sales due to blocking and the cost of customer's waiting time in queue for service. In practice, these costs may be difficult to estimate. In such situations, we may still use the previously mentioned approach to determine the costs for which the current staffing level may be optimal. Managers can then determine whether the results are reasonable. Alternately, we may set upper bounds on the average fraction of arrivals that will be blocked or the maximum waiting time that we would like to permit and then try to determine the minimum buffer capacity or processing capacity that will be needed to accomplish these goals.

8.8 Variability in Process Performance

Our entire discussion thus far has focused on the *average* queue length and the *average* waiting time as measures of the process performance. In this section, we show why considering only the average values of these performance measures may not be sufficient.

In a queuing process, the average waiting time includes both customers with very long waits and those with short or no waits. Now a customer who in fact has to wait 30 minutes for service is not likely to be comforted to know that the *average* waiting time of all customers was only three minutes, and in fact 20% of all customers did not have to wait at all! Typically, customers' tolerance for waiting decreases with the duration of the wait. Those who have to wait for longer times are disproportionately more dissatisfied than those who have to wait for shorter times. Ideally, we would like to look at the entire probability distribution of the waiting time across all customers, not just its average. At least we would like to know the probability that a customer may have to wait longer than a specified duration that we consider acceptable. It is important to know, therefore, what fraction of customers may experience an extraordinarily long wait because that would highlight problematic or unacceptable service. Thus, we need to focus on the *upper tail* of the probability distribution of the waiting time, not just its average value. To illustrate, consider Example 8.11.

Example 8.11

The pharmacy department of WalCo Drugs is staffed by one pharmacist, Dave. On average, 20 customers come to the pharmacy every hour to get their prescriptions filled. Dave takes an average of 2.5 minutes to fill a prescription, so his processing rate is 24 per hour. If we assume exponentially distributed interarrival and processing times, we have a single-phase, single-server exponential model of Section 8.3, and the *average* total time in the process is given by $T = 1/(R_p - R_i) = 1/(24 - 20) = 0.25$ hours, or 15 minutes. Figure 8.8 shows the probability distribution of the actual total time that a customer spends in the process (obtained by simulation). Note that 15 minutes corresponds roughly to the 65th percentile of this distribution; that is, 65% of customers will spend 15 minutes or less in the process, or 35% of all customers will experience

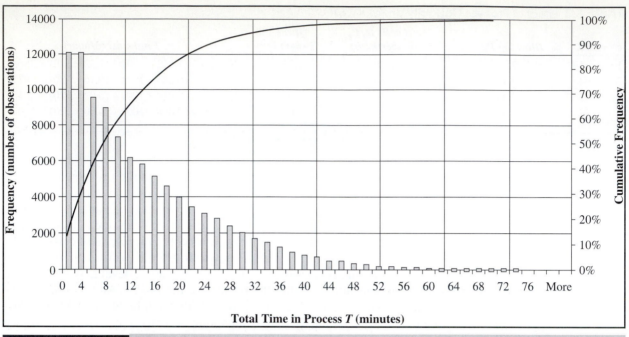

■ ■ ■ ■ ■ ■ ■ ■ ■ ■ ■ **FIGURE 8.8** Probability Distribution of Total Time in Process

total time in process of more than 15 minutes. Note also from Figure 8.8 that approximately 95% of all customers are served in less than 40 minutes, or 5% of all customers will have to wait more than 40 minutes before getting their prescriptions filled. For these 5% of customers, it is cold comfort to know that an average customer spends only 15 minutes in the system. These 5% of customers will also be the ones who will complain most bitterly about the delay. Thus, in addition to the average value, the 95th percentile of the distribution of the actual total time in process provides important information about the process performance. It qualifies the average total time of 15 minutes with a caution that 5% of customers will experience delays of 40 minutes or more.

Since a large fraction of customers may experience delays longer than the average *T*, the process manager may not wish to announce *T* as what most customers *will* experience (even though that is what a typical customer *should* expect to spend in the process). As a service promise, a firm may wish to quote that customers will be served within some, conservatively high, duration $T_{duedate}$, so that it will meet that promise most of the time. Equivalently, the firm can set a service level (*SL*), which is the probability of fulfilling the stated promise, and derive the corresponding time $T_{duedate}$ to promise. For example, if $SL = 0.95$, the firm is promising that the total time that a customer spends in process will be no more than $T_{duedate}$ for 95% of its customers. Given a service level *SL*, we can calculate the corresponding promised time $T_{duedate}$ from the probability distribution of the total time in process, as was illustrated in Example 8.9. Usually, the desired service level will be high enough (more than 0.65) so that $T_{duedate}$ will be greater than the average total time in process (*T*). We can then define safety time (analogous to safety inventory and safety capacity) as

$$T_{safety} = T_{duedate} - T \qquad \textbf{(8.11)}$$

or

$$T_{duedate} = T + T_{safety}$$

Thus, **safety time** *is the time margin that we should allow over and above the expected time to deliver service in order to ensure that we will be able to meet the promised date with high probability.* Just as in Chapter 7, the amount of safety time required for a desired SL will depend on the probability distribution of the total time in process:

$$\text{Prob(Total time in process} \le T_{duedate}) = SL \tag{8.12}$$

Clearly, the larger the safety time, the greater the probability of fulfilling the promise. In make-to-order manufacturing operations (as in job shops), *the practice of promising a time frame within which the product will be delivered after an order has been placed is called* **due date quotation**.

In a single-phase single server service process and exponentially distributed inter-arrival and processing times, it turns out that the actual total time that a customer spends in the process is exponentially distributed with mean T. Therefore,

$$SL = \text{Prob(Total time in process} \le T_{duedate}) = 1 - \text{EXP}(-T_{duedate}/T)$$

which is the fraction of customers who will be delayed no longer than the promised duration $T_{duedate}$. Therefore, $T_{duedate} = -T \ln(1 - SL)$, where ln denotes the natural logarithm with $e^{\ln(x)} = x$. The exponential distribution is also a good approximation of the distribution of the total time in process for many other interarrival and processing time distributions. Alternately, for more complex processes, the probability distribution of the total time in process can be estimated through simulation.

Example 8.12

Suppose that WalCo Drugs prides itself on superior customer service and would like to promise their customers that their prescriptions will be filled within a short time after they approach the pharmacy. The WalCo management would like to meet this promise for 95% of its customers, so that $SL = 0.95$. Assuming that the probability distribution of the total time that a customer spends in the pharmacy is exponential, we get the desired promised duration

$$T_{duedate} = -T \ln(0.05) = 3T$$

In other words, the flow time for the 95th percentile of the exponential distribution is *three* times the average total time in process. Recall from Example 8.9 that $T = 15$ minutes, so that $T_{duedate} = 3 \times 15 = 45$ minutes. Thus, 95% of the customers will get their prescriptions filled within 45 minutes, and 5% of customers may have to wait more than 45 minutes—even though the actual time to fill a prescription is only 2.5 minutes! Note that by promising $T_{duedate} = 45$ minutes, we are allowing a safety time of $T_{safety} = T_{duedate} - T = 45 - 15 = 30$ minutes, which is the extra margin that WalCo Drugs should allow as protection against variability in arrival and processing.

Relating Utilization and Safety Time   Since both the average total time in process and its probability distribution depend on the capacity utilization, the safety time needed to provide a given level of service will change with capacity utilization. Table 8.4 shows the effect of capacity utilization on safety time for $SL = 0.95$, where the average waiting time (T_i), promised time or due date ($T_{duedate}$), and safety time (T_{safety}) are all expressed as functions of the processing time (T_p).

Observe that the higher the utilization, the longer the promised time and safety time allowed. Recall that utilization is closely related to safety capacity; safety capacity decreases as the capacity utilization increases. Table 8.4 also indicates the relationship between the safety capacity and safety time. A larger safety capacity allows us to have a smaller safety time and hence promise a shorter wait.

TABLE 8.4 Safety Time versus Capacity Utilization for $SL = 0.95$

Capacity utilization ρ	60%	70%	80%	90%
Waiting time T_i	$1.5T_p$	$2.33T_p$	$4T_p$	$9T_p$
Total flow time $T = T_i + T_p$	$2.5T_p$	$3.33T_p$	$5T_p$	$10T_p$
Promised time $T_{duedate}$	$7.5T_p$	$10T_p$	$15T_p$	$30T_p$
Safety time $T_{safety} = T_{duedate} - T$	$5T_p$	$6.67T_p$	$10T_p$	$20T_p$

▮▮▮ 8.9 Managing Customer Perceptions and Expectations

In practice, delays, queues, and congestion are facts of life that cannot be eliminated completely. However, their adverse impact on customer satisfaction can often be reduced through behavioral strategies. Making the waiting customers comfortable, creating distractions to take their minds off the ordeal of waiting, offering them some form of entertainment, and managing their expectation of the wait are some of the strategies. The goal is to make the customer less sensitive to waits, thereby reducing the cost of waiting in terms of customer dissatisfaction and loss of future business.

Various approaches are detailed in Maister (1985), each dealing with the management of customer perceptions and expectations of waiting time. One approach calls for occupying the customer with some activity of interest while she waits. Hotel guests complain much less about the wait for elevators in hotels that have installed nearby mirrors: the experience of waiting, it seems, is much less disagreeable when you are admiring yourself. Similarly, restaurants often keep customers occupied by letting them look at menus and order drinks while waiting for tables (which has the added advantage of generating extra revenues and reducing the serving times required once guests arrive at tables). Some restaurants even provide customers with pagers and inform them when a table becomes available, allowing them to occupy themselves with other activities while waiting.

Several studies have shown that uncertainty about the length of wait ("blind waits") seems to make customers more impatient. They tolerate waits better if they are informed of the expected waiting time when they join the queue. Florida Power and Light Company found that customers were willing to wait up to 94 seconds for a service representative to respond to a call. If, however, the customers are informed of the expected wait at the outset, then they were willing to wait an additional 105 seconds, for a total of 199 seconds, without complaining. Another example comes from waiting lines at rides in amusement parks. Managers of these establishments found that customer complaints dropped significantly after they started displaying the expected waiting times. It is often wise to post pessimistic estimates, as customers are especially pleased when the actual wait turns out to be less than expected.

Customers are often willing to wait longer if the service itself is time consuming. At supermarkets, customers with full carts are willing to wait longer than those purchasing only a few items. (Incidentally, keeping special checkout counters for customers with fewer items is also an example of reducing the mean as well as variability in processing times, thus reducing the average overall wait.) Another key factor in managing customer expectations is the perceived fairness of wait. Customers often complain more readily if they perceive that later arrivals have been served first (even if their own wait is not long). Conversely, if customers are served in the order of their arrival, they accept it as a fair practice and usually elicit fewer complaints even if their waits are long. Thus, managing customer perceptions of the wait could be as important a lever as reducing the actual waiting time itself.

SUMMARY ▮▮▮▮▮▮▮

In this and in the previous chapter, we considered the fundamental problem of matching available supply with variable demand in managing process flows. In Chapter 7, we saw how safety inventory can be used to achieve this objective in make-to-stock processes, while in this chapter we concentrated on the role of safety capacity in make-to-order processes. In these processes, we have seen that flow units may have to wait in input buffers if resources required for processing them are not immediately available, which increases flow times and input buffer inventories.

In particular, in this chapter we focused on managing service operations where customer arrivals have to wait for servers, leading to delays and queues that lead to customer dissatisfaction. We saw that waiting occurs because of (1) high variability in inter-arrival and processing times; (2) high capacity utilization, which may be due to high inflow rate or low processing capacity; and (3) lack of synchronization between available capacity and variable demand. The queue length formula gives an approximation to the average number of customers waiting in a queue as a function of utilization, the number of servers, and the variability parameters. Safety capacity is a measure of excess capacity in the process available to handle customer inflows. Appropriate managerial levers for reducing the cost of waiting and long lines therefore include (1) decreasing variability in inflows (by using reliable suppliers, better forecasts, reservations, and appointments) and in processing (by employing standardized operating procedures, better training, and specialized servers), (2) managing safety capacity (by increasing the process scale through more servers and/or speed through process improvement and by pooling safety capacity), and (3) improving synchronization of capacity with demand (by scheduling, peak load pricing, and use of part-time workers).

Capacity investment decisions include investments in buffer and processing capacity. They should consider the trade-offs between the cost of capacity, the cost of waiting, and the potential lost sales due to abandonment and busy signals (as appropriate).

While quoting due dates to customers, however, variability in flow time needs to be considered. Depending on the desired service level, which measures the confidence with which the process manager wishes to meet the due date, a safety time may have to be added in the quoted due date. As long as there is underlying variability in the arrival and service processes, the safety time will increase with utilization.

Finally, in addition to reducing the queues and waits, customers' perceptions of actual waiting can also be managed. This can be achieved in several ways, including making their waits more comfortable, distracting their preoccupation with the wait by entertaining them, explaining the reasons for their wait, and somewhat overstating the wait involved so that customers are pleasantly surprised when the actual wait turns out to be less than announced.

KEY EQUATIONS AND SYMBOLS ▮▮▮▮▮▮▮

(8.1) $R_p = \dfrac{c}{T_p}$

(8.2) $R = \min(R_i, R_p)$ (throughput without blocking and abandonment)

(8.3) $\rho = \dfrac{R}{R_p}$

(8.4) $R_s = R_p - R_i$

(8.5) $T = T_i + T_p$

(8.6) $I_i = R \times T_i$

(8.7) $I_p = R \times T_p$

(8.8) $I = R \times T$

(8.9) $I_i = \dfrac{\rho^{\sqrt{2(c+1)}}}{1-\rho} \times \dfrac{C_i^2 + C_p^2}{2}$ (queue length formula)

(8.10) $R = \min[R_i(1 - P_b)(1 - P_a), R_p]$ (throughput rate with blocking and abandonment)

(8.11) $T_{safety} = T_{duedate} - T$

(8.12) Prob(Total time in Process $\leq T_{duedate}$) = SL

where

R_p = Processing rate
c = Number of servers
T_p = Processing time
R = Throughput rate
R_i = Inflow (arrival) rate
ρ = Capacity utilization
R_s = Safety capacity
T = Average total time in process
T_i = Average time in input buffer

I_i = Average number of flow units waiting in input buffer
I_p = Average number of flow units in process
I = Average total number of flow units in process
C_i = Coefficient of variation in interarrival times
C_p = Coefficient of variation in processing times
P_b = Probability of blocking
P_a = Probability of abandonment
T_{safety} = Safety time
$T_{duedate}$ = Promised time (or due date)
SL = Service level

KEY TERMS ▮▮▮▮▮▮▮

- Abandonment
- Blocking
- Buffer capacity
- Coefficient of variation
- Demand management strategies
- Due date quotation
- Inflow rate
- Interarrival time

- Pooling capacity
- Processing rate
- Processing time
- Proportion abandoning
- Proportion blocked
- Queue length formula
- Safety capacity
- Safety time

- Service order discipline
- Service rate
- Single-phase service process
- Stability condition
- Stochastic variability
- Throughput delay curve

DISCUSSION QUESTIONS ▮▮▮▮▮▮▮

8.1 A fundamental problem in operations management is that of matching supply and demand. What possible strategies can process managers use to address this problem?

8.2 Why are different strategies used to manage make-to-stock and make-to-order processes?

8.3 In service operations such as supermarkets and medical clinics, process managers strive to make sure that they have sufficient resources on hand to process arriving customers. In spite of this effort, why do we often experience long lines?

8.4 In organizing resources to meet variable demand, service process managers can either pool resources so that each resource unit is available for processing any customer, or they can assign specific resources to specific types of customers. Discuss the pros and cons of each strategy and state which strategy you would recommend under what circumstances.

8.5 What is the effect of limited buffer capacity on the number of customers who cannot get in and the waiting time of those who do get in?

8.6 Discuss and contrast the following three statements:
- "The goal of every process manager should be to satisfy as many customers as possible as quickly as possible."
- "The goal of every process manager should be to minimize inventories."
- "The goal of every process manager should be to maximize product availability."

8.7 In this chapter, we emphasized strategies for improving the process performance in terms of the average flow time and average inventory. Give examples in which it may be inadequate to consider only the average values of these measures.

8.8 In this chapter, we considered mostly *quantitative* measures of process performance in operational terms (such as flow time and inventory) as well as economic terms (including operating revenues and costs). Give five examples of strategies that would improve the perception of the process performance in *qualitative* terms by reducing the psychological impact on customer satisfaction.

8.1 A call center has a total of 12 WATS lines coming into its customer service department, which is staffed by 5 customer service representatives. On average, 2 potential customers call every minute. Each customer service representative requires, on average, 2 minutes to serve a caller. After great deliberation, management has decided to add another WATS line, increasing the total to 13. As a result, the call center can expect the following:

a. The proportion of potential customers getting a busy signal will
  increase
  decrease
  be unchanged

b. Average flow time experienced by customers will
  increase
  decrease
  be unchanged

c. Average utilization of customer service representatives will
  increase
  decrease
  be unchanged

8.2 A mail-order company has one department for taking customer orders and another for handling complaints. Currently, each department has a separate telephone number. Each has 7 WATS lines served by 2 customer service representatives. Calls come into each department at an average rate of 1 per minute. Each representative takes, on average, 1.5 minutes to serve a customer. Management has proposed merging the two departments and cross-training all workers. The projected new department would have 14 WATS lines served by 4 customer service representatives. As process manager, you expect the following:

a. The proportion of callers getting a busy signal will
  increase
  decrease
  be unchanged

b. Average flow time experienced by customers will
  increase
  decrease
  be unchanged

8.3 Entrepreneur John Doe has just founded Pizza-Ready Inc., which will accept pizza orders for pickup over the phone. Pizza-Ready's strategy is to compete with established pizza restaurants by offering superior, fresh, made-to-order deep-dish pizza and excellent service. As part of his advertising campaign, Doe will publish an ad stating, "If your pizza is not ready in 20 minutes, that pizza plus your next order are on us." Doe has done extensive research on the pizza-cooking process and knows that all fresh deep-dish pizzas require 15 minutes of oven time and 2 minutes of preparation. Moreover, as part of its excellent service, Pizza-Ready will accept orders whenever customers place them, and a marketing study estimates that Pizza-Ready can count on an average demand of 20 pizzas per hour. Doe, therefore, has ordered five pizza ovens, each of which is able to bake one pizza at a time. Doe is now looking for a silent partner to help carry the financial burden of his start-up company. Given the structure of this business, a potential partner has asked you whether Pizza-Ready would be a profitable investment. What would you recommend, and why?

8.4 M.M. Sprout, a catalog mail-order retailer, has one customer service representative (CSR) to take orders at an 800 telephone number. If the CSR is busy, the next caller is put on hold. For simplicity, assume that any number of incoming calls can be put on hold and that nobody hangs up in frustration over a long wait. Suppose that, on average, one call comes in every 4 minutes and that it takes the CSR an average of 3 minutes to take an order. Both interarrival and activity times are exponentially distributed. The CSR is paid $20 per hour, and the telephone company charges $5 per hour for the 800 line. The company estimates that each minute a customer is kept on hold costs it $2 in customer dissatisfaction and loss of future business.

a. Estimate the following:
- The proportion of time that the CSR will be busy
- The average time that a customer will be on hold
- The average number of customers on line
- The total hourly cost of service and waiting

b. More realistically, suppose that M.M. Sprout has four telephone lines. At most, therefore, three callers can be kept on hold. Assume, too, that any caller who gets a busy signal because all four lines are occupied simply hangs up and calls a competitor. M.M. Sprout's average loss, in terms of current and potential future business, is $100 per frustrated caller. Estimate the total cost of the following:
- Providing service
- Waiting
- Average hourly loss incurred because customers cannot get through

c. Suppose that M.M. Sprout is considering adding another line in order to reduce the amount of lost business. If the installation cost is negligible, can the addition of one line be justified on economic grounds? How would it affect customer waiting time?

d. In addition to adding another line, suppose M.M. Sprout wants to hire one more CSR to reduce waiting time. Should the firm hire another CSR?

8.5 Heavenly Mercy Hospital wants to improve the efficiency of its radiology department and its responsiveness to doctors' needs. Administrators have observed that, every hour, doctors submit an average of 18 X-ray films for examination by staff radiologists. Each radiologist is equipped with a conventional piece of viewing equipment that reads one film at a time. Because of complications that vary from case to case, the actual time needed for report preparation is exponentially distributed with a mean of 30 minutes. Together, the cost of leasing one piece of viewing equipment and each radiologist's salary is $100 per hour. Although it is difficult to put a dollar value on a doctor's waiting time, each doctor would like to get a radiologist's report within an average of 40 minutes from the time the film is submitted.

a. Determine the number of radiologists that the hospital should staff in order to meet doctors' requirements regarding job flow time. Compute the resulting hourly cost of operating the radiology department.

b. The hospital could also change its diagnostic procedure by leasing more sophisticated X-ray viewing devices. Administrators estimate that the new procedure would reduce a radiologist's average film-processing time to 20 minutes. At the same time, however, higher equipment rental and salaries for additional support personnel would boost the hourly cost per radiologist to $150.

   Determine the number of radiologists that the hospital should staff under this new arrangement. Would the new arrangement be economically advantageous?

8.6 First Local Bank would like to improve customer service at its drive-in facility by reducing waiting and transaction times. On the basis of a pilot study, the bank's process manager estimates the average rate of customer arrivals at 30 per hour. All arriving cars line up in single file and are served at one of 4 windows on a first-come/first-served basis. Each teller currently requires an average of 6 minutes to complete a transaction. The bank is considering the possibility of leasing high-speed information-retrieval and communication equipment that would cost $30 per hour. The new equipment would, however, serve the entire facility and reduce each teller's transaction-processing time to an average of 4 minutes per customer. Assume that interarrival and activity times are exponentially distributed.

a. If our manager estimates the cost of a customer's waiting time in queue (in terms of future business lost to the competition) to be $20 per customer per hour, can she justify leasing the new equipment on an economic basis?

b. Although the waiting-cost figure of $20 per customer per hour appears questionable, a casual study of the competition indicates that a customer should be in and out of a drive-in facility within an average of 8 minutes (including waiting). If First Local wants to meet this standard, should it lease the new high-speed equipment?

8.7 Since deregulation of the airline industry, increased traffic and fierce competition have forced Global Airlines to reexamine the efficiency and economy of its operations. As part of a campaign to improve customer service in a cost-effective manner, Global has focused on passenger check-in operations at its hub terminal. For best utilization of its check-in facilities, Global operates a common check-in system: passengers for all Global flights queue up in a single "snake line," and each can be served at any one of several counters as clerks become available. Arrival rate is estimated at an average of 52 passengers per hour. During the check-in process, an agent confirms the reservation, assigns a seat, issues a boarding pass, and weighs, labels, and dispatches baggage. The entire process takes an average of 3 minutes. Agents are paid $20 per hour, and Global's customer relations department estimates that for every minute that a customer spends waiting in line, Global loses $1 in missed flights, customer dissatisfaction, and future business.

  a. How many agents should Global staff at its hub terminal?
  b. Global has surveyed both its customers and its competition and discovered that 3 minutes is an acceptable average waiting time. If Global wants to meet this industry norm, how many agents should it hire?

8.8 When customers of Henniker Bank believe a mistake has been made on their account statements, their claims are forwarded to the bank's research department, whose trained clerks carefully research and document the transactions in question. On completing her investigation, a clerk phones the customer with her findings. The research department has three clerks. Each handles claims from a separate geographic district and never works on claims from outside her own district. The average number of complaints arising from each district is the same, 3.5 per week. The clerks are equally experienced and completely process the average claim in 1.2 days. Assume a five-day week.

  a. Across all districts, how many claims are waiting to be processed on average? What fraction of claims is completed in less than 10 business days?
  b. The bank is considering introducing a new information system that would reduce the standard deviation of the service distribution by 50%, although the mean would remain unchanged. How would your answers to part a change?

8.9 Burrito King, a new fast-food franchise, has had problems with its drive-through window operations. Customers arrive at an average rate of one every 30 seconds. Current service time has averaged 25 seconds with a standard deviation of 20 seconds. A suggested process change, when tested, results in an average service time of 25 seconds with a standard deviation of 10 seconds. Assume that no customers are blocked or abandon the system.

  a. As a result of implementing this change, will the average waiting time in queue increase, decrease, or remain unchanged?
  b. As a result of implementing this change, will the average server utilization increase, decrease, or remain the same?

8.10 V.V. Ranger is a seller of industrial products. All purchases by customers are made through call centers where Ranger representatives take orders. Currently, Ranger has over 350 warehouses in the United States, each with its own call center. Customers call one of the call centers and wait on hold until a representative at that call center becomes available. Ranger is evaluating a switching system where customers will call one 800 number from where they will be routed to the first available representative in any of the call centers. If Ranger installs the switching system, will the average waiting time of customers increase, decrease, or remain the same? Explain.

8.11 Master Karr is a supplier of industrial parts. All orders are received at a call center. The call center has 15 phone lines, so that a maximum of 15 callers may be in the system at a time. Calls arrive at an average of 4 calls per minute. The call center currently has 5 service representatives (SRs). Each SR averages 1 minute a customer. Master Karr estimates that waiting costs incurred are $1 per customer per minute in terms of phone charges and loss of future business. Also assume that callers who get a busy signal take their business elsewhere, resulting in a loss to Master Karr of $50 per lost call. Assume that callers do not abandon once they enter the system. SRs are paid $15 per hour.

    a. What is the hourly cost to Master Karr of the current configuration of the call center?

    b. What is the hourly cost to Master Karr if they decide to hire another SR? Do you recommend this move?

8.12 BizTravel.com is a travel Web site that recently announced "BizTravel Guarantee," putting money behind customer-service guarantees.

    a. One of the items in the BizTravel guarantee states, "If your customer service e-mail is not responded to within two hours, we'll pay you $10." Customers currently send e-mails to service@biztravel.com. The e-mail server of BizTravel equally distributes these e-mails to the specific address of each of the five CSRs. For example, one-fifth of the e-mails are directed to the mailbox of CSR1@biztravel.com, another one-fifth to CSR2@biztravel.com, and so on. Collaborative Inc. has developed collaborative software for customer relationship management that allows the firm to keep all customer service requests in a central mailbox and dynamically route the e-mails based on agent availability. Do you think the software from Collaborative Inc. will help BizTravel meet its customer guarantee better? Explain.

    b. Another service guarantee offered is, "If your phone call is not answered within 90 seconds, we'll pay you $10." Peak arrival rate of calls to BizTravel is during the lunch hour from 12 to 1, and averages one customer every minute. A transaction takes on average 5 minutes to service. The manager decides to schedule 5 agents during this period. Do you expect the BizTravel to have to pay out any money?

8.13 Drive-through window operations are becoming an increasing source of competitive advantage for the fast-food restaurant business. McBerger's has performed poorly in this area compared to Mandy's, the leader in drive-through operations. The service from a drive-through window is staged. At the first stage, the customer places an order. At the second stage, the customer makes a payment at the payment window. Finally, at the third stage, the customer picks up the order. The time between consecutive customer arrivals is exponentially distributed with an average of 45 seconds. Currently, McBerger's total service time (across three stages) averaged 55 seconds with a standard deviation of 35 seconds. Several new process changes were made. Assume that no customers are blocked or abandon the system after entry in either system (before or after the change).

    a. Competitors have experimented with a separate kitchen to service the drive-through orders. When McBerger's implemented this new "plant-within-a-plant" strategy, average service time remained at 55 seconds but with a standard deviation of 25 seconds. As a result of this change, did the average waiting time in queue increase, decrease, or remain the same?

    b. McBerger's began testing the installation of a transponder on a customer's windshield that allowed the restaurant to scan the identification of the car. Using this technology, the customers were billed directly instead of paying at the window. As a result of this technology, do you think the average waiting time increased, decreased, or remained the same?

MODELING EXERCISE ▮▮▮▮▮▮▮

www.prenhall.com/anupindi

For exercises and models using the evaluation software of iGrafx Process, insert the CD-ROM that is packaged with this book. An electronic copy of the User Guide is included on the CD. For more information on iGrafx, visit www.iGrafx.com. Detailed descriptions of the models may also be found at www.prenhall.com/anupindi.

Model

In Exercise 8.4, you studied the call center process at M.M. Sprout, a catalog mail-order company. For various configurations of the call center, you estimated operational performance like percentage of busy callers, average waiting time, and average number of callers waiting. Using these measures, you estimated the financial performance of the call center. In this modeling exercise, the M.M. Sprout call center of Exercise 8.4 is simulated using iGrafx Process. The performance of various configurations of the call center can now be evaluated via simulation.

Simulation

To simulate the flow of calls in the call center, double-click on iGrafx document CH8EX4. This loads the simulation model within iGrafx Process. The main screen should have two panes. The left pane shows the Explorer bar with the following contents: Processes, Scenarios, and Reports. (If you do not see this, click on View and the Explorer bar from the menu item and ensure that the All Components view is chosen at the top of the Explorer bar.) You may view the model for this exercise by double-clicking on M.M. Sprout Call Center under Processes. Details of the simulation parameters for each of the four call center configurations are available under Scenarios. Finally, results of a simulation run may be viewed by double-clicking on Report 1 under the Reports tab in the Explorer bar.

There are four scenarios implemented corresponding to Exercises 8.4a, 8.4b, 8.4c, and 8.4d. To simulate the model for a particular scenario, first load the scenario by selecting it from a drop-down menu in the second row below the top iGrafx menu line. You may also double-click on Scenario in the Explorer bar to open and select a particular scenario. Then, from the Model menu, point to Run and choose Start. A Simulation Progress window pops up at the right end of the screen. As soon as the simulation ends, the results of the simulation are displayed as a report. There are five tabs in a report. Select the Custom tab to see the customized report for this exercise. Since the results in the custom report are sequentially appended to results from previous scenarios, it is recommended that you run the models in the sequence of 8.4a (first) through 8.4d (last).

Implementation

The process flow diagram is illustrated at the beginning of this section. Calls arrive into the call center through the Call M.M. Sprout activity. If the line is not busy, calls proceed to be answered by a CSR in the Take Order activity. Completed calls leave the process through the End Call activity. If all lines are busy, then the customer leaves the process through the Hang Up and Call Competitor activity.

iGrafx Process software is naturally suited for implementing queuing processes. The built-in Worker resource is used to model the CSRs. In the scenarios for questions 8.4a, 8.4b, and 8.4c, the worker count is set to 1. In the 8.4d scenario, the worker count is increased to 2. The simulation is set up for 30 days with the first two days' worth of data discarded for performance measurement in the custom report.

Refer to the document in the CD for detailed explanations on the modeling approach for this exercise.

Performance Interpretation

The performance of the process is illustrated in the custom report[1] and consists of the following:

- *Busy proportion of CSR(s)* gives the proportion of CSRs busy. Recall from the chapter description that this also represents the resource utilization.
- *Average number of minutes a customer is on hold* gives the average waiting time of customers.
- *Average number of calls in the system* is the sum of the average number of calls waiting and in process (being served by the CSR).
- *Hourly costs* table gives the total hourly costs of CSR, phone line, lost calls, customer waiting, and finally the system cost.
- *Statistics used in calculating hourly costs* gives the values of the operational performance metrics needed to estimate the costs that are given in the earlier table and include the total number of CSRs, the number of lost calls, lost calls per hour, average waiting time, total cumulative waiting time of all customers who wait (measured in days), the simulation time (less two days of start-up data discarded), and finally the total average number of customers waiting.

SELECTED BIBLIOGRAPHY

Bhat, U. N. 1984. *Elements of Applied Stochastic Processes.* New York: John Wiley & Sons.

Chase, R., F. R. Jacobs, and N. Aquilano. 2004. *Production and Operations Management.* 10th ed. New York: McGraw-Hill/Irwin.

Hopp, W. J., and M. L. Spearman. 1996. *Factory Physics.* Chicago: Irwin.

Kleinrock, L. 1975. *Queueing Systems.* New York: John Wiley & Sons.

Larson, R. C. "Perspectives on Queues: Social Justice and the Psychology of Queuing." *Operations Research* 35, no. 6: 895–905.

Maister, D. 1985. "The Psychology of Waiting Lines." In *Service Encounter,* ed. J. A. Czepiel, M. R. Solomon, and C. F. Suprenant. Lexington, Ky.

McClain, J. O., L. J. Thomas, and J. B. Mazzola. 1992. *Operations Management.* 3rd ed. Upper Saddle River, N.J.: Prentice Hall.

[1]The performance parameters estimated in the custom report discard the first two days of simulation data, whereas other tabs in the report element report statistics based on the entire simulation period (without discarding start-up data); hence, there may be some discrepancy between the two.

▪▪▪▪▪▪▪ Appendix: The Exponential Model ▪▪▪▪▪▪▪

with Finite Buffer Capacity

Suppose:

- Interarrival and processing times are exponentially distributed with the mean arrival rate R_i and the mean processing rate $R_p = c/T_p$ (so that the mean interarrival time $= 1/R_i$ and the mean processing time $= T_p$).
- There are c servers, each processing customers joining a single queue in FIFO order.
- Input buffer capacity is K (so that $K + c$ is the maximum number of customers that can be in the system).

Explicit formulas are available for computing performance characteristics of such a system (for details, see Kleinrock, 1975)—in particular, the probability P_n that there are n customers in the system or, equivalently, that inventory $I = n$ is

$$
P_n = \begin{cases}
\dfrac{1}{n!}(T_p R_i)^n P_0 & \text{if } \quad 0 \le n < c \\[2ex]
\dfrac{1}{c! \, c^{n-c}}(T_p R_i)^n P_0 & \text{if } \quad c \le n \le c + K,
\end{cases}
$$

where P_0 is the probability that there is no one in the system, which is given by

$$
\frac{1}{P_0} =
$$

$$
\begin{cases}
\displaystyle\sum_{n=0}^{c-1} \frac{1}{n!}(T_p R_i)^n + \frac{(T_p R_i)^c}{c!} \, \frac{\left(1 - (T_p R_i)^{K+1}\right)}{\left(1 - T_p R_i\right)} & \text{if } R_i \ne R_p \\[3ex]
\displaystyle\sum_{n=0}^{c-1} \frac{1}{n!}(T_p R_i)^n + \frac{(T_p R_i)^c}{c!}(K+1) & \text{if } R_i = R_p
\end{cases}
$$

Note that the blocking probability P_b is the probability that there are $K + c$ customers in the system. Thus, $P_b = P_{K+c}$. Capacity utilization of such a service process is given by

$$
\rho = \frac{R}{R_p} = \frac{R_i(1 - P_b)}{R_p} = \frac{T_p R_i(1 - P_{K+c})}{c}
$$

Define $r = R_i T_p$. We then have

$$
I_i = \frac{P_0 (cr)^c \, r}{c!(1-r)^2}\left[1 - r^{K+1} - (1-r)(K+1)r^K\right],
$$

$$
I = I_i + c - P_0 \sum_{n=0}^{c-1} \frac{(c-n)(rc)^n}{n!}; \quad T_i = \frac{I_i}{R}; \quad T = \frac{I}{R}.
$$

These formulas may also be used when there is no limit on buffer capacity by setting the buffer capacity K to be a very large number. As mentioned earlier, these formulas have been programmed on a spreadsheet called Performance.xls that can be downloaded from the MBPF Web site at www.prenhall.com/anupindi. From these, other performance measures follow by their definitions and by Little's law.

CHAPTER 9

Managing Flow Variability: Process Control and Capability

Introduction

MBPF Inc., which you will recall from previous chapters, is a high-tech manufacturer of steel doors sold to industrial warehouses as well as to those looking for a residential garage door. MBPF uses the latest computer-aided design and manufacturing (CAD/CAM) methods for developing and producing steel doors to exact customer specifications. They pride themselves on the high quality of their products and their professional after-sales service and have built a solid reputation as a premier steel door manufacturer, commanding 15% share of the market.

At their recent holiday company party, MBPF employees were celebrating the company's success over the year past. During the many speeches given, executives were congratulating one another for the job well done. However, the sales manager stunned everyone by announcing, "Ladies and gentlemen, I do not wish to spoil your mood, but I have some disturbing news! Lately, I have been talking to some of our major customers, and I have found, much to my surprise, that many of them are less than satisfied with our products and services. In fact, someone said to me the other day that our overall quality stinks! Although *we* think our products are great and that our service is unsurpassed, if what I am hearing is right, it is only a matter of time before we lose our loyal customer base to the competition, which is working hard to provide newer and better products, cheaper and faster." Typically a messenger of bad news like this would be ignored, if not fired, especially given everybody's perception of the company as a successful enterprise. However, the chief executive officer (CEO) of MBPF was not an ordinary individual; she was a thoughtful leader with vision, wisdom, and an open mind. So she asked the sales manager to elaborate further. He explained that several customers that he talked to were unhappy with their door quality in terms of safety, durability, and ease of operation; others were annoyed that our doors cost much more than the competition; and still others complained about the difficulty in getting their orders delivered on time or receiving prompt service when something went wrong with installation or operation. The CEO listened carefully and concluded that it was time to be proactive by identifying and eliminating root causes of customer dissatisfaction with the company's products and services.

The CEO pointed out that the sales manager's observations were based primarily on a subjective assessment and that in the spirit of "management by fact," the next logical step should be to collect and analyze some hard data. This would enable her to take specific actions based on quantitative scientific evidence rather than on mere intuition or hearsay. Accordingly, the CEO formed an interdisciplinary team comprised of the sales manager, production engineer, product designer, steel supplier, and service manager. She assigned the team the task of collecting and analyzing concrete data on critical performance measures that drive customer satisfaction with the goal of identifying, correcting, and preventing the sources of future problems.

All products and services vary in terms of their cost, quality, availability, and flow times, and this variability often leads to customer dissatisfaction, as the story above illustrates. In this chapter, we study graphical and statistical methods for measuring, analyzing, controlling, and reducing this variability in product and process performance to improve customer satisfaction. In Section 9.1, we discuss the impact of variability on customer satisfaction. In Section 9.2, we present simple graphical and statistical methods for measuring, organizing, visualizing, and analyzing performance variability. Although the concepts and methods throughout this chapter are applicable to managing variability in any measure of product or process performance—including cost, quality, availability, and response time—for purposes of illustration we will stress quality as the key attribute since we have already concentrated on the others in the previous chapters.

In Chapters 7 and 8, we analyzed the effects of variability in supply (lead time and processing time) and demand (quantities and customer arrivals) on process performance in terms of product availability and response time. There we assumed that the statistical nature of variability was stable and known in terms of its probability distribution. Our response to this variability was then a *static* plan of building in safety nets (such as safety inventory, safety capacity, or safety time margin) that would absorb variability in the actual supply or demand so as to provide a desired level of performance most of the time. In practice, however, the statistical laws governing variability may themselves be unknown, and, moreover, they may change over time. In Section 9.3, we study online *process control,* based on the principle of *feedback control,* which involves *dynamically* monitoring the actual process performance over time and taking corrective actions in light of the observed deviation from the planned performance. Process control involves tracking a key performance measure, comparing it with the expected level of performance, and signaling the need for a corrective action whenever the observed performance seems to deviate excessively from the expected one. In particular, we outline the general structure of a *control limit policy* that specifies investigation and correction when—and only when—the observed performance measure exceeds certain critical thresholds. We discuss *statistical process control* as a prominent example of such a policy for managing quality and indicate its application to controlling inventory, flow time, and cost.

The objective of process control is an *internal* one of identifying and eliminating abnormal variability so as to maintain the process in a stable state of statistical equilibrium that displays only normal variability in its performance. *Process capability*, in contrast, measures how well the process output meets *external* customer requirements, which is the subject of Section 9.4. Greater process capability means a more precise process that provides a greater safety margin in relation to customer specifications, so that the process output will meet customer needs even if there are unexpected shifts in the process settings. In contrast with short-term process control, improving process capability requires long-term investment in resources to reduce normal process variability, as discussed in Section 9.5. In Section 9.6, we show how careful design of products and processes through simplification, standardization, and mistake-proofing minimizes sources of process variability and its impact on product performance. We conclude the chapter with a summary of the levers for planning and controlling product and process variability.

▮▮▮ 9.1 Performance Variability

All measures of product and process performance—both external and internal—display variability. Results of external measurements (such as customer satisfaction indices, relative product rankings, and number of customer complaints) vary from one market survey to the next. Internally, flow units in all business processes vary with respect to cost, quality, and flow times. For instance, no two cars rolling off an assembly line are exactly identical. Even under identical circumstances, the time and cost required to produce and deliver the same product may be quite different. Two different customers (in fact, the same customer on two different occasions) may experience (or perceive) the quality of a restaurant dining experience quite differently. The cost of operating a department within a company also varies from one quarter to the next. Bank customers conducting apparently identical transactions may in fact need different processing times. Even with carefully planned safety inventory, a department store may run out of stock of an item one month and have excess inventory the next. Sources of all this variability may be either internal to the process (e.g., imprecise equipment, untrained workers, or lack of standard operating procedures) or external (e.g., inconsistent raw material, supplier delivery delays, changing economic conditions, or changing customer tastes and requirements).

In general, variability refers to a discrepancy between the actual and the expected performance, which usually leads to higher costs, longer flow times, reduced product availability, lower quality, and, ultimately, dissatisfied customers. A powerful multimedia computer that crashes unexpectedly may be judged as inferior to a basic no-frills model that is nevertheless reliable. A highly skilled carpenter who often misses or is late for appointments cannot be recommended for a house remodeling job. A sharpshooter whose shots are, *on average*, centered on the bull's-eye but widely dispersed around it cannot be considered a dependable bodyguard. As we saw in Chapter 7, a raw material supplier with consistent delivery lead time would permit the manufacturer to reduce the safety inventory required to assure desired availability. Finally, recall from Chapter 8 that customers often prefer predictable—even if long—waits (e.g., in a restaurant or on the telephone) over "blind" waits. Thus, processes that display greater performance variability are generally judged less satisfactory than those with consistent, predictable performance. An old adage reminds us that one may in fact drown in a lake that is, *on average*, only five feet deep! In short, variability in product and process performance—not just its average—matters to customers.

Although some may enjoy the surprise of the unexpected, generally customers perceive any variation in product or service from its expected performance as a loss in value. Japanese quality engineer Genichi Taguchi suggests measuring this loss by the *squared* deviation in the actual performance from its target, implying that product value drops rapidly as its actual performance deviates further from the planned target. In fact, product quality or customer satisfaction with it may be defined broadly in terms of the discrepancy between customers' expectation of product performance and their actual experience with it. It may be due to a gap between the following:

- What the customer wants and what the product is designed for
- What the product design calls for and what the process for making it is capable of producing
- What the process is capable of producing and what it actually produces
- How the produced product is expected to perform and how it actually performs
- How the product actually performs and how the customer perceives it

Each of these gaps ultimately leads to customer dissatisfaction.

In general, we may classify a product as being "defective" if its cost, quality, availability, or flow time differ significantly from their expected values, leading to dissatisfied customers. In quality management literature, **quality of design** refers to *how well product specifications aim to meet customer requirements.* **Quality function deployment (QFD)** is a *conceptual framework for translating customers' functional requirements of a product* (such as the ease of operation of a door or its durability) *into concrete design specifications* (such as the door weight should be between 75 and 85 kg). The objective of QFD is to provide a common platform for incorporating the "voice of the customer" into the product design process. Details about QFD may be found, for example, in Hauser and Clausing (1988).

Quality of conformance, on the other hand, refers to *how closely the actual product conforms to the chosen design specifications.* Thus, a well-made Toyota Tercel has a better quality of conformance than a poorly made Camry, although Camry has a better quality of design in terms of more power and comfort and safety features. Quality of design thus refers to *what* we promise to customers (in terms of what the product can do), while quality of conformance measures *how well* we keep our promise (in terms of how it in fact performs). Measures of the quality of conformance, therefore, include such criteria as "number of defects per car" and "fraction of the output that meets specifications." In a bank, for instance, the degree of conformance can be measured by the error rate in check processing and in monthly statements mailed or the percentage of customers who have to wait longer than 5 minutes for a transaction. In evaluating performance of the information services department of a company, conformance measurements might include the number of errors per 1,000 lines of code, the percentage of project milestones met on time, the frequency and magnitude of project cost overruns, the number of software program rewrites, or the frequency of system crashes. In an airline, conformance may be measured in terms of the percentage of flights delayed by more than 15 minutes, the number of bags lost per thousand flown, or the number of reservation errors made. The degree of product conformance to design specifications depends on variability in process performance that results in defective products and customer dissatisfaction, leading to a loss of reputation, market share, and competitive position. It is therefore critical to measure, analyze, control, and reduce this variability.

▪▪▪ 9.2 Analysis of Variability

In this section, we first present some simple graphical methods for collecting, organizing, and displaying information about variability in product and process performance. Statistics is the science of variability, so we will then outline some statistical methods for analyzing observed variability. Our goal is to provide diagnostic tools to help us monitor the actual process performance over time, analyze variability in it, uncover the root causes of that variability, eliminate them, and prevent them from recurring in the future. Throughout, we will illustrate the key concepts and methods by examining operations at the steel door manufacturer MBPF Inc., whose business motto is "Guaranteed Total Satisfaction." MBPF managers want to know how their customers perceive the total experience of doing business with the company and how it can be improved. Accordingly, they have tried to identify factors that affect customer satisfaction with MBPF's products and services and understand how to measure, analyze, and improve them.

9.2.1 Check Sheets

A **check sheet** is simply *a tally of the types and frequency of problems with a product or a service experienced by customers,* as illustrated in Example 9.1.

Example 9.1

Suppose MBPF's customer service department surveyed 1,000 current and past customers, asking them to rate their experiences with each of the following aspects of MBPF's products and services:

- Cost of purchasing and maintaining a door
- Response time from ordering a door until its installation
- Degree of door customization permitted in accommodating individual preferences
- Service quality in terms of order placement experience and after-sales service
- Door quality in terms of its

    Fit and finish

    Ease of operation

    Durability

If customers rate their experience as "unsatisfactory" along any of these dimensions (indicating a gap between their expectation and experience), the pertinent flow unit (customer order) would be considered "defective." MBPF then compiled a check sheet of defectives shown in Figure 9.1.

▪▪▪▪▪▪▪▪▪▪▪▪ **FIGURE 9.1 Check Sheet**

Type of Complaint	Number of Complaints
Cost	卌 卌
Response Time	卌
Customization	‖‖
Service Quality	卌 卌 卌
Door Quality	卌 卌 卌 卌 卌

9.2.2 Pareto Charts

After counting defects by type, our next step is to determine which problem should be tackled first. All defects are not equal in terms of either their importance or their frequency of occurrence. So, given the limited time and resources at our disposal, we should identify and focus on a few critical ones. We may rank-order types of defects by the frequency of their occurrence or, better yet, according to the frequency weighted by their importance. Problems usually distribute themselves according to the principle of "vital few and trivial many." Thus, the **80-20 Pareto principle** states that *20% of problem types account for 80% of all occurrences.* A **Pareto chart** is simply *a bar chart that plots frequencies of occurrences of problem types in decreasing order.* Example 9.2 illustrates the Pareto chart and its use in the analysis of performance variability.

Example 9.2

The customer survey record from the check sheet in Figure 9.1 can be graphed as a column chart in Figure 9.2. As you can see, it identifies door quality as the major problem that MBPF should address first.

   The Pareto chart tells us, for example, that it is better to focus our process improvement efforts first at reducing the tallest bar (door quality) by one-half rather than trying to completely eliminate a short bar (such as response time or even cost).

   Once the dominant problem is solved, we may collect new data in order to uncover a new tallest bar on which to focus our efforts next. A Pareto chart can thus serve as a dynamic tool for making continuous improvement by continually identifying, prioritizing, and fixing problems. Thus, after identifying door quality as the main concern voiced by MBPF customers, we could try to pin down exactly what aspects of door quality trouble them most. We could again use a check sheet, this time classifying each defective door according to a new list—poor fit and finish, not easy or safe to operate, not durable, and so forth.

   Suppose the second Pareto chart reveals that customers assess door quality first in terms of the ease of operation, followed by its durability. MBPF might assign an engineering team to determine the factors that contribute to these two main problems. Suppose all this detective work ultimately leads to identifying the weight of a garage door as the critical quality characteristic that affects both problems: if a door is too heavy, it's difficult and unsafe to balance and lift; if it's too light, it tends to break down frequently or not close properly. Suppose the design engineers determine that a standard garage door should weigh a minimum of 75 kg and a maximum of 85 kg, which thus specifies its design quality. To determine the quality of conformance, the

FIGURE 9.2 Pareto Chart

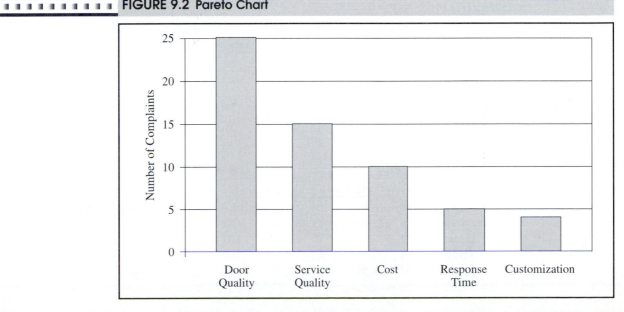

MBPF team will now have to collect data on the actual weights of 100 standard garage doors sampled randomly from monthly production of almost 2,000 doors.

9.2.3 Histograms

A **histogram** is *a bar plot that displays the frequency distribution of an observed performance characteristic.* A preliminary statistical analysis of the performance characteristic involves summarizing the frequency distribution in terms of its *average* (or *mean*, or *expected value*) at which the distribution is balanced, and the *standard deviation,* which measures the spread of the distribution around this mean. Example 9.3 illustrates the histogram for door weights for MBPF Inc.

Example 9.3

Suppose five doors from each of the past 20 days' production runs were weighed at two-hour intervals and recorded as in Table 9.1. As we can see, door weights display variability from door to door *within* each day's sample as well as *between* samples from different days. Our ultimate goal is to analyze this variability, determine what action, if any, is necessary to keep it in control, and finally how it can be reduced to improve conformance of actual door weights to design specifications.

The garage door weight data in Table 9.1 can be displayed as a histogram in Figure 9.3, which shows that 14% of the doors weighed about 83 kg, 8% weighed about 81 kg, and so forth.

We can summarize the entire distribution of door weights in terms of its two key statistics, the overall average weight $\overline{A}$ = 82.5 kg and standard deviation s = 4.2 kg (or the *variance* s^2 = 17.64 kg^2), based on our 100 observations. Thus, $\overline{A}$ estimates the expected weight of a garage door produced, and s is an estimate of variability in weights from door to door. A higher value of $\overline{A}$ shifts the entire distribution to the right, indicating that doors are consistently heavier. An increase in the value of s means a wider spread of the distribution around the mean, implying that there are many doors that are much heavier or lighter than the average.

The discrete distribution depicted by isolated bars in Figure 9.3 may be conveniently approximated by a continuous curve, which in this instance would appear as a bell-shaped normal distribution that is symmetric around its mean. Recall the properties of normal distribution that we discussed in the context of safety inventory in Chapter 7 (see also Appendix II). From these properties, we know, for example, that 68.26% of all doors will weigh within ±1 standard deviation from the average weight—that is, within 82.5 ± (1)(4.2), or between 78.3 and 86.7 kg. Likewise, we know that weights of 95.44% of doors will fall within ±2 standard deviations from the mean (between 74.1 and 90.9 kg), and 99.73% of door weights will be within ±3 standard deviations from the mean (between 69.9 and 95.1 kg). Standard deviation (or variance) of the output is thus a measure of the variability in the door-making process. A precise, consistent

TABLE 9.1 Garage Door Weight Data

					Day					
Time	*1*	*2*	*3*	*4*	*5*	*6*	*7*	*8*	*9*	*10*
9 a.m.	81	82	80	74	75	81	83	86	88	82
11 a.m.	73	87	83	81	86	86	82	83	79	84
1 p.m.	85	88	76	91	82	83	76	82	86	89
3 p.m.	90	78	84	75	84	88	77	79	84	84
5 p.m.	80	84	82	83	75	81	78	85	85	80

					Day					
Time	*11*	*12*	*13*	*14*	*15*	*16*	*17*	*18*	*19*	*20*
9 a.m.	86	86	88	72	84	76	74	85	82	89
11 a.m.	84	83	79	86	85	82	86	85	84	80
1 p.m.	81	78	83	80	81	83	83	82	83	90
3 p.m.	81	80	83	79	88	84	89	77	92	83
5 p.m.	87	83	82	87	81	79	83	77	84	77

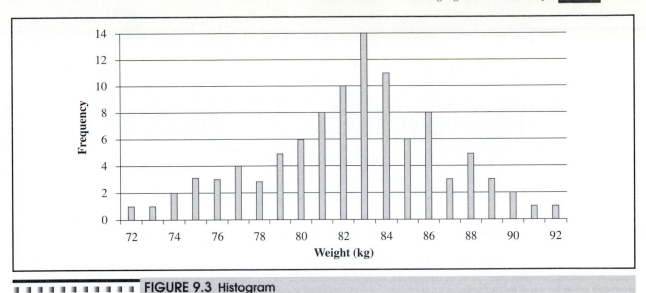

■ ■ ■ ■ ■ ■ ■ ■ ■ ■ ■ ■   **FIGURE 9.3** Histogram

process would produce doors of nearly identical weights, resulting in predictable quality in terms of the ease of operation and durability.

Similar statistical analysis can be performed on the probability distribution of response time, cost, and customer experience with the order fulfillment process as well as any other performance measure that may be important to MBPF's customers. The key fact is that process performance along any dimension varies from one flow unit to another, and we would like to measure, control, and reduce this variability, with the goal of making process performance more predictable and consistent with customers' expectations.

Although a histogram summarizes the overall process performance *in the aggregate,* it does not show how it varies *over time,* information that is often useful in identifying and reducing overall variability.

Example 9.3 (Continued)
Suppose that over the past 20 days there has been a steady upward trend in door weights from an average of 80 to 85 kg, or 0.25 kg per day. When we aggregate the 20-day data, we may get the same histogram, mean, and variance that we would get if we had made all our observations from the output of day 10, which also has an average weight of 82.5 kg. What can we say, then, if we had to predict door weights on day 21 of production? On the basis of the histogram alone, we would think that it will be a random sample from the normal distribution with a mean of 82.5 kg and a standard deviation of 4.2 kg. With knowledge of the upward trend over time, on the other hand, our estimate of the mean weight on day 21 should be 85.25 kg.

Thus, if we rely solely on the performance measurement summarized by a histogram, we lose the "time value" of information. In the next section, therefore, we emphasize the importance of tracking process performance over time, which is consistent with our flow perspective adopted throughout this book.

9.2.4   Run Charts

A **run chart** is *a plot of some measure of process performance monitored over time.* It displays variability in the process output *across time.* It also helps identify *structural variability* such as trend and seasonality (to be distinguished from *stochastic variability* due to random noise). A run chart of door weights is illustrated in Example 9.4.

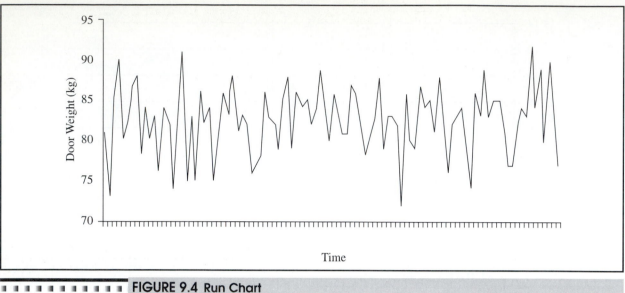

Example 9.4

To track variability in door weights over time, we may plot weights of doors sampled at two-hour intervals from each day's production. If we plot the 100 door weights recorded over time in the past 20 days, the resulting run chart appears as in Figure 9.4.

9.2.5 Multi-Vari Charts

To analyze the observed variability in process performance further, we may try to separate (1) variability *among* flow units produced at one time and (2) variability *between* flow units produced across time. Isolating the dominant type of variability would then facilitate our search for and elimination of its source. To distinguish between the two types of variability, we take N samples of process performance over time, each sample containing n observations. For each sample, we then compute the highest, the lowest, and the average measurement.

A **multi-vari chart** *is a plot of high-average-low values of performance measurement sampled over time.* The range between high and low measurements within each sample indicates variability in flow units produced at one time, while fluctuations in sample averages show variability across time.

Example 9.5

From the data in Table 9.1, we compute the high, low, and average weights in $N = 20$ samples, each containing $n = 5$ observations, and summarize the results in Table 9.2.

The high, low, and average values can now be plotted as a multi-vari chart in Figure 9.5. The length of each vertical line represents the range of variation in weights sampled on a given day, which indicates the amount of variability among the doors *within* that day's production. The dot on each vertical line shows the average weight of doors produced on that day. Fluctuation in the average weight from one day to the next then indicates variability *between* doors produced from one day to the next, which is tracked by lines connecting the dots across time.

From this multi-vari chart, we see that there is relatively little fluctuation in averages observed across time. We may therefore conclude that there is no apparent trend or cyclical pattern over time that affects door weights between days (ruling out, e.g., "Friday afternoon" or "Monday morning" effects on worker performance). Similarly, the lengths of vertical lines also seem to vary little from one day to another, so that variability in weights within each day appears stable as well. Thus, we may conclude that each day looks more or less the same as any other.

TABLE 9.2 Variation Between and Within Samples

	Day									
	1	*2*	*3*	*4*	*5*	*6*	*7*	*8*	*9*	*10*
High	90	88	84	91	86	88	83	86	88	89
Low	73	78	76	74	75	81	76	79	79	80
Average	81.8	83.8	81.0	80.8	80.4	83.8	79.2	83.0	84.4	83.8

	Day									
	11	*12*	*13*	*14*	*15*	*16*	*17*	*18*	*19*	*20*
High	87	86	88	87	88	84	89	85	92	90
Low	81	78	79	72	81	76	74	77	82	77
Average	83.8	82.0	83.0	80.8	83.8	80.8	83.0	81.2	85.0	83.8

However, variability between days appears to be less pronounced than variability within each day, so in our search to reduce overall variability, we should look for causes of variability that are common to all days.

The basic idea of separating variability between and within batches is also useful in disaggregating variability between and within worker teams, work shifts, and so forth. The goal is to isolate different types of variability so that we can identify, control, and eliminate causes of the most prevalent type. However, aside from displaying variability within and across samples, multi-vari charts do not provide any guidance for taking actions.

FIGURE 9.5 Multi-Vari Chart

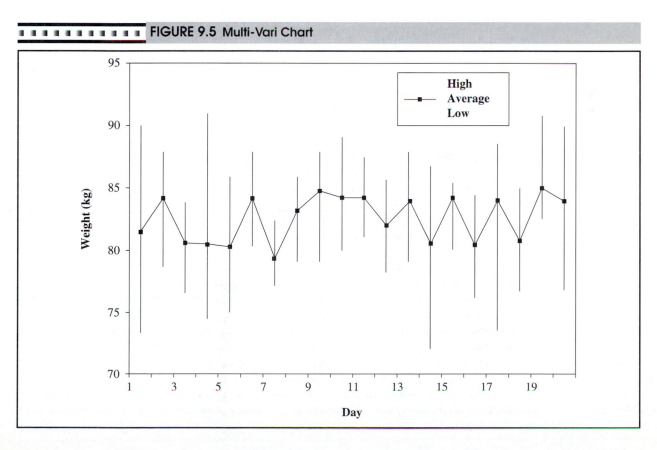

Example 9.5 (Continued)

From Figure 9.5, we note that on day 19, the average door weight observed was 85 kg—the highest of all averages observed so far and 3.8 kg above the previous day's average. Should we have taken any action back on day 19 to try to reduce the door weight? Well, we didn't, but luckily the average came down to 83.8 kg on day 20. In retrospect, it was good that we didn't panic and act hastily. But what should we do if, on day 21, we observe an average weight of 86 kg? Is that too high to be ignored?

We need some operational decision rule for taking actions based on observed variability. The same problem arises when tracking any series of data evolving over time to make decisions. For example, an investor has to decide when to buy or sell a stock as its price fluctuates; the central bank has to decide when to raise or lower interest rates on the basis of economic data collected over time. We devote the next section to the analysis of this important problem of deciding when to act and when not to act.

▪ ▪ ▪ ▪ **9.3   Process Control**

As we saw in Chapter 1, there are two aspects to process management: process planning and process control. *Process planning* involves structuring the process, designing operating procedures and developing such key competencies as process capability, flexibility, capacity, and cost efficiency. The long-run goal of process planning is to produce and deliver products that satisfy targeted customer needs. The goal of *process control,* on the other hand, is to continually ensure that, in the short run, the actual process performance conforms to the planned performance. Now the actual performance varies from the planned performance because of various disturbances. Process control involves tracking these deviations between the actual and the planned performance and taking corrective actions to identify and eliminate sources of these variations.

9.3.1   The Feedback Control Principle

Central to managing process performance over time is the general principle of feedback control of dynamical systems, which involves two steps:

1. Collecting information about a critical performance measure over time
2. Taking necessary corrective actions based on the observed performance to steer and maintain it at some desired level

Figure 9.6 displays the feedback control principle.

A house thermostat is a classic example of a feedback control mechanism. We set it at a desired temperature and a thermometer monitors the actual temperature, which may fluctuate because of air leaks, door openings, wind conditions, and so forth. Depending on the actual temperature, the controller automatically turns the air conditioner or furnace on and off over time. Automobile cruise control is another example of a feedback control mechanism. It maintains the car speed by monitoring the actual speed and adjusting the fuel supply to ensure that the actual speed stays close to the desired speed in spite of uneven hills encountered along the highway.

Applying the feedback control principle to **process control** *involves periodically monitoring the actual process performance (in terms of cost, quality, availability, and response time), comparing it to the planned levels of performance, identifying causes of the observed discrepancy between the two, and taking corrective actions to eliminate those causes.*

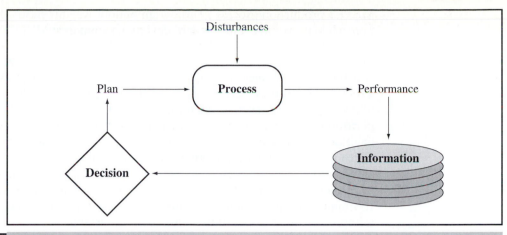

FIGURE 9.6 The Feedback Control Principle

Conceptually, process planning and control are similar to the **Plan-Do-Check-Act (PDCA) cycle** for problem solving and continuous improvement. The PDCA cycle *involves planning the process, operating it, inspecting its output, and adjusting it in light of the observation.* These four activities are then repeated continuously to monitor and improve the process performance.

The main problem in process control is deciding *when* to act in light of the observed performance. In practice, process managers often compare the current period's performance with that of the previous (or comparable) period in the past. Thus cost and productivity variance reports typically show percentage gains or losses from one month to the next. Managers then base actions (such as granting rewards and reprimands) on whether the observed variances are favorable. Unfortunately, some variances may be due to factors beyond a subordinate's control, so any incentive scheme based on such variance reports may be unfair. According to the late quality guru W. Edwards Deming, incentives based on factors that are beyond a worker's control (which he called "system causes") is like rewarding or punishing workers according to a lottery. To use observed performance data rationally, we must separate which variability is due to factors that are within a subordinate's control and which are beyond his or her control. We must understand different types of performance variability and their causes because appropriate managerial actions that are required to tackle each are very different.

9.3.2 Types and Causes of Variability

Performance of every process displays variability. Some of this variability is *normal*—to be expected of any process of a given design, operating in a given environment—while *abnormal* variability also occurs unexpectedly from time to time.

Normal variability *is statistically predictable and includes both structural variability and stochastic variability.* Recall that structural variability refers to systematic changes in the process performance, including seasonality and trend patterns. Stochastic variability arises from chance and is due to a stable system of *random* (or *common*) causes that are inherent to every process. Random causes are many in number, but each has only a small and unpredictable effect on the process performance. They cannot be easily isolated or removed without redesigning the entire process. For example, the weight of garage doors produced varies from door to door because of many factors bearing on the precision of

MBPF's production process. A histogram of door weights shows the frequency distribution, while its average and standard deviation summarize MBPF's process target weight and precision in achieving it. Beyond that we cannot say why two consecutive doors from the same day's output have different weights; the production process is inherently imprecise. If the performance variability is normal, due to random causes only, the process is in a stable state of statistical equilibrium—that is, parameters of the probability distribution of its performance (such as the mean and the variance) are unchanging—the process is performing as expected, given its design. How can we remove these random causes and increase consistency of our process performance? Only by improving the process design, which involves purchasing more precise equipment, hiring better skilled workers, training them better, purchasing better quality materials, and so forth. All this takes time and investment of resources over the long term and is therefore management's responsibility. It is unfair to expect operators to produce consistent output when the process provided is imprecise and the operating environment is unstable.

In contrast, **abnormal variability** *is unpredictable and disturbs the state of statistical equilibrium of the process by changing parameters of its distribution in an unexpected way.* Abnormal variability results from *assignable* or *special* causes that are externally superimposed from time to time. The existence of abnormal variability means that one or more of the factors affecting the process performance—architecture, procedures, or environment—may have changed. Although assignable causes are few in number, each has a significant effect on process performance. On the upside, however, they can be isolated, investigated, and eliminated, even in the short run. A particular batch of raw material might be defective, the machine may be incorrectly set, or the operator may be ill on that day. Because such causes are identifiable and correctable in the short run, at the local level, and without large capital expenditures, they are the operator's responsibility. The goal of process control is to identify whether the observed variability is normal or abnormal, so that an appropriate action can be taken at an appropriate level to eliminate it.

Ironically, another source of abnormal variability is process *tampering*—unnecessary adjustments made in trying to compensate for normal variability. Deming's "marble experiment" illustrates this principle beautifully. A subject is asked to drop a marble through a funnel repeatedly with the goal of hitting a target on the floor underneath. If the marble misses the target, a naive subject tries to compensate for the deviation by moving the funnel in the opposite direction. This unnecessary tinkering, however, results in an *increase* in the variability of the marble's final position. The correct strategy, of course, is to aim the funnel right on the target and let the marble land around it, its final position exhibiting stochastic variability due to random causes. The idea is to avoid overreacting to random fluctuations in the short run. In the long run, we may wish to reduce even random fluctuations by redesigning the process—for example, by lowering the funnel, using a less bouncy marble, or leveling and changing the composition of the landing surface.

In statistical terms, normal variability is observed among random draws from a fixed probability distribution of process performance. Abnormal variability occurs when the parameters of this distribution (such as its mean or variance) are changed. Thus, in the short run, our goal is fourfold:

1. To estimate normal stochastic variability, separated from structural variability
2. To accept it as an inevitable part of the given process and avoid unnecessary tampering to counteract it
3. To detect the presence of abnormal variability in process performance
4. To identify and eliminate assignable causes of abnormal variability

Our long-term goal then is to reduce normal variability as well by improving the process precision. Short-term process adjustments could and should be delegated to those workers who are closest to the sources of abnormal variability. Long-term process improvements, which may involve considerable investment, time, and effort, are the manager's responsibility.

We deal first with the problem of short-term process control. In the following sections, we assume that structural variability has already been accounted for and that tampering is avoided. As we monitor the process over time, we wish to determine whether the observed performance variability is normal or abnormal. If it is normal—due to random causes only—we say that the *process is in control.* We should then accept the observed variability as an aspect of the process performance that is to be expected and that cannot be eliminated in the short run. It represents the best effort of the process, and we should leave it alone. If, on the other hand, performance variability appears to be abnormal—due to an assignable cause—we conclude that the *process is out of control.* In this case, we should stop the process and investigate, identify, and remove assignable causes so as to bring it back into the state of control. The fundamental problem, therefore, is how to decide whether observed variability is normal or abnormal.

9.3.3   Control Limit Policy

The structure of this type of "threshold policy" for making decisions based on observed performance has an intuitive appeal, and is known to be optimal in a wide variety of situations. At the most basic level, if the process performance varies "too much" from a planned level, we should conclude that this variability is abnormal and we should look for an assignable cause. To quantify what we mean by "too much," we establish a **control band**, *a range within which any variation in process performance is to be interpreted as normal, due to known structural or random causes that cannot be readily identified or eliminated in the short run.* Therefore, if the process performance varies within this band, we should consider it an unavoidable fact of life, leave the process alone and not tamper with it. Any variability outside this range, on the other hand, should be considered abnormal, due to an assignable cause, warranting a detailed investigation and correction.

As an example of a control limit policy, we might monitor the performance of our car by tracking the gas mileage we get from one fill-up to the next. If we get 25 miles per gallon on average, a combination of random causes (weather and traffic conditions, gasoline quality) and assignable causes (incorrect ignition timing, burned spark plugs, leaky gas tank, untrained driver) will cause actual mileage to deviate from 25 mpg. Our decision rule may be to set a lower limit of acceptable mileage (say, 20 mpg). If the actual mileage falls below this limit, we should take the car to a mechanic for a checkup; if it is above this limit, we should continue to drive it as is. Similarly, in the house thermostat example, the controller may be set at 20°C, and may turn the furnace on if the temperature drops 2°C below the set temperature and shut it off if the temperature rises 2°C above the set value. As a result, the house temperature will be maintained within the control band between 18°C and 22°C. A more precise controller may be more expensive but would maintain the temperature closer to the setting by turning the furnace on and off more frequently.

Although the concept of process control is usually applied to managing product quality, the principle is applicable to controlling *any* measure of process performance over time. For example, we have already seen an application of control limit policy in managing inventory and capacity. In Chapter 7, we saw that inventory control with uncertain demand involves monitoring the inventory level over time and ordering Q units as soon as the inventory depletes to a preestablished reorder point (ROP) level. In this context, the ROP constitutes a "control limit," and the action taken, when necessary, consists of ordering Q units. The ROP determines the safety inventory, which controls the product availability in terms of the probability of stockout.

Similarly, in managing process capacity and flow time, as in Chapter 8, we may monitor the length of the waiting line (or the duration of a customer's waiting time). As soon as it reaches some upper limit, we may increase the process capacity by adding a server, and when it reaches a lower limit, we may decrease the capacity. Such operating policies are routinely followed in opening and closing checkout counters in supermarkets. In establishing the queue control limits, the goal is to limit the customer's waiting time.

In the area of cost management, accountants use cost and productivity variance reports to track a department's performance and to specify managerial actions when the observed cost exceeds a certain threshold or productivity drops below a critical level. In short-term cash management, a firm's (or an investor's) cash position might fluctuate over time. If it falls below a certain level, the firm may liquidate some of its assets in order to raise cash, while if the cash position reaches some higher level, the firm may invest the excess cash in an asset. Finally, in stock trading, investors can place "limit orders" to purchase (or "stop loss" orders to sell) a stock if and when its price drops to a specific level. Computerized "program trading" automatically executes trades when prices reach prespecified trigger levels. Thus, in a wide variety of business applications, a control limit policy provides guidelines in the form of critical thresholds for taking actions online, in real time, in light of current information.

9.3.4 Control Charts

Statistical process control involves setting a range of acceptable variation in process performance around its mean. As long as the observed performance varies within this range, we accept the variation as normal and conclude that we do not have sufficient evidence to suspect the presence of an assignable cause, so we refrain from tampering with the process. Any performance variation outside this range, however, should be regarded as abnormal, warranting an action; we should stop the process, search for an assignable cause, and eliminate it.

In setting an acceptable control band around the expected performance μ, we should take into account two factors:

1. The normal variability in process performance, as measured by its standard deviation σ
2. How tightly we wish to control the process, as represented by a positive number z; the smaller the value of z, the tighter the control desired

We then set z standard deviations around the mean as an acceptable band of process variability. We thus specify a **lower control limit (LCL)** and an **upper control limit (UCL)** and denote the **control band** as $[LCL, UCL]$. The general formulas for determining the two **control limits**, therefore, are

$$LCL = \mu - z\sigma \quad \text{and} \quad UCL = \mu + z\sigma \tag{9.1}$$

Figure 9.7 shows a generic **control chart**, which *displays how process performance varies over time in relation to the control limits.* It is like a run chart of process performance with control limits overlaid to give it decision-making power. If the observed performance varies within the control band, we infer that the performance variability

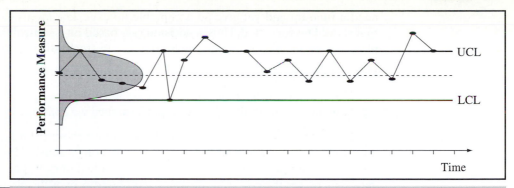

FIGURE 9.7 Process Control Chart

is normal, the process is in control and therefore take no action. Performance variation outside the control band is to be interpreted as abnormal, indicating that the process is out of control, signaling probable existence of an assignable cause that should be identified and removed. In addition to comparing the observed performance against the control limits, we may also try to identify any structural variability in terms of trend or seasonal patterns over time and use this information to make decisions. Various additional rules of thumb may be used to make inferences about variability to decide when to act. For example, one rule recommends that if seven consecutive observations are above (or below) the average performance, we should investigate the process even though the variation is within the control band and the process appears to be in control.

Statistical Interpretation   A reader familiar with statistics may recognize the relationship of control limits to *hypothesis testing*. We start with a *null hypothesis* that the process is in control (i.e., stable) at some level μ, the *alternate hypothesis* being that the process mean has in fact shifted to some other level. Based on the observed performance, we must determine if the process mean has shifted. The decision rule is to accept the null hypothesis if the observed performance falls within the control limits. If it falls outside the control limits, we conclude that there is statistically significant evidence to reject the null hypothesis and infer that the mean has shifted because of some assignable cause.

This decision rule is not mistake-proof because the presence of stochastic variability may result in misinterpretation of observed variability, leading to wrong decisions. Sometimes, even when the process is in control, its performance measure may fall outside the control band simply because of normal variability. In that case, we may conclude—wrongly—that the process is out of control and look for an assignable cause when in fact none exists, leading to an expensive wild-goose chase. *The probability of false alarm due to mistaking normal variability as abnormal* is called **type I (or α) error**. Conversely, our process performance measure may fall within the control band by chance even if there is an assignable cause. In this case, we conclude—again wrongly—that the observed variability is normal and warrants no investigation when in fact it is abnormal and we should be looking for an assignable cause. *The probability of missed signal due to mistaking abnormal variability as normal is called* **type II (or β) error**. In our car gas mileage example, suppose we usually get an average of 25 mpg and set a lower control limit at 20 mpg, so we take the car to a mechanic whenever the mileage drops below 20 mpg. It is possible that even when nothing is wrong with the car, our mileage may drop below 20 mpg purely by chance because of environmental conditions, and hence we erroneously conclude that the car needs repair, which of course costs us unnecessarily in terms of time, effort, and money. On the other hand, the car may in fact need a tune-up and yet give an acceptable mileage, leading us to overlook a problem that should be corrected. Thus, a decision rule based on a control limit policy—although plausible—may lead to wrong conclusions due to stochastic variability.

Optimal Degree of Control   The degree of control exercised depends on two factors:

1. How frequently we monitor the process performance
2. How much variability in process performance we consider acceptable

In automatic control systems (such as a house thermostat and car cruise control) monitoring and adjustment are performed continuously. In business processes, however, continuous control may not be economical or even possible. Frequent observation increases the cost of monitoring but also improves the chance of quickly discovering any degradation in performance, leading to speedy recovery. The optimal frequency of monitoring should balance these costs and benefits. For example, the heart rate and cholesterol levels of a person with heart disease are monitored more closely than those of a healthy person, because the cost of monitoring is insignificant in relation to the risk of a heart attack.

Similarly, responsiveness of process control depends on the width of the control band, as measured by z, which also determines the magnitude of type I and type II errors and the resulting costs. Recall that a smaller value of z means a narrower control band, which leads us to look for assignable causes more often than we should, resulting in frequent unnecessary investigation. At the same time, however, the tighter control band ensures that assignable causes, when present, will be detected faster, which would reduce the cost of nonconformance. Conversely, a larger z—and a wider control band—means looser control, infrequent investigation, and a lower cost of control but also a higher cost of nonconformance. The correct choice of z would balance these costs of investigation and failure to eliminate assignable causes of variability. On one hand, we would like to avoid a knee-jerk reaction to normal variability, while, on the other hand, we would like to discover and act promptly to eliminate any abnormal variability.

In summary, the optimum degree of control—in terms of the frequency of observation and the sensitivity of the decision rule—is based on tradeoffs between the costs of control and the benefits of conformance to the planned performance, as displayed in Figure 9.8.

▪ ▪ ▪ ▪ ▪ ▪ ▪ ▪ ▪ ▪ ▪ ▪ **FIGURE 9.8** Optimal Degree of Control

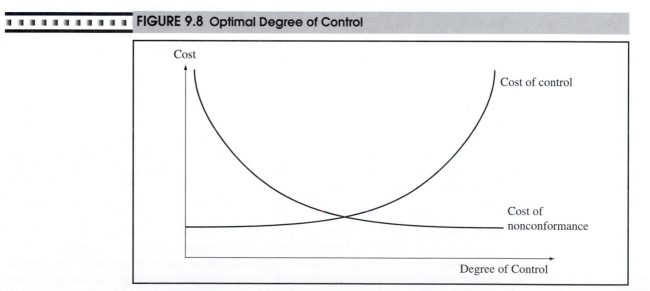

Although ideally, the optimal value of z should balance the costs of type I and type II errors involved, traditionally and in the practice of statistical process control, a value of $z = 3$ is often used. Recall that if a performance measure is normally distributed, 99.73% of all measurements will fall within the mean ±3 standard deviations. Therefore, as long as the actual performance varies within this range, we conclude that the process is in control and take no action, while any variation outside this range is considered statistically significant, indicating an out-of-control process that needs to be investigated and corrected.

In practical application of process control, we often do not know if a performance measure is normally distributed, nor do we know its true mean or standard deviation. We must therefore ascertain these by sampling the actual performance and establish control limits based on sample estimates, as discussed in the next section.

Average and Variation Control Charts   We monitor process performance by taking random samples over time. As we saw in Section 9.2.5, multi-vari charts display performance variability *within* each sample and *between* samples, but they do not tell us which variability is normal to be left alone, and which is abnormal that warrants an action. Average and variation control charts accomplish this by establishing bands of acceptable variability.

As before, we take N random samples of process performance over time, each containing n observations. We compute two summary statistics for each sample:

- Sample average A of the n measurements
- Sample variation V, which is the difference between the highest and the lowest measurements among n observations

Thus we obtain sample averages $A_1, A_2, \ldots A_N$ and sample variations $V_1, V_2, \ldots V_N$. Each sample average is an estimate of the *expected* (or *mean*) performance of the process, whereas a sample variation indicates *variability* in process performance (which is directly related to—but not the same as—the *standard deviation* and is easier to compute). As in a multi-vari chart, we can plot these N sample averages and sample variations over time, displaying variability *between* and *within* samples, respectively. To decide whether observed variability is normal or abnormal we establish control bands on sample averages and sample variations.

The **average control chart** *shows the average process performance as well as a band of acceptable variability in averages with the goal of identifying abnormal variability that changes the process mean.* An important result in probability theory, known as the *central limit theorem*, states that the probability distribution of sample averages will be approximately normal, *even if* individual observations are not. Therefore we can assume that sample averages are normally distributed with some mean μ_A and some standard deviation σ_A. It turns out that $\mu_A = \mu$, the mean of each individual observation, and $\sigma_A = \sigma / \sqrt{n}$, which is smaller than the process standard deviation of an individual observation (that is, sample averages display less variability than individual observations). We can therefore apply the generic control limits of Equation 9.1 to obtain

$$LCL = \mu - z\sigma / \sqrt{n} \quad \text{and} \quad UCL = \mu + z\sigma / \sqrt{n}$$

where μ and σ are the true mean and the true standard deviation of individual observations, both of which are typically unknown.

We therefore estimate μ by the overall average $\overline{A} = (A_1 + A_2 + \ldots + A_N)/N$, and σ by s, the standard deviation of all $N \times n$ observations. With these estimates, we can obtain the control limits for the **average control chart** as

$$LCL = \overline{A} - zs/\sqrt{n} \quad \text{and} \quad UCL = \overline{A} + zs/\sqrt{n} \tag{9.2}$$

If all of the observed sample averages $A_1, A_2, \ldots A_N$ fall within this control band, we say that "the average chart is in control" and conclude that the process mean is stable; the observed variability *between* sample averages must therefore be due to normal causes only. If a sample average falls outside the control band, we conclude that the observed variability is abnormal, signaling that we should look for an assignable cause that has changed the process mean.

In addition to controlling the process mean, we would also like to make sure that variability in process performance is stable over time. As indicated before, a greater variability means a wider range of variation V in the observed performance *within* each sample. Given the observed variations $V_1, V_2, \ldots V_N$ in N samples, we can compute the *average sample variation* $\overline{V} = (V_1 + V_2 + \ldots + V_N)/N$, which is a measure of the expected variability, and s_V, the standard deviation of the sample variation. With these estimates of the expected value and variability in sample variations, we apply the generic control limits to sample variations to get the **variation control chart** as

$$LCL = \overline{V} - zs_V \quad \text{and} \quad UCL = \overline{V} + zs_V \tag{9.3}$$

If all observed sample variations fall within this band, we say that the "variation chart is in control" and conclude that the process variability is stable, so that any observed variability *within* samples must be due to normal causes only. If an observed sample variation falls above the upper control limit, we should look for an assignable cause for excessive variability, while if it is below the lower control limit, the process performance is significantly less variable than expected.

We illustrate construction of the average control and variation control charts for the data in Example 9.6.

Example 9.6

As shown in Table 9.1, we have taken $N = 20$ samples over time, each containing $n = 5$ observations. As in Table 9.2, we can compute the average door weight in the sample of five on day 1 as

$$A_1 = (81 + 73 + 85 + 90 + 80)/5 = 81.8 \text{ kg}$$

and the range of variation between the heaviest and the lightest door in that sample as

$$V_1 = 90 - 73 = 17 \text{ kg}$$

Similarly, the average weight on day 2 is $A_2 = 83.8$ kg with the range of variation $V_2 = 10$ kg and so on. These sample averages and variations are tabulated in Table 9.3.

Note that both the averages and variations in weights vary from one sample to the next. With the twenty averages from Table 9.3 we can now compute the average of the twenty averages as

$$\overline{A} = 82.5 \text{ kg}$$

which, of course, matches with the overall average weight in all 100 doors sampled, as calculated in Example 9.3, where the overall standard deviation of weights was also calculated as $s = 4.2$ kg.

TABLE 9.3 Sample Averages and Variations in Door Weights over Time

					Day					
Sample	***1***	***2***	***3***	***4***	***5***	***6***	***7***	***8***	***9***	***10***
A	81.8	83.8	81.0	80.8	80.4	83.8	79.2	83.0	84.4	83.8
V	17	10	8	17	11	7	7	7	9	9

					Day					
Sample	***11***	***12***	***13***	***14***	***15***	***16***	***17***	***18***	***19***	***20***
A	83.8	82.0	83.0	80.8	83.8	80.8	83.0	81.2	85.0	83.8
V	6	8	9	15	7	8	15	8	10	13

With the standard practice of setting $z = 3$, our control limits on sample averages in Equation (9.2) become

$$LCL = \overline{A} - zs/\sqrt{n} = 82.5 - (3)(4.2)/\sqrt{5} = 76.87 \text{ kg}$$
$$UCL = \overline{A} + zs/\sqrt{n} = 82.5 + (3)(4.2)/\sqrt{5} = 88.13 \text{ kg}$$

If we compare the 20 values of sample averages in Table 9.3 against these limits, we see that all of them fall within our control band. Equivalently, we can plot the observed sample averages and the upper and lower control limits on the chart in Figure 9.9. Since all of the observations fall between $LCL = 77.7$ and $UCL = 87.3$, we conclude that the process mean is stable; there is no statistical evidence to indicate the presence of an assignable cause of variability that affects the process mean. In other words, there is no reason to believe that door weights vary significantly *between* days.

Likewise, we can compute from Table 9.3 the average of sample variations

$$\overline{V} = 10.1 \text{ kg}$$

and standard deviation of sample variations

$$s_V = 3.5 \text{ kg}$$

We can then establish control limits on values of the observed ranges of variation as

$$LCL = \overline{V} - 3s_V = (10.1) - (3)(3.5) = -0.4$$
$$UCL = \overline{V} + 3s_V = (10.1) + (3)(3.5) = 20.6$$

■ ■ ■ ■ ■ ■ ■ ■ ■ ■ ■   **FIGURE 9.9 Average Control Chart**

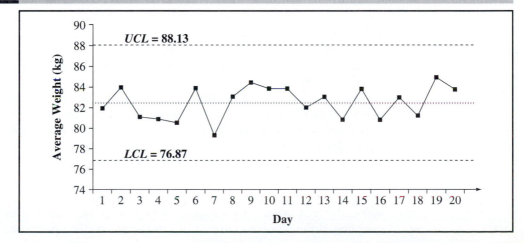

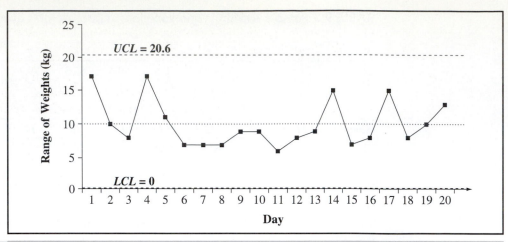

FIGURE 9.10 Variation Control Chart

Note that we should set the *LCL* of –0.4 to 0 because the range of variation within a sample cannot be negative. Again, when we compare the 20 observed ranges against these control limits, we see that they are all less than 20.6 kg. Equivalently, we can plot the 20 observed ranges of variation against the upper and lower control limits as shown in Figure 9.10. Observe that all points are below *UCL* = 20.6. We therefore conclude that there is no reason to believe that any day's output is varying significantly either. In other words, there is no assignable cause of variability *within* each day's performance. Thus, we conclude that our production process seems to display only normal variability within as well as between days. In other words, *the process is in control,* and as far as door weights are concerned, the door-making process appears to be statistically stable.

In order to highlight the essence of statistical process control, we have described the terminology and technical details of control charts in a simplified form. A complete exposition involves using the average range of variations to estimate the standard deviations of process output and its range. Details may be found, for example, in Grant and Leavenworth (1988).

Extensions   Although we have described process control in terms of the quality of its output, the same principles would apply if we considered the performance measure as the unit flow time or cost. Likewise, our performance measure may be a continuous variable (such as door weight, customer waiting time, or processing cost) or a discrete variable (such as whether a flow unit is defective, number of defects per flow unit produced, or number of customer complaints). In the continuous case, we assume normal distribution, as illustrated previously, whereas in the discrete case, we use an appropriate discrete probability distribution such as *binomial* or *Poisson*. Although the control limit formulas differ, the basic principles of establishing control limits remain the same.

For example, suppose we wish to monitor and control the number of order processing errors at MBPF. If MBPF processes a large number of orders and if the chance of making an error on each order is small, we may model the number of monthly errors by a Poisson distribution with some mean μ, which is also equal to its variance (see Appendix II). We can then set control limits on the observed number of errors per month as (called the *number of defects chart*):

$$\mu \pm z\sqrt{\mu} \qquad\qquad (9.4)$$

where the true mean μ is estimated by m, the average number of errors observed by sampling. If the observed number of errors exceeds the upper control limit, it indicates statistically significant degradation in performance that should be investigated. Similarly, a number of errors less than the lower control limit would indicate better-than-expected performance that should be recognized and rewarded—and perhaps institutionalized. In either case, whenever we get a signal that performance variability is abnormal, we should look for an assignable cause—favorable or unfavorable—and act on it.

Note that in order to establish control limits as mean $\pm z$ standard deviations, we first need to estimate the true mean and the true standard deviation of process performance based on observed samples. To ensure that our estimates are reliable, it is essential that samples are randomly selected and drawn from a stable probability distribution with constant mean and standard deviation, which means the process is in control. Thus, the logic of control charts may appear somewhat circular: control limits are based on estimates of process parameters assuming that the process is in control but then the same observations are compared against these control limits to determine whether the observed variability is normal! The apparent contradiction disappears if we view process control as an ongoing activity which uses control charts as a dynamic tool for continually monitoring and estimating process performance. We compare the observed performance against the currently established control limits which are based on the estimates obtained from the data observed thus far. We then take action to stabilize the process if the current control limits are exceeded. As we continue to observe and stabilize the process performance over time, we keep improving our estimates of the parameters of the probability distribution of the performance measure. We adjust the control limits accordingly, and compare newly observed performance against these more reliable limits, and continue.

What do we do if process performance falls outside control limits? How do we investigate and correct causes of abnormal variability? We indicate a couple of tools for systematically analyzing and correcting sources of abnormal variability.

9.3.5 Cause–Effect Diagrams

On detecting the presence of abnormal variability, we may use a **cause–effect diagram** (also known as a **fishbone diagram** or **Ishikawa diagram**) to identify the root cause(s) of the observed variability. A cause–effect diagram *shows a chain of cause–effect relationships that ultimately leads to the observed variability*. Through discussion and brainstorming, we first try to generate hypotheses about possible causes. According to one guideline, if we diligently pursue a sequence of five *Why?* questions, we will ultimately arrive at the root cause of a problem. For example:

- Why are these doors so heavy? *Because the sheet metal used to make them was too thick.*
- Why was the sheet metal too thick? *Because the rollers at the supplier's steel mill were set incorrectly.*
- Why were the supplier's rollers incorrectly set? *Because the supplier is incapable of producing to our specifications.*
- Why did we select a supplier who can't meet our specifications? *Because our project supervisor was too busy "getting the product out" to invest time in vendor selection.*
- Why did he find himself in these circumstances? *Because he gets paid by his performance in meeting production quotas.*

Thus, the root cause of the door weight problem might be MBPF's incentive structure. A simplified fishbone diagram of this problem may look like the one in Figure 9.11. The tail of each arrow shows a possible cause of the effect indicated at the head of that arrow.

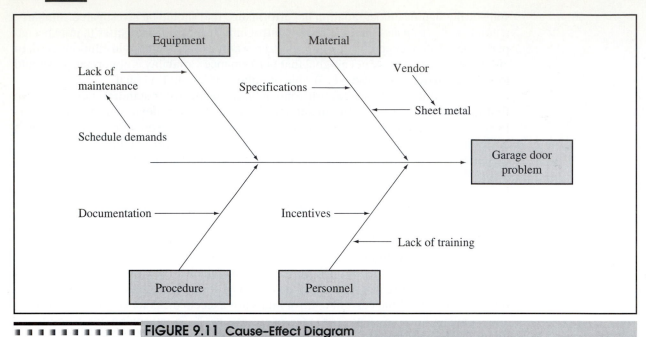

Although a cause–effect diagram enables us to identify a *qualitative* relationship between a process variable and its effect on the product characteristic that customers care about, in order to take a concrete action, we need to understand the precise *quantitative* relationship between the two, as indicated in the next section.

9.3.6 Scatter Plots

Suppose we have identified the supplier's sheet metal rolling process as the root cause of the door weight problem (which affects the ease of door operation and its durability that customers value). We would now like to measure the exact relationship between the two so that we will be able to control the door weight by changing the settings on the supplier's rolling mill.

To estimate this relationship, we may experiment with various settings on the rolling mill, measure the effect on the garage door weights, and plot the results on a graph, which is called a **scatter plot**. Formally, a scatter plot is *a graph showing how a controllable process variable affects the resulting performance characteristic.* In the scatter plot shown in Figure 9.12, the horizontal axis represents the sheet metal thickness setting in millimeters, and the vertical axis shows the weight of garage doors produced. The two variables seem to be "positively correlated"—higher roller settings tends to be associated with increased door weights. One could continue with statistical *regression analysis* to estimate the strength of this relationship, but we will not go into details here.

To summarize this section, process control involves dynamically monitoring process performance over time to ensure that variability in performance is due to normal random causes only. It enables us to detect abnormal variability so that we can identify and eliminate its root causes. A process being "in control" simply means that variability in its performance is stable through time so that variability in its output is statistically predictable. Being in control makes a statement about the *internal* stability of the process. However, it is important to note that being in control does *not* necessarily mean that the process performance is satisfactory in terms of its output from the

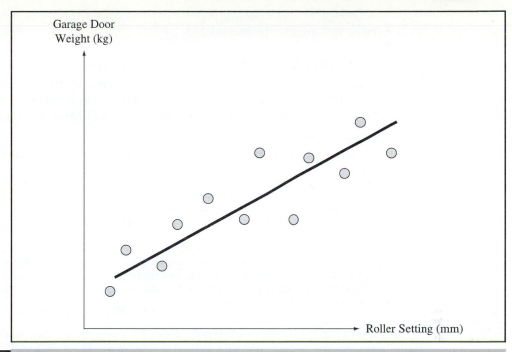

Garage Door
Weight (kg)

Roller Setting (mm)

FIGURE 9.12 Scatter Plot

external customer's perspective. Therefore, in addition to maintaining the process in a state of internal control, it is important for process managers to make sure that process performance also meets the external customer requirements—a topic that we take up in the next section.

9.4   Process Capability

In our study of process planning and control at MBPF Inc., we first identified the external product measures that customers desire (such as the ease of door operation and durability) and linked them to internal measures (door weight) that the manufacturer can control. We then translated the product performance desired by customers into the necessary **upper specification (*US*)** and **lower specification (*LS*)** limits (from 75 to 85 kg) of the product design. *These specifications indicate the range of performance variation that a customer is willing to accept.* Thus, product specification limits refer to performance variability acceptable from the external perspective of the customer. On the other hand, process control limits represent the range of performance variability that is acceptable from the internal perspective of maintaining process stability. Thus it is important to note that process control limits and product specification limits serve very different roles and should not be mixed together, for example, by plotting the two on the same chart. Thus in an average control chart, we plot and compare sample averages with *control limits*, and not with *specification limits*. Similarly, *individual* units—not just sample *averages*—must meet customer specifications.

Once we have a process in control so that its output variability is normal and statistically predictable, our estimates of the process mean and standard deviation are reliable. Based on these estimates, we may determine the **process capability**, which may be defined broadly as *the ability of the process to meet customer specifications.*

Although we can measure process capability in a variety of ways, here we describe three that are closely interrelated.

9.4.1 Fraction of Output within Specifications

One measure of process capability is the fraction of the process output that meets customer specifications. We can compute this fraction either by actual observation or by using a theoretical probability distribution, as illustrated in Example 9.7.

Example 9.7

Recall that in the MBPF example, specifications of the garage door weight are $US = 85$ kg and $LS = 75$ kg. Also recall that in Figure 9.3, the height of each bar corresponds to the fraction of doors with a specific weight. Adding all the bar weights between 75 and 85 kg, therefore, yields the total fraction of door output that meets design specifications. We see that 74 out of the 100 doors observed fall within the specifications. We may therefore say that *the process is currently 74% capable of meeting customer requirements*; it is producing approximately 26% defectives.

Alternatively, we may use the normal distribution as a continuous approximation and compute the area under the normal probability density curve between 75 and 85 kg. If door weight W is a normal random variable with mean $\mu = 82.5$ kg and standard deviation of $\sigma = 4.2$ kg, then the proportion of doors falling within the specification limits is given by

$$\text{Prob}(75 \leq W \leq 85) = \text{Prob}(W \leq 85) - \text{Prob}(W \leq 75)$$

If we let Z denote the standard normal variable (with mean 0 and standard deviation of 1), we can use the standard normal tables in the Appendix II (or Microsoft Excel, as described in Chapter 7) to compute $\text{Prob}(W \leq 85)$ in terms of

$$Z = (W - \mu)/\sigma$$

as

$$\text{Prob}[Z \leq (85 - 82.5)/4.2] = \text{Prob}(Z \leq 0.5952) = 0.724$$

(In Microsoft Excel, Prob $(W \leq 85) = \text{NORMDIST}(85, 82.5, 4.2, \text{True}) = 0.724158$.)
Similarly, we find from the standard normal tables that

$$\text{Prob}(W \leq 75) = \text{Prob}(Z \leq (75 - 82.5)/4.2) = \text{Prob}(Z \leq -1.79) = 0.0367$$

(In Microsoft Excel, Prob $(W \leq 75) = \text{NORMDIST}(75, 82.5, 4.2, \text{True}) = 0.037073$.)
Then

$$\text{Prob}(75 \leq W \leq 85) = 0.724 - 0.0367 = 0.6873$$

(or by Microsoft Excel we get $0.724158 - 0.037073 = 0.687085$). With normal approximation, therefore, MBPF's process is capable of producing about 69% of doors within the specifications, or MBPF is delivering about 31% defective doors!

Note that, on average, doors weigh 82.5 kg, which is well within the specification limits, but that is not a relevant criterion in meeting customer requirements. Specifications refer to *individual* doors, *not* averages: MBPF cannot comfort an individual customer by assuring that, *on average*, its doors do meet specifications because there is a 30% chance that the customer may have received a door that is either too light or too heavy. It is the variability in *individual* doors—not just their *average* weight—that matters in determining how capable the process is in meeting customer requirements.

9.4.2 Process Capability Ratios (C_{pk} and C_p)

A related measure of process capability that is easier to compute is called the *process capability ratio,* denoted as C_{pk}. This ratio is based on the observation that in a normal distribution, if the mean is 3 standard deviations above the lower specification LS

(or below the upper specification *US*), there is very little chance of a product falling below *LS* (or above *US*). We therefore compute

$$(US - \mu)/3\sigma$$

and

$$(\mu - LS)/3\sigma$$

as surrogate measures of how well process output would fall within our specifications. The higher these values, the more capable the process is in meeting specifications. In fact, to be on the conservative side, we may take the smaller of these two ratios and define a single measure of process capability as

$$C_{pk} = \min[(US - \mu)/3\sigma, (\mu - LS)/3\sigma] \tag{9.5}$$

A process with a higher value of C_{pk} is more capable than one with a lower value. Typically, a process with of C_{pk} of 1 or more represents a capable process that will produce most of the output meeting customer specifications.

The C_{pk} measure is also useful when our product specifications are one sided—that is, when we need to ensure that performance measurements are not too high (or too low). For example, if we need to measure the processing cost, delivery time delay, or the number of errors per transactions processed, we may specify only the upper specification limit *US* because lower values mean only better-than-expected quality. The C_{pk} is then given by the single term in the previous expression that is relevant, the first one in these examples.

As a special case, if the process is properly centered at the middle of the specification range, we may define C_{pk} by either

$$(US - \mu)/3\sigma$$

or

$$(\mu - LS)/3\sigma$$

as both are equal for a centered process. Therefore, for a correctly centered process, we may simply define the *process capability ratio* denoted by C_p as

$$C_p = (US - LS)/6\sigma \tag{9.6}$$

This ratio has a nice interpretation. Its numerator specifies the range of variability that the customer is willing to tolerate (and so represents the "voice of the customer"). The denominator, meanwhile, denotes the range of variability that the process is capable of delivering (which represents the "voice of the process"). Recall that with normal distribution, most process output—99.73%—falls within ±3 standard deviations from the mean. That is, most of the process variability is within 6 standard deviations around the mean. Consequently, 6σ is sometimes referred to as the *natural tolerance of the process*. Example 9.8 illustrates the computations of the process capability ratio for our door problem.

Example 9.8
In our garage door example, since the mean is 82.5 kg and the standard deviation is 4.2 kg, we can compute

$$\begin{aligned}
C_{pk} &= \min[(US - \mu)/3\sigma, \ (\mu - LS)/3\sigma] \\
&= \min\{(85 - 82.5)/[(3)(4.2)], (82.5 - 75)/[(3)(4.2)]\} \\
&= \min\{0.1984, 0.5952\} = 0.1984
\end{aligned}$$

TABLE 9.4 Relationship between Process Capability Ratio and Proportion Defective

Defects (ppm)	10,000	3,000	1,000	100	10	1	2 ppb
C_p	0.86	1	1.1	1.3	1.47	1.63	2

If the process is correctly centered at $\mu = 80$ kg, we compute the process capability ratio as

$$C_p = (US - LS)/6\sigma$$
$$= (85 - 75)/[(6)(4.2)] = 0.3968$$

It is important to note that $C_{pk} = 0.1984$ (or $C_p = 0.3968$) does *not* mean that the process is capable of meeting customer needs 19.84% (or 39.68%) of the time; we computed that figure in Example 9.7 to be about 69%. There is, however, a close relationship between the process capability ratio and the proportion of the process output that meets customer specifications. Table 9.4 summarizes this relationship, wherein defects are counted in parts per million (ppm) or parts per billion (ppb), and the process is assumed to be properly centered. Thus, if we would like no more than 100 defects per million (0.01% defectives), we should have the probability distribution of door weights so closely concentrated around the mean that the standard deviation is 1.282 kg, which then corresponds to $C_p = 1.3$.

9.4.3 Six-Sigma Capability

A third equivalent measure of process capability that is used by Motorola, General Electric, Sun Microsystems, and other quality-conscious companies is called the *sigma measure,* which is computed as

$$S = \min[(US - \mu)/\sigma, (\mu - LS)/\sigma] \tag{9.7}$$

and the process is called an *S-sigma process.* If the process is correctly centered at the middle of specifications, Equation 9.7 is equivalent to

$$S = [(US - LS)/2\sigma] \tag{9.8}$$

Example 9.9

Currently the sigma capability of MBPF's door-making process is

$$S = \min[(85 - 82.5)/4.2, (82.5 - 75)/4.2] = 0.5952$$

By centering the process correctly, its sigma capability increases to

$$S = (85 - 75)/[(2)(4.2)] = 1.19$$

Thus, with a three-sigma process that is correctly centered, the upper and lower specifications are 3 standard deviations away from the mean, which corresponds to $C_p = 1$, and 99.73% of the output will meet the specifications. Similarly, a correctly centered **six-sigma process** has a standard deviation so small that the upper and lower specification limits are 6 standard deviations from the mean each. This level of performance consistency represents an extraordinarily high degree of precision. It corresponds to $C_p = 2$, or only two defective units per billion produced! In order for MBPF's door-making process to be a six-sigma process, its standard deviation must be

$$\sigma = (85 - 75)/[(2)(6)] = 0.833 \text{ kg}$$

which is about one-fifth of its current value of 4.2 kg.

TABLE 9.5 Fraction Defective and Sigma Measure

Sigma S	3	4	5	6
Capability Ratio C_p	1	1.33	1.667	2
Defects (ppm)	66810	6210	233	3.4

Adjusting for Mean Shifts   Actually, given the sigma measure, Motorola computes the fraction defective more conservatively by allowing for a shift in the mean of ±1.5 standard deviations from the center of specifications. Allowing for this shift, a six-sigma process amounts to producing an average of 3.4 defective units per million units. Thus, even if the process is not correctly centered, the six-sigma process will produce only 3.4 ppm defectives. Such a high standard represents, although not quite "zero defects," "virtual perfection" and a goal to strive for.

With these three measures of process capability and allowing for a *1.5-sigma* shift in the process mean, we can determine the relationship between the sigma measure, C_p, and defective ppm produced, tabulated as in Table 9.5.

Why Six-Sigma?   From the table, note that improvement in the process capability from a three-sigma to a four-sigma process calls for a 10-fold reduction in the fraction defective, while going from a four-sigma process to a five-sigma process requires a 30-fold improvement, and improving from a five-sigma to a six-sigma process means a 70-fold improvement. Thus further improvements in process capability become increasingly more challenging. Experts estimate that an average company delivers about four-sigma quality, whereas best-in-class companies aim for six-sigma.

Why should we insist on such high—and perhaps unattainable—standards? For one thing, even if individual parts (or processing steps) are of extremely high quality, the overall quality of the entire product (or process) that requires *all* of them to work satisfactorily will be significantly lower. For example, if a product contains 100 parts and each part is 99% reliable, the chance that the product (all its parts) will work is only $(0.99)^{100} = 0.366$, or 36.6%!

Moreover, even if defectives are infrequent, the cost associated with each may be very high. Deaths caused by faulty heart valves, automobile brake failures, or defective welds on airplane bodies, however infrequent, are too expensive to the manufacturers (in terms of lawsuits and lost reputation), customers (in terms of lives), and ultimately society. Moreover, the competition and customer expectations keep rising constantly, and ambitious companies and their leaders continue to set such stretch goals.

Safety Capability   In general, we may also express process capability in terms of the *design margin* $[(US - LS) - z\sigma]$ and interpret it *as safety capability*, analogous to safety inventory, safety capacity, and safety time studied in Chapters 7 and 8. Each of these safety margins represents an allowance planned to meet customer requirements of product quality, availability, and response time in the face of variability in supply and/or demand.

Greater process capability means less variability and less chance of product failing to meet customer specifications. Moreover, if the process output is closely clustered around its mean, in relation to the width of customer specifications, most of the output will fall within the specifications, even if the mean is not centered exactly at the middle of the specifications. Higher capability thus means less chance of producing defectives even if the process goes out of control because of a shift in the mean off from the center of the specifications. Thus, process capability measures *robustness* of the process in meeting customer specifications. A robust process will produce satisfactory output even when it is out of control.

9.4.4 Capability and Control

As we saw in Example 9.7, MBPF's production process is not performing well in terms of meeting the customer specifications; only 69% of the output meets the specifications. Yet recall from Example 9.6 that we concluded that the MBPF process was "in control"! *It is therefore important to emphasize that being in control and meeting specifications are two very different measures of process performance.* Whereas the former indicates *internal* stability and statistical predictability of the process performance, the latter indicates its ability to meet *external* customer requirements. Being in control is a necessary but not sufficient condition for satisfactory performance of a process. Observations of a process in control ensure that the resulting estimates of the process mean and standard deviation are reliable so that our measurement of the process capability is accurate. The next step is then to improve the process capability so that its output will be satisfactory from the customers' viewpoint as well.

▪▪▪ 9.5 Process Capability Improvement

Since each measure of process capability defined previously depends on both process mean and standard deviation, we must try to adjust one or the other or both to improve the process capability.

9.5.1 Mean Shift

Given the probability distribution of process output, changing the process mean will shift the distribution and increase the proportion of output that falls within the specifications as well as the process capability ratio.

Example 9.10

MBPF's process mean of 82.5 kg is much too high in relation to the company's specifications of 75 to 85 kg. The histogram in Figure 9.3 reveals a symmetric shape of the door weight distribution around its mean. If we can shift the process mean to the center of the specifications, it would bring a greater proportion of the output within the specifications. Thus, if our supplier turns down the thickness setting on his sheet rolling mill, he may be able to reduce the average door weight down to $\mu = 80$ kg, thereby shifting the entire distribution of door weights to the left. Under these conditions, the proportion of sheets falling within the specifications increases to

$$\text{Prob}(75 \le W \le 85) = \text{Prob}(-1.19 \le Z \le 1.19) = (2)(0.383) = 0.766$$

Figure 9.13 shows the improvement in the proportion meeting specifications by shifting the process mean from 82.5 to 80.

As we saw in Example 9.8, the process capability index C_{pk} increases from 0.1984 to 0.3968.

Thus, centering the process appropriately improves its capability. Any further improvement must come from reduction in the normal process variability.

9.5.2 Variability Reduction

Currently, there is too much variability in weights from one door to the next, as measured by the standard deviation of 4.2 kg. This lack of consistency may be due to any number of causes—perhaps the door fabrication equipment is too old, poorly maintained, and

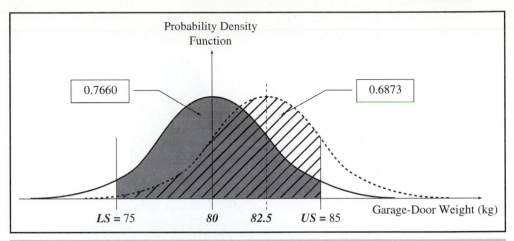

FIGURE 9.13 Process Improvement from the Mean Shift

imprecise; perhaps the operator has not been trained properly; or perhaps the steel rolls delivered by the supplier are inconsistent from batch to batch because of imprecision in the rolling mill.

If such causes of variability were corrected—through investment in better equipment, worker training, or supplier selection—the process output would be more consistent. In turn, that consistency would be reflected in a smaller standard deviation and a greater concentration of the frequency distribution closer to the mean. A greater fraction of output would fall within the specifications. In this case, note that reducing the process average is much easier and can be done quickly by the appropriate worker (or at least the supervisor). Reducing process variability, however, requires considerable time, effort, and investment in resources and is therefore management's responsibility. Sometimes even reducing the process mean might require considerable effort. For example, reducing the average unit flow time in manufacturing or waiting time in a service operation usually requires considerable investment in process capacity.

Example 9.11

Returning to our door weight problem at MBPF, if we can reduce σ from its current estimate of 4.2 to 2.5 kg, the proportion of the output meeting specifications will increase to

$$\text{Prob}(75 \le W \le 85) = \text{Prob}(-2 \le Z \le 2) = 0.9544$$

with corresponding

$$C_p = (85 - 75)/[(6)(2.5)] = 0.67$$

Figure 9.14 shows improvement in the proportion of output meeting specifications that comes from reducing the process variability.

If we would like 99% of our output to fall within the specifications, how much must we reduce σ? To achieve this level, σ must be such that the upper and lower specifications are $z = 2.58$ standard deviations from the mean. In other words, we must have

$$2.58\sigma = 5$$

or

$$\sigma = 1.938 \text{ kg}$$

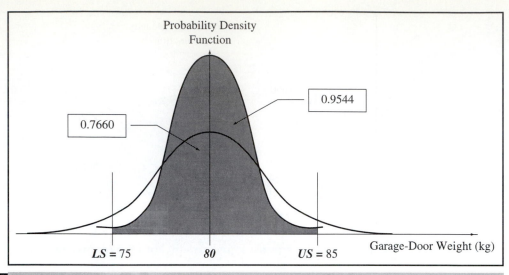

FIGURE 9.14 Process Improvement from Variability Reduction

which corresponds to

$$C_p = (85 - 75)/[(6)(1.938)] = 0.86$$

9.5.3   Effect of Process Improvement on Process Control

It is important to note that, as the process capability is improved by shifting its mean μ or reducing its variability σ, its control limits must also be adjusted accordingly.

Example 9.12
On adjusting the process mean from 82.5 kg down to 80 kg, the new control limits would be

$$80 \pm (3)(4.2)/\sqrt{5} = (74.37, 85.63)$$

From then on, we would compare observed average weights of five doors against these new control limits to identify the presence of an assignable cause of abnormal variability.

Similarly, if we reduce the standard deviation from 4.2 to 2.5 kg, we need to revise control limits to

$$80 \pm (3)(2.5)/\sqrt{5} = (76.65, 83.35)$$

Thus, process control limits should be readjusted each time the process parameters are changed. Note that control limits on a more precise process are tighter since we expect normal variability to be less. It is important to stress again that process control charts plot *sample averages*, whereas process capability refers to the ability of the process to meet specifications on *individual* units; the two should not be plotted on the same graph.

Figure 9.15 shows the progression in managing process variability from being (1) out of control to (2) in control by eliminating abnormal variability and, finally, to (3) greater capability through proper centering and reduced normal variability.

Although progression from (1) to (2) can be achieved in the short run, further improvement from (2) to (3) is a long-term journey. The next section indicates some steps in that direction through improved product and process design.

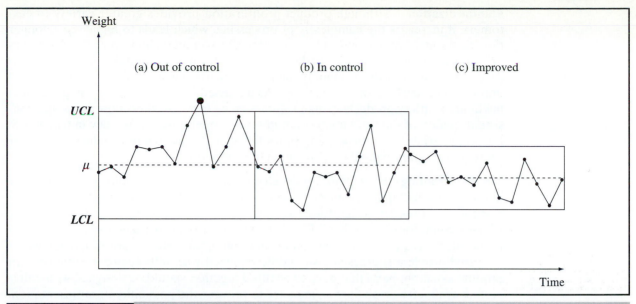

FIGURE 9.15 From Control to Capability Improvement

9.6   Product and Process Design

Often sources of performance variability can be traced to the design of the product and the process producing it. In this section, we indicate two general principles of design for minimizing process variability and its impact on product performance.

9.6.1   Design for Processing

We outline three general principles of product and process design aimed at minimizing chances of variability: product or process simplification, standardization, and mistake-proofing.

Simplification   As the term suggests, the objective here is to simplify product (or process) design so that it has fewer parts (or processing stages), which would then require fewer suppliers and reduced chances of confusion and error. If a product (or process) contains n parts (or stages) and each has probability p of performing successfully, then the probability that the *entire* product (process) will perform successfully—that *all n* parts will work—is p^n, which decreases geometrically as n increases, so that reducing n will improve its reliability.

Product simplification without foregoing product variety can be achieved through use of interchangeable parts and modular designs. They not only permit a greater variety at the assembly stage but also simplify materials handling and inventory control. Recall from Chapter 7 the benefits of inventory pooling as a result of parts commonality, which reduces the amount of safety inventory needed.

Process simplification by eliminating non-value-adding steps in processing not only reduces the processing cost and flow time but also reduces opportunities for making mistakes. In general, "keep it simple, stupid!" (KISS) is an important design principle that requires ingenious and innovative ways of identifying opportunities to eliminate unnecessary, non-value-adding parts and processing steps.

Standardization Although product proliferation provides greater variety to customers, it increases the complexity of processing, which leads to higher cost, longer flow times, and lower quality. Using standard, proven parts and procedures removes operator discretion, ambiguity, and opportunities for making mistakes. Likewise, standard operating procedures simplify the tasks of recruiting and training employees and improve their performance consistency. As discussed in Chapter 2, flow shops producing limited variety products in high volumes enjoy low cost, short flow times, and consistent quality of output. Finally, even in service operations, as we saw in Chapter 8, reducing variability in processing times through standardization reduces customer waiting times, improving their perception of service quality.

Mistake-Proofing By minimizing the chance of human error, foolproofing a process improves product quality, reduces rework, and thus reduces both flow time and processing cost. Product design for ease of assembly is critical in assembly operations, which account for two-thirds of all manufacturing costs and are a major source of quality problems. Fasteners (such as screws and bolts), for instance, are widely known as potential problem sources and should be replaced with self-locking mechanisms. In product assembly, parts that have to be fitted together should be designed with either perfect symmetry or obvious asymmetry to prevent the possibility of misorientation. Workers and equipment should always have adequate clearance, unobstructed vision, and easy access to facilitate assembly. Such techniques as alphanumeric coding, color coding, and bar coding parts help make processing operations error resistant. Use of automation generally reduces labor costs, as well as chances of human error, and increases processing speed and consistency of the output.

Although many of these design principles appear obvious, their implementation in practice requires ingenuity, patience, and experimentation, with a lot of cooperation and contribution from workers, suppliers, and customers.

9.6.2 Robust Design

Until now, we focused on ways to eliminate assignable variability in the short run and reduce normal variability in the long run. Sometimes, however, variability reduction may not be possible or economical. An alternate approach to dealing with variability is through **robust design**. The idea is to *design the product in such a way that its actual performance will not suffer despite any variability in the production process or in the customer's operating environment.* The goal is to develop a design that is robust in resisting effects of variability.

In general, product performance is determined by internal (process-related) and external (environment-related) noise factors along with its own design parameters. The designer's goal is to identify a combination of design parameters that will protect product performance from the internal and external noise factors to which it may be subjected. In statistically planned experiments, different combinations of design factors are tested in conjunction with combinations of different levels of noise factors. The challenge is to identify the right combination of design parameters (without trying them all) that works well, on average, in spite of noise factors. More details may be found in Taguchi and Clausing (1990).

SUMMARY ▪▪▪▪▪▪▪

In this chapter, we emphasized how *variability* in performance—and not just its *average*—is an important determinant of customer satisfaction. We first presented some simple graphical and statistical tools—such as check sheets, Pareto charts, and histograms—for documenting, organizing, and summarizing information about observed variability. We then extended this *static* analysis to *dynamic* tools such as run charts, multi-vari charts and, most importantly, control charts to track performance variability over time.

We outlined the *feedback control principle* for monitoring and acting on the observed variability over time. We learned that a deviation in process performance from its expected value may be due to *normal* or *abnormal* variability. We studied *process control charts* as a prime application of this principle that enables us to detect the presence of abnormal variability. Setting up a control chart involves (1) estimating the average process performance measure and normal variability around it and (2) establishing limits of acceptable variability in performance around its average. Implementing a control chart involves (1) monitoring and plotting the actual process performance against these limits and (2) signaling the presence of abnormal variability that warrants an action when these limits are exceeded. We indicated *cause–effect diagrams* and *scatter plots* as simple tools for identifying and correcting causes of abnormal variability. Thus, the goal of process control is to detect when a process goes "out of control" and eliminate causes of abnormal variability to bring the process back "in control" so it displays only normal variability, which signifies a state of internal stability.

We then studied *process capability* in terms of its ability to meet external customer requirements. We defined the fraction of the output that meets customer specifications, the process capability ratio, and sigma capability as three related measures of process capability, all of which try to quantify the magnitude of process variability in relation to customer specifications. We outlined a few strategies for improving process capability by reducing its normal variability through better *product and process design* to facilitate error-proof processing through simplification, standardization, and mistake-proofing. Finally, we indicated the concept of *robust design* of products, which desensitizes their performance to sources of process variability.

Although variability will always plague every process, it becomes troublesome when it leads to process instability, lower capability, and customer dissatisfaction. In this chapter, our goal has been to study how to measure, analyze, and minimize sources of this variability so as to improve consistency in product and process performance, ultimately leading to total customer satisfaction and superior competitive position.

KEY EQUATIONS AND SYMBOLS ▪▪▪▪▪▪▪

(9.1) $LCL = \mu - z\sigma$ and $UCL = \mu + z\sigma$ (generic control limits)

(9.2) $LCL = \bar{A} - zs/\sqrt{n}$ and $UCL = \bar{A} + zs/\sqrt{n}$ (average control chart limits)

(9.3) $LCL = \bar{V} - zs_V$ and $UCL = \bar{V} + zs_V$ (variation control chart limits)

(9.4) $\mu \pm z\sqrt{\mu}$ (number of defects control chart limits)

(9.5) $C_{pk} = \min[(US - \mu)/3\sigma, (\mu - LS)/3\sigma]$ (process capability ratio)

(9.6) $C_p = (US - LS)/6\sigma$ (process capability ratio for a centered process)

(9.7) $S = \min[(US - \mu)/\sigma, (\mu - LS)/\sigma]$ (sigma capability)

(9.8) $S = (US - LS)/2\sigma$ (sigma capability of a centered process)

where
LCL = Lower control limit
UCL = Upper control limit
μ = Process mean
σ = Process standard deviation
z = Measure of tightness of control
A = Sample average
$\bar{A}$ = Average of sample averages
s = Sample standard deviation of all observations
V = Range of variation in a sample
$\bar{V}$ = Average variation in all samples
s_V = Standard deviation of variation in a sample
C_{pk} = Process capability ratio (for noncentered process)
C_p = Process capability ratio (for centered process)
US = Upper specification
LS = Lower specification

KEY TERMS ▪ ▪ ▪ ▪ ▪ ▪ ▪

- 80-20 Pareto principle
- Abnormal variability
- Cause–effect diagram
- Check sheet
- Control band
- Control chart
- Control limits
- Feedback control principle
- Fishbone diagram
- Histogram
- Ishikawa diagram

- Lower control limit (*LCL*)
- Lower specification (*LS*)
- Multi-vari chart
- Normal variability
- Pareto chart
- Plan-Do-Check-Act (PDCA) cycle
- Process capability
- Quality function deployment (QFD)
- Quality of conformance

- Quality of design
- Robust design
- Run chart
- Scatter plot
- Sigma capability
- Six-sigma process
- Type I (or α) error
- Type II (or β) error
- Upper control limit (*UCL*)
- Upper specification (*US*)

DISCUSSION QUESTIONS ▪ ▪ ▪ ▪ ▪ ▪ ▪

9.1 Discuss three examples from everyday life where variability in product or process performance leads to customer dissatisfaction even though the average performance is considered good.

9.2 Suppose you are managing a grocery store and would like to provide a first-rate shopping experience to your customers. Outline how you would go about determining factors that are important to them, how well you are doing in meeting their needs and expectations, and how you can improve your operations to give them total customer satisfaction. Specifically, discuss which of the tools that you learned in this chapter can be used and how.

9.3 In operating an airline, on-time performance is a critical measure that customers value. Suppose you plot a histogram of actual arrival and departure times in relation to the scheduled times. What information will it provide that you can use to improve the process?

9.4 What information do run charts, multi-vari charts, and control charts provide in addition to that contained in a histogram that shows variability in process performance?

9.5 Give three everyday life examples of situations where the feedback control principle can be applied for collecting information and making decisions.

9.6 What are the two main types of process variability? How can we identify and remove the sources of this variability?

9.7 What factors should one consider in setting control limits? What are the trade-offs involved in determining the width of a control band?

9.8 How can the process be "in control" but have dissatisfied customers? It sounds like "the operation was successful, but the patient died." Comment on this apparent paradox.

9.9 What are two concrete ways of measuring process capability? How are they related? How can they be improved?

9.10 What does six-sigma capability mean? Why is it important to insist on such high standards?

9.11 It has been observed that in the airline industry, baggage handling is about a four-sigma process, whereas frequency of airline fatalities corresponds to a seven-sigma capability. How can two processes within the same industry be so different?

9.12 Give three examples of improving process capability through better design.

EXERCISES ▪ ▪ ▪ ▪ ▪ ▪ ▪

9.1 Costello Labs supplies 500-cc bottles of treated Elixir plasma solution to Mercy Hospital. Several factors are important in assessing plasma quality, such as purity, absence of AIDS or hepatitis virus, and bacterial count. The most important quality characteristic, however, is protein concentration. Protein concentration is measured by a sophisticated electronic process known as electrophoresis. American Medical Association (AMA) standards specify that a 500-cc plasma bottle should contain between 30 and 35 grams of protein. Both concentrations under and over this range may be hazardous to a patient's health.

Hospital administrators have instructed Costello Labs to straighten out its plasma production operation and to demonstrate evidence of tighter process controls prior to the renewal of its supply contract. Costello's plasma production equipment consists of a protein injector and a mixer that determine protein concentration in each bottle. Process capability depends on the precision of these pieces of equipment.

a. Suppose that the hospital and the lab have agreed that at least 98% of the plasma bottles supplied by Costello should conform to AMA specifications (i.e., should contain between 30 and 35 grams of protein). Determine the standard deviation of the amount of protein that it must inject into each bottle in order to produce 98% of process output within the specifications.

    Also compute corresponding process capability ratio C_p.

b. Costello Labs production manager Phil Abbott wants to establish statistical process control charts to monitor the plasma-injection process. Set up these control charts based on average protein readings taken from randomly selected samples of 12 bottles from each batch.

9.2 Natural Foods sells Takeoff, a breakfast cereal, in one-pound boxes. According to Food and Drug Administration (FDA) regulations, a one-pound box must contain at least 15.5 ounces of cereal. However, Natural Food's box-filling process is not perfect: its precision, expressed in terms of the standard deviation of the weight of a one-pound box filled, is 0.5 ounces.

a. Where should Natural Foods center its process in order to ensure that 98% of boxes filled meet FDA requirements? What proportion of boxes would be overfilled beyond 16 ounces?

b. While underweight boxes might prompt FDA action, overweight boxes certainly cost Natural Foods in terms of higher material costs. Therefore, quality control manager Morris Nerdstat wants to monitor the cereal-filling process in order to ensure that its mean does not deviate from the level established in part a. He plans to weigh nine randomly selected boxes at regular time intervals and plot the average weight on a chart. At one point, he finds an average weight of 15.9 ounces. The company's legal staff is pleased that this performance is better than the FDA requirement of 15.5 ounces. What action, if any, should Nerdstat take?

c. What targets (in terms of the mean and the standard deviation) would result in the process with six-sigma capability?

9.3 In measuring and evaluating the quality of banking services, analysts have found that customers regard accuracy, timeliness, and responsiveness as the most important characteristics. Accordingly, First Chicago Bank constantly monitors and charts almost 500 performance measures of these quality characteristics. Accuracy, for example, is measured by the error/reject rate in processing transactions, timeliness by delays in collecting funds, and responsiveness by speed in resolving customer inquiries or complaints. For each measure, First Chicago also sets a level called Minimal Acceptable Performance (MAP), which serves as an early warning signal to management, as a basis for comparison with the banking-industry competition, and as a constantly upgraded goal for ensuring continuous improvement of service quality.

Over one six-month period, First Chicago recorded, on a weekly basis, errors per thousand items processed in all types of collection transactions. The resulting 26 numbers were as follows: 0, 2, 0, 17, 2, 4, 0, 2, 1, 0, 0, 5, 6, 5, 15, 5, 10, 5, 2, 2, 0, 2, 0, 0, 0, and 1. The Bank Administration Institute reports that the average error rate for such transactions is 1.5%.

a. Determine the appropriate process control limits on the fraction of transactions in error, or the number of errors per thousand transactions.

b. By way of comparison, plot the observations, process average, control limits, and industry standard. Is First Chicago's process in control? How does its performance compare with the industry standard?

9.4 Government regulations mandate that Belgian chocolate bars sold in packages of ½ kilogram cannot weigh less than ½ kilogram, the specified weight on the package. If regulations are violated, the company is fined. The chocolate machine at the Cote d'Or chocolate company fills packages with a standard deviation of 5 grams regardless of the mean setting. To be sure that government regulations are met, the operator decides to set the mean at 515 grams.

a. To check if the process is in control, the operator plans to take samples where each sample consists of 25 chocolate bars. The average weight of this sample of 25 bars is used to determine if the process is in control. Following industry practice, what control limits should the operator use?

b. If the process is in control, approximately what fraction of chocolate bars will weigh less than 500 grams (this is the fraction that would violate government regulation)?

c. Clearly, producing an excess average chocolate weight of 15 grams just in order to prevent regulation fines is costly in terms of chocolate "given away for free." Cote d'Or management wants to reduce the average excess weight to 3 grams while staying in line with regulations "practically always," which means 99.87% of the time. In what sense will this require improved process technology? Give an explanation in words as well as a specific numeric answer.

9.5 Consider a machine producing drive shafts with a mean diameter of 6 cm and a standard deviation of 0.01 centimeters. To see if the process is in control, we take samples of size 10 and evaluate the average diameter over the entire sample. Customer specifications require drive shafts to be between 5.98 and 6.02 centimeters. Establish the appropriate control limits.

9.6 If product specifications remain unchanged, as the sigma capability of a process improves from being 1-sigma to 4-sigma process, what is the effect on the range between the control limits ($UCL - LCL$)? Does it become narrower, wider, or remain unchanged? Why?

9.7 A bank has recently taken over the billing function of a company. An agreement stipulates that the bank should process 99.2% of the bills within 4 hours. A study of the current process indicates that the processing time averages 2.2 hours per bill with a standard deviation of 0.8. A process improvement team has suggested a change. Experiments indicate that the change will lower the average processing time to 2 hours but raise the standard deviation to 1.2. Should this change be implemented? Why?

9.8 Balding Inc. is the official producer of basketballs used in NBA tournaments. The Dallas Mavericks have placed a large order for Balding's Fusion basketballs of 29.5-inch diameter, which feature exclusive micropump technology. Jennifer Boling, the Mavericks' head of basketball operations, says she will accept only basketballs within 0.2-inch tolerance (i.e., those with diameters between 29.3 and 29.7 inches). Balding's production manager sets the mean of its basketball manufacturing process at 29.5 inches and would like to ensure that 95% of its output will meet Boling's requirements. What should be Balding's process capability ratio?

9.9 Evaluate with explanation the following statements, circle the appropriate response, and explain briefly.

a. Suppose the control limits for a process are set at 3 standard deviations from the mean. If the process is in control, 99.73% of its output will meet the specifications. True or false?

b. As the sample size increases, the upper control limit for a process should be decreased. True or false?

c. Suppose control limits for a process are set at 3 standard deviations from the mean. If the process is in control, the probability of observing a sample outside the control limits is independent of the sigma capability of the process. True or false?

d. If a process improves its sigma capability (e.g., moves from being a 3-sigma to a 4-sigma process), will the width of its control band ($UCL - LCL$) increase, decrease, or remain unchanged?

e. A six-sigma process is always "in control." True or false?

SELECTED BIBLIOGRAPHY ■ ■ ■ ■ ■ ■ ■

Deming, W. E. 1986. *Out of the Crisis.* Cambridge, MA: MIT Center for Advanced Engineering Study.

Feigenbaum, A. V. 1961. *Total Quality Control.* New York: McGraw-Hill.

Garvin, D. A. 1988. *Managing Quality.* New York: Free Press.

Grant, E. L., and R. S. Leavenworth. 1988. *Statistical Quality Control.* 6th ed. New York: McGraw-Hill.

Hauser, J., and D. Clausing. 1988. "The House of Quality." *Harvard Business Review,* May–June, 63–73.

Joiner, B., and M. Gaudard. 1990. "Variation, Management, and W. Edwards Deming." *Quality Progress*. Special Issue on Variation, December.

Juran, J. M., and F. M. Gryna. 1988. *Quality Control Handbook.* 4th ed. New York: McGraw-Hill.

Juran, J. M., and F. M. Gryna. 1980. *Quality Planning and Analysis.* 2nd ed. New York: McGraw-Hill.

Ott, E. R., and E. J Schilling. 1990. *Process Quality Control: Troubleshooting and Interpretation of Data.* 2nd ed. New York: McGraw-Hill.

Taguchi, G., and D. Clausing. 1990. "Robust Quality." *Harvard Business Review,* January–February, 65–75.

Wadsworth, H. M., K. Stephens, and B. Godfrey. 1986. *Modern Methods for Quality Control and Improvement.* New York: John Wiley & Sons.

PART IV

Process Integration

CHAPTER 10
Lean Operations: Process Synchronization and Improvement

CHAPTER 10

Lean Operations: Process Synchronization and Improvement

Introduction

In the late 1990s, the aerospace industry—an industry long known for high costs and delays—embraced the ideas of lean operations perfected by the Japanese automaker Toyota to achieve dramatic efficiency gains. According to Pollack (1999), using ideas from lean operations a Northrop Grumman Corporation mechanic who required 8.4 hours to apply 70 feet of tape to the B-2 bomber was able to finish the job in only 1.62 hours. Originally, the mechanic walked away from the plane 26 times and took three hours to gather required material just to get started. In the revised process, the factory made kits with all required parts, allowing the mechanic to work without having to leave the plane. At the Boeing factory in Chula Vista, California, metal skins for the Boeing 717 fan cowls, a part of the engine housing, used to travel 17,000 feet as they moved between workstations and take 43 days to produce. By rearranging production in cells, the travel distance was reduced to 4,300 feet, and the product was completed in seven days. Between 1997 and 1999, the factory went from producing enough parts for fewer than two Boeing 737-700s a month to producing enough for 23 while simultaneously reducing the number of employees from 18 to 14.

Doig et al. (2003) discuss how some airlines have used lean operations techniques to improve aircraft and component turnaround times during maintenance by 30% to 50% and maintenance productivity by 25% to 50%. Such dramatic improvements have also been observed in service operations. According to Swank (2003), Jefferson Pilot Financial, a full-service life insurance company, applied lean production techniques to the process of handling applications from its premier partners. The result was a 26% reduction in labor costs and a 40% reduction in the rate of reissues due to errors. These outcomes increased new annualized premiums collected in the company's life insurance business by 60% over two years. According to Wysocki (2004), Allegheny General Hospital in Pittsburgh used the quality at source idea from lean operations to cut infections by 90% within 90 days.

Many industries have used the principles of lean operations to improve performance in terms of cost, quality, and response time within their plants and supply chains. What are the basic principles of lean operations? How can they be used to improve flows within a factory? How can these ideas be applied to improve flows across the supply chain?

We examine these concepts in this chapter. In Section 10.1, we discuss how factories and supply chains can be represented as processing networks. In Section 10.2, we characterize the ideal performance of a processing network in meeting customer requirements in terms of flow synchronization and cost efficiency. In Section 10.3, we view any deviation from this ideal as waste and examine its sources and consequences. We define the goal of process improvement as bringing the process performance closer to the ideal by identifying and eliminating waste. In Section 10.4, we study methods of lean operations designed to improve plant-level performance by increasing flexibility, reducing variability, and improving information and material flows. In Section 10.5, we extend lean ideas toward the goal of achieving synchronization and efficiency across the entire supply chain. Finally, in Section 10.6, we look at the process of improvement and compare two general approaches to attaining ideal performance: continuous improvement and process reengineering. We also indicate the role of benchmarking in setting process-improvement goals and the importance of managing the organizational change that always accompanies process improvement.

▪▪▪ 10.1 Processing Networks

As discussed in Chapter 1, any organization can be viewed as a business process that transforms inputs into outputs to satisfy customer needs. A firm satisfies customers by providing them what they want, when they want it, and where they want it at a price they are willing to pay. Theoretically, satisfying all these criteria would mean developing, producing, and delivering individually customized products of the highest quality, in the shortest time, and at the lowest cost. In reality, given the firm's capabilities and constraints, trade-offs must be considered. In most industries, as discussed in Chapter 2, there exists an operations frontier in the competitive product space defined by the four product attributes—cost, quality, variety, and response time. This frontier reflects the optimal trade-offs given the current state of technology and management practices. Competition forces firms operating below the industry's operations frontier to improve and move toward the frontier. World-class firms already operating at the frontier can stay ahead of competitors only by improving and pushing the frontier further. Thus, firms at every level have the scope and necessity to improve process performance along the four dimensions that customers value.

This chapter extends the concepts and principles developed thus far for individual processes to improve performance of a **processing network** that *consists of information and material flows of multiple products through a sequence of interconnected processes.* Figure 10.1 illustrates two product flows through a typical processing network. The overall goal of this network is to satisfy customer demand in the most economical way by producing and delivering the *right* products, in the *right* quantities, at the *right* times,

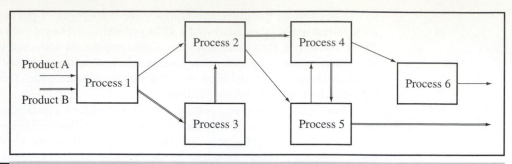

▪▪▪▪▪▪▪▪▪▪▪▪ **FIGURE 10.1** Product Flows in a Processing Network

to the *right* places. It requires the synchronization of flows between processes in a cost-effective manner.

Plants and Supply Chains   Our discussion focuses on performance at two different levels—*plant* and *supply chain*. A **plant** *is any singly owned, independently managed and operated facility, such as a manufacturing site, a service unit, or a storage warehouse.* A **supply chain** is *a network of interconnected facilities of diverse ownership with flows of information and materials between them.* It can include raw materials suppliers, finished-goods producers, wholesalers, distributors, and retailers. For example, the supply chain that makes a detergent available in a supermarket includes chemical plants, warehouses for storing chemicals, factories for producing and packaging detergents, distributors, wholesalers, and, finally, retailers. Each facility represents a plant, whereas all of them together form the detergent supply chain.

If we view the facilities in greater detail, each plant in the supply chain is also a processing network. Within the detergent maker's factory, the purchasing, production, storage, and shipping departments are all processes, each handling a variety of detergents and cleaners. In this chapter, we first examine how to manage processing network operations within a given plant and then extend the key principles to coordinate the operations of the entire supply chain. The core ideas that apply to both levels of operation are the same and draw on the process-improvement levers that we have discussed in earlier chapters. However, the operational details differ because of differences in scale, scope, geographical dispersion, and incentives of diverse process owners involved.

▪▪▪ 10.2   The Process Ideal: Synchronization and Efficiency

Customers want a wide variety of high-quality products from convenient locations at low prices. Performance of an **ideal process**—*a process that achieves synchronization at the lowest possible cost*—can thus be summarized in terms of two closely related operating characteristics:

1. **Process synchronization** refers to *the ability of the process to meet customer demand in terms of their quantity, time, quality, and location requirements.*
2. **Process efficiency** is *measured in terms of the total processing cost.*

The Four "Just Rights" of Synchronization   A well-synchronized detergent supply chain produces and delivers the right quantities of defect-free boxes of the detergent to widely dispersed supermarkets so that just enough is available to satisfy all customer demand without delay. For manufactured goods, customer demand can always be satisfied by producing in advance and carrying large inventories of all products, of verified quality, in all locations. This approach, however, is not synchronized with demand and not very efficient. We therefore define a perfectly synchronized process as one that is *lean* in that it develops, produces, and delivers the following only on demand:

- Exactly *what* is needed (not wrong or defective products)
- Exactly *how much* is needed (neither more nor less)
- Exactly *when* it is needed (not before or after)
- Exactly *where* it is needed (not somewhere else)

A perfectly synchronized process always supplies just the right *quantity* of the right *quality* product, at just the right *time*, and in just the right *place*—just as desired by customers. These four "just rights" of synchronization form the core of the **just-in-time (JIT)** paradigm. Just-in-time refers to *an action taken only when it becomes necessary. In manufacturing, it means production of only necessary flow units in necessary quantities at necessary times*.

These four criteria define the ultimate in process capability, flexibility, capacity, and speed. Producing any product without defects requires the process to be extremely versatile and precise. The ability to produce any desired quantity requires flexibility to produce one unit at a time. In order to satisfy demand arising at any time—without entailing inventories—a process must have instant, complete, and accurate information on demand and must be able to react by producing and delivering instantly as well. An ideal process can satisfy all these requirements and do so at the lowest possible cost. In short, an ideal process is infinitely capable, flexible, fast, and frugal.

Synchronized Networks   This concept of an ideal process extends naturally to a *network* of processes—once we recognize that in such a network, the outflow of one process (a supplier) is the inflow to another (a customer). Perfect synchronization of an entire network of processes requires precise matching of supply and demand of various flow units at each processing stage. It means that each stage must satisfy—precisely—the quality, quantity, time, and place requirements of the next stage.

We can define synchronization at the level of an individual process (as a network of activities), a plant (as a network of processes), or a supply chain (as a network of plants). In each case, the goal of ideal performance requires that individual processing stages be capable, flexible, fast, and frugal. Synchronization requires all stages to be tightly linked in terms of the flow of information and product. The result is a precisely balanced system of inflows and outflows at all stages through which units flow smoothly and continuously without disruption or accumulation along the way. In particular, for a perfectly synchronized process, the output of every stage will precisely match (external) end-customer demand. In an ideal network, this synchronization of processing stages is achieved at the lowest possible cost.

Although the ideal may seem unattainable in a practical sense, the long-run goal—and challenge—of process management should be to approach this ideal by improving products, processes, and practices. In the next section, we examine the causes and consequences of failure to attain the ideal.

10.3   Waste and Its Sources

It is important to focus on the ideal because anything short of ideal performance represents an opportunity for us to improve the process—or for the competition to move in. Operationally, low efficiency is reflected in high processing costs. Lack of synchronization manifests itself in defective products, high inventories, long delays, or frequent stockouts.

Sources of Waste   Regarding any deviation from the ideal as **waste**, we paraphrase the goal of process improvement as *the elimination of all waste.* Thus, waste means *producing inefficiently, producing wrong or defective products, producing in quantities too large or too small, and delivering products too early or too late—that is, failing to match customer demand most economically.* Taiichi Ohno, the main architect of the Toyota Production System, classified seven types of waste in manufacturing (1988):

- Producing defective products
- Producing too much product
- Carrying inventory
- Waiting due to unbalanced workloads
- Unnecessary processing
- Unnecessary worker movement
- Transporting materials

All this waste results in high costs, low quality, and long response times, ultimately leading to customer dissatisfaction and loss of business to the competition. Producing defective units results not only in unhappy customers but also in additional cost and time required to receive, inspect, test, rework, and return those units. Producing too much or too early builds up excess inventory, which increases holding costs (including the costs of capital, storage, and possible obsolescence) and the unit flow time. In turn, long flow times mean delays in responding to changes in customer tastes and in getting new product designs to market. In processing networks, inventory buffers between stages increase total flow time, thus delaying feedback on quality problems, obstructing traceability of root causes, and diffusing accountability for errors.

Producing too little or too late results in stockouts, delays, and increased expediting costs. In processing networks, insufficient inflows starve some stages, resulting in idleness and inefficient utilization of resources. Finally, delivering wrong products to wrong places creates excess inventories of wrong products, shortages of right ones, or both. Corrective transfers then result in additional costs and delays.

The sources of all this waste can ultimately be traced to underlying process imperfections, demand and supply variability, or management practices discussed throughout this book. We saw in Chapter 4 that *non-value-adding activities,* such as transportation, movement, inspection, and rework, increase theoretical flow time and processing costs. Similarly, we learned in Chapters 5 and 8 that *insufficient capacity* at bottlenecks reduces process throughput and increases waiting time. In Chapter 6, we observed that a *lack of flexibility* to switch between products, measured in terms of fixed setup (or changeover) costs, necessitates producing in large batches even though demand is continuous, a mismatch giving rise to *cycle* inventories. Likewise, we found in Chapter 7 that *stochastic variability* in supply and demand, together with long and uncertain lead times, requires us to hold safety inventory to protect against stockouts. If demand is predictable and all stages in a supply chain are both flexible in processing different products and predictable in terms of operating without variability, buffer inventories are unnecessary and flows synchronized. As discussed in Chapter 8, it is the *variability* in demand and processing times that causes both waiting and inflow inventory, thereby requiring safety capacity at an added cost. In Chapter 9, we saw that *insufficient process capability* in terms of high normal variability results in defective units. Meanwhile, abnormal variability in terms of *process instability* over time necessitates expensive process control. Finally, lack of synchronization from delivering wrong products to wrong locations is often due to inadequate transmission of information and materials through the network.

Waste Elimination   Cycle and safety inventories, safety capacity, and non-value-adding activities including transportation, inspection, rework, and process control are short-term tactical actions that process managers take in order to work with imperfect processes suffering from inflexibility, variability, and inefficient logistics. In the short term, we accept these process limitations as given and try to deal with them by processing in batches, incorporating safety stocks and safety capacity, monitoring processes, and correcting defects. All these measures, however, increase total cost, inventory, and flow time, resulting in less-than-ideal performance.

A long-term strategy is to improve the underlying process to make it more flexible, predictable, and stable, which eliminates the need for such temporary measures as batch processing, safety allowances, and process control. For example, recall from Chapter 6 that the optimal batch size (hence the cycle inventory and flow time) are directly related to the (square root of) setup cost. A long-term solution to reducing cycle inventories is to reduce the setup cost itself (i.e., improve process flexibility) so that it is economical to produce various products in small batches. Such an action improves synchronization by reducing cycle inventory and flow time.

Similarly, recall from Chapters 7 and 8 that the amount of safety inventory and safety capacity needed to provide a given level of service depends directly on the degree of variability in the system. A long-term solution calls for making flows more regular and predictable—in other words, for reducing variability. In so doing, we reduce the required safety cushion—thereby reducing cost while improving synchronization.

In Chapter 9 we identified two principles governing the relationship between variability and process stability. In the short run, the following holds:

1. Greater normal variability (i.e., lower process capability) results in more defective products
2. More abnormal variability (i.e., greater process instability) requires tighter process control to maintain stability

It follows, then, that reducing variability (by increasing process capability and stability) does the following:

1. Decreases the number of defective products, inspection, and rework
2. Reduces the need for online process control, thereby improving synchronization and reducing overall cost

Thus, the long-run goal of process improvement is to identify and eliminate the root causes of waste rather than to compensate for them with short-term solutions. The idea is to diagnose and remove the roots of an ailment, seeking a permanent cure, rather than superficially treating symptoms with temporary fixes.

The River Analogy   Figure 10.2 illustrates the concept of waste and its sources by using a *river analogy* that has been popularized in the literature on the Toyota Production System. Visualize process imperfections—defective materials, machine breakdowns, long setup times, unreliable suppliers, inefficient layouts—as rocks lying on a riverbed. The water level in the river represents waste in the form of short-term measures such as excess cycle and safety inventories, safety capacity, time allowance, safety quality, inspection, rework, and process control. They provide an operating cushion to facilitate smooth sailing for the process manager despite underlying problems. The appropriate long-term response is to uncover and remove these rocks so that we

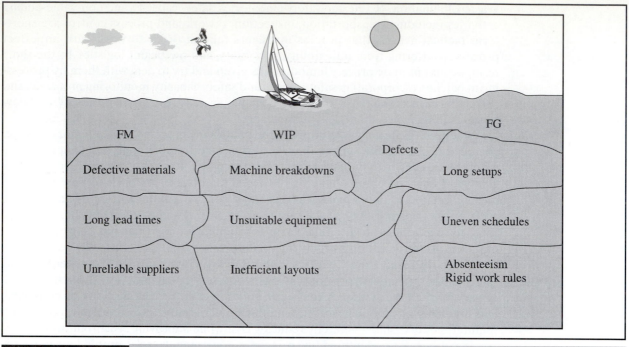

▮▮▮▮▮▮▮▮▮▮▮▮ **FIGURE 10.2** The River Analogy: Waste and Its Sources

can sail smoothly even in shallow water (which symbolizes lean operations). Three factors, however, impede us from achieving the long-term solution: (1) a high water level covers up rocks, reduces problem *visibility,* and clouds the root causes on the bottom; (2) smooth sailing because of the safety cushion dampens our *incentives* to look for root causes; and (3) lack of problem-solving skills makes it difficult to eliminate the root causes. The challenge of process management is to overcome these three obstructions and bring actual performance closer to the ideal. The river analogy suggests lowering the water level slowly until the top rocks are visible. Eliminating these rocks now provides smooth sailing with a lower level of water. The pressure for improvement is maintained by lowering the water level further until more rocks become visible. As rocks are constantly eliminated, a low level of water is sufficient to provide smooth sailing.

In the next two sections, we examine *specific* methods for improving process synchronization and efficiency, first within a plant and then within an entire supply chain. Although the operational details in the two contexts are different, the basic principles are the same. To improve process synchronization, we need to do the following:

- Synchronize flows of material and information
- Increase resource flexibility
- Reduce process variability

To improve process efficiency, we need to do the following:

- Reduce processing cost and flow time

These improvements at the plant and supply chain level require a long-term investment in the process, including equipment, technology, workers, and suppliers.

▮▮▮ 10.4 Improving Flows in a Plant: Basic Principles of Lean Operations

Any plant, whether a manufacturing or a service facility, is a network of processing stages through which materials or customers flow before emerging as finished products or serviced customers. An ideal plant is synchronized and efficient: the outflow of each stage meets—precisely and economically—the inflow requirements of the next, without defects, inventories, delays, or stockouts. Methods for achieving efficiency and synchronization within a plant have been discussed in the operations management literature under such headings as *lean operations, just-in-time production, zero inventory program, synchronous manufacturing, agile manufacturing,* and the *Toyota Production System (TPS).*

The basic objective of TPS is "to shorten the time it takes to convert customer orders into deliveries" (Ohno, 1988) by synchronizing production with customer demand. Because there will always be a gap between actual and ideal synchronization, the *process* of approaching the ideal is an important aspect of lean operations. TPS, for example, *strives to make small but constant changes and improvements* (called **kaizen**) by continuously identifying and eliminating sources of waste (i.e., by gradually lowering the water level to expose the rocks and then crushing them). We discuss this philosophy of *continuous improvement* further in Section 10.6. In this section we focus primarily on concrete methods of *lean operations* to achieve synchronization and efficiency.

A lean operation has four ongoing objectives:

1. *To improve process flows* through efficient plant layout and fast and accurate flow of material and information
2. *To increase process flexibility* by reducing equipment changeover times and cross-functional training
3. *To decrease process variability* in flow rates, processing times, and quality
4. *To minimize processing costs* by eliminating non-value-adding activities such as transportation, inspection, and rework

The first three goals improve process synchronization, and the fourth improves cost efficiency. These goals are achieved through process-improvement levers discussed earlier in this book. Although the methods for achieving them will often be illustrated in the specific context of (automobile) manufacturing, the basic ideas work well in any stable, high-volume, limited-variety, sequential-processing environment including service industries.

The classic example of efficiency and synchronization for mass production was Henry Ford's Rouge, Michigan, plant in the 1910s. It was a totally integrated facility (including a steel mill and a glass factory), equipped with modern machine tools, electrical systems, and an automated assembly line and operated by highly paid, well-trained workers. Process efficiency was achieved by applying Frederick W. Taylor's principles of "scientific management," including time-and-motion studies, work rationalization, and best work methods (discussed in Chapter 2, Section 2.7). Streamlined to minimize the total flow time and cost, the moving assembly line was the ultimate in synchronizing production without buffer inventories between workstations. In fact, the roots of TPS can be traced to Henry Ford's system, except for one vital distinction, namely, the ability to handle product *variety.* Whereas Henry Ford's plant produced only the Model T (and only in black because the color dries fastest), modern automobile manufacturers must offer a wide variety of models and options, all of which must be of high quality and competitively priced, to satisfy contemporary customers' ever-rising expectations. We explore some of Toyota's tactics for meeting this challenge. However, we keep our exposition at a more general level to address how a plant can achieve synchronization and efficiency through lean operations.

10.4.1 Improving Process Architecture: Cellular Layouts

A plant's *process architecture* (the network of activities and resources) has a significant impact on both the flow of work through the process and the ability of the process to synchronize production with demand. As indicated in Chapter 1, in a conventional *functional layout,* resources ("stations") that perform the same function are physically pooled together. Depending on their individual processing requirements, different product types follow different routings through these resource pools, and each flow unit may be sent to any available station in the pool.

A major advantage of the functional layout is that it pools all available capacity for each function, thereby permitting a fuller utilization of the resource pool in producing a variety of products. It also facilitates worker training and performance measurement in each well-defined function. Most important, it benefits from division of labor, specialization, and standardization of work within each function, thereby increasing the efficiency of each function. As we discussed in Chapter 1, a functional layout is ideal for job shops that process a wide variety of products in small volumes.

In terms of synchronization, however, the functional layout has several drawbacks. Flow units often travel significant distances between various resource pools, so their flow times are longer and it is harder to move them in small lots. The result is an intermittent jumbled flow with significant accumulation of inventories along the way. In addition, because each worker tends to be narrowly focused on performing only a part of the total processing task, he or she rarely sees the whole picture, leading to narrow, technology-focused process improvements.

An alternative to the process-based functional layout is the product-focused **cellular layout**, *in which all workstations that perform successive operations on a given product (or product family) are grouped together to form a "cell."* In order to facilitate a linear, efficient flow of both information and materials, different workstations within the cell are located next to one another and laid out sequentially. A cell is focused on a narrow range of customer needs and contains all resources required to meet these needs. Henry Ford's assembly line for the Model T is the classic example of such a product-focused layout. In a general hospital, trauma units, cancer care centers, and emergency rooms are examples of cells set up to process only patients with specific needs.

Advantages of Cellular Layouts   The cellular layout facilitates synchronous flow of information and materials between processing stations. Physical proximity of stations within a cell reduces transportation of flow units between them and makes it feasible to move small batches (the ideal is one) of flow units quickly. It also facilitates communication among stations and improves synchronization by permitting each station to produce parts only if and when the following station needs them. Moreover, because any differences in workloads at different stations become immediately apparent, targeted improvements can be made to balance them. Similarly, if a station encounters a defective unit, that information can be reported to the supplier station immediately; because the supplier station has just handled the unit in question, the cause of the defect can be determined more easily. In short, the cellular layout facilitates synchronized flows and improved defect visibility, traceability, and accountability—which, in turn, leads to fast detection, analysis, and correction of quality problems.

Close interaction among different functions within a cell also encourages crossfunctional skill development and teamwork among workers, which may lead to more satisfying jobs. Because the entire team works on the same product, workers can experience a sense of ownership of the total product and process. The interchangeability of flexible workers also allows them to cooperate and smooth out any flow imbalances resulting from station variability. Finally, a cross-trained workforce improves synchronization by making it possible to adjust production volume to conform to changes in demand.

Disadvantages of Cellular Layouts   Because resources are dedicated to specific cells, they cannot be used by other cells. Consequently, we lose the advantage of resource pooling that a functional layout enjoys. This loss of pooling can be countered with resources that are flexible and cross functional. Cells without flexible resources can be justified only if product volume is sufficiently high.

The stronger interdependence of cellular stations also means that worker incentives have to be based on team—rather than individual—performance. Because individual effort is only indirectly related to the team performance and rewards, workers have less incentive to do their share of work. One solution to this "free rider problem" relies on peer pressure to control the productivity of team members.

Thus, there are advantages and disadvantages to both functional and cellular layouts. Ideally, cellular structure is appropriate for products or product families with similar work-flow patterns and sufficiently high volume, as in automobile and electronic-goods manufacturing. In some cases it may be appropriate to set up a cell of very flexible resources that is assigned a large variety of low-volume parts. The focus of the cell is then on flexibility, and it produces all low-volume parts so that the rest of the plant can focus on producing the high-volume parts efficiently. If resources are not very flexible, it is inefficient to set up a cell to handle a variety of products with different work-flow requirements and high changeover times and costs, as in a job shop. There, the functional layout is more appropriate.

10.4.2   Improving Information and Material Flow: Demand Pull

Given a system of interconnected stations in a processing network, managing flows means informing each station *what* to produce, *when* to produce, and *how much* to produce. There are two approaches to managing information and material flows: push and pull. *In the* **push** *approach, input availability triggers production,* the emphasis being on "keeping busy" to maximize resource utilization as long as there is work to be done. For example, using a popular planning tool called **material requirements planning (MRP)**, *the end-product demand forecasts are "exploded" backward to determine parts requirements at intermediate stations, based on the product structure ("bills of materials"), processing lead times, and levels of inventories at those stations.* A centralized production plan then tells each station when and how much to produce so that output will meet the planned (not the actual) requirements of downstream stations. In implementing the plan, each station processes whatever input quantity is on hand and pushes its output on to the next station. This push operation synchronizes supply with demand at each stage only under the following conditions:

- *If* all information (about the bill of materials, processing lead times, and parts inventories) is accurate
- *If* forecasts of finished goods are correct
- *If* there is no variability in processing times

Failure to meet any one of these conditions at any stage disturbs planned flow and destroys synchronization throughout the process, which then experiences excess inventories and/or shortages at various stages. Because each process bases output not on demand but on input availability, it is not surprising that production often fails to synchronize with demand.

An alternative method for ensuring synchronization is **pull**, where *demand from a customer station triggers production* so that each station produces only on demand from its customer station. Work at an upstream station is initiated by *actual* downstream demand from its customer station. Flow units are "pulled" from each process by its customer process only as they are needed rather than being "pushed" by the supplier process on to the customer process as they are produced. Under pull, the supplier process does not produce or deliver anything until the customer process really needs it and thus avoids inventories of unwanted outputs by refraining from processing inputs even if they are available.

Toyota's Taiichi Ohno (1988) characterized the pull system in terms of supermarket operations:

> From the supermarket, we got the idea of viewing the earlier process in a production line as a store. The later process (customer) goes to the earlier process (supermarket) to acquire the required parts (commodities) at the time and in the quantity needed. The earlier process immediately produces the quantity just taken (restocking the shelves).

The distinction between the push and pull systems of work flow is illustrated in Figure 10.3. Note that information that drives a push system is often a central plan based on the forecast of end-product demand. Information needed to determine flows in a pull system, in contrast, is local from the succeeding station only, and flows are controlled in a decentralized fashion.

There are two key requirements to making a pull system work:

1. Each process must have a well-defined customer, and each customer must have a well-defined supplier process.
2. Each process must produce the quantity needed only when signaled to do so by its customer.

▪▪▪▪▪▪▪▪▪▪▪▪ **FIGURE 10.3 Synchronization: Supply Push versus Demand Pull**

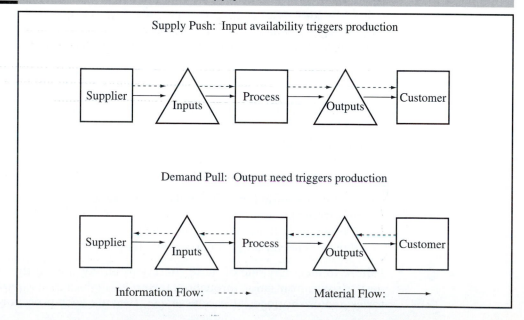

Supply Push: Input availability triggers production

Demand Pull: Output need triggers production

Information Flow: ----▸   Material Flow: ———▸

Demand Signaling   In a push system, input availability is sufficient to trigger production. In a pull system, however, the customer needs a signaling device with which to inform the supplier of its need.

Toyota has formalized its signaling **kanbans**, *a device that allows the customer to inform the supplier of its need. It is a card attached to an output flow unit in the buffer between customer and supplier processes and lists the customer process, the supplier process, parts description, and production quantity.* Kanbans are attached to output flow units in the buffer between customer and supplier processes, and each card lists the following information:

- Customer process
- Supplier process
- Parts description
- Production quantity

As the customer withdraws output flow units from the buffer, the attached kanban goes back to the supplier, which signals an authorization for the supplier to produce the listed quantity. On producing the stipulated quantity, the supplier returns the output with an attached kanban to the buffer. (There are actually two types of kanbans—one to authorize withdrawal and one to authorize production; however, here we will skim over the details.) Because each kanban corresponds to a fixed quantity of flow units to be produced and passed on, the number of kanbans in the buffer between the customer and the supplier determines the maximum size of the buffer. A station can produce a prescribed quantity only if it receives a production authorization kanban. Thus, kanbans control buffer inventory and provide information and discipline to the supplier as to when and how much to produce. The end customer's demand starts a chain reaction of withdrawals and replenishments of intermediate parts that ripples back through upstream stations. The EOQ-ROP system discussed in Chapters 6 and 7 can also be viewed as a pull system with the ROP triggering production at the supplier and the EOQ determining the quantity produced.

In the case of a process that handles multiple products, in addition to when and how much to produce, each supplier station must also know what to produce next. In an automobile assembly plant, for example, cars of different colors and options have different parts and processing requirements. A station that installs inner trim in 1 of 10 options needs to know which trim to install in the car next in line; likewise, its supplier needs a signal to produce that particular trim. One solution for handling variety is to create separate kanbans for each option—a system where 10 different buffers are controlled by 10 different kanbans. As the assembly station installs a particular trim, the released kanban signals its supplier to replenish that unit.

In order for the assembly station to know which trim unit to install on the car at hand, it needs to know the exact production sequence of cars rolling down the line. There is an alternative to maintaining multiple kanbans and complete information at each station if the trim supplier's response time is short enough to produce and deliver the trim to the assembly station in the period between when the production sequence is fixed and the time at which the car reaches the assembly station. Knowing the production sequence for the cars, the supplier can deliver different trims in the correct sequence. The assembly station can simply pick up the trim at the head of the buffer and install it into the next car without knowing the *entire* production sequence because the delivered trim sequence matches the car sequence coming down the line. In this case, only the trim supplier must know the production sequence to determine what to produce and in what sequence to deliver it. We refer to this *approach of delivering parts in sequence as* **synchronized pull**. This approach requires a greater capability on the part of the supplier and very tight coordination between the supplier and customer processes. At the same time, however, it achieves synchronization within a plant with minimal flow of material and information.

10.4.3 Improving Process Flexibility: Batch-Size Reduction

In addition to knowing what and when to produce, each station in a processing network needs to know *how much* to produce at a time. Consider, for example, an automobile assembly line that produces two different models—say, sedans and station wagons. Suppose that monthly demand for each model is 10,000 units. One way to meet this demand is to spend the first half of the month producing 10,000 sedans and the second half producing 10,000 station wagons. This pattern of production will not synchronize supply with demand because actual monthly demand is unlikely to look like this. Moreover, this approach places an uneven workload on the upstream processes (typically, suppliers) that feed parts for the two models: parts suppliers for station wagons have no orders in the first half of the month, and those for sedans have no orders in the second half of the month.

Level Production   At the other extreme, we can achieve perfect synchronization if we alternate sedan and station wagon production one at a time. This results in **level production** (**heijunka** in TPS terminology) *where small quantities are produced frequently to match with customer demand.* If monthly demand called for 10,000 sedans and 5,000 SUVs, a level production system calls for producing two sedans followed by one SUV and then repeating the sequence. If the demand pattern is stable, level production achieves perfect synchronization, producing flow units on demand and in the quantity demanded. Moreover, level production places an even workload on both the production process itself and all supplier processes feeding it.

Changeover Costs and Batch Reduction   Level production in a multiproduct setting requires reducing the batch size produced of each product. As observed in Chapter 6, this reduction is economical only if the fixed cost associated with producing each batch can be reduced. The fixed cost results from the changeover cost and time required to switch production from one model to the other. Thus, a fundamental requirement of level production is reduction of changeover cost. Otherwise, excessive changeover costs from producing small quantities will drive up total production costs.

This concept of small-batch production is a focus for Toyota when introducing suppliers to lean operations. Changeover costs can be reduced by studying and simplifying the changeover process itself, using special tools to speed it up, customizing some machines, and keeping some extra machines that are already set up. All changeover activities that can be performed with the machine running (e.g., obtaining tools required for the changeover) should be completed without shutting down the machine. This reduces the time that a machine is not operating during the changeover, thus decreasing the changeover cost and time. The goal is to externalize as much of the setup as possible and perform these tasks in parallel with actual machine operation. By focusing on improvements to the changeover process itself, Toyota and other auto manufacturers have successfully reduced changeover times and costs by orders of magnitude. This increased ability to economically produce small batches without hurting the throughput results in low flow times and inventory.

The concept of small-batch production within a plant can be extended to small-batch pickups and deliveries made from several suppliers to several plants. One of two procedures is normally used: either a single truck from one supplier carries deliveries to multiple plants, or a single truck destined for one plant carries small quantities of supplies from multiple suppliers. In either case, it is feasible to ship in smaller batches because the fixed cost of a shipment is spread over several suppliers or several plants.

We should reemphasize, however, that although level production is the goal of synchronization, it can be achieved economically only through reduction of the fixed setup (i.e., changeover) or transportation costs associated with each batch. Recall that reduction of changeover cost was among the key levers explained in Chapter 6 and that it may not be optimal for every process to achieve level production with batches of one. In automobile manufacturing, for instance, expensive parts like seats are produced and delivered in batches of one. In contrast, windshield wipers, fasteners, and other low-cost items arrive in larger batches because it makes little economic sense to reduce batch sizes once the costs of doing so outweigh the benefits. In general, reducing batch size is most beneficial for large, expensive inputs; smaller, less expensive inputs are better handled in larger batches.

10.4.4   Quality at Source: Defect Prevention and Early Detection

Synchronization means more than supplying correct quantities at correct times as required by customers: it also means meeting their quality requirements. Supplying defective flow units increases average flow time and cost because it necessitates inspection and rework. Moreover, in order to avoid starving the customer station, the production process must compensate for defective units by holding extra safety inventory in the buffer. In turn, this requirement further increases average flow time and cost. Thus, a key requirement of lean, synchronous operations is producing and passing only defect-free flow units between workstations. It requires planning and controlling quality at the source rather than after the fact (in final inspection) and can be accomplished in two ways:

1. By preventing defects from occurring in the first place
2. By detecting and correcting them as soon as they appear

Defect Prevention   As discussed in Chapter 9, defect prevention requires careful design of both product and process. The goal is to use simplification, standardization, and mistake-proofing to minimize the chance of errors. Two techniques used by TPS to guard against defects are *mistake-proofing* (**poka yoke**) and *intelligent automation* (**jidoka**). Under poka yoke, for example, parts are designed to minimize chances of incorrect assembly. Under jidoka, machines are designed to halt automatically when defective units are fed into them. Product and process design for defect prevention requires clearly defined and documented processing steps, thus removing worker discretion to the extent possible. Integrated design requires joint cooperation and input of all players: customers, designers, engineers, suppliers, as well as production workers. Each of them may have unique ideas and suggestions for product and process improvement that should be encouraged and rewarded.

Defect Visibility   Even though all defects cannot be prevented, their early detection and correction is more effective and economical than catching them during final inspection. Early detection of defects not only improves our chances of tracing them to their sources but also minimizes waste of economic value that is added during the process until they are caught and must be discarded as scrap. Early detection contributes to better synchronization and lower costs in the long run by reducing the number of defectives introduced into the process stream.

Fast detection and correction of quality problems requires constant vigilance and monitoring of feedback. As discussed in Chapter 9, statistical process control can be used to monitor process performance so that any abnormal variation can be detected and eliminated early to maintain process stability.

Decentralized Control   In addition, employees must be equipped with both the authority and the means to identify and correct problems at the local level without administrative and bureaucratic delays. The main idea behind making problems visible is to minimize the cost and delay associated with identifying, searching for, and eliminating their sources. For example, in a Toyota plant, workers pull a rope conveniently located next to their stations if they detect a problem. Pulling the rope lights a *lamp on a signboard that immediately calls the supervisor's attention to the worker's location* (like a flight attendant's light in an airplane) called an **andon**. The supervisor then rushes to the station to help correct the problem. If the supervisor is unable to correct the problem quickly, the line shuts down, alerting more people about the problem. The system is designed to increase attention to a problem until it is resolved. (One should consider the trade-off between the benefits of detecting and fixing problems early and the costs of lost production due to line stoppages.) Compare this practice to that of conventional plants in which resource utilization is given the top priority, work stoppage is permitted only on rare occasions, and only managers are empowered to take action. In fact, in a typical conventional plant, line workers do not feel the responsibility, motivation, or security to point out problems.

In summary, poor quality disturbs flow synchronization through a process. The basic strategy of lean operations, therefore, is threefold:

1. Preventing problems through better planning
2. Highlighting problems as soon as they occur
3. Delegating problem solving to the local level

The goal is to take permanent, corrective action immediately, minimizing future recurrences of problems, thus ensuring quality at source.

10.4.5   Reducing Processing Variability: Standardization of Work, Maintenance, and Safety Capacity

Variability in processing often results from imprecise specification of the work, equipment malfunction, and breakdown. The first step in reducing processing variability is to standardize work at each stage and specify it clearly. At a Toyota plant, each station has posted next to it a standardized work chart showing the flow time at the station, the sequence of activities performed, and the timing to perform them for each car processed. Green and red lines mark the beginning and end of each workstation, and a yellow line in between marks a point by which 70% of the work should be complete. The advantage of this standardization is threefold. First, the standardization reduces variability that arises from changing personnel. Second, the standardization reduces variability from one production cycle to the next. Finally, standardization makes it easier to identify sources of waste that can be eliminated. It is much harder to identify waste if the process itself is not clearly specified.

Given the vulnerability of a process operating without inventories to downstream equipment failure, planned preventive maintenance is an important prerequisite for synchronizing supply and demand. In fact, TPS calls for workers themselves to handle light maintenance of their equipment on an ongoing basis with more complete maintenance scheduled during off-hours.

It is impossible to eliminate all sources of variability; some are simply beyond the manager's control. For example, labor strikes, snowstorms, fires, and other acts of nature can disrupt supply deliveries. As discussed in Chapters 7 and 8, there are only two practical means of dealing with supply or demand variability if delays are to be avoided: carrying safety inventory or keeping some safety capacity. Although processes should consider the trade-off between carrying safety inventory and safety capacity, lean operations try to minimize carrying *safety inventory* because it increases flow time and jeopardizes synchronization. Consequently, a lean process must maintain some *safety capacity* as protection against variability.

Safety capacity may be in the form of extra machines, workers, or overtime. Toyota, for example, does not schedule production for all 24 hours in the day. The residual capacity is used as overtime if scheduled production is not completed by the end of the day. Ideally, safety capacity in the form of machines or workers should be flexible so that it can be used as needed.

10.4.6 Visibility of Performance

As discussed by Swank (2003), a fundamental principle of lean operations is to measure process performance from the customer's perspective. For example, when process performance is evaluated by measuring average time per call at a call center, customer-service representatives are eager to get the customers off the phone. However, this may lead to customers having to make repeat calls because their concerns were not fully resolved the first time. To measure process performance from the customer's perspective, it is more effective to measure the percentage of customers whose problems are resolved in a single call. This ensures that customer-service representatives are focused on resolving customer problems as opposed to doing their best to keep the calls as short as possible. Similarly, measuring internal flow time within the picking process at a mail-order warehouse is of little interest to a customer. The customer cares about the flow time from when she places an order to when it is delivered. Thus, all processes at the warehouse should be geared to reducing the overall flow time. It is important to ensure that goals at all levels of the organization are linked to each other. The metric used to measure a manager's performance should be directly affected by the metric used to measure the people working under her.

One of the most important principles of lean operations is that actual performance, along with expectations, be very visible for each work cell. For example, the numbers are often posted on electronic or whiteboards close to the cell so that employees can see the level of current performance. The goal of this visibility is not to assign blame and punish low performers but to provide quick feedback for corrective action in case of a problem and to give teams an opportunity for celebrating success in case of high performance. The visibility of expectations and performance also clarifies for employees that they will be evaluated and rewarded for objective results that they can track themselves.

10.4.7 Managing Human Resources: Employee Involvement

Implementing synchronization within a plant requires cooperation, contribution, and commitment on the part of all employees to work in a tightly linked, highly interdependent environment. Managing human resources is therefore a critical factor in lean operations.

Behavioral studies since Elton Mayo's famous "Hawthorne experiments" at Western Electric in the 1940s have shown that if workers are involved in the decision-making processes that affect their jobs, they are better motivated to contribute substantially to productivity improvement. The key concept behind these theories of employee involvement is the recognition that workers have talents, education, and experience that can be harnessed to improve the process.

Worker participation in problem-solving and process-improvement efforts (as in "quality circles") is an important component of lean operations. Based on the premise that the workers closest to the job have the most expertise to provide suggestions for improvement, the employee-involvement approach suggests involving workers in all phases of the improvement cycle. It also argues that employees possess the most current and accurate information about a given problem. It stands to reason, therefore, that providing them the necessary training and tools—and, just as important, "empowering" them with the authority and responsibility to make job-related decisions—is the fastest method of implementing decentralized control. The authority to stop production when a defect is detected at Toyota is an example of such an approach.

In lean operations, workers are cross-trained both to provide the company with flexible workers and to give workers greater variety through job rotation. In addition to their regular jobs, work teams in cells may also be authorized to perform certain managerial duties, such as work and vacation scheduling, material ordering, and even hiring new workers.

Worker participation in such initiatives requires that employees not only have basic skills and education but also are willing to learn multiple tasks, work in team environments, and be committed to the success of the entire process. Lean operations, therefore, places a great importance on the recruiting and training of workers.

10.4.8   Supplier Management: Partnerships

Outsourcing materials—that is, buying them from someone else rather than making them—provides a flexible alternative to vertical integration. In modern manufacturing, purchased materials not only account for a major portion of the product cost but also represent a major source of quality problems. With lean operations, reliable, on-time deliveries of defect-free parts assume critical importance. External suppliers, therefore, constitute an essential resource that impacts product cost, quality, and flow time.

A conventional approach to supplier management calls for selecting several suppliers, making them compete against one another on price alone, and then monitoring them closely to ensure that they do not neglect quality and timely delivery. It often leads to adversarial and even hostile relationships between the supplier and the manufacturer. Synchronizing flow becomes very difficult if the product is sourced from many suppliers. The lean approach to supplier management, in contrast, calls for choosing only a few capable, reliable suppliers with whom to cultivate cooperative, long-term relationships. The buyer works to make the suppliers an extension of the plant by sharing information and helping them improve their own processes through training, technical, and even economic assistance and by extending long-term contracts as incentives to induce cooperation in synchronizing flows of inputs with the plant requirements.

In terms of actual deliveries, the conventional approach seeks quantity discounts by purchasing in large volumes and tries to ensure quality through extensive inspection of incoming material. Lean operations, in contrast, involve processing without inventories or quality inspection. Plant synchronization with supplier requires that defect-free material be delivered frequently, in small batches, and directly to the point of usage. In turn, small, frequent, reliable deliveries require supplier proximity and simplified buying and accounts-payable procedures. They also require that the supplier's process be able to produce small quantities on demand—that the supplier's plant be synchronized with the buyer's. Ensuring quality at source (without the non-value-adding activity of inspection) requires supplier capability and commitment to producing quality parts. It also requires open communication between the buyer's plant and the supplier on such matters as product design changes and possible improvements.

Supplier management involves treating suppliers as partners—which is quite a change from the conventional approach that regards suppliers as outsiders not to be trusted. Even now, firms often interpret lean operations to mean requiring *suppliers* to produce and hold the parts inventory and supply just-in-time to the plant so that the plant can operate without raw materials inventory. Such a policy amounts to simply pushing the plant's raw materials inventory back on to the suppliers. In fact, the goal of lean operations should be to reduce inventories in the total supply chain by synchronizing both the supplier's process and the buyer's process. It is thus critical to manage suppliers as a part of one's business, working with them closely to help them improve their quality, delivery, and cost so that they are able to meet the plant's requirements and remain economically viable.

In Brazil, supplier factories surround the Blue Macaw assembly plant of General Motors (Wilson, 2000). The factories produce instrument panels, seats, and other components for the Chevrolet Celta, a low-priced vehicle for the Brazilian market. The suppliers are responsible for the design and engineering of their components. Suppliers control a portion of the assembly line where they handle assembly of an entire system that has typically been designed and engineered by them. For example, Lear Corporation controls door assembly at Blue Macaw and installs locks, windows, and other components onto the door. Similar ideas have been used by the Ford Motor Company and Volkswagen in Brazil. The increased involvement of suppliers in the design, engineering, and assembly phase has led to significant savings.

In summary, lean operations aim to sustain continuous flow processing in an economical manner by implementing four closely related principles:

1. *Synchronize material and information flows* by means of cellular layouts and demand pull mechanisms (Sections 10.4.1 and 10.4.2)
2. *Increase flexibility* by means of fast changeovers that permit smaller batches to level production (Section 10.4.3)
3. *Reduce variability* by means of work standardization and improved supplier reliability and quality, coupled with safety capacity, preventive maintenance, and fast feedback and correction (Sections 10.4.4 and 10.4.5)
4. *Decrease processing costs* by improving quality and eliminating non-value-added activities such as transportation, inspection, and rework (Chapters 4 and 5)

Each of these principles are further facilitated by setting goals that are consistent with customer needs, establishing visibility of performance (Section 10.4.6), and making long-term investment in workers and suppliers (Sections 10.4.7 and 10.4.8) leading to successful lean operations. As many companies have realized, any efforts to implement just-in-time operations that ignore these prerequisites are sure to fail. For example, if a process has a high setup cost and a high degree of variability, it will be uneconomical and inefficient to operate without cycle or safety inventories (for further discussion, see Zipkin, 1991).

10.5 Improving Flows in a Supply Chain

Producing and distributing goods to meet customer demand involves flows through a complex network of processes that include raw materials suppliers, finished-goods producers, wholesalers, distributors, and retailers. This entire value-adding network is the supply chain. Managing a supply chain involves storing and moving products and information along the entire network in order to make products available to customers when and where they are desired at the lowest possible cost. The goal of a supply chain is to synchronize flows throughout the network to meet customer demand most economically.

In the previous section, we discussed key issues in achieving synchronization and efficiency within a plant—which is just one node in the entire supply chain. The plant, however, can be considered a network of processing stages through which raw materials, components, and subassemblies flow to emerge as finished products. Its structure, in other words, is similar to that of a supply chain. Therefore, the concepts we applied at the plant level are equally applicable in synchronizing flows in supply chains. There are, however, three special challenges in managing a supply chain:

1. **Scale magnification:** This implies that issues that arise within a plant (relating, for instance, to economies of scale, inventory levels, and flow times) are magnified in a supply chain. For example, flow times between nodes in a supply chain could be orders of magnitude larger than those between processes within a plant. Similarly, economies of scale in transporting goods from one node to another in a supply chain are much larger because of the geographical distances involved.
2. **Multiple decision makers:** Because different nodes in a supply chain may have separate ownership, each with its own objectives, the supply chain consists of multiple decision makers. Aligning incentives among different agents is much more difficult and results in suboptimization of nodes: locally optimal decisions made at one node may not be globally optimal for the entire supply chain.
3. **Asymmetric information:** Each (independent) decision maker may possess only private information and lack the global information necessary to synchronize its flows with the rest of the supply chain. Thus, even if a decision maker wishes to act in the best interests of the chain, he or she may not be able to do so.

In this section, we discuss the consequences of unsynchronized flows in a supply chain, identify their root causes, and propose some measures for improving synchronization and efficiency in a supply chain. For a more detailed discussion of this topic, see Chopra and Meindl (2004).

10.5.1 Lack of Synchronization: The Bullwhip Effect

A supply chain can be analyzed in terms of product and information flows. Products primarily flow toward the customer, whereas information flows in both directions. Information regarding orders flows upstream towards the supplier, whereas information on prices and product availability flows downstream to the customer. Matching supply and demand involves synchronizing *product flows* with customer demand. The ability to synchronize is affected by *information flows* in a supply chain.

Consider a simple, linear supply chain that consists of a manufacturer, a distributor, a wholesaler, and a retailer. Customer demand at the retailer starts a chain reaction of orders upstream all the way back to the manufacturer. Figure 10.4 shows typical order patterns faced by each node in such a supply chain. Note that the retailer's orders to the wholesaler display greater variability than the end-consumer sales, the wholesaler's orders to its distributor show even more oscillation, and the distributor's orders to the manufacturer are most volatile. Thus, the pattern of orders received at upstream stages becomes increasingly more variable than consumption patterns at the retail end.

This *phenomenon of upstream variability magnification* is referred to as the **bullwhip effect** *and indicates lack of synchronization among supply chain members.* Even a slight disturbance in consumer sales sends back magnified oscillations, as does the flick of a bullwhip. In a perfectly synchronized supply chain, the order pattern at each stage would mimic the consumption pattern at the retail end. In a supply chain

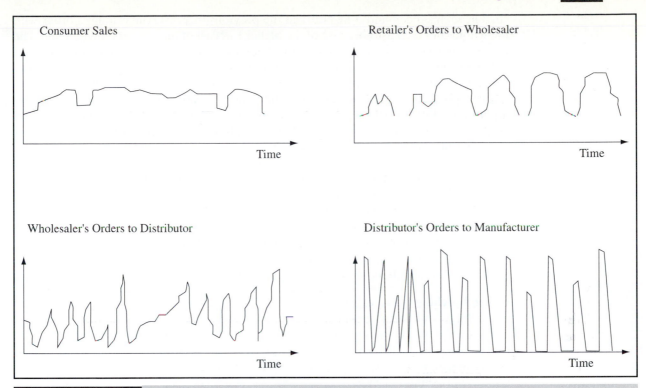

FIGURE 10.4 The Bullwhip Effect: Order Variability in a Supply Chain

that is not synchronized, however, information flows are distorted, leading to inventory accumulation at some stages and shortages and delays at other stages. The bullwhip effect has been observed by firms in numerous industries, including Procter & Gamble (P&G) in consumer products, Hewlett-Packard in electronics, General Motors (GM) in automobiles, and Eli Lily in pharmaceuticals.

10.5.2   Causes of the Bullwhip Effect

Four main causes of the bullwhip effect have been identified by Lee et al. (1997):

1. Demand signal processing
2. Order batching
3. Price fluctuations
4. Rationing or shortage gaming

In the following sections, we discuss each cause briefly and show how it leads to an increase in the variability of the order pattern as compared to the demand pattern faced by each node in the supply network. The bullwhip effect is then a result of these four causes, as the variability cascades across the nodes as orders move upstream.

Demand Signal Processing   Most firms rely on some form of demand forecasting to plan procurement, production, and capacity. Usually, short-term forecasting involves extrapolating the history of past sales and demand, with every observation of current demand factored into future demand projections. Consider a retailer who satisfies end-customer demand by ordering from a wholesaler. If demand in the current period is higher than expected, the retailer adjusts his forecast of the future lead time demand (including both the mean and the error). The new forecast is adjusted upward because current realized demand is higher than the previous forecast. The retailer's order with the wholesaler increases because of the higher forecast of mean lead time demand. The increase in order size is exacerbated by the delay in material and information flow between the two stages. The retailer's order is higher-than-realized demand to compensate for the delay in replenishment. The same phenomenon recurs when the wholesaler receives the retailer's order: the wholesaler's order to his or her supplier is also amplified relative to the retailer's order (whose order was amplified relative to the change in customer demand). Order amplifications cascade upstream in the supply chain because each stage forecasts demand based on orders it receives.

Conversely, if the current demand is lower than the forecast amount, the retailer adjusts the forecast of lead time demand downward. This adjustment leads to a reduction in order, thus creating a distortion in the ordering pattern. Observe that the order amplification is exacerbated by the fact that each stage in the supply chain makes plans according to a different information set—namely, the order stream from the immediately downstream stage—and not according to the ultimate customer demand. Thus, we see an interplay of all three difficulties discussed earlier—scale magnification, diverse decision makers, and private information.

Order Batching   The practice of batching occurs when a node in the supply chain places large and infrequent orders. Firms may place orders in some periodic fashion— say, on a weekly, biweekly, or monthly basis. This practice results from some form of economy of scale in procurement, production, or transportation, as discussed in Chapter 6. Firms also place orders in large batches in response to incentives (say, quantity discounts) offered by a supplier.

Although batching may be optimal for the buyer, it creates a distortion in the demand pattern experienced by the supplier. As discussed in Chapter 6, when demand rates are known and constant, the use of an economic order quantity (EOQ) model creates an order pattern with large spikes. If a supplier expects this pattern of ordering from a buyer (perhaps through information sharing), he or she can account for the unevenness. Often, however, this is not the case because only orders and not demand information are passed along the supply chain.

Whenever a process at one stage in the supply chain places orders in batches, the process at the upstream stage sees orders that are much more variable than end-customer demand. This effect is exacerbated when multiple retailers place large orders simultaneously with the same upstream supplier (numerous retailers, for instance, may place their orders every Monday).

Price Fluctuations   When prices offered by an upstream stage to a downstream stage fluctuate often, the downstream stage may order more than it immediately needs when prices are low and postpone purchases when they are high. In Chapter 6, we showed how buyers forward buy and increase order quantities by a large amount when suppliers offer small short-term price discounts. Forward buying makes orders even more variable than demand, thus exacerbating the bullwhip effect. Short-term price discounts and forward buying are fairly common for several commodity products, such as dry goods in the grocery industry.

Rationing or Shortage Gaming   When total orders placed by retailers exceed product availability, manufacturers use some form of *rationing* to allocate their products to buyers. If retailers know that a product will be in short supply (and thus rationed), they may exaggerate their needs when placing orders. When demand turns out to be lower than the inflated order quantities, retailers start canceling orders—leaving large levels of inventories with manufacturers. This pattern can set in even if shortages are not real: orders may be amplified at the slightest *perception* of a shortage by retailers. Because orders do not reflect actual consumer demand, such "gaming" behavior on the part of downstream stages produces the bullwhip effect.

In November 2003, *Off the Record Research* reported wide shortages of Nokia phones in Europe. Buyers were quoted as saying, "We're seeing a lot of supply problems affecting almost all vendors at the moment. When I order 50,000, I'll probably get 20,000 from Nokia; it's the same with Samsung and Siemens." The result of widespread shortages was double ordering by network operators hoping to increase available supply. The double ordering was expected to affect inventory levels in early 2004, when the additional units were delivered.

10.5.3   Levers to Counteract the Bullwhip Effect

A typical supply chain is characterized by independent players who optimize their own objectives according to limited private information. As we have seen thus far, even when these players behave rationally, information distortion in the supply chain can produce the bullwhip effect. Having understood some of the causes of the bullwhip effect, we now outline some levers to counteract them. The root causes of the bullwhip effect can be traced to the following factors:

1. Inefficient processes (resulting, for example, in long flow times between stages or in high fixed costs)
2. Inconsistency of available information (due to poor timing, inaccuracy)
3. Local actions by individual players that are suboptimal for the overall system

Likewise, we can put the levers for counteracting the bullwhip effect into three categories:

1. Operational effectiveness
2. Information sharing
3. Channel alignment

Operational Effectiveness   Throughout this book, we have considered operational effectiveness in terms of cost, quality, and response time and suggested levers to achieve effectiveness in these terms. Several of these levers also help counter the bullwhip effect as outlined here:

- **Reduce (material and information) flow time:** The bullwhip effect is reduced if material and information flow times are decreased. Some technologies, such as *electronic data interchange* (*EDI*) and the Internet, permit various stages in the supply chain to transmit information electronically, thereby reducing delays in information flows. *Cross-docking,* which is widely practiced by Wal-Mart and many other firms (see Example 2.1 in Chapter 2), calls for moving material directly from receiving to shipping with minimum dwell time in the warehouse—a practice that helps decrease the transportation flow time and pipeline inventory between suppliers and retailers.
- **Reduce economies of scale:** The bullwhip effect can be diminished if batch sizes of purchases are reduced. The various levers for decreasing batch size discussed earlier can be applied to reduce batch sizes in a supply chain:

  Reduce fixed costs: Fixed procurement, production, and transportation costs create the bullwhip effect by encouraging large batch order sizes. EDI and the Internet reduce fixed procurement costs by allowing firms to place orders electronically. Several principles that we have attributed to lean operations reduce changeover cost and encourage production in smaller batches. For example, **single minute exchange of dies (SMED)** *is a system by which the changeover times can be reduced to less than 10 minutes,* and **flexible manufacturing systems (FMS)** *is a reprogrammable manufacturing system capable of producing a large variety of parts.* Both permit level production (heijunka) by reducing production setup and changeover costs.

Give quantity discounts for assortments: Suppliers often offer quantity discounts based on the batch size of purchase. These discounts, however, are typically offered for *individual* items. For example a firm may offer a 3% discount for purchases in a full truckload. When these discounts are offered separately for each product family, customers have an incentive to purchase full truckloads of each family. The result is a distortion of ultimate demand information. If suppliers offer discounts on *assortments* of items, thus allowing the customer to obtain the same 3% discount as long as they fill a truckload of the assortment, there is little need to exaggerate batch sizes for individual items. Such a policy reduces distortion in item-level demand information while still permitting the supplier to exploit economies of scale in transportation. Following this approach, P&G now offers discounts to distributors as long as they fill a truckload with an assortment of P&G products.

Form logistical alliances: Another way to exploit transportation economies is to form an alliance with a third-party logistics firm. Such providers achieve economies of scale in transportation by consolidating the needs of multiple suppliers/customers. Consolidating shipments lessens the need to increase batch sizes by allowing each supplier/customer to ship/receive less than a full truckload of quantities. Firms should, however, consider other coordination and strategic issues before deciding to outsource the logistics function.

Information Sharing The presence of multiple decision makers working with private information affects the product/information flows in the supply chain. Sharing of information among supply chain members can reduce the magnitude of the bullwhip effect:

- **Share consumption information with upstream players:** Each stage in the supply chain processes its demand information to construct a forecast for the future (a strategy that we have labeled *demand signal processing*). However, only the last stage in the chain is privy to *sales data* regarding the end-consumer demand, which is usually collected through *point-of-sale* (*POS*) technology. Forecasts at all other stages are based on the orders they receive. Consequently, each stage in the chain is trying to forecast demand based on a different set of data. A first step in information sharing is to make sales data available to all players in the supply chain so that every member's plans are based on the same data set. In fact, as described in Chapter 2, Wal-Mart shares its sales data with suppliers.
- **Share availability information with downstream players:** Shortage gaming results when retailers do not know the actual availability or capacity of their suppliers. Although sharing capacity/availability information will eliminate mistaken perceptions of shortages, it will also reveal the existence of real shortages. Thus, it may not be a perfect instrument to counteract the bullwhip effect. When shortages do exist, allocation policies should be based on past sales and not current orders.

Channel Alignment Although operational improvements and information sharing may assist independent supply chain players in making decisions that improve their own performance, these practices alone are usually insufficient to synchronize the entire supply chain. Other explicit coordination/incentive mechanisms are needed to align the priorities of individual members with those of the system:

- **Coordinate replenishment and forecasting decisions:** Even if every stage in the supply chain possesses customer sales data, differences in forecasting methods and buying practices can still lead to fluctuations in orders. One solution is for a single upstream stage to control the replenishment of material to the downstream stage. This tactic works when the upstream stage has access to downstream demand and inventory information and replenishes its stock accordingly. **Vendor managed inventory (VMI)** and **Continuous Replenishment Program (CRP)** are two techniques used by the consumer-products industry to implement these practices. VMI *is a partnership program under which the supplier decides the inventory levels to be maintained at its customer locations and arranges for replenishments to maintain these levels.* P&G and Wal-Mart have been at the forefront of VMI program initiated in 1985. Under CRP, *the supplier automatically replenishes its customer inventories based on contractually agreed-on levels.* The Campbell Soup Company uses a CRP program with its retailers to coordinate replenishment.

    Under such programs, however, a downstream stage, which no longer decides on how much to order, may perceive a loss of control. Another solution, therefore, is to adopt a coordinated forecasting and replenishment methodology for all stages in the chain. **Collaborative Planning, Forecasting, and Replenishment (CPFR)** *is an initiative in the consumer-goods industry designed to coordinate planning, forecasting, and replenishment across the supply chain.* Details on CPFR can be found at www.cpfr.org.
- **Stabilize prices:** Short-term price reductions provide an incentive to the retailers to "forward buy" and thereby distort the supplier's demand information. A manufacturer can reduce forward buying by the following methods:

    1. Establish a uniform wholesale-pricing policy
    2. Limit the amount that can be purchased under forward buys
    3. Credit retailers for promotional discounts based on customer sales during a given period rather than on orders placed

    In the grocery industry, for instance, major manufacturers like P&G and Kraft have adopted *everyday low purchase pricing* (*EDLPP*) strategies, a practice discussed in Chapter 6.
- **Change allocation policies:** We have already observed that sharing upstream capacity/availability information is not a perfect instrument for reducing the bullwhip effect due to gaming. Allocation mechanisms based on current orders encourage downstream stages to exaggerate their orders. Other allocation mechanisms, however—such as GM's policy of basing allocations on past sales—may remove incentives to inflate orders.

To summarize, the ability to synchronize flows in a supply chain is affected by such factors as operational efficiency, information availability, and level of coordination. Organizations must understand the root causes of the inefficiency that results from the bullwhip effect and take measures to remedy them. Implementation of the solutions like those proposed in this chapter is challenging because the process often involves interorganizational issues in coordination, information sharing, and change of incentive structures.

10.6   The Improvement Process

Although we have identified various levers for process improvement (i.e., what to do), we have not yet described any process or framework for achieving such improvement (i.e., *how* to do it). In this section, we conclude by discussing the *process* of process improvement. We describe an improvement process that begins by maintaining process stability in the short run, gradually improving it over time, and occasionally revamping it in the long run. Managers should keep in mind that the workers closest to the job are in the best position to identify opportunities for process improvement. They should, therefore, be encouraged—even prodded—to make suggestions. Including workers in the improvement process makes them feel not only comfortable and secure in exposing and facing up to new problems but also disciplined and ambitious enough to overcome complacency in approaching the ideal.

10.6.1   Process Stabilization: Standardizing and Controlling the Process

The first step in process improvement is to define the process by standardizing the various activities. Because process performance usually displays variability, reliable measurement requires that the observed performance be *statistically predictable*. The second step in process improvement is to bring the process under control, as discussed in Chapter 9. Statistical process control involves monitoring performance over time and providing fast feedback when variability appears to be abnormal. This practice identifies and corrects sources of abnormal variation, thus ensuring that our estimates of its performance characteristics are reliable. At this stage we have a well-defined process and a reliable measurement of its performance in relation to the ideal. This is a base from where improvement should start.

10.6.2   Continuous Improvement: Management by Sight and Stress

For a process that has been stabilized, any gap between actual and ideal performance can be reduced by making **continuous improvement**, *ongoing incremental improvement in process performance,* which is an important aspect of lean operations and TPS. As we mentioned in Section 10.4, it is often referred to as *kaizen,* which means "a good change." Kaizen has also been characterized as "continuous, incremental improvement in the process by everyone involved" (Imai, 1986). We next discuss three drivers of continuous improvement.

Management by Sight   Management by sight focuses on driving continuous improvement by making problems and opportunities visible and providing incentives and tools to eliminate the former and take advantage of the latter. A natural short-term tendency in process management is to cover up process imperfections (such as inflexibility or variability) by building in safety cushions (such as cycle or safety inventory). This approach obstructs our view of process imperfections and reduces our sense of urgency to remove them. The principle of management by sight calls for constantly removing—not inserting—safety cushions such as inventory in order to expose and contend with process problems (as opposed to covering up these problems). Both removing safety cushions and exposing problems are treated as an opportunity to improve the process.

Management by Stress   Management by stress focuses on constantly stressing the system, thus forcing it to improve performance to reduce the stress. In the river analogy, as the water level is lowered, new problems surface, and we are forced to deal with them. As soon as we have solved these newly visible problems, the water level is lowered again, exposing yet more rocks to be dealt with. Our goal is to refuse to be content with smooth sailing in ample water. Rather than using extra resources as a safety cushion to protect against imperfections, we keep on reducing their level, relentlessly exposing more problems, and eliminating their root causes. The idea is to keep the process under constant pressure by gradually removing the security blanket.

The management-by-stress philosophy teaches us that by keeping the system under constant stress, we force new problems to become visible and so increase our own responsibility for eliminating root causes rather than simply reacting to them as they occur. At Toyota, for example, the rope-pull (*andon*) system is a tool for making problems visible. If a problem repeatedly prompts rope pulls, it is clearly in the supervisor's best interest to get to the root cause of the problem and eliminate it once and for all. To ensure sufficient visibility, Toyota tracks the number of rope pulls per shift. Similarly, the production process is kept under constant stress by removing *kanbans* (and hence the inventory buffer) between stages so that stages or nodes are forced to devise methods to work with less and less inventory.

Recall, however, that the success of continuous improvement requires a gradual lowering of the water level; otherwise, the boat will scrape the bottom against a rock and spring a leak. In fact, the failure to appreciate the importance of *gradual* stress is one reason why lean operations sometimes fail in practice: firms set arbitrarily high targets for inventory reduction without correspondingly improving the process. Ultimately, it is process improvement—not merely inventory reduction in itself—that is the goal. Inventory reduction is merely a means for exposing problems.

Management by Objective   Another approach to continuous improvement is to regularly set *targets* (say, every quarter or every year) for critical performance measures. These targets should reflect both the demands of the marketplace and the performance of competitors. The purpose of such targets is to guide the firm in its efforts to *do better* than competitors with the same level of resources or to do as well *with fewer* resources. In either case, targets, once achieved, are then revised, and the process (and the pressure) continues. This approach to continuous improvement is sometimes called *management by objective*. The major difference between this approach and that of management by sight and stress is a matter of *focus*. In managing by sight and stress, we focus on making problems visible and then treat them as drivers for change. In management by objective, we focus on achieving an objective and let the desire to hit targets drive change. In either case, the basic tool kit for process improvement contains the same levers that we have been describing throughout this book.

10.6.3 Business Process Reengineering: Process Innovation

Sometimes gradual improvement toward the ideal process may not be enough: a significant jump in process performance may be necessary to catch up to or overtake the competition. In that case, the solution might be **reengineering**, which Hammer and Champy (1993) (who popularized the term in the early 1990s) define as "*fundamental rethinking and radical redesign of business processes in order to achieve dramatic improvements in critical contemporary measures of performance such as cost, quality, service and speed.*"

Consider some of the key terms of this definition:

- *Fundamental* rethinking means reexamining and questioning traditional practices and assumptions that may have become obsolete, erroneous, or inappropriate over time. At each stage of a business process, one asks why it is done and how it can be done differently or, better yet, how it can be eliminated completely.

- *Radical* redesign means *reinventing the process from scratch, not just tweaking the existing one.* It means channeling a new river without rocks rather than trying to uncover and remove the rocks one by one in the current river. It thus requires starting with a "clean slate" and asking what an ideal process would look like if we had to start all over again.
- *Dramatic* improvements mean substantial changes aimed at, say, 10-fold, not 10%, improvements in performance measures. For example, the goal of a typical reengineering project would be to design, produce, and deliver a product with *half* as many defectives, in *half* as much time, at *half* as much cost as the one we now market. The *six-sigma philosophy* that we discussed in Chapter 9 is an example of setting such "stretch goals." Improvements of such magnitude require "out-of-the-box" innovative thinking.
- *Critical* measures of performance that are *important to the customer*—cost, quality, and response time—should be the focus of process improvement. It is a waste of energy to make improvements that the customer does not see or value.

Reengineering versus Continuous Improvement As a framework for improvement, reengineering differs from continuous improvement in three elements: magnitude and time frame of desired improvement and change drivers. In continuous improvement, the change drivers (visibility or targets) are *internal* components of the existing process. In process reengineering, a complete rethinking of the process itself is forced by something *external*—either a dramatic change in customer needs or a change in technology. We strive not merely to make the existing process better but, potentially, to invent a new process that will do the job significantly better than the current process.

Hammer and Champy (1993) cite the accounts payable process at Ford Motor Company as a classic example of successful reengineering. During the early 1980s, the department employed over 500 people in North America. Management hoped for a 20% reduction in head count by improving the existing processes. That process, however, focused on processing invoices sent in by suppliers, and Ford discovered that by eliminating invoices altogether and basing payments on receipts of shipments, it could radically alter the entire procurement process. The result was a 75% reduction in the personnel. Note, however, that although the popular press tended to equate "reengineering" with "downsizing" in the early 1990s, reducing head count and cost are not the only projects in which reengineering may be useful. Reengineering may also make dramatic improvements in terms of time, quality, and flexibility. Hammer and Champy discuss several illuminating examples.

Reengineering and continuous improvement are not necessarily antithetical approaches. Both are valuable as components of the same long-term improvement program. In fact, along with the design for a new process, reengineering effort should also include a program for continuous improvement. Similarly, while continuous improvement takes a process toward ideal performance in regular, incremental steps, reengineering is needed from time to time to make a radical change—especially when significant changes occur in the external environment and technology. Thus, reengineering is called for when there is a dramatic change in customer expectations or a change in technology that makes possible a completely different process design.

10.6.4 Benchmarking: Heeding the Voices of the Best

Process improvement requires setting and approaching specific goals—a project that can be aided greatly by studying others' processes and emulating their best practices; it can save you time and money by not having to "reinvent the wheel." Robert Camp (1995) defines **benchmarking** as *"the process of continually searching for the best* *methods, practices, and processes, and adopting or adapting the good features to become 'the best of the best.'"* We may benchmark someone else's products (in terms of price, quality, or response time), key processes (in terms of cost, flow time, or inventory turns), or support processes (such as warehousing, billing, or shipping).

In search of best practices, we may look either within our own organization or to outside competitors. We may even turn to noncompetitors in other industries. We have already seen, for instance, how the Japanese devised the pull system of material flow based on observations of U.S. supermarket operations. Xerox Corporation benchmarked mail-order retailer L.L. Bean for its efficient logistics and distribution system. In an effort to expedite aircraft turnaround times at the gate, Southwest Airlines studied the National Association for Stock Car Auto Racing (NASCAR) pit stops. The use of bar coding, so prevalent at supermarket checkout counters, is now widely used by manufacturers to manage parts inventories and flows.

The key to successful benchmarking is not merely duplicating the activities of others: benchmarking means identifying the basic concepts underlying what world-class companies do, understanding how they do it, and adapting what we have learned to our own situation. It requires external orientation to identify the best in class, open-mindedness to understand their approach, and innovativeness to modify their solution to fit our problem.

10.6.5 Managing Change

Process improvement means changing our way of doing business, which is accompanied by uncertainty. It is a natural human tendency, however, to prefer the status quo and predictability. In managing change, the challenge is to encourage people to accept change and to motivate them to take the kinds of risks that bring about change for the better.

Ironically, it is easier to motivate people to change when times are bad; change is then perceived as a survival imperative rather than an option to improve. By that time, however, it may be too late to improve the firm's competitive position merely by making gradual improvements to the existing process; it may be necessary to reengineer the whole process. It is also unfortunate that when times are good, the natural tendency is to be complacent—and perhaps oblivious to potential environmental changes and competitive threats. The challenge then is to make people feel dissatisfied enough with the status quo to seek change and yet feel secure enough to take risks associated with a change. As we saw in our discussion of continuous improvement, this motivational balance can be spurred by increasing visibility of waste (management by sight), gradually reducing available resources (management by stress), or gradually raising goals (management by objective).

Finally, any organizational change is easier to bring about if everyone affected by it is involved in a participatory spirit, in a nonthreatening environment, with open lines of communication.

SUMMARY   ▪ ▪ ▪ ▪ ▪ ▪ ▪

In this chapter we examined problems of managing flows of multiple products through a network of processes. The overall goal of such a processing network is to match its supply with demand in terms of cost, quality, variety, and availability of products when and where customers want them. The ideal is to achieve this synchronization of supply and demand at the lowest cost. We studied principles of lean operations to accomplish this at the plant level and extended them to managing the entire supply chain. The objective is to eliminate waste of all kind: excess costs, defects, delays, and inventories by increasing process capability and flexibility and decreasing variability. Furthermore, different processes must be coordinated to facilitate fast and accurate flow of information and materials between them.

Concrete methods for accomplishing these objectives at the plant level include the following:

1. Improve process architecture with a cellular layout
2. Coordinate information and material flow using a demand pull system
3. Decrease batch sizes and improve process flexibility by reducing changeover times
4. Ensure quality at source
5. Reduce processing variability by work standardization, preventive maintenance, and safety capacity
6. Increase visibility of performance to identify areas for improvement
7. Involve all employees in the improvement process
8. Coordinate information and align incentives with suppliers

Similar principles apply in managing flows in a supply chain, with added complications due to scale magnification and multiple decision makers having different information and incentives. This results in an increased variability in orders due to divergent forecasts, order batching, price fluctuations, and shortage gaming. Levers to synchronize the supply chain include the following:

1. Reduce information and material flow times through technology and logistics
2. Decrease fixed costs of production and ordering and reduce quantity discounts
3. Share information on customer demand and product availability
4. Coordinate forecasts and replenishment between various parties
5. Avoid short-term price fluctuations

Improvement in the process at the plant or supply chain level requires (1) stabilization through process standardization and control; (2) continuous improvement through management by sight, stress, and objectives; and (3) process reengineering through completely rethinking and radically redesigning the process for dramatic improvements in critical performance measures such as cost, quality, and response time that are important to the customers. Benchmarking accomplishments of the best in class in these areas helps set and achieve concrete goals for process improvement by identifying, adapting, and adopting their practices. Finally, it is important to recognize that every process-improvement effort entails an organizational change that must be motivated and internalized.

KEY TERMS ▮▮▮▮▮▮▮

- Andon
- Benchmarking
- Bullwhip effect
- Cellular layout
- Collaborative Planning, Forecasting, and Replenishment (CPFR)
- Continuous improvement
- Continuous Replenishment Program (CRP)
- Flexible manufacturing systems (FMS)
- Heijunka
- Ideal process
- Jidoka
- Just-in-time (JIT)
- Kaizen
- Kanbans
- Level production
- Material requirements planning (MRP)
- Plant
- Poka yoke
- Process efficiency

- Process synchronization
- Processing network
- Pull
- Push
- Reengineering
- Single minute exchange of dies (SMED)
- Supply chain
- Vendor managed inventory (VMI)
- Waste

DISCUSSION QUESTIONS

10.1 How does the use of kanbans result in a pull system?

10.2 A manufacturer of auto parts has just learned about the Toyota Production System and is trying to implement lean operations. Traditionally, there has been no control on the amount of work-in-process inventory between stages (it has been known to exceed 500 parts between some stages). As a first step, the amount of work-in-process inventory between stages is limited to a maximum of 20 parts. What, if any, impact does this have on the output from the factory in the short term? Using lessons learned from the river analogy, how should the manufacturer manage buffers?

10.3 Taiichi Ohno, architect of the Toyota Production System, claims to have been inspired by U.S. supermarkets in his use of kanban cards. Describe how a supermarket dairy section fits in with use of kanbans in the Toyota Production System.

10.4 List conditions under which a cellular layout is most beneficial. Under what conditions is a functional layout to be preferred?

10.5 What are some mechanisms to implement a pull system in a multiproduct plant? What are the pros and cons of each mechanism?

10.6 What are some advantages of heijunka, or level production? Why are short changeover times essential if heijunka is to succeed?

10.7 At each stage of a supply chain, why do forecasts based on orders received lead to the bullwhip effect, especially if lead times are long? What countermeasures can improve the situation?

10.8 Why do price promotions exacerbate the bullwhip effect? What countermeasures can improve the situation?

10.9 What actions can a firm like Wal-Mart take to help diminish the bullwhip effect on its supply chain?

10.10 What actions can a firm like P&G take to help diminish the bullwhip effect in its supply chain?

SELECTED BIBLIOGRAPHY

Camp, R. 1995. *Business Process Benchmarking.* Milwaukee: ASQ Quality Press.

Chopra, S., and P. Meindl. 2004. *Supply Chain Management: Strategy, Planning, and Operation.* Upper Saddle River, N.J.: Prentice Hall.

Doig, S. J., A. Howard, and R. C. Ritter. 2003. "The Hidden Value in Airline Operations." *McKinsey Quarterly,* no. 4, 105–15.

Gualandi, G., R. Hatfield, J. King, H. Leuschner, P. Ridgewell, and G. Shao. 2003. "Nokia Feels the Squeeze from Shortage." *Off the Record Research: Sound Byte,* November 13.

Hammer, M., and J. Champy. 1993. *Reengineering the Corporation: A Manifesto for Business Revolution.* New York: Harper Press.

Imai, M. 1986. *Kaizen: The Key to Japan's Competitive Success.* New York: Random House.

Lee, H. L., V. Padmanabhan, and S. Whang. 1997. "Information Distortion in a Supply Chain: The Bullwhip Effect." *Management Science* 43: 546–58.

Mishina, Kazuhiro. 1992. *Toyota Motor Manufacturing, U.S.A., Inc.* Harvard Business School Case Study 1-693-019. Boston, MA: Harvard Business School Publishing, 1–23.

Ohno, T. 1988. *Toyota Production System: Beyond Large-Scale Production.* Cambridge, Mass.: Productivity Press.

Pollack, A. 1999. "Aerospace Gets Japan's Message: Without Military Largess, Industry Takes the Lean Path." *New York Times,* March 9.

Schoenberger, R. 1982. *Japanese Manufacturing Techniques: Nine Hidden Lessons in Simplicity.* New York: Free Press.

Spear, Steven, and H. Kent Bowen. 1999. "Decoding the DNA of the Toyota Production System." *Harvard Business Review,* September–October, 96-106.

Swank, C. K. 2003. "The Lean Service Machine." *Harvard Business Review,* October, 1–8.

Wilson, A. 2000. "Blue Macaw: GM's Factory of the Future." *Automotive News International,* September 1.

Womack, J. P., D. Jones, and D. Roos. 1990. *The Machine That Changed the World: The Story of Lean Production.* New York: Macmillan.

Wysocki, B., Jr. 2004. "To Fix Healthcare, Hospitals Take Tips from Factory Floor." *Wall Street Journal,* April 9.

Zipkin, P. 1991. "Does Manufacturing Need a JIT Revolution?" *Harvard Business Review,* January–February, 40–50.

⠿⠿⠿⠿⠿ MBPF Checklist ⠿⠿⠿⠿⠿

Here we provide a summary of key points from the book. This appendix is meant to serve as a checklist for managing business process flows.

Process Flow Measures

- **Key concepts:** Flow time (T), inventory (I), throughput (R), process cost (c)
- **Key relation:** Inventory = Throughput × Flow time: $I = R \times T$
- **Key management activity:** Select process flow measures to manage for improvement
- **Key metric:** Net present value, return on total assets

Because the three operational measures (flow time, inventory, and throughput) are interrelated, defining targets on any two of them defines a target for the third. The basic managerial levers for process improvement are the following:

1. Increase in throughput (decrease in flow time)
2. Decrease in inventory (decrease in flow time)
3. Decrease in process cost

Levers for Managing Theoretical Flow Time

- **Key concepts:** Critical path, critical activity, theoretical flow time
- **Key management activity:** Identify and manage activities on all critical paths
- **Key metric:** Length of critical paths

Because the theoretical flow time of a process is determined by the total work content of its critical path(s), the only way to decrease it is by shortening the length of *every* critical path. The basic approaches to decreasing the work content of a critical path are the following:

1. **Eliminate:** Reduce the work content of an activity on the critical path:
   - Eliminate non-value-adding aspects of the activity ("work smarter")

- Increase the speed at which the activity is done ("work faster"):
     - Acquire faster equipment
     - Increase incentives to work faster
   - Reduce the number of repeat activities ("do it right the first time")
2. **Work in parallel:** Move some of the work content off the critical path:
   - Move work from a critical path to a noncritical path (i.e., perform work in parallel rather than in sequence)
   - Move work from a critical path to the "outer loop" (pre- or postprocessing)
3. **Select:** Modify the product mix:
   - Change the product mix to produce products with smaller work content with respect to the specified activity

Levers for Managing Throughput

- **Key concepts:** Throughput, capacity (theoretical and effective), bottleneck resource
- **Key management activity:** Identify and manage bottleneck resource(s)
- **Key metric:** Contribution margin per unit time on bottleneck(s)

To increase the *throughput* of a process:

1. Decrease *resource idleness*:
   - Synchronize flows within the process to reduce starvation
   - Set appropriate size of buffers to reduce blockage
2. Increase the *net availability* of resources to increase effective capacity:
   - Improve maintenance policies, perform preventive maintenance outside periods of scheduled availability, and institute effective problem-solving measures that reduce frequency and duration of breakdowns
   - Institute motivational programs and incentives to reduce absenteeism, increase employee morale

3. Reduce *setup waste*:

- Reduce the frequency of setups
- Reduce the time required for a single setup

4. Increase the *theoretical capacity*:

- Decrease unit load on the bottleneck resource pool:

    Work faster, work smarter, do it right the first time, change produce mix
    Subcontract or outsource
    Invest in flexible resources

- Increase the load batch of a resources in the bottleneck resource pool (increase scale of resource)
- Increase the number of units in the bottleneck resource pool (increase scale of process)
- Increase the scheduled availability of the bottleneck resource pool (work longer)
- Modify the product mix

Levers for Reducing Waiting Time

- **Key concepts:** Waiting time, buffer, variability, flow-time efficiency, cycle inventory, safety inventory, safety capacity
- **Key management activity:** Manage buffers to reduce waiting time
- **Key metric:** Waiting time in buffers

Buffers build up primarily because of batching or variability. The basic approaches to reducing waiting time can be summarized as follows:

1. Reduce *cycle inventory* (reduce batch size):

- Reduce setup or order cost per batch
- Reduce forward buying

2. Reduce *safety inventory*:

- Reduce demand variability through improved forecasting
- Reduce the replenishment lead time
- Reduce the variability in replenishment lead time
- Pool safety inventory for multiple locations or products through either physical/virtual centralization or specialization or some combination thereof
- Exploit product substitution
- Use common components
- Postpone the product differentiation closer to the point of demand

3. Manage *safety capacity*:

- Increase safety capacity
- Decrease variability in arrivals and service
- Pool available safety capacity

4. Synchronize flows:

- Manage capacity to synchronize with demand
- Manage demand to synchronize with available capacity
- Synchronize flows within the process

5. Manage the psychological perceptions of the customers to *reduce the cost of waiting*

Levers for Controlling Process Variability

- **Key concepts:** Normal and abnormal variability, process capability, robust design
- **Key management activity:** Monitor and adjust process performance dynamically over time, reduce variability and its effects
- **Key metrics:** Quality, cost, time, inventory

1. Measure, prioritize, and analyze variability in key performance measures over time

2. Feedback control to limit abnormal variability:

- Set control limits of acceptable variability in key performance measures
- Monitor actual performance and correct any abnormal variability

3. Decrease normal process variability:

- Design for processing (simplify, standardize, and mistake-proof)

4. Immunize product performance to process variability through robust design

Levers for Managing Flows in Processing Networks

- **Key concepts:** Waste, non-value-adding activities, product (cellular) layout, demand pull, quality at source, employee involvement, supplier partnership, bullwhip effect, information flows, incentives, level production, river analogy, continuous improvement, reengineering
- **Key management activity:** Synchronize process flows while maintaining efficiency, set up a framework for process improvement
- **Key metric:** Cost, quality, time, flexibility

1. Managing flows in a plant:

- Process structure: Cellular layout
- Information and material flow: Demand pull system

- Level production: Batch size reduction
- Quality at source: Defect prevention, visibility, and decentralized control
- Supplier management: Partnership with information sharing and aligned incentives
- Supply consistency: Maintenance of safety capacity
- Human resource management: Employee involvement

2. Managing flows in a supply chain:

- Reduce information and material flow times through technology and efficient logistics

- Reduce fixed costs of ordering and quantity discounts
- Share information on customer demand and product availability
- Coordinate forecasts between various parties
- Stabilize prices

3. Improving processes:

- Frameworks: Continuous improvement and reengineering
- Tools: Increased visibility, incentives, improvement engine (PDCA cycle), and benchmarking

Appendix II

▪▪▪▪▪▪▪▪ Background Material in ▪▪▪▪▪▪▪▪ Probability and Statistics

This appendix summarizes basic material in probability and statistics used in the text.

Random Variables, Mean, Variance, and Covariance

Random Variable

A random variable (r.v.) is a numerical outcome whose value depends on chance.

- We denote random variables with **BOLDFACE UPPERCASE LETTERS**.
- We denote the realized values of random variables with *lowercase italicized letters*.

For example, let us say that we are trying to forecast demand for sweaters during the next month. We use **X** to represent the uncertain demand which is anywhere between 0 and 1,000 units; that is, **X** is a number in the interval [0, 1,000]. At the end of next month, we discover that the actual demand was 734 units, or $x = 734$.

Density and Distribution Functions of a Random Variable. The expression $\{\mathbf{X} \le x\}$ is the *event* that the random variable **X** assumes a value less than or equal to the real number x. This event may or may not occur, depending on the outcome of the experiment or phenomenon that determines the value of the random variable **X**. The *probability* that the event occurs is denoted as $\Pr\{\mathbf{X} \le x\}$. Allowing x to vary, this probability defines a function:

$$F(x) = \Pr\{\mathbf{X} \le x\}, \qquad -\infty < x < \infty$$

which is called the *distribution function* of the random variable **X**. Sometimes, F is also called the *cumulative distribution function*. (We may write $F_{\mathbf{X}}(x)$ to highlight the correspondence between the random variable and its distribution function.) The distribution function contains all the information available about a random variable before its value is determined or realized by experiment.

A random variable **X** is called *discrete* if it can assume only a finite or denumerable set of distinct values $x_1, x_2, \ldots$, such that $p_i = \Pr\{\mathbf{X} = x_i\}$ for $i = 1, 2, \ldots$, and $\Sigma_i\, p_i = 1$. The function

$$f(x_i) = \Pr\{\mathbf{X} = x_i\} = p_i, \quad \text{for } i = 1, 2, \ldots$$

is called the *probability mass function* of the random variable **X**. It is related to the distribution function via

$$F(x) = \sum_{x_i \le x} f(x_i)$$

A random variable **X** is called *continuous* if $\Pr\{\mathbf{X} = x\} = 0$ for every value of x. Then its distribution function is a continuous function of x. Often there exists a *probability density function $f(x)$* such that

$$F(x) = \int_{-\infty}^{x} f(u)\,du$$

Mean

The mean, average, or "expected value" of a random variable **X** is

$$E(\mathbf{X}) = \begin{cases} \sum_i x_i f(x_i) & \text{if } \mathbf{X} \text{ is a discrete r.v.} \\[2mm] \int_{-\infty}^{\infty} u f(u)\,du & \text{if } \mathbf{X} \text{ is a continuous r.v.} \end{cases}$$

We also will denote the average of **X** by the *italicized* font X or by $\mu_{\mathbf{X}}$.

Variance

The variance of a random variable **X** measures the average squared deviation of **X** from its mean $\mu_{\mathbf{X}}$ and is denoted by

$$V(\mathbf{X}) = E((\mathbf{X} - \mu_{\mathbf{X}})^2)$$

316

Standard Deviation. The standard deviation of a random variable $\mathbf{X}$ is the square root of its variance and is denoted by

$$\sigma_{\mathbf{X}} = \sqrt{V(\mathbf{X})} = \sqrt{E((\mathbf{X} - \mu_{\mathbf{X}})^2)}$$

Coefficient of Variation. The coefficient of variation of a random variable $\mathbf{X}$ is the ratio of its standard deviation to its mean and is denoted by

$$C_{\mathbf{X}} = \frac{\sigma_{\mathbf{X}}}{\mu_{\mathbf{X}}}$$

The variance, standard deviation, and the coefficient of variation are all measures of the amount of uncertainty or variability in $\mathbf{X}$. With these basic definitions, we can now consider some concepts and results that involve multiple random variables.

Independence of Random Variables. Two random variables $\mathbf{X}_1$ and $\mathbf{X}_2$ are said to be independent if and only if knowledge about the value of $\mathbf{X}_1$ does not change the probability of any event involving $\mathbf{X}_2$. Formally, two random variables $\mathbf{X}_1$ and $\mathbf{X}_2$ are *independent if and only if for any two events A and B,*

$$\Pr(\mathbf{X}_1 \in A \text{ and } \mathbf{X}_2 \in B) = \Pr(\mathbf{X}_1 \in A)\,\Pr(\mathbf{X}_2 \in B)$$

If this relationship is not satisfied, then $\mathbf{X}_1$ and $\mathbf{X}_2$ are said to be dependent.

It then follows that if $\mathbf{X}_1$ and $\mathbf{X}_2$ are independent, then

$$E(\mathbf{X}_1\mathbf{X}_2) = E(\mathbf{X}_1)E(\mathbf{X}_2)$$

Covariance and Coefficient of Correlation

Let $\mathbf{X}_1$ and $\mathbf{X}_2$ be two random variables with means μ_1 and μ_2 and standard deviations σ_1 and σ_2, respectively. The *covariance* of $\mathbf{X}_1$ and $\mathbf{X}_2$ is defined to be the expected value of $(\mathbf{X}_1 - \mu_1)(\mathbf{X}_2 - \mu_2)$ and is denoted by

$$Cov(\mathbf{X}_1, \mathbf{X}_2) = E[(\mathbf{X}_1 - \mu_1)(\mathbf{X}_2 - \mu_2)]$$

The *coefficient of correlation* is defined as

$$\rho = \frac{Cov(\mathbf{X}_1, \mathbf{X}_2)}{\sigma_1 \sigma_2}$$

The value of the correlation coefficient always lies between -1 and $+1$. A positive covariance or correlation coefficient implies that if $\mathbf{X}_1$ increases, then, on average, so does $\mathbf{X}_2$. Alternately, a negative covariance or correlation coefficient implies that if $\mathbf{X}_1$ increases, then $\mathbf{X}_2$ decreases, on average. If $\mathbf{X}_1$ and $\mathbf{X}_2$ are independent, then

$$Cov(\mathbf{X}_1, \mathbf{X}_2) = 0$$

Sums of Random Variables. Consider two random variables $\mathbf{X}_1$ and $\mathbf{X}_2$. Then

$$E(\mathbf{X}_1 + \mathbf{X}_2) = E(\mathbf{X}_1) + E(\mathbf{X}_2)$$
$$V(\mathbf{X}_1 + \mathbf{X}_2) = V(\mathbf{X}_1) + V(\mathbf{X}_2) + 2Cov(\mathbf{X}_1, \mathbf{X}_2)$$

Recall that if $\mathbf{X}_1$ and $\mathbf{X}_2$ are independent, then $Cov(\mathbf{X}_1, \mathbf{X}_2) = 0$. It then follows that *the expected value and variance of sums of independent random variables is equal to the sum of their expectations and variances, respectively.*

Also, if $\mathbf{X}_1$ and $\mathbf{X}_2$ have identical distributions (and thus identical means and standard deviations) but are correlated with a correlation coefficient ρ, then the standard deviation of the sum $\mathbf{X}_1 + \mathbf{X}_2$ is

$$\sigma_{\mathbf{X}_1 + \mathbf{X}_2} = \sqrt{2(1 + \rho)}\,\sigma$$

where σ is the standard deviation of $\mathbf{X}_1$ and $\mathbf{X}_2$.

Some Probability Distributions
The Poisson Probability Distribution

Consider a sequence of random events occurring in time. Suppose that these events occur at an average rate of R events per unit of time. Let $\mathbf{N}(t)$ be the discrete random variable representing the number of events that occur in a time interval of duration t. We say that $\mathbf{N}(t)$ follows a *Poisson distribution* if

$$\Pr(\mathbf{N}(t) = n) = e^{-Rt}\frac{(Rt)^n}{n!}$$

The mean number of events in time period t is given by $E(\mathbf{N}(t)) = Rt$, and the standard deviation of the number of events in time period t is also given by Rt. Thus, the coefficient of variation of a Poisson random variable is equal to 1. The Poisson probability mass function and cumulative distributions can also be evaluated in Excel with the "Poisson" function as follows:

$$f_{\mathbf{N}(t)}(n) = \Pr(\mathbf{N}(t) = n) = \text{Poisson}(n, Rt, 0)$$

$$F_{\mathbf{N}(t)}(n) = \sum_{0 \le i \le n} \Pr(\mathbf{N}(t) = i) = \text{Poisson}(n, Rt, 1)$$

The Exponential Probability Distribution

Consider a sequence of random events occurring in time. Let **T** be the continuous random variable representing the time elapsed between two consecutive events. If the mean elapsed time between two consecutive events is given by m, then the probability density function of **T**, denoted by $f(t)$, is said to be exponentially distributed if

$$f(t) = \frac{1}{m} e^{-t/m}$$

The standard deviation of the elapsed time between consecutive events is also m. Therefore, the coefficient of variation of an exponential random variable is equal to 1.

The exponential probability density function and cumulative distributions can also be evaluated in Excel with the "Expondist" function as follows:

$$f(t) = \text{Expondist}(t, 1/m, 0)$$
$$F(t) = \text{Expondist}(t, 1/m, 1)$$

From this, one may guess that there should be a relationship between the Poisson and the exponential distributions. In fact, if the distribution of the number of events in a time interval is Poisson, then the times between consecutive events are independent and exponentially distributed and vice versa.

The Normal Probability Distribution

A continuous random variable **X** has a normal distribution if for some μ and $\sigma > 0$, its probability density function is given by

$$f_{\mathbf{X}}(x) = \frac{1}{\sigma\sqrt{2\pi}} \exp\left[-\frac{(x-\mu)^2}{2\sigma^2} \right]$$

The mean of the normally distributed random variable **X** is μ and its variance is σ^2. Such a random variable is often denoted as $N(\mu, \sigma^2)$. Two important properties of the normal distribution are the following:

- It is symmetric around its mean.
- A sum of a fixed number of normally distributed random variables is also normally distributed.

In applications, one is often interested in computing the probability, say p, that a normal random variable $\mathbf{X} = N(\mu, \sigma^2)$ is smaller than a given quantity x or vice versa. we now discuss two techniques for doing this: one is a direct numeric technique using the spreadsheet software Excel, while the other uses an analytic technique, called standardization.

To find a probability p that $\mathbf{X} = N(\mu, \sigma^2)$ is smaller than a given quantity x:

1. Using the Excel function Normdist:

$$p = \text{Normdist}(x, \mu, \sigma, 1)$$

2. Using "standardization": Transform the random variable **X** and the number x into a new random variable **Z** and number z as

$$\mathbf{Z} = \frac{\mathbf{X} - \mu}{\sigma} \quad \text{and} \quad z = \frac{x - \mu}{\sigma}$$

Then **Z** is also normally distributed but has a mean equal to 0 and a standard deviation equal to 1: $\mathbf{Z} = N(0, 1)$. Such a random variable is called a *standard normal* random variable, and clearly

$$p = \Pr\{\mathbf{X} \leq x\} = \Pr(\mathbf{Z} \leq z)$$

as shown in Figure A2.1.

FIGURE A2.1 A Graphic Representation of the Probability *p* (Shaded Area) That a Standard Normal Random Variable Z Is Less Than or Equal to a Number *z*

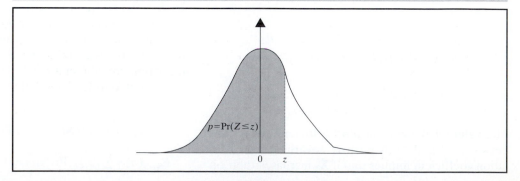

TABLE A2.1 The Cumulative Standard Normal Distribution

z	0.00	0.01	0.02	0.03	0.04	0.05	0.06	0.07	0.08	0.09
0.0	0.5000	0.5040	0.5080	0.5120	0.5160	0.5199	0.5239	0.5279	0.5319	0.5359
0.1	0.5398	0.5438	0.5478	0.5517	0.5557	0.5596	0.5636	0.5675	0.5714	0.5753
0.2	0.5793	0.5832	0.5871	0.5910	0.5948	0.5987	0.6026	0.6064	0.6103	0.6141
0.3	0.6179	0.6217	0.6255	0.6293	0.6331	0.6368	0.6406	0.6443	0.6480	0.6517
0.4	0.6554	0.6591	0.6628	0.6664	0.6700	0.6736	0.6772	0.6808	0.6844	0.6879
0.5	0.6915	0.6950	0.6985	0.7019	0.7054	0.7088	0.7123	0.7157	0.7190	0.7224
0.6	0.7257	0.7291	0.7324	0.7357	0.7389	0.7422	0.7454	0.7486	0.7517	0.7549
0.7	0.7580	0.7611	0.7642	0.7673	0.7704	0.7734	0.7764	0.7794	0.7823	0.7852
0.8	0.7881	0.7910	0.7939	0.7967	0.7995	0.8023	0.8051	0.8078	0.8106	0.8133
0.9	0.8159	0.8186	0.8212	0.8238	0.8264	0.8289	0.8315	0.8340	0.8365	0.8389
1.0	0.8413	0.8438	0.8461	0.8485	0.8508	0.8531	0.8554	0.8577	0.8599	0.8621
1.1	0.8643	0.8665	0.8686	0.8708	0.8729	0.8749	0.8770	0.8790	0.8810	0.8830
1.2	0.8849	0.8869	0.8888	0.8907	0.8925	0.8944	0.8962	0.8980	0.8997	0.9015
1.3	0.9032	0.9049	0.9066	0.9082	0.9099	0.9115	0.9131	0.9147	0.9162	0.9177
1.4	0.9192	0.9207	0.9222	0.9236	0.9251	0.9265	0.9279	0.9292	0.9306	0.9319
1.5	0.9332	0.9345	0.9357	0.9370	0.9382	0.9394	0.9406	0.9418	0.9429	0.9441
1.6	0.9452	0.9463	0.9474	0.9484	0.9495	0.9505	0.9515	0.9525	0.9535	0.9545
1.7	0.9554	0.9564	0.9573	0.9582	0.9591	0.9599	0.9608	0.9616	0.9625	0.9633
1.8	0.9641	0.9649	0.9656	0.9664	0.9671	0.9678	0.9686	0.9693	0.9699	0.9706
1.9	0.9713	0.9719	0.9726	0.9732	0.9738	0.9744	0.9750	0.9756	0.9761	0.9767
2.0	0.9772	0.9778	0.9783	0.9788	0.9793	0.9798	0.9803	0.9808	0.9812	0.9817
2.1	0.9821	0.9826	0.9830	0.9834	0.9838	0.9842	0.9846	0.9850	0.9854	0.9857
2.2	0.9861	0.9864	0.9868	0.9871	0.9875	0.9878	0.9881	0.9884	0.9887	0.9890
2.3	0.9893	0.9896	0.9898	0.9901	0.9904	0.9906	0.9909	0.9911	0.9913	0.9916
2.4	0.9918	0.9920	0.9922	0.9925	0.9927	0.9929	0.9931	0.9932	0.9934	0.9936
2.5	0.9938	0.9940	0.9941	0.9943	0.9945	0.9946	0.9948	0.9949	0.9951	0.9952
2.6	0.9953	0.9955	0.9956	0.9957	0.9959	0.9960	0.9961	0.9962	0.9963	0.9964
2.7	0.9965	0.9966	0.9967	0.9968	0.9969	0.9970	0.9971	0.9972	0.9973	0.9974
2.8	0.9974	0.9975	0.9976	0.9977	0.9977	0.9978	0.9979	0.9979	0.9980	0.9981
2.9	0.9981	0.9982	0.9982	0.9983	0.9984	0.9984	0.9985	0.9985	0.9986	0.9986
3.0	0.9987	0.9987	0.9987	0.9988	0.9988	0.9989	0.9989	0.9989	0.9990	0.9990
3.1	0.9990	0.9991	0.9991	0.9991	0.9992	0.9992	0.9992	0.9992	0.9993	0.9993
3.2	0.9993	0.9993	0.9994	0.9994	0.9994	0.9994	0.9994	0.9995	0.9995	0.9995
3.3	0.9995	0.9995	0.9995	0.9996	0.9996	0.9996	0.9996	0.9996	0.9996	0.9997

This table represents the cumulative distribution function of a standard normal random variable. That is, it gives the probability p that the standard normal random variable $N(0,1)$ is less than a quantity z. For example, if $z = 1.65$, then $p = 0.9505$.

For any given z, the corresponding value of p can be read from Table A2.1 or can be computed with Excel. (For negative values of z, notice that $\Pr(Z \le z) = 1 - \Pr(Z \le -z)$.)

To find a quantity x such that $p = \Pr(X = N(\mu, \sigma^2) \le x)$ for a given probability p:

1. Using the Excel function Norminv:

$$x = \text{Norminv}(x, \mu, \sigma)$$

2. Using "standardization": Transform the random variable X and the number x into their "standard" counterparts Z and z as described previously. Then read z from Table A2.1 such that $\Pr(Z \le z) = p$ and find the quantity x by transforming back:

$$x = \mu + z\sigma$$

▮▮▮▮▮▮▮ iGrafx® FlowCharter™ ▮▮▮▮▮▮▮
Quick Reference Guide

User Interface

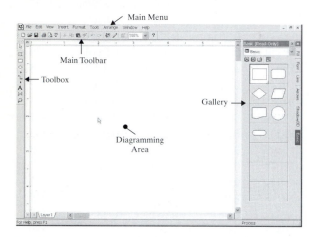

Toolbars

1. Main Toolbar

A B C D E F   G H   I

2. Toolbox

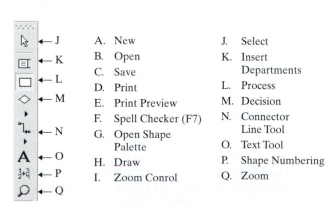

←J	A. New	J.	Select
←K	B. Open	K.	Insert Departments
←L	C. Save		
←M	D. Print	L.	Process
	E. Print Preview	M.	Decision
	F. Spell Checker (F7)	N.	Connector Line Tool
←N	G. Open Shape Palette		
←O	H. Draw	O.	Text Tool
←P	I. Zoom Conrol	P.	Shape Numbering
←Q		Q.	Zoom

How to Create a New Basic Diagram

1. Open iGrafx FlowCharter.

2. Click New Document.

3. From the drop-down list, select Basic Diagram.

How to Select the Desired Shape

1. Left-mouse click shape buttons (L or M) to select from the Toolbox, or

2. Left-mouse click a shape to select from the Gallery, or

3. Left-mouse click on the page, outside a shape, to quickly re-select the last shape used, or

4. Double left click, as in #1 above, to "permanently" select a shape for quick multiple placements.

How to Place and Auto-Connect Shapes

1. Left-mouse click on the Process button (J) on the Toolbox.

Note the cursor now displays ✎ as an indicator of being in SHAPE PLACEMENT MODE.

2. Move the cursor over the diagramming area.

3. Left-mouse click to add a process shape.

Note the cursor now displays I as an indicator of being in TEXT ENTRY MODE.

4. Type desired text in shape.

5. Left-mouse click outside the shape to deselect it. YOU ARE STILL IN SHAPE PLACEMENT MODE AND HAVE SELECTED THE LAST

SHAPE USED ✎ .

6. Place cursor over the middle of the previously placed Process shape.

Note the cursor now displays ✎ as an indicator of being in AUTO SHAPE CONNECT MODE.

7. Left-mouse down and drag to the right. Release the left-mouse button to place the shape.

8. Repeat steps 4–7 to place additional shapes.

How to Exit Shape Placement Mode

1. Press ESC or left-mouse click another button, or
2. If you have left-mouse double clicked a shape button (L or M) you must left-mouse click FINISHED on the small open window.

How to Add a Shape between Lines

1. Left-mouse click on the desired shape—decision shape shown (M).
2. Left-mouse click on top of the connector.
3. Type desired text in new shape.

Note that by default the "No" output is assigned to the resulting connector.

How to Delete Shapes

1. Left-mouse click to select the desired shape.
2. Press Delete.

How to Place a Decision Shape and Outputs

1. Left-mouse click the Process button (J).
2. Place the cursor over the middle of the decision shape.
3. Left-mouse down and drag the cursor straight down. *DO NOT RELEASE LEFT-MOUSE BUTTON.*
4. Press the SPACE BAR to alternate through the OUTPUT text on the resulting connector.

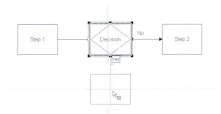

How to Change Outputs on an Existing Decision Shape

1. Right-mouse click on the "Yes" from the decision shape.
2. Select either "No" / "Yes" / "No label."

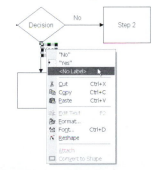

How to Change the Output Text on a Decision Shape

1. Left-mouse double click the decision shape.
2. Left-mouse click the Output tab.
3. Left-mouse click the Output text field and enter new text.
4. Left-mouse click OK.

— Note you can have more than 2 outputs by entering a new "#Cases" value.

How to Add Text to Shapes

1. Select the shape into which you would like to input text.
2. Start typing.
3. Note that there is no need to switch to a writing tool due to iGrafx auto-sensing features.

How to Add Shape Numbers

1. Left-mouse click the Shape Numbering button (P).
2. Choose Show all shape numbers.

Note that iGrafx places the shape numbers according to the order in which the shapes were created.

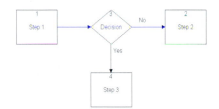

How to Renumber Shapes

1. Left-mouse click the Shape Numbering button (P).
2. Select Manual Renumber.
3. From the Renumber window, choose 1.
4. Click on the individual shapes to renumber the shapes as desired.
5. Click Finished.

Note that with Auto Renumber you can renumber the shapes by flow, left to right, or across departments, and by a defined start number.

How to Attach a Note to a Shape

1. Select the shape.
2. Click F6 or alternatively choose View → Note.
3. Start typing on the note space provided.

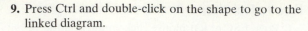

Note an "-N" will be shown on the shape as a visual indicator that a note is present.

How to Add Links to Other Diagrams or Documents

1. Select the shape.
2. Choose Insert → Link.
3. Under Link to, click on File or Web Page (or Diagrams).
4. Enter the file location or browse to find your file or webpage.
5. Click Open.
6. Place your mouse in the Key Modifiers text box.
7. Press Ctrl (or other key).
8. Click OK.

9. Press Ctrl and double-click on the shape to go to the linked diagram.

Note a SHADOW is associated with the shape as a VISUAL indicator of the link.

How to Use Zoom Control to View a Document

1. Left-mouse click the Zoom Control (i) drop-down arrow and select Best Fit.
2. To view the diagram Full Screen, choose View → Full Screen.
3. Press Esc to exit.

Using the Help Content

1. Choose Help → iGrafx Help (maximize window if necessary).

iGrafx® Process Simulation
Quick Reference Guide

Five-Step Process to Simulation Analysis

The basic methodology for analyzing a process with simulation includes these five basic steps:

1. *Identify goals,* objectives, and scope for the project. *This is the most important step*.
2. *Gather data* on the existing process through interviews and measurements.
3. *Build a model* of the current process, which, when simulated, approximates the process performance.
4. *Perform simulation "What-if?" analysis* by making changes to the model and running simulations.
5. *Present your results* and recommendations for potential changes to the current process.

These five basic steps are shown in Diagram A4.1.

The purpose of this document is to provide a guideline for using iGrafx Process or Process for Six Sigma to build and simulate a process model (step 3). It is not an exhaustive review of features but rather a general guideline for getting a process model built and simulating quickly.

Step 3: Build a Process Model

Using iGrafx Process to build a process model involves four basic activities, shown in Diagram A4.2.

1. *Create the process diagram* by using departments, shapes, and connection lines.
2. *Describe the behavior of each activity* (such as time duration) through the Properties dialog box.
3. *Describe the simulation environment* the process lives in by using the Scenario.
4. *Execute a simulation* and analyze the results in the Report.

Create a Process Diagram (Map or Flowchart)

The Process Diagram type supports all the features and functionality discussed in this guide. When the tool presents the welcome guide, choose the New Document button, and then choose Process.

⌕ Selector cursor: Click the left mouse button to select an object.

✎ Placement cursor: Click the left mouse button to place a shape/symbol.

▤ Insert/Add Department

- Choose the "Insert Department" icon in the Toolbox toolbar (the vertical toolbar on the left side of the window), which opens the Insert Departments dialog box.

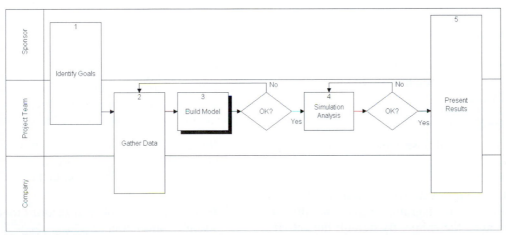

DIAGRAM A4.1

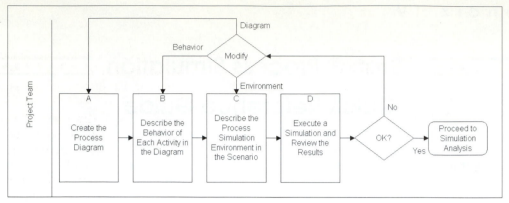

DIAGRAM A4.2

- Choose the Add button, which opens the Insert Department dialog box.
- Enter a name for the department, and choose OK.

Add a Shape/Symbol

- Click on a Shape icon in the Toolbox toolbar.
- Move the cursor into the process window. The cursor changes to the placement cursor (a pencil and shape).
- Press, drag, and release the left mouse button to place the shape on the diagram.
- To enter text, simply type. The text will be placed in the shape automatically.

Connect Shapes/Symbols

- Move the Selector tool's *arrow cursor* (or connector line tool's line cursor) inside the source, or origin, shape.
- Press and hold the left mouse button.
- Drag the cursor to the destination shape. The cursor automatically changes to the line cursor (pencil and line).
- Position the cursor just inside the destination shape, and release the mouse. The line is automatically routed.

A Text Tool

- Select the shape, if it isn't already selected. Type the text.

Display Shape/Activity Numbers When a shape is placed on the diagram, a number is automatically assigned to the shape. By default the activity numbers are not displayed. To display activity numbers on the shapes,

- Choose Show All Shape Numbers on the Shape Numbering button in the Toolbox toolbar.

To automatically renumber the shapes,

- Choose Auto Renumber on the Shape Numbering button in the Toolbox toolbar and choose OK.

Describe the Behavior of Each Shape/Activity

Most shapes represent activities, and will contain behavioral information. As a general rule, during simulation a transaction enters the activity and visits each tab starting on the left (Inputs) and proceeding to the right (Summary). The most commonly used tabs are Inputs, Resources, Task, and Outputs.

Display the Properties Dialog Box

- Double-click the left mouse button on a shape, or click the right mouse button and choose Properties.

Inputs **Inputs Tab** The Inputs tab allows for the collection of transactions (see Diagram A4.3). The default is no collection or None. The most common forms of collection are used in modeling:

Batch: Collect multiple transactions in a basket and carry them through the process. The Outputs tab contains a command to Unbatch the transactions.

Join: Merge multiple transactions together into a single transaction.

DIAGRAM A4.3   **DIAGRAM A4.4**

Gate: Hold transactions at the gate until a condition is met and the gate is opened.

Start Point   Specifies an entry point for transactions. The transactions may arrive at the process from a Generator (see Section C, the Scenario) or a higher-level process. To specify a Start Point, place a check in the start point box (see Diagram A4.3) and then choose a start point name in the scroll-down menu or type a new name.

Resources   **Resources Tab**   The Resources tab identifies the resources required to do work in the activity (see Diagram A4.4). iGrafx has a built-in resource named *Worker*. The Worker resource belongs to each department. When a department is added to the Process diagram, a worker is automatically created and allocated to the department. Creating other Labor or Equipment (non-worker) resources is done in the Scenario; see Section C.

There are many options that may be specified for a resource; however, these three are the most important:

- Choose the resource by name using the scroll-down menu (default Worker).
- Specify how the resource is used. Usually the resource works for the activity, which is the default.
- Specify the number of resources required to work on *each* transaction processed. The default is 1.

To specify that more than one type of resource is required for an activity, choose the Add button in the Resource tab. To remove a specified resource from participating in an activity, choose the Remove button.

Attributes   **Attributes Tab**   The Attributes tab allows the user access to Transaction (local) and Scenario (global) location attributes. For details on building expressions, search the software Help system using the key word "duration expressions."

Task   **Task Tab**   The Task tab defines the type of task represented by the activity (see Diagram A4.5). It is used on most activities.

Types of Tasks.   There are three types of tasks:

Work: This task will use a resource to work on a transaction for the duration of the Task.

Delay: This task blocks the transaction for the duration of the Task. Delay Tasks do not usually use a resource.

Process: This task is linked to a sub-process. During simulation, the transaction will move from this activity to a start activity on another diagram (sub-process). The transaction returns to this activity when it completes the sub-process. To create a sub-process,

- Choose Process from the drop-down menu for task type.
- Click on the New Process button.
- Enter a name for the process, and choose OK.

To view a sub-process, hold down the Shift key and double-click.

Duration.   If the activity is Work or Delay, then task will have duration; default is zero (0). The duration may be

Constant: The same (constant) duration value for all transactions.

Distributed: The duration value will vary between two values. The distributed duration may be uniformly or normally distributed between the two numbers.

- Uniform specifies every number between the two numbers has an equal probability of being used.
- Normal specifies a normal (bell curve) distribution, which is centered between the two numbers.

Expression.   Equations may be defined to describe the duration of the activity. For details on

DIAGRAM A4.5   **DIAGRAM A4.6**

building expressions, search the software Help system using the key word "duration expressions."

Activity Value. This is an opportunity to classify the activity. You are free to define these classifications as you desire:

VA: Value added

NVA: No value added

BVA: Business value added

Outputs Tab The Outputs tab describes how transactions leave the activity (see Diagram A4.6). A transaction will follow directed connection line(s) to the Inputs of the next activity. Typical outputs are as follows:

All: This sends the transaction down *all* paths that leave the activity. This is the default. If there is more than one path, then an implicit split occurs, creating *identical* transactions to be sent down each path.

Decision: This sends the transaction into one of the paths specified, based on percentages or expressions.

Split: This divides a transaction into multiple (count) *identical* transactions. The "All" still applies.

Unbatch: This undoes the "Batch" collection of transactions; each transaction is removed from the basket.

Describe the Process Environment in the Scenario

A Scenario describes the simulation environment for the process. A single file may contain multiple Scenarios. The first four topics in the Scenario (Run Setup, Generators, Resources, and Schedules/Calendars) are the most important in getting started.

View Scenario You may view information in the Scenario "at a glance" in the Scenario window. To open the Scenario window, choose the View Scenario button in the Modeling toolbar. Alternately, use the File menu and choose Components, and in the Components dialog, select the Scenario and click on the View button.

Run Setup The Run Setup topic sets simulation timing and how the results of simulation are placed in a report. Double-click on the Run Setup information in the Scenario to invoke the Run Setup Dialog (see Diagram A4.7). There are many options; the most important two are the following:

Simulation Time Tab

- **Simulation start:** Specify when the simulation starts (default Weekday).
- **Simulation end:** The default is Transactions Complete. Most often you'll want to specify a specific duration for simulation (Custom). To specify a custom end for simulation,

> Choose Custom from the Simulation End scroll-down menu.
>
> Choose a duration time unit (Hours, Days, Months, etc.).
>
> Enter a duration (simulation end) value.

Initialization/Reports Tab. Specify how the simulation results are to be saved to the report (default is Create).

Generators During simulation, generators insert transactions into the process. There are many options, and the most important is Generator Type; the generator type dictates other data to specify.

Completion: The Completion generator introduces transaction(s) into the process when the

DIAGRAM A4.7

DIAGRAM A4.8

DIAGRAM A4.9

DIAGRAM A4.10

previous transaction(s) has completed processing. It will place one or one group of transaction(s) at a time in the process until it reaches the Maximum count. The default is a Max of 1.

Demand: The Demand generator introduces a transaction whenever the named resource (e.g., Worker) is available or not acquired in the department that has the Start activity for this generator.

Interarrival: The Interarrival generator specifies the time or duration between transactions arriving in the process. There are many options; you may want to start with a simple Constant or Distributed interarrival time.

- **Constant:** The same (constant) time between transaction entering the process.
- **Distributed:** The time between transactions entering the process will vary between two values.
- **Expression:** The expression can use math functions, such as ExponDist() for exponential arrivals.

Timetable: The Timetable generator introduces transactions at intervals over a span of time. The table may be repeated. To modify the timetable generator, choose the Modify Timetable button; a bar chart is displayed. The X-axis shows the time intervals and the overall time span, and the Y-axis shows the number of transactions introduced each interval. The values of interest are the following:

- **Total span:** The total span of time covered by the timetable pattern given. For example, 1d (1 day) indicates that every day the given pattern should repeat.
- **Time resolution:** The smallest interval of time unit of time in the bar chart.

 Resources The Resources topic is where resources used by the process are created, modified, and managed. Double click the left mouse button on the Resources topic/data in the Scenario to obtain the Resources dialog box (see Diagram A4.9).

To add a resource, choose the Add button, which brings up the Add New Resource dialog box:

- Enter a name under Resource Name. You *cannot* use spaces in the name.
- Choose a Resource Type (Labor or Equipment). Don't use Other as a resource type; it has limited use.

To modify a resource, select the resource in Existing Resources list. If it is a Worker resource and multiple departments are defined, double-click on a department name to access the resource data:

- **Resource count:** Specify the number of that resource available to the process.
- **Schedule:** Specify the schedule the resources are on.
- **Resource cost:** Specify the hourly and/or overtime hourly rate and/or the per-use cost for the resource.

Schedules Schedules are spans of time. The time will be either active or inactive. There are several built-in schedules (see Diagram A4.10). The default schedule is the Standard schedule, which is Monday through Friday, 8 a.m. to 5 p.m., with 1 inactive hour for lunch. For details on creating and modifying schedules, search the software Help system using the key word "schedules."

Execute Simulation and Analyze Results in the Report

▶ or ◑▸ **Run a Simulation** To execute a simulation, from the Model menu, choose Run and then Start. You can "trace" simulation by first entering Trace mode, *and then* running simulation. The Control menu's Trace Colors command shows the colors' meanings. When simulation is complete, a Report is presented for review.

Report Structure. Four of the Report tabs (Time, Cost, Resource, and Queue) contain sets of commonly used statistics captured during simulation. The fifth tab (Custom) is blank; you may add a report element (table or graph) to the Custom tab by copying and pasting an existing report element or creating a new report element from the Report menu.

TABLE A4.1 Commonly Used Statistics Captured in the Report

Resource (Process Performance from the Resource's Perspective)	Transaction (Process Performance from the Transaction's Perspective)	Activity (Detailed Information about What Occurred at Each Shape/Activity)
Workers (count)	Cycle time (avg, tot.)	Cycle time (min, max, avg)
Resource utilization (util. %)	Service time (avg, tot.)	Service time (min, max, avg)
Resource cost (avg, tot.)	Service wait time (avg, tot.)	Service wait time (min, max, avg)
Elapsed time	Wait time (avg, tot.)	Wait time (min, max, avg)
	Blocked time (avg, tot.)	Blocked time (min, max, avg)
	Resource wait time (avg, tot.)	Resource wait time (min, max, avg)
	Work time (avg, tot.)	Work time (min, max, avg)
	Inactive time (avg, tot.)	Cost (VA, NVA, BVA)
	Completion count	Number of transactions

Report Results. Basic statistics are gathered about process times, costs, resources, and queues. You may also create your own custom statistics. The basic statistics are further categorized depending on whether they apply to transactions, resources, or activities (see Table A4.1).

Basic Time Statistics. There are four basic time statistics:

- **Blocked time:** The time accumulated waiting in collection (Inputs tab) and in delay (Task tab).
- **Resource wait time:** The time accumulated waiting to obtain a resource (Resources tab).
- **Work time:** The time accumulated doing work (Task tab Duration).
- **Inactive time:** The time accumulated waiting for a resource that is inactive or out of schedule.

Composite Time Statistics. The following statistics are constructed from the basic statistics:

- **Service wait time:** Blocked time + resource wait time
- **Service time:** Blocked time + resource wait time + work time
- **Cycle time:** Blocked time + resource wait time + work time + inactive time
- **Wait time:** Blocked time + resource wait time + inactive time

Add a New Report Element
- From the Report menu, choose Add Element.
- Follow the wizard to define the Statistic Category, Structure, Filter, and Format of the Report Element.

Turn a Tabular Report Element into a Graph
- Double-click on the Report Element to obtain the Edit Report Element dialog box.

- Choose the Format tab.
- Choose Graph in the Display As scroll-down menu.
- Choose the style of graph you wish to display, for example, a 2D bar chart.
- Choose OK.

Resource Utilization %	
ShipLineTech1	77.73
ShipLineTech2	96.86
ShipLineTech3	99.82

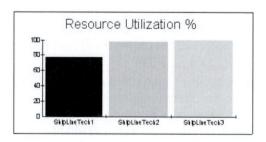

For more information on iGrafx, please use the following contact information:

iGrafx, a division of Corel Inc.
7585 SW Mohawk St.
Tualatin, OR 97062
Phone: (503) 404-6050
E-mail: info@igrafx.com
Web: www.igrafx.com

Glossary

80-20 Pareto principle A principle that states that roughly 20% of problem types account for 80% of all occurrences.

Abandonment A situation when a customer, having waited in queue for some time, leaves the process before being served.

Abnormal variability Unpredictable variability that disturbs the state of statistical equilibrium of the process by changing parameters of its distribution in an unexpected way.

Activity The simplest form of transformation; the building block of a process.

Activity time The time required by a typical flow unit to complete the activity once.

Aggregation, principle of A statistical principle that states that the standard deviation of the sum of random variables is less than the sum of the individual standard deviations.

American system of manufacturing The manufacturing system begun in 1810 that introduced the use of interchangeable parts, thereby eliminating the need to custom fit parts during assembly.

Andon Literally, andon means a display board. In the Toyota Production System, a worker is empowered to stop the line by pulling a cord. A display board identifies the station that pulled the cord, enabling the supervisor to locate it easily.

Availability loss factor Resource availability loss as a fraction of scheduled availability.

Average flow rate The average number of flow units that flow through (into and out of) the process per unit over time. Also called *throughput*.

Average flow time The average of the flow times across all flow units that exit the process during a specific span of time.

Backlogged The situation in which customers must wait to have their demand satisfied.

Batch The size of an order or production in response to the economies of scale.

Benchmarking The process of continually searching for the best methods, practices, and processes, and adopting or adapting the good features to become "the best of the best."

Blockage An event that occurs when resources are prevented from producing more flow units because there is no place to store the already processed flow units or because additional processing has not been authorized.

Blocking A situation that occurs because input buffers have only limited capacity to accommodate arrivals waiting to be processed.

Bottleneck Slowest resource pool. See also Theoretical bottleneck; Effective bottleneck.

Buffer The part of the process that stores flow units that have finished with one activity but are waiting for the next activity to start.

Buffer capacity The maximum number of flow units that can wait in a buffer.

Bullwhip effect The phenomenon of upstream variability magnification that indicates a lack of synchronization among supply chain members.

Business process A network of activities performed by resources that transform inputs into outputs.

Business strategy The aspect of strategic planning that defines the scope of each division or business unit in terms of the attributes of the products that it will offer and the market segments that it will serve.

Capacity utilization of a resource pool The degree to which resources are utilized by a process; the ratio of throughput and theoretical capacity of resource pool.

Capital Fixed assets, such as land, building, facilities, equipment, machines, and information systems.

Cascading Representing a given process at several levels of detail simultaneously in a process flowchart.

Causal models Forecasting methods that assume data plus other factors influence demand.

Cause–effect diagram An illustration that shows a chain of cause–effect relationships that allows one to find the root causes of the observed variability. Also called *fishbone diagram* or *Ishikawa diagram*.

Cellular layout A layout of resources where all stations that perform successive operations on a product (or product family) are grouped together and organized according to the sequence of activities.

Changeover The cleaning, resetting, or retooling of equipment in order for it to process a different product. Also called *setup*.

Chase demand strategy A strategy to deal with demand fluctuations whereby a firm produces quantities to exactly match demand.

Check sheet A tally of the types and frequency of problems with a product or a service experienced by customers.

Coefficient of variation A measure of variability relative to its mean. It is obtained by computing the ratio of the standard deviation to the mean.

Collaborative Planning, Forecasting, and Replenishment (CPFR) An initiative in the consumer-goods industry designed to coordinate planning, forecasting, and replenishment across the supply chain.

Competitive product space A representation of the firm's product portfolio as measured along four dimensions or product attributes: product cost, response time, variety, and quality.

Continuous improvement Ongoing incremental improvement in process performance. See also Kaizen.

Continuous Replenishment Program (CRP) A partnership program under which the supplier automatically replenishes its customer inventories based on contractually agreed-on levels.

Continuous review, reorder point policy An order policy wherein a process manager, having initially ordered a fixed quantity, monitors inventory level continuously and then reorders once available inventory falls to a prespecified reorder point.

Control band A range within which any variation is to be interpreted as a normal, unavoidable aspect of any process.

Control chart A run chart of process performance with control limits overlaid to give it decision-making power.

Control limits The lower and upper range of the control band.

Corporate strategy The aspect of strategic planning that defines the businesses in which the corporation will participate and specifies how key corporate resources will be acquired and allocated to each business.

Critical activities Activities that lie on the critical path.

Critical path The longest path in the flowchart.

Cycle inventory The average inventory arising from a specific batch size.

Cycle service level The probability that there will be no stockout within an order cycle. Also called *service level*.

Delayed differentiation A strategy in which part of a process is delayed in order to reduce the need for safety inventory. Also called *postponement*.

Demand management strategies Actions by a firm that attempt to influence demand pattern.

Division of labor The breakdown of labor into its components and the distribution of labor among people and machines to increase efficiency of production.

Due date quotation The practice of promising a time frame within which the product will be delivered after an order has been placed.

Economic order quantity The optimal order size that minimizes total fixed and variable costs.

Economies of scale A process exhibits economies of scale when the average unit cost of output decreases with volume.

Effective bottleneck The resource pool with least effective capacity.

Effective capacity of a process The effective capacity of the effective bottleneck.

Effective capacity of a resource unit The maximum flow rate of a resource unit if it were fully utilized during its net availability, that is, if there were no periods of resource idleness.

Everyday low pricing (EDLP) The retail practice of charging constant, everyday low prices with no temporary discounts.

Everyday low purchase prices (EDLPP) The wholesale practice of charging constant, everyday low prices with no temporary discounts.

Feedback control The process of periodically monitoring the actual process performance, comparing it to planned levels of performance, investigating causes of the observed discrepancy between the two, and taking corrective actions to eliminate those causes.

Fill rate The fraction of total demand satisfied from inventory on hand.

Fishbone diagram See Cause–effect diagram.

Fixed order cost The administrative cost of processing an order, transporting material, receiving the product(s), and inspecting the delivery regardless of order size.

Fixed setup cost The time and materials required to set up a process.

Flexible manufacturing system (FMS) A reprogrammable manufacturing system capable of producing a large variety of parts.

Flexible mass production A method of high-volume production that allows differences in products.

Flow rate The number of flow units that flow through a specific point in the process per unit of time.

Flow shop A type of process architecture that uses specialized resources to produce a low variety of products at high volumes.

Flow time The total time that a flow unit spends within process boundaries.

Flow-time efficiency The ratio between theoretical flow time and the average flow time that indicates the amount of waiting time associated with the process.

Flow unit The item being analyzed within a process view. Examples of flow units include an input unit, such as a customer order, or an output unit, such as a finished product. A flow unit can also be the financial value of the input or output.

Focused process A process in which products all fall within a small region of the competitive product space. This process supports a focused strategy.

Focused strategy A business process that is committed to a limited, congruent set of objectives in terms of demand and supply.

Forecasting The process of predicting the future.

Forward buying The taking advantage of price discounts to purchase for future needs.

Functional layout A type of process design that groups organizational resources by processing activity or "function" in "departments." Also called *process layout*.

Functional specialization A process and organizational structure where people are specialized by function, meaning each individual is dedicated to a specific task. (The other organizational structure is *product specialization*.)

Functional strategy The part of strategic planning that defines the purpose of marketing, operations and finance—the three main functions of organizations.

Heijunka See Level production.

Histogram A bar plot that displays the frequency distribution of an observed performance characteristic.

Ideal process A process that achieves synchronization at the lowest possible cost.

Inflow rate The average rate of flow unit arrivals per unit of time.

In-process inventory An inventory classification; flow units that are being processed. See Work-in-process inventory; In-transit inventory.

Inputs Any tangible or intangible items that flow into the process from the environment and are transformed; they include raw materials, component parts, energy, data, and customers in need of service.

Inputs inventory An inventory classification; flow units that are waiting to begin processing.

Instantaneous inventory accumulation rate The difference between instantaneous inflow rate and outflow rate, written $\Delta R(t)$. Also called *instantaneous inventory buildup rate*.

Instantaneous inventory buildup rate See Instantaneous inventory accumulation rate.

Interarrival time The time between consecutive customer arrivals.

In-transit inventory A category of in-process inventory; flow units being transported. Also called *pipeline inventory*.

Inventory The total number of flow units present within process boundaries.

Inventory buildup diagram An illustration that depicts inventory fluctuation over time.

Inventory holding cost The financial cost of carrying inventory. Its two main components are *physical holding cost* and the *opportunity cost* of capital.

Inventory turns The ratio of throughput to average inventory. It is the reciprocal of average flow time. Also called *turnover ratio*.

Ishikawa diagram See Cause–effect diagram.

Jidoka Intelligent automation whereby the ability to detect errors is automatically built into the machine.

Job shop A type of process architecture that uses flexible resources to produce low volumes of customized, high-variety products.

Just-in-time An action taken only when it becomes necessary to do so. In the context of manufacturing, it means production of only necessary flow units in necessary quantities at necessary times.

Kaizen Improvement by continuously identifying and eliminating sources of waste in a process, such as inventory, waiting time, or defective parts.

Kanban The signaling device formalized by Toyota that allows the customer to inform the supplier of its need. It is a card attached to an output flow unit in the buffer between customer and supplier processes and lists the customer process, the supplier process, parts description, and production quantity.

Labor Human resource assets, such as engineers, operators, customer service representatives, and sales staff.

Lead time The time lag between the arrival of the replenishment and the time the order was placed.

Lead time demand The total flow unit requirement during replenishment lead time.

Level production A production schedule where small quantities of different products are produced frequently to match with customer demand. Also called *heijunka*.

Level-production strategy The maintenance of a constant processing rate when demand fluctuates seasonally and thus the building of inventories in periods of low demand and the depleting of inventories when demand is high.

Little's law The law that describes the relationship among the three performance measures. It states that *average inventory equals average throughput times average flow time.*

Load batching The phenomenon of a resource processing several flow units simultaneously; the number of units processed simultaneously is called the load batch.

Lot size The number of units processed consecutively after a setup. Also called *setup batch*.

Lower control limit (LCL) Lower range of the *control limits*.

Lower specification (LS) Lower range of acceptable performance.

Make-to-order Produce in response to customer orders.

Make-to-stock Produce in anticipation of customer orders.

Manufacturing The process of producing goods. Also called *product operations.*

Marginal analysis The process of comparing expected costs and benefits of purchasing each incremental unit.

Market-driven strategy One of two approaches to strategic fit wherein a firm starts with key competitive priorities and then develops processes to support them. (The other approach to strategic fit is *process-driven strategy.*)

Mass production The production of products in large (massive) quantities.

Material requirements planning (MRP) A planning tool in which the end-product demand forecasts are "exploded" backward to determine parts requirements at intermediate stations based on the product structure ("bills of materials"), processing lead times, and levels of inventories at those stations.

Multi-vari chart A plot of high, average, and low values of performance measurement sampled over time.

Net availability of a resource The actual time during which a resource is available for processing flow units; the difference between the scheduled availability and resource availability loss of a resource unit.

Net marginal benefit The difference between the unit price of the product and unit marginal cost of procurement.

Net marginal cost The difference between unit marginal cost of procurement and its salvage value.

Net present value A measure of expected aggregate monetary gain or loss that is computed by discounting all expected future cash inflows and outflows to their present value.

Network of activities and buffers Process activities linked so that the output of one becomes an input into another, often through an intermediate buffer.

Newsvendor problem A basic model of decision making under uncertainty whereby the decision maker balances the expected costs of ordering too much with the expected costs of ordering too little to determine the optimal order quantity

Non-value-adding activities Activities that are required by a firm's process that do not directly increase the value of a flow unit.

Normal variability Statistically predictable variability. It includes both *structural variability* and *stochastic variability.*

On-order inventory The inventory represented by outstanding orders not yet delivered.

Operational effectiveness The measure of how well a firm manages its processes.

Operations Business processes that design, produce, and deliver goods and services.

Operations frontier The smallest curve that contains all industry positions in the competitive product space.

Operations strategy The aspect of strategic planning that configures and develops business processes that best enable a firm to produce and deliver the products specified by the business strategy.

Opportunity cost The forgone return on the funds invested in a given activity rather than in alternative projects.

Outputs Any tangible or intangible items that flow from the process back into the environment. Examples include finished products, processed information, material, energy, cash, and satisfied customers.

Outputs inventory An inventory classification; processed flow units that have not yet exited process boundaries.

Pareto chart A bar chart that plots frequencies of problem-type occurrence in decreasing order.

Physical centralization The consolidation of all of a firm's stock into one location from which it services all customers.

Physical holding cost The out-of-pocket expense of storing inventory.

Pipeline inventory A category of in-process inventory; flow units being transported. Also called *in-transit inventory.*

Plan-Do-Check-Act (PDCA) cycle A tool to implement continuous improvement. It involves planning the process, operating it, inspecting its output, and adjusting it in light of the observation.

Plant Any singly owned, independently managed and operated facility, such as a manufacturing site, a service unit, or a storage warehouse.

Plant-within-a-plant (PWP) A plant in which the entire facility is divided into several "miniplants," each devoted to its own specific mission by performing a process that focuses strictly on that mission.

Poka yoke Mistake-proofing; design of a part, product, or a process that prevents its user from making a mistake.

Pooling capacity The sharing of available capacity among various sources of demand (or arrivals).

Pooling inventory The sharing of available inventory among various sources of demand.

Postponement See Delayed differentiation.

Precedence relationships The sequential relationships that determine which activity must be finished before another can begin.

Preventive maintenance Scheduled maintenance activities for resources.

Process Any organization or *any part* of an organization that transforms inputs into outputs.

Process capability The ability of a process to meet customer specifications.

Process capacity The maximum sustainable flow rate of a process.

Process control The aspect of process management that is focused on continually ensuring that, in the short run, the actual process performance conforms to the planned performance.

Process cost The total cost incurred in producing and delivering outputs.

Process design The system of selecting the process architecture that best develops the competencies that will meet customer expectations.

Process efficiency Process performance measured in terms of total processing cost.

Process flexibility The ability of the process to produce and deliver desired product variety.

Process flowchart A graphical representation of a process that identifies the inputs, outputs, flow units, network of activities and buffers, resources allocated to activities, and information structure.

Process flow management A set of managerial policies that specifies how a process should be operated over time and which resources should be allocated over time to the activities.

Process flow measures Internal measures of process performance that managers can control. Together, these measures—flow time, flow rate, and inventory—capture the essence of process flow.

Process flow time See Flow time.

Process layout See Functional layout.

Process planning Identifying internal measures that track process competence and specifying the managerial policies that improve process competence along desired dimensions.

Process quality The ability of the process to produce and deliver quality products.

Process synchronization The ability of the process to meet customer demand in terms of their quantity, time, quality, and location requirements.

Process-driven strategy One of two approaches to strategic fit wherein a firm starts with a given set of process competencies and then identifies which market position is best supported by those processes. (The other approach to strategic fit is *market-driven strategy.*)

Processing network A system that consists of information and material flows of multiple products through a sequence of interconnected paths.

Processing rate The rate at which customers are processed by a server. Also called *service rate.*

Processing time See Activity time.

Procurement batch A *batch size* arising in procurement.

Product attributes The properties of a product that customers consider important.

Product cost The total cost that a customer incurs in order to own and experience the product.

Product delivery response time The total time that a customer must wait before receiving a product for which he or she has expressed a need to the provider.

Product layout A type of process design in which the location of resources is dictated by the processing requirements of the product.

Product quality The degree of excellence of a product; how well a product performs.

Product specialization A process and organizational structure where people are specialized by product, meaning each individual is dedicated to a specific product line. (The other organizational structure is *process or functional specialization.*)

Product value The price a specific customer is willing to pay for a product.

Product variety The range of choices offered to the customer to meet his or her needs.

Production batch A *batch size* arising in production.

Productivity dilemma The choice between manufacturing goods with higher variety at a lower rate of productivity or manufacturing goods with lower variety at a higher rate of productivity.

Product–process matrix A tool used to match processes to products proposed by Hayes and Wheelwright (1979).

Proportion abandoning The number of customers who enter the process but abandon it before being served.

Proportion blocked The average fraction of arrivals blocked from entering the process because the input buffer is full.

Pull A process where the signal to produce is triggered by the customer so that each station produces only on demand from its customer station.

Push A process where input availability, as opposed to customer need, triggers production.

Quality function deployment (QFD) A conceptual framework that can be used to translate customers' functional requirements of a product into concrete design specifications.

Quality of conformance How well the actual product conforms to the chosen design specifications.

Quality of design How well product specifications aim to meet customer requirements.

Queue length formula A formula for the average queue length as a function of the utilization, number of servers, and variability.

Rate of return The reward that an investor demands for accepting payment delayed by one period of time.

Reengineering Fundamental rethinking and radical redesign of business processes in order to achieve dramatic improvements in critical contemporary measures of performance, such as cost, quality, service, and speed.

Reorder point The available inventory at the time a reorder is placed.

Resource availability loss A category of factors that affect process capacity in which the resource itself is not available for processing.

Resource breakdown The unavailability of a resource for processing due to equipment malfunctioning.

Resource idleness A category of factors that affect process capacity in which the resource is available but is not processing units. Examples of factors include starvation and blockage.

Resource pool A collection of interchangeable resources that can perform an identical set of activities.

Resource pooling Making separate resource pools flexible to handle tasks performed by each other.

Resource unit Each unit in a resource pool.

Resources Tangible assets that help transform inputs to outputs in a process. They are usually divided into two categories: capital, which includes fixed assets such as land, building, facilities, equipment, machines, and information systems, and labor, which includes people such as engineers, operators, customer service representatives, and sales staff.

Return on total assets A common financial measure that shows how well a firm uses its assets to earn income for the stakeholders who are financing it.

Robust design The designing of a product in such a way that its actual performance will not suffer despite any variability in the production process or in the customer's operating environment.

Run chart A plot of some measure of process performance monitored over time.

Safety capacity The excess processing capacity available to handle customer inflows.

Safety inventories Inventories maintained to insulate the process from disruptions in supply or uncertainty in demand. Also called *safety stock.*

Safety stock See Safety inventories.

Safety time The time margin that should be allowed over and above the expected time to deliver service in order to ensure that a firm will be able to meet the promised date.

Scatter plot A graph showing how a controllable process variable affects the resulting product characteristic.

Scheduled availability The amount of time that a resource unit is scheduled for operation.

Seasonal inventories Inventories that act as buffers to absorb seasonal fluctuations of supply and demand.

Server order discipline The sequence in which waiting customers are served.

Service operations Processes that deliver services.

Service rate See Processing rate.

Setup See Changeover.

Setup batch See Lot size.

Single minute exchange of dies (SMED) A system by which the changeover times can be reduced to less than 10 minutes.

Single-phase service process A service process in which each customer is processed by one server and all tasks performed by that server are combined into a single activity.

Six-sigma A process that produces only 3.4 defective units per million opportunities.

Slack time of an activity The extent to which an activity could be delayed without affecting process flow time.

Square root law The law states that the total safety inventory required to provide a specified level of service increases by the square root of the number of locations in which it is held.

Stability condition The requirement that the average inflow rate should be strictly less than the average processing rate to ensure a *stable process.* It is necessary to limit delays or queues.

Stable process A process in which, in the long run, the average inflow rate is the same as the average outflow rate.

Starvation The forced idleness of resources due to the unavailability of necessary inputs.

Statistical quality control A management approach that relies on sampling of flow units and statistical theory to ensure the quality of the process.

Stochastic variability The unpredictable or random variability experienced by service processes.

Strategic fit Having consistency between the competitive advantage that a firm seeks and the process architecture and managerial policies that it uses to achieve that advantage.

Subprocess Activities that are exploded into a set of subactivities that is then considered a process in its own right, with its own set of inputs, outputs, activities, and so forth.

Supply chain An entire network of interconnected facilities of diverse ownership with flows of information and materials between them. It can include raw materials suppliers, finished-goods producers, wholesalers, distributors, and retailers.

Theoretical bottleneck A resource pool with minimum theoretical capacity.

Theoretical capacity of a process The theoretical capacity of the theoretical bottleneck.

Theoretical capacity of a resource pool The sum of the theoretical capacities of all the resource units in that pool.

Theoretical capacity of a resource unit The maximum sustainable flow rate of the resource unit if it were fully utilized (without idle periods, resource availability loss, and time lost to setups).

Theoretical flow time The minimum amount of time required for processing a typical flow unit without any waiting.

Theoretical inventory The minimum amount of inventory necessary to maintain a process throughput rate in equilibrium.

Throughput See Average flow rate.

Throughput delay curve A graph displaying the average flow time of a process as a function of capacity utilization.

Time-series analyses Forecasting methods that rely solely on past data.

Trade promotion A form of price discount wherein a discount is offered for only a short period of time.

Trade-off On the operations frontier, a decreasing of one aspect to increase another.

Transfer batch A *batch size* arising in transportation or movement.

Turnover ratio See Inventory turns.

Type I error A situation when process performance falls outside the control band even with normal variability.

Type II error A situation when process performance measure falls within the control band, even though there is an assignable cause of abnormal variability.

Unit load of a resource unit The amount of time required by the resource to process each flow unit.

Upper control limit (UCL) Upper range of the *control limits*.

Upper specification (US) Upper range of acceptable performance.

Value-adding activities Those activities that increase the economic value of a flow unit because the customer values them.

Vendor managed inventory (VMI) A partnership program under which the supplier decides the inventory levels to be maintained at its customer locations and arranges for replenishments to maintain these levels.

Virtual centralization A system in which inventory pooling in a network of locations is facilitated using information regarding availability of goods and subsequent transshipment of goods between locations to satisfy demand.

Waste The failure to match customer demand most economically by, for example, producing inefficiently, producing defective products, producing in quantities too large or too small, and delivering products too early or too late.

Work content of an activity The activity time multiplied by the average number of visits at that activity. It measures the total amount of time required to perform an activity during the transformation of a flow unit.

Work-in-process inventory A category of in-process inventory; flow units being processed in a manufacturing or service operation.

Index

Page references followed by *t* or *f* denote tables or figures.

COREL CORPORATION END USER LICENSE AGREEMENT

ATTENTION: THIS IS A LICENSE, NOT A SALE. THIS PRODUCT IS PROVIDED UNDER THE FOLLOWING END USER LICENSE AGREEMENT ("EULA") AND ALL APPLICABLE ADDENDA ("LICENSE") WHICH DEFINE WHAT YOU MAY DO WITH THE PRODUCT AND CONTAIN LIMITATIONS ON WARRANTIES AND/OR REMEDIES. THIS LICENSE IS GRANTED BY COREL CORPORATION ("Corel") AND INCLUDES THE FOLLOWING:

1. General License Agreement
2. Corel Guidelines for the Use of Clipart and Stock Photo Images
3. Trial Version Addendum to the General License Agreement
4. Academic Version Addendum to the General License Agreement
5. OEM Version Addendum to the General License Agreement
6. SDK Addendum to the General License Agreement
7. Beta Version Addendum to the General License Agreement
8. iGrafx® Process Central™ 2003, Starter Edition, Addendum to the General License Agreement
9. iGrafx® Process Central™ 2003, Standard Edition, Addendum to the General License Agreement

IF YOU ARE DOWNLOADING THIS PRODUCT:

(i) you certify that you are not a minor and that you agree to be bound by all of the terms and conditions set out in this License. Downloading and/or using the Product will be an irrevocable acceptance of the terms and conditions of the License;

(ii) you agree to be responsible for any and all Internet service provider fees, telecommunication and other charges that may apply as a result of your download of the Product; and

(iii) you represent and warrant to Corel, if you are accepting on behalf of a company, or other legal entity, that you have full authority to bind such entity.

IF YOU DO NOT AGREE WITH THE ABOVE, DO NOT DOWNLOAD THIS PRODUCT

1. GENERAL LICENSE AGREEMENT

IMPORTANT: CAREFULLY READ THIS LICENSE BEFORE USING THIS PRODUCT. INSTALLING, COPYING, OR OTHERWISE USING THIS PRODUCT INDICATES YOUR ACKNOWLEDGMENT THAT YOU HAVE READ THIS LICENSE AND AGREE TO BE BOUND BY AND COMPLY WITH ITS TERMS. IF YOU DO NOT AGREE AND THIS PRODUCT IS TANGIBLE STORAGE MEDIA (i.e. CD), RETURN THE COMPLETE PRODUCT TO COREL CUSTOMER SERVICE, 1600 CARLING AVENUE, OTTAWA, ONTARIO, CANADA, K1Z 8R7, WITHIN TEN (10) DAYS OF THE DATE YOU ACQUIRED IT FOR A FULL REFUND. THIS EULA IS YOUR PROOF OF LICENSE. PLEASE TREAT IT AS VALUABLE PROPERTY.

1.1 LICENSE:

COREL ("we" or "us") provides you with a computer program, computer software, including its code, objects including their APIs as well as any images, photographs, templates, animations, video, audio, music, text and "applets" incorporated into the software, the accompanying printed materials, a License, and "online" or electronic documentation (together called the "Product") and we grant you a License to use the Product in accordance with the terms of this License. Any supplemental software code and supporting materials provided to you as part of support services provided by Corel for the Product shall be considered part of the Product and subject to the terms and conditions of this License. The copyright and all other rights to the Product shall remain with us or our licensors. You must reproduce any copyright or other notice(s) marked on the Product on all copies you make.

1.2 YOU MAY:

(i) install and use one copy of the Product on a single computer. You may also make and use a second copy of the Product on a home or portable computer provided that copy is never loaded in the RAM of the home or portable computer at the same time it is loaded in the RAM of the primary computer;

(ii) also store or install a copy of the Product on a storage device, such as a network server, used only to install or run the Product on your other computers over an internal network; however, you must acquire and dedicate a license for each separate computer on which the Product is installed or run from the storage device. A license for the Product may not be shared or used concurrently on different computers;

(iii) make one copy of the Product for archive or backup purposes;

(iv) if this Product includes Clipart and/or Photo Images, use the Clipart and/or Photo Images only if you comply with the terms set out in the Corel Guidelines for the Use of Clipart and Stock Photo Images in Section 2 below;

(v) except in the case of Academic and OEM edition Products which are non-transferable (see Academic Version Addendum and OEM Version Addendum to this License), transfer the Product to someone else only if you assign all of your rights under this License, cease all use of the Product, erase or destroy any copy (including the hard disk copy) made in support of your use of the Product, and ensure that the person to whom you wish to transfer the Product agrees to the terms of this License;

(vi) if you have purchased this Product as an upgrade of either a Corel product or another vendor's product, you may continue to use your upgraded product with this Product. If you transfer this Product, you must either transfer the upgraded product at the same time you transfer the Product or destroy the upgraded product at the same time you transfer the Product. If the Product you have purchased is an upgrade of a Corel product, you now may use that upgraded product only in accordance with this License; and

(vii) use only one (1) of the language versions if the Product provides you with a selection of multiple language versions.

1.3 YOU MAY NOT:

(i) use the Product or make copies of it except as permitted in this License;

(ii) translate, reverse engineer, decompile, or disassemble the Product except to the extent the foregoing restriction is expressly prohibited by applicable law;

(iii) rent, lease, assign, or transfer the Product except as set out in Section 1.2 above;

(iv) modify the Product or merge all or any part of the Product with another program;

(v) redistribute the fonts or sound files included with the Product;

(vi) separate the component parts of the Product for use on more than one computer; and if this Product is OEM:

(vii) use or copy the Product if you received the Product as a standalone. The Product must be purchased in conjunction with the Corel approved partner products or services described in the Warning located on the Product storage media.

1.4 UNISYS TECHNOLOGY LIMITATION:

Corel products that provide PDF and/or TIFF-LZW and/or GIF and/or Postscript-LZW and/or LZW graphics capability utilize technology covered by U.S. Patent No. 4,558,302, and all foreign counterparts ("Unisys Patent"). The License granted to you hereunder permits you to use the Unisys Patent in conjunction with your use of this Product only. Use of any other product or the performance of any other activity involving the compression/decompression technology covered by the Unisys Patent requires a separate license from Unisys Corporation.

1.5 PRODUCT PATCH, PLUG OR UPDATE

If this is a patch, plug, update or other file located at this site (if you are downloading from the Web) or contained on this storage media (if you are receiving software on CD-ROM) (the "Software"), the Software is designed for use with a Corel application software product (the "Original Application") and is subject to Corel's Limitations of Warranties and Liability (as set out in Section 1.8) and Eligibility provisions (as set out in Section 1.11), as applicable. You are granted a non-exclusive license to use such Software only with the Original Application provided that you still possess a valid license from Corel for the Original Application. Except as provided below, the Software is subject to the terms and conditions of the License from Corel accompanying the Original Application. If you are downloading this Software, all risk of damage to the Software during transmission and download is assumed by you.

1.6 TERM:

This License shall remain in effect only for so long as you are in compliance with the terms and conditions of this License. This License will terminate if you fail to comply with any of its terms or conditions. You agree, upon termination, to destroy all copies of the Product. The Limitations of Warranties and Liability set out below shall continue in force even after any termination. If you have purchased this product as part of the Student Campus Reward Option for Learning (SCROL) Program, you are bound by the conditions as stated in Section 4.2 herein.

1.7 WARRANTY:

IF THIS PRODUCT IS TANGIBLE STORAGE MEDIA (i.e. CD) COREL WARRANTS THAT THIS PRODUCT WILL BE FREE FROM DEFECT IN MATERIALS AND WORKMANSHIP FOR NINETY (90) DAYS FROM THE DATE YOU ACQUIRE IT. IF SUCH A DEFECT OCCURS, RETURN THE MEDIA TO US AT COREL CUSTOMER SERVICE, 1600 CARLING AVENUE, OTTAWA, ONTARIO, CANADA, K1Z 8R7, AND WE WILL REPLACE IT FREE OF CHARGE. THIS REMEDY IS YOUR EXCLUSIVE REMEDY FOR BREACH OF THIS WARRANTY. IT GIVES YOU CERTAIN RIGHTS AND YOU MAY HAVE OTHER LEGISLATED RIGHTS WHICH MAY VARY FROM JURISDICTION TO JURISDICTION.

1.8 LIMITATION OF WARRANTIES AND LIABILITY:

EXCEPT FOR THE EXPRESS WARRANTY ABOVE, THE PRODUCT IS PROVIDED ON AN "AS IS" BASIS, WITHOUT ANY OTHER WARRANTIES OR CONDITIONS, EXPRESS OR IMPLIED, INCLUDING, BUT NOT LIMITED TO, WARRANTIES OF MERCHANTABLE QUALITY, SATISFACTORY QUALITY, MERCHANTABILITY OR FITNESS FOR A PARTICULAR PURPOSE, OR THOSE ARISING BY LAW, STATUTE, USAGE OF TRADE, COURSE OF DEALING OR OTHERWISE. THE ENTIRE RISK AS TO THE RESULTS AND PERFORMANCE OF THE PRODUCT IS ASSUMED BY YOU. NEITHER COREL NOR ITS DEALERS OR SUPPLIERS SHALL HAVE ANY LIABILITY TO YOU OR ANY OTHER PERSON OR ENTITY FOR ANY INDIRECT, INCIDENTAL, SPECIAL, OR CONSEQUENTIAL DAMAGES WHATSOEVER, INCLUDING, BUT NOT LIMITED TO, LOSS OF REVENUE OR PROFIT, LOST OR DAMAGED DATA OR OTHER COMMERCIAL OR ECONOMIC LOSS, EVEN IF WE HAVE BEEN ADVISED OF THE POSSIBILITY OF SUCH DAMAGES, OR THEY ARE FORESEEABLE. WE ARE ALSO NOT RESPONSIBLE FOR CLAIMS BY A THIRD PARTY. OUR MAXIMUM AGGREGATE LIABILITY TO YOU AND THAT OF OUR DEALERS AND SUPPLIERS SHALL NOT EXCEED THE AMOUNT PAID BY YOU FOR THE PRODUCT. THE LIMITATIONS IN THIS SECTION SHALL APPLY WHETHER OR NOT THE ALLEGED BREACH OR DEFAULT IS A BREACH OF A FUNDAMENTAL CONDITION OR TERM OR A FUNDAMENTAL BREACH. SOME STATES/COUNTRIES DO NOT ALLOW THE EXCLUSION OR LIMITATION OF LIABILITY FOR CONSEQUENTIAL OR INCIDENTAL DAMAGES, SO THE ABOVE LIMITATION MAY NOT APPLY TO YOU.

1.9 U.S. GOVERNMENT RIGHTS:

The Product under this License is "commercial computer software" as that term is described in 48 C.F.R. 252.227-7014(a)(1). If acquired by or on behalf of a civilian agency, the U.S. Government acquires this commercial computer software and/or commercial computer software documentation subject to the terms of this License as specified in 48 C.F.R. 12.212 (Computer Software) and 12.211 (Technical Data) of the Federal Acquisition Regulations ("FAR") and its successors. If acquired by or on behalf of any agency within the Department of Defense ("DOD"), the U.S. Government acquires this commercial computer software and/or commercial computer software documentation subject to the terms of this License as specified in 48 C.F.R. 227.7202 of the DOD FAR Supplement ("DFAR") and its successors.

1.10 EXPORT CONTROLS:

If the Product is identified as a not-for-export product (for example, on the box, media or in the installation process), then, unless you have exemption from the United States Department of Commerce or other regulatory authority as designated from time to time the following applies: EXCEPT FOR EXPORT TO CANADA FOR USE IN CANADA BY CANADIAN CITIZENS, THE PROGRAM MAY NOT BE EXPORTED OUTSIDE OF THE UNITED STATES OR TO ANY FOREIGN ENTITY OR "FOREIGN PERSON" AS DEFINED BY THE U.S. GOVERNMENT REGULATIONS, INCLUDING WITHOUT LIMITATION, ANYONE WHO IS NOT A CITIZEN, NATIONAL OR LAWFUL PERMANENT RESIDENT OF THE UNITED STATES. BY AGREEING TO THE TERMS OF THIS LICENSE YOU ARE WARRANTING TO COREL THAT YOU ARE NOT A "FOREIGN PERSON" OR UNDER THE CONTROL OF A "FOREIGN PERSON."

1.11 ELIGIBILITY:

If you are downloading this Product from the Web, to be eligible to download the Product you must be in compliance with applicable export laws. By accepting the EULA you are representing and warranting to Corel you are compliant with the following statements: (i) you are not a citizen, national or resident of, and are not under the control of, the government of: Cuba, Iran, Iraq, Libya, North Korea, Sudan, Syria, Serbia, Taliban-controlled areas of Afghanistan, nor any other country to which the United States has prohibited export; (ii) you will not download or otherwise export or re-export the Product, directly or indirectly, to the countries mentioned in clause (i) nor to citizens, nationals or residents of those countries; (iii) you are not listed in the United States Department of Treasury lists of Specially Designated Nationals, Specially Designated Terrorists, and Specially Designated Narcotic Traffickers, nor are you listed on the United States Department of Commerce Table of Denial Orders; (iv) you will not download or otherwise export or re-export the Product, directly or indirectly, to persons on the lists mentioned in clause (iii); and (v) you will not use the Product for, and will not allow the Product to be used for, any purposes prohibited by United States law, including, without limitation, for the development, design, manufacture or production of nuclear, chemical or biological weapons of mass destruction.

If you cannot represent and warrant that you are in compliance with the above statements, you are not eligible to download the Product.

1.12 GENERAL:

This License is the entire agreement between us, superseding any other agreement or discussions, oral or written other than a separate, valid and existing license agreement entered into between you and Corel or any of its subsidiaries of affiliates (the "Other License") in which case that Other License governs to the extent of any inconsistency between this License and that Other License, and may not be changed except by a signed agreement. This License shall be governed by and construed in accordance with the laws of the Province of Ontario, Canada, unless there is an Other License, in which case the choice of law specified in that Other License shall prevail, excluding that body of law applicable to choice of law and excluding the United Nations Convention on Contracts for the International Sale of Goods and any legislation implementing such Convention, if otherwise applicable. If any provision of this License is declared by a Court of competent jurisdiction to be invalid, illegal, or unenforceable, such a provision shall be severed from the License and the other provisions shall remain in full force and effect. The parties have requested that this Agreement and all documents contemplated hereby be drawn up in English. Les parties aux présentes ont exigé que cette entente et tous autres documents envisagés par les présentes soient rédigés en anglais.

2. COREL GUIDELINES FOR THE USE OF CLIPART AND STOCK PHOTO IMAGES:

Corel products contain numerous clipart and photo images (collectively referred to as the "Images") which are either owned by Corel or licensed from a third party. As a user of Corel products you are free to use, modify and publish the Images as you wish subject to the restrictions set out below. If you are uncertain as to whether your intended use is in compliance with the Guidelines set out below, we recommend that you seek the advice of your own attorney or legal counsel. Corel will not provide you with an opinion as to whether your use is in compliance with these Guidelines.

2.1 YOU MAY, subject to any restrictions set out below:
(i) incorporate any Image(s) into your own original work and publish, display and distribute your work in any media; provided you include a copyright notice in your work reflecting on the copyright ownership of both you and Corel as follows:

"Copyright © 200_ [your name] and its licensors. All rights reserved."
You may not, however, resell, sublicense or otherwise make available the Image(s) for use or distribution separately or detached from a product or Web page. For example, the Image(s) may be used as part of a Web page design, but may not be made available for downloading separately or in a format designed or intended for permanent storage or re-use by others. Similarly, clients may be provided with copies of the Image(s) (including digital files) as an integral part of a work product, but may not be provided with the Image(s) or permitted to use the Image(s) separately or as part of any other product; and
(ii) make one (1) copy of the Image(s) for backup or archival purposes.

2.2 YOU MAY NOT:
(i) create scandalous, obscene, defamatory or immoral works using the Image(s) nor use the Image(s) for any other purpose which is prohibited by law;
(ii) use or permit the use of the Image(s) or any part thereof as a trademark or service mark, or claim any proprietary rights of any sort in the Image(s) or any part thereof;
(iii) use any of the Images related to identifiable individuals or entities for any commercial purpose or in a manner which suggests their association with or endorsement of any product or service;
(iv) use the Image(s) in electronic format, on-line or in multimedia applications unless the Image(s) are incorporated for viewing purposes only and no permission is given to download and/or save the Image(s) for any reason.
(v) rent, lease, sublicense or lend the Image(s), or a copy thereof, to another person or legal entity. You may, however, transfer all your License to use the Image(s) to another person or legal entity, provided that (i) you transfer the Image(s) and this License, including all copies (except copies incorporated into your work product as permitted under this License), to such person or entity, (ii) that you retain no copies, including copies stored on a computer or other storage device, and (iii) the receiving party agrees to be bound by the terms and conditions of this License; and
(vi) use any Image(s) except as expressly permitted by this License.

2.3 GOVERNMENT CRESTS, SEALS AND OTHER INSIGNIA
The national and municipal insignia contained in this product are protected by various laws against misuse. Generally speaking, all logos, insignia, patches, seals, flags and coats of arms are for official use only. It is your responsibility to obey all national and international laws regulating display of the insignia, seals, flags and coats of arms contained herein.

3. TRIAL VERSION ADDENDUM TO THE GENERAL LICENSE AGREEMENT:

IF THIS PRODUCT IS IDENTIFIED AS A TRIAL VERSION, YOUR USE OF THE TRIAL VERSION PRODUCT IS GOVERNED BY THE TERMS OF THE GENERAL LICENSE AGREEMENT AS MODIFIED BY THE TERMS OF THIS TRIAL VERSION ADDENDUM. IN THE EVENT OF ANY CONFLICT BETWEEN THE TERMS OF THE GENERAL LICENSE AGREEMENT AND THIS TRIAL VERSION ADDENDUM, THE TERMS OF THE TRIAL VERSION ADDENDUM SHALL GOVERN.

THE PRODUCT IS A 120 DAY TRIAL VERSION ONLY AND WILL BECOME INOPERABLE 120 DAYS AFTER YOU LAUNCH THE PROGRAM. AFTER THIS DATE, YOU WILL NOT BE ABLE TO ACCESS ANY FILES CREATED WITH THIS TRIAL VERSION UNLESS YOU HAVE INSTALLED A FULL VERSION OF THE PRODUCT. IF YOU WISH TO PURCHASE A FULL VERSION OF THE PRODUCT, PLEASE CONTACT US AT (503) 404-6050, INFO@IGRAFX.COM OR VISIT WWW.IGRAFX.COM.

END USERS OF THIS EVALUATION VERSION SHALL NOT BE CONSIDERED "REGISTERED OWNERS" OF A COREL PRODUCT AND THEREFORE SHALL NOT BE ELIGIBLE FOR UPGRADES, PROMOTIONS, TECHNICAL SUPPORT OR OTHER BENEFITS AVAILABLE TO "REGISTERED OWNERS" OF COREL PRODUCTS.

THIS TRIAL VERSION CONTAINS A LIMITED NUMBER OF MAJOR MODULE(S) INCLUDED IN THE RETAIL VERSION OF THE PRODUCT AND THESE ARE THE ONLY MODULE(S) YOU WILL BE ABLE TO INSTALL. EXTRA VALUE COMPONENTS AND APPLICATIONS OF THE RETAIL VERSION OF THE PRODUCT ARE NOT INCLUDED. ALL REFERENCES TO OTHER APPLICATIONS, EXTRA LIBRARIES OR OTHER CD-ROMS THAT MAY APPEAR IN THIS TRIAL VERSION OF THE PRODUCT ARE NOT APPLICABLE.

YOU ARE GRANTED A LICENSE TO USE THE TRIAL VERSION OF THE PRODUCT ONLY. SUCH LICENSE SHALL CONTINUE FOR THE PERIOD SET OUT ABOVE, AFTER WHICH TIME YOUR LICENSE TO USE THE TRIAL VERSION SHALL TERMINATE.

ANY ATTEMPT TO CIRCUMVENT ANY EXPIRY DATE TECHNOLOGY/TIME BOMB MECHANISM OR OTHER MECHANISM CONTAINED WITHIN THE SOFTWARE WHICH IS INTENDED TO LIMIT YOUR ABILITY TO USE THE SOFTWARE FOR A SPECIFIED PERIOD IS A VIOLATION OF THIS LICENSE. ANY ATTEMPT TO CIRCUMVENT ANY SUCH EXPIRY DATE TECHNOLOGY/TIME BOMB MECHANISM SHALL RESULT IN THE IMMEDIATE TERMINATION OF YOUR LICENSE TO USE THE SOFTWARE.

4. ACADEMIC EDITION ADDENDUM TO THE GENERAL LICENSE AGREEMENT:

4.1 IF THIS PRODUCT IS IDENTIFIED AS AN ACADEMIC EDITION, YOUR USE OF THIS PRODUCT IS GOVERNED BY THE TERMS OF THE GENERAL LICENSE AGREEMENT AS MODIFIED BY THE TERMS OF THIS ACADEMIC EDITION ADDENDUM TO THE GENERAL LICENSE AGREEMENT. IN THE EVENT OF ANY CONFLICT BETWEEN THE TERMS OF THE GENERAL LICENSE AGREEMENT AND THIS ACADEMIC EDITION ADDENDUM, THE TERMS OF THIS ACADEMIC ADDENDUM TO THE GENERAL LICENSE AGREEMENT SHALL GOVERN.

7.2 TERMINATION: The license granted under this Beta Addendum will terminate thirty (30) days following Corel's release of a commercial release of the Product. The license will terminate automatically if you fail to comply with the limitations described herein. You must destroy all copies of the Product upon termination.

7.3 DISCLAIMER OF WARRANTIES: USER ACKNOWLEDGES THAT THE PRODUCT IS A PRE-RELEASE PRODUCT AND IS PROVIDED ON AN "AS IS" BASIS AND WITHOUT WARRANTY. THE PRODUCT MAY CONTAIN BUGS, ERRORS AND OTHER PROBLEMS THAT COULD CAUSE SYSTEM FAILURES OR MAY NOT PERFORM ALL FUNCTIONS FOR WHICH IT IS INTENDED OR REPRESENTED AND THE USE OF THE PRODUCT IS ENTIRELY AT THE USER'S RISK. THIS DISCLAIMER IS IN LIEU OF ALL WARRANTIES WHETHER EXPRESS OR IMPLIED, ARISING BY STATUTE, OPERATION OF LAW OR OTHERWISE, INCLUDING IMPLIED WARRANTIES AND CONDITIONS OF MERCHANTABILITY, MERCHANTABLE QUALITY, SATISFACTORY QUALITY OR FITNESS FOR A PARTICULAR PURPOSE.

8. IGRAFX® PROCESS CENTRAL™ 2003, STARTER EDITION, ADDENDUM TO THE GENERAL LICENSE AGREEMENT:

If the product is the iGrafx Process Central 2003, Starter Edition, notwithstanding anything to the contrary in the General License Agreement, the following applies:

8.1 You may create iGrafx Process Central 2003, Starter Edition, repositories on a single Server. If the Server has more than one processor, you must obtain a separate license for each processor on that Server.

8.2 You may install the Client, Server Administrator, and Web Central components of iGrafx Process Central 2003, Starter Edition, on any internal device. In addition, iGrafx Process 2003 Viewer Software may be installed on any internal device.

8.3 Five concurrent users may access the iGrafx Process Central 2003, Starter Edition, repositories so long as you have acquired a valid license for each processor on the Server where the iGrafx Process Central 2003, Starter Edition, repositories reside. The five user limit is automatically enforced by the iGrafx Process Central 2003, Starter Edition.

Please contact a Corel sales representative if you wish to upgrade your license to iGrafx Process Central 2003, Standard Edition, which allows an unlimited number of concurrent users.

9. IGRAFX® PROCESS CENTRAL™ 2003, STANDARD EDITION, ADDENDUM TO THE GENERAL LICENSE AGREEMENT:

If the product is iGrafx Process Central 2003, Standard Edition, notwithstanding anything to the contrary in the General License Agreement, the following applies:

9.1 You may create iGrafx Process Central 2003, Standard Edition, repositories on a single Server. If the Server has more than one processor, you must obtain a separate license for each processor on that Server.

9.2 You may install the Client, Server Administrator, and Web Central components of iGrafx Process Central 2003, Standard Edition, on any internal device. In addition, iGrafx Process 2003 Viewer Software may be installed on any internal device.

9.3 Any number of users may access iGrafx Process Central 2003, Standard Edition, repositories so long as you have acquired a valid license for each processor on the Server where the iGrafx Process Central 2003, Standard Edition, repositories reside.

April 2004

NOTWITHSTANDING ANYTHING TO THE CONTRARY IN THE GENERAL LICENSE AGREEMENT, YOU MAY NOT TRANSFER OR ASSIGN THE PRODUCT OR ANY COPY THEREOF, OR YOUR LICENSE TO USE THE PRODUCT TO A THIRD PARTY.

4.2 If you have purchased this Product as part of the Student Campus Reward Option for Learning (SCROL) Program, Section 1.6 of the License shall be deleted and replaced with the following:
1.6 TERM: This License shall remain in effect only for so long as you are a registered full-time student or a faculty member at an accredited higher education institution. This License shall terminate in the event you are no longer a registered full-time student or a faculty member at an accredited higher education institution. For the purposes of this License, "accredited higher education institution" shall mean either a publicly or privately owned vocational or correspondence school; junior college; college; university or scientific or technical institute recognized by the appropriate ministry or department of education. In addition this License will terminate if you fail to comply with any of its terms or conditions. You agree, upon termination, to destroy all copies of the Product. The Limitations of Warranties and Liability set out in Section 1.8 shall continue in force even after any termination.

5. OEM EDITION ADDENDUM TO THE GENERAL LICENSE AGREEMENT:

OEM PRODUCT IS SOLD UNDER LICENSE IN CONJUNCTION WITH COREL APPROVED PARTNER PRODUCTS OR SERVICES WHICH ARE DESCRIBED IN THE WARNING LOCATED ON THE STORAGE MEDIA. IF THIS PRODUCT IS IDENTIFIED AS AN OEM EDITION, YOUR USE OF THIS PRODUCT IS GOVERNED BY THE TERMS OF THE GENERAL LICENSE AGREEMENT AS MODIFIED BY THE TERMS OF THIS OEM EDITION ADDENDUM TO THE GENERAL LICENSE AGREEMENT. IN THE EVENT OF ANY CONFLICT BETWEEN THE TERMS OF THE GENERAL LICENSE AGREEMENT AND THIS OEM EDITION ADDENDUM, THE TERMS OF THIS OEM ADDENDUM TO THE GENERAL LICENSE AGREEMENT SHALL GOVERN.

NOTWITHSTANDING ANYTHING TO THE CONTRARY IN THE GENERAL LICENSE AGREEMENT, YOU MAY NOT TRANSFER OR ASSIGN THE PRODUCT OR ANY COPY THEREOF, OR YOUR LICENSE TO USE THE PRODUCT TO A THIRD PARTY.

6. SDK ADDENDUM TO THE GENERAL LICENSE AGREEMENT:

IF THIS PRODUCT CONTAINS A COREL SOFTWARE DEVELOPER'S TOOLKIT ("SDK"), YOUR USE OF THE SDK PORTION OF THE PRODUCT IS GOVERNED BY THE TERMS OF THE GENERAL LICENSE AGREEMENT AS MODIFIED BY THE TERMS OF THIS SDK ADDENDUM TO THE GENERAL LICENSE AGREEMENT. IN THE EVENT OF ANY CONFLICT BETWEEN THE TERMS OF THE GENERAL LICENSE AGREEMENT AND THIS SDK ADDENDUM, THE TERMS OF THIS SDK ADDENDUM TO THE GENERAL LICENSE AGREEMENT SHALL GOVERN.

It is Corel's intention in designing the Software Developer's Kit to make it compatible with other versions of the Software Developer's Kit. However, since it is constantly being modified and reorganized, with certain capabilities added to or eliminated from any particular version or product, Corel makes no representations or warranties concerning compatibility with other versions or products.

You are solely responsible for determining the usefulness of the Software Developer's Kit for your particular purpose. The Software Developer's Kit is provided to software developers with the expectation that the developers are capable of writing and debugging their own programs; Corel does not assume any support obligations with respect to the Software Developer's Kit or the use thereof. Any research, development, or evaluations you perform are done entirely at your own risk.

6.1 YOU MAY:
(i) use the SDK solely for the purpose of developing, manufacturing, marketing and supporting one or more applications software package(s) ("Software Application Product"); and
(ii) reproduce and sublicense the software program files included in the SDK's 'Redistributables' folder ("SDK files"), provided the files are in executable format and incorporated into a Software Application Product developed by you. Any sublicense of the SDK files shall be granted solely for the use of these SDK files in connection with and as a sublicensed part of a Software Application Product for any support, service, upgrades or other assistance.

6.2 YOU MAY NOT:
(i) remove or alter any copyright notice, trademark, or other proprietary rights notice placed by Corel on the SDK or any portion thereof.

6.3 INDEMNIFICATION: You agree to indemnify and hold Corel harmless from and against any and all costs, liabilities, claims, or demands (including reasonable attorney's fees and expenses of any kind whatsoever) that arise or result from the use, reproduction or distribution of your Software Application Product, documentation, or promotional or sales materials.

6.4 COREL TRADEMARKS AND TRADENAMES: You may not refer to Corel or include any Corel trademarks in or on any material except for the sole purpose of stating that a Software Application Product may be utilized in connection with the specific Corel software product. In the event you refer to Corel or include the trademarks in or on any program materials or any packaging, marketing, or advertising materials, the trade name or trademarks must be accompanied with the following footnote disclaimer printed in a clearly legible manner on the same page in no smaller than ten-point type:

"This product is not manufactured, approved, or supported by Corel Corporation."

7. BETA VERSION ADDENDUM TO THE GENERAL LICENSE AGREEMENT:

IF THIS PRODUCT IS IDENTIFIED AS A BETA VERSION, YOUR USE OF THIS PRODUCT IS GOVERNED BY THE TERMS OF THE GENERAL LICENSE AGREEMENT AS MODIFIED BY THE TERMS OF THIS BETA VERSION ADDENDUM TO THE GENERAL LICENSE AGREEMENT. IN THE EVENT OF ANY CONFLICT BETWEEN THE TERMS OF THE GENERAL LICENSE AGREEMENT AND THIS BETA VERSION ADDENDUM, THE TERMS OF THIS BETA VERSION ADDENDUM TO THE GENERAL LICENSE AGREEMENT SHALL GOVERN. IN THE EVENT THAT YOU ARE AN AUTHORIZED COREL BETA TEST SITE AND HAVE BEEN AUTHORIZED TO TEST A BETA VERSION PRODUCT THAT HAS NOT BEEN MADE PUBLICLY AVAILABLE BY COREL, YOUR USE OF THE BETA VERSION PRODUCT SHALL BE GOVERNED BY THE TERMS OF THE BETA TEST SITE LICENSE AGREEMENT ENTERED INTO BETWEEN COREL AND YOURSELF AND THE PROVISIONS SET OUT BELOW SHALL NOT APPLY.

7.1 LICENSE GRANT: Corel grants to you a non-exclusive license to use the Product for evaluation and trial purposes only for a limited time. This license does not entitle you to hard-copy documentation, support or telephone assistance. While Corel intends to distribute a commercial release of the Product, Corel reserves the right at any time not to release a commercial release of the Product or, if released, to alter prices, features, licensing terms, or other characteristics of the commercial release.